Interpreting Late Antiquity

INTERPRETING LATE ANTIQUITY

Essays on the Postclassical World

G. W. BOWERSOCK

PETER BROWN

OLEG GRABAR

Editors

The Belknap Press of Harvard University Press

Cambridge, Massachusetts, and London, England · 2001

Library of Congress Cataloging-in-Publication Data

Interpreting late antiquity : essays on the postclassical world / G. W. Bowersock, Peter Brown,
Oleg Grabar.
     p.   cm.
   Includes bibliographical references and index.
   ISBN 0-674-00598-8 (alk. paper)
     1. Civilization, Greco-Roman.   2. Byzantine Empire—Civilization—To 527.
  3. Rome—History—Germanic Invasions, 3rd–6th centuries.
  4. Church history—Primitive and early church, ca. 30–600.
  I. Bowersock, G. W. (Glen Warren), 1936– II. Brown, Peter Robert Lamont.
  III. Grabar, Oleg.
  DE3 .I6 2001
  938—dc21   2001035271

CONTENTS

INTRODUCTION

In the year 250 C.E., the most populous and long-settled regions of western Eurasia, which stretched in a great arc from the Atlantic coasts of France, Portugal, and Morocco across the Mediterranean, the Balkans, and the Middle East as far as Afghanistan, were subject to the control of two—and only two—immense imperial systems: the Roman empire and the Sassanian empire of Persia. Over five hundred years later, around 800 C.E., the populations of the same area still lived largely in the shadow of empire. The Roman empire was still there. From Calabria, across the southern Balkans, and deep into Anatolia, the territories of what we call, by a modern misnomer redolent of ill-informed contempt, the "Byzantine" empire, had been ruled continuously for over eight hundred years by the direct successors of Emperor Augustus. In Rome itself, the pope was still a "Roman." Every document emanating from the papal chancery was dated by the regnal date of the Roman emperor who reigned at Constantinople and by the *Indictio,* a fifteen-year tax cycle that had started in 312.

In 800, also, from Central Asia to the plateau of Castile, an Islamic caliphate, created at headlong speed by the Arab conquests of the 7th century, had gained stability by settling back into the habits of the ancient empires it had replaced. The tax system of the Islamic empire continued with little break the practices of the Roman and Sassanian states. Its coins were *denarii, dinar*s. The system of post-horses and of governmental information on which its extended rule depended was called after its Roman predecessor *veredus, al-barīd.* Its most significant enemy was still known, in Arabic, as the empire of *Rum*—the empire of Rome in the east, centered on Constantinople.

For all the startling and self-conscious novelty of their religion, the early Muslim conquerors of the Middle East found themselves heirs to a past of extraordinary density. This past piled up around them in every city they had occupied. The first great public mosque was created, at the Umayyad capital at Damascus, by the simple and dramatic expedient of embracing, in a single enclosure made of porticoes sheathed in shimmering east Roman mosaics, the former temple precinct of Jupiter/Haddad and its recent Christian rival, the shrine of St. John the Baptist. A thousand years of unbroken urban history, and the history of two religions, were thus encased in a new, Muslim place of worship. In 762, the center of what would become the medieval Islamic caliphate was created by the founding of Baghdad. Baghdad stood on ground heavy with the past. It lay upriver from the ruins of the former Sassanian capital of Ctesiphon. These ruins were dominated by the Taq-i Kesra, the immense shell of the Sassanian Palace Arch ascribed to Khosro I Anushirvan (530–579). The awesome height and apparent indestructibility of that great arch of brick was a permanent reminder of an ancient, pre-Islamic style of rule, indelibly associated with the memory of Khosro, the contemporary and rival of the east Roman emperor Justinian (527–565)—himself no mean creator of enduring legacies, the builder of the Hagia Sophia and the definitive codifier of the laws of Rome.

Only at the western tip of Eurasia, in what we call western Europe, did it seem as if the long summer's afternoon of empire had begun to fade. Yet from Ireland to the upper Danube, the clergy shared a common Catholicism, first formed in the Christian Roman empire of Constantine and Theodosius I. Even on the outer periphery of Europe, the clergy still thought of themselves as part of a wider world embraced by great empires. To enter the library of Iona, on the southwest coast of Scotland, and to consult its books was to share in a sacred geography of Christendom that still stretched along the entire length of the old Roman empire and beyond: it included not only Jerusalem and the Holy Places, but also Alexandria, Damascus, Edessa, and memories of Christian martyrs yet farther to the east, in Mesopotamia and northern Iraq.

Although alternately decried and romanticized by scholars of the 18th and 19th centuries as pure "barbarians," the ruling classes of the postimperial kingdoms of the west had, in fact, inherited a basically Roman sense of social order and a Roman penchant for extended empire. Power still wore a Roman face. The acclamation of the Frankish king, Charlemagne, by the Roman people and by the pope as "their" emperor, in 800 (and the deadly seriousness with which Charlemagne accepted the compliment) was yet another case of a successful state-builder from a once peripheral region easing himself into the comfortable seat provided by half a millennium of empire. Charlemagne's contemporary, Caliph Hārūn al-Rashīd, viewed the indestructible arch of Khosro with much the same mixture of awe and proud entitlement as did Charlemagne when faced with a Rome heavy with pagan and Christian memories. They were both, each in his own distinctive way, inheritors of a remarkable Age of Empires.

We should not take this for granted. Back in 250 it was far from certain that an Age of Empires lay in the immediate future. Torn by civil war and largely unprepared for large-scale mobilization, the Roman empire seemed doomed to disintegrate. Nor could anyone have foretold that the Sassanian dynasty, which emerged so rapidly from Fars in the 220s, would eventually mold the sub-kingdoms of the Iranian plateau and Mesopotamia into the formidable world power of the age of Khosro Anushirvan, and in so doing would provide a model of empire as enduring, for the populations of Islamic Asia, as was the myth of Rome for the Christians of western Europe. By the end of the 7th century, it seemed as if the Arab conquerors would destroy themselves through reckless civil wars within fifty years of their conquests. Yet none of these possible events happened. In each case, the immediate future lay not with chaos but with the reassertion of strong, extended empires. The reformed Roman empire of Diocletian and Constantine was the most formidably governed state ever created in the ancient world. It survived largely intact in its eastern regions until 640. The consolidation of the Iranian territories under the Sassanian King of Kings involved a similar, if less clearly documented achievement. After a period of civil wars, the Islamic caliphate emerged, under the Abbasid dynasty at Baghdad, to form what has rightly been called the last great empire of antiquity. As a result, the populations of western Eurasia (even those of western Europe) could look back, in the year 800, to find their horizon blocked by the massive outlines of great empires, frequently overhauled since 250 yet still irreplaceable.

But there was more to it than that. Today, as Jews, Zoroastrians, Christians, and Muslims, millions of persons are the direct heirs of religions either born or refashioned in late antiquity. Some religions took the form in which they are still recognizable—as was the case with the Jews—within communities bounded by the Roman and the Sassanian empires. Others grasped the fact of empire with spectacular results. Zoroastrians look back to the age of the Sassanians as the time of the restoration of their orthodoxy and of the formation of their religious literature. The Christians embraced with zeal the Christian Roman empire of Constantine and his successors. The Muslims created rapidly, from the remnants of the Roman and the Sassanian states, an empire of their own.

This, very briefly, is what we mean when we talk of "late antiquity." The essays in this volume, commissioned for the reference work *Late Antiquity: A Guide to the Postclassical World,* share the frank assumption that the time has come for scholars, students, and the educated public in general to treat the period between around 250 and 800 as a distinctive and quite decisive period of history that stands on its own. It is not, as it once was for Edward Gibbon, a subject of obsessive fascination only as the story of the unraveling of a once glorious and "higher" state of civilization. It was not a period of irrevocable Decline and Fall; nor was it merely a violent and hurried prelude to better things. It cannot be treated as a corpse to be dragged quickly offstage so that the next great act of the drama of the Middle Ages should begin—with the emergence of Catholic Europe and the creation of the Arabic civilization associated with the golden age of medieval Islam.

Not only did late antiquity last for over half a millennium; much of what was created in that period still runs in our veins. It is, for instance, from late antiquity, and not from any earlier period of Roman history, that we have inherited the codifications of Roman law that are the root of the judicial systems of so many states in Europe and the Americas. The forms of Judaism associated with the emergence of the rabbinate and the codification of the Talmud emerged from late antique Roman Palestine and from the distinctive society of Sassanian Mesopotamia. The basic structures and dogmatic formulations of the Christian church, both in Latin Catholicism and in the many forms of eastern Christianity, came from this time, as did the first, triumphant expression of the Muslim faith. Even our access to the earlier classics of the ancient world, in Latin and Greek, was made possible only through the copying activities of late antique Christians and their early medieval successors, locked in an endless, unresolved dialogue with their own pagan past.

Compared with the solid, almost unseen ground-course of institutions and ideas created in late antiquity that still lie at the foundations of our own world, the earlier classical period of the ancient world has a surreal, almost weightless quality about it. It is the Dream Time of western civilization. It can act as a never failing source of inspiration. But we cannot claim to come from that classical world alone, for whole segments of the modern world had no place in it. These emerged, rather, in the period between 250 and 800: a Europe in which the non-Roman north and the Roman south came to be joined in a common Catholic Christianity; a Greek-speaking world that stood at the western pole of a widely extended federation of Christian communities which ranged from Georgia to Ethiopia, and from Mesopotamia to Kerala and western China; a Middle East in which Constantinople/Istanbul and Baghdad were founded (in 324 and in 762) and have remained among the most emotionally charged cities of Asia; a paganism that lived on, no longer in temples, but in austere philosophical systems that summed up an ancient wisdom which continued to fascinate and to repel Christians, Jews, and Muslims for centuries to come; a Middle East in which Islam had, by 800, become an overwhelming presence. Nothing like this was to be seen before 250. These developments belong to late antiquity. If we do not like what we see in late antiquity, it is often because the ideas and the structures that first emerged at that time are still with us. They have the power to move or to repel us even today. The period which has bequeathed to us such living legacies deserves attention in its own right.

This volume also attempts to treat as a single whole the vast geographic space covered by the Roman and the Sassanian empires. And even this extensive space must be seen as no more than a vivid cluster of settlements set in a yet wider world. For, in this period, societies as far apart as Scandinavia and the Hadramawt, Saharan Africa and western China were touched by events along that great arc of imperially governed societies and interacted decisively, at crucial moments, with those societies.

Above all, these essays draw on the advances in scholarship that have enabled scholars for the first time to treat, with even-handed erudition, the very different regions of western Europe, the eastern empire, the Sassanian empire, and the early caliphate, as well as the many more distant societies that were implicated in the overall development of the late antique period.

For if there is one thing which we as the editors of *Late Antiquity* and this volume would wish to bring about, it is that its readers should begin the 21st century with fewer artificial barriers in their minds, erected between periods and regions which have proved, in the light of modern research, to be more continuous with each other than we had once thought. For instance, we go out of our way to encourage readers to join the history of the later Roman empire in the east with the subsequent evolution of the first centuries of Islam. We also encourage the reader to stand on both sides of the political frontiers of the empires of that time. For if they do this, they will be able better to appreciate the all-important process of symbiosis that led to the creation, and to the eventual triumph over the traditional empires, of new societies, created in the "war zones" of the Rhine and the Danube, of Sassanian Central Asia and of the steppelands of Syria and Iraq.

We hope that the interested reader will travel from the world of Constantine to the seemingly very different world of the Damascus of 'Abd al-Malik—and may be surprised to see that not everything had changed. We wish our readers to make a habit of crossing the political frontier that separated late Roman Syria from the busy world of Sassanian Iraq, and of traveling to the steppes of Central Asia and eastern Europe to take up an unexpected viewpoint upon the Roman empire. We also hope to remind students of religion and of the history of ideas of the unexpected, long-term consequences of many of the better-known achievements of the period. They will find, for instance, that texts of Greek philosophy, science, and medicine written at the beginning of our period will, by the end of it, be circulating in more copies in Syriac and Arabic than in their Greek original. They will be struck by the tenacity and by the long-term implications of the philosophical and theological issues debated in the period. Such themes can be appreciated only when seen in the long term, as they endure and change over many centuries and in very different environments. Not least of the surprises in store for the reader will be the extent to which religious groups, who throughout this period made a point of distinguishing themselves from each other with singular ferocity, continued, in fact, to be drawn together by the mute force of common intellectual preoccupations and, even when they fought most fiercely (by attacking the cult sites of their rivals), by the oceanic weight of shared notions of the sacred. Whether they liked each other or not, they remained not only "Christians," "Jews," and "pagans," "orthodox" and "heretics," "clergy" and "laity": they breathed the same heavy air of a common civilization—that of late antiquity.

Travel of this kind is calculated to broaden the mind. Students of well-known topics in much-studied regions—for instance, those interested in the Christianization of western Europe—will here be reminded of the working out of analogous processes in other parts of the Christian world. To take one example, the recent remarkable increase of archaeological discoveries in the countries of the Middle East adds a new dimension to such study. It is now possible to compare phenomena well known to the student of the postimperial west, such as the explosion of church building in the cities of Merovingian Gaul, with evidence for a similar explosion among the Christian communities of the Middle East. Fifteen late antique churches, mainly from the 6th century, have been discovered in Jerash (Jordan) alone. The splendid mosaics recently uncovered at Mefaa, modern Umm ar-Rasas (also in Jordan) have made us all sit up and take notice. These are recognizably late antique productions. They contain scenes that lovingly depict the classical facades of neighboring cities. Yet they were laid down in 718 C.E., that is, by exact contemporaries of the Venerable Bede. They were the work of Christians who had already lived for almost eighty years as subjects of the Islamic empire. It is in such small details, unavailable to us until only a few decades ago, that we can gain, through comparison across widely separated regions, a sense of scale and of the pace of a worldwide phenomenon, such as the establishment and survival of the Christian church in its many regions.

Through recent archaeological discoveries, it is now possible to grasp an entire world no longer in its broad outlines, through the magisterial sweep of narratives such as Edward Gibbon's *Decline and Fall of the Roman Empire* or, as in a magnificent bird's eye view, through A. H. M. Jones's *The Later Roman Empire*, but rather in the accumulation of vivid details on the ground. An entire landscape has filled up with the traces of villages and unpretentious bathhouses, with the jolly mosaics of the petty gentry and with hundreds of little churches and synagogues dedicated by pious notables. Scattered across the entire sweep of the late antique Mediterranean and the Middle East, these recently discovered remains remind us that late antiquity did, indeed, happen. We are dealing with a distinctive civilization, whose density and sheer tenacity, on a humble level that we had hitherto barely suspected, demands some form of overall treatment.

In these essays, we have not wished to sacrifice the vividness of a personal introduction to selected themes to the harmless drudgery of a comprehensive survey. The essays are meant to provoke thought. They are not there to repeat, under the guise of providing comprehensive information, the narrative stereotypes that have weighed particularly heavily on our interpretation of the period. It is the frank intention of the authors of these essays to encourage readers to travel further in new directions. For it is their opinion that new directions have, indeed, been opened up for the period of late antiquity in a manner which would barely have been thinkable only a century ago; and that these directions point firmly away from many commonly accepted stereotypes of the period.

It has long been recognized that the late antique period stands at the crossroads of many histories. The great highroads of many well-established disciplines traverse our period: dictionaries of the classical world end in late antiquity, dictionaries of Judaism and Christianity inevitably pass through it, dictionaries of Islam, Byzantium, and the Middle Ages make it their starting point. Besides our own *Late Antiquity: A Guide to the Postclassical World*, we can refer the reader to many exhaustive dictionaries, encyclopedias, and lexicons that deal competently with themes that are central to late antiquity. To take an obvious example: those interested in the history of the Christian church are urged to turn to works such as *The Oxford Dictionary of the Christian Church*, the *Dictionnaire de Spiritualité*, the *Prosopographie chrétienne* (which has already produced one precious volume for Africa), the *Reallexikon für Antike und Christentum* and, now, to *The Coptic Encyclopedia*—to mention only a few. And for those in whom these essays have instilled a salutary zest for further information, we need only point out *The Oxford Dictionary of Byzantium*, the *Prosopography of the Later Roman Empire*, and the new edition of

The Oxford Classical Dictionary, not to mention *The Encyclopedia Judaica*, the *Encyclopedia of Islam*, and the *Reallexikon für germanische Altertumskunde*, among many other reliable and largely up-to-date works of reference. If this volume inspires in its readers a wish to continue to study the distinctive period of late antiquity in its many aspects and to follow the directions into new territory to which it points, then the editors will consider that this volume will have served its purpose.

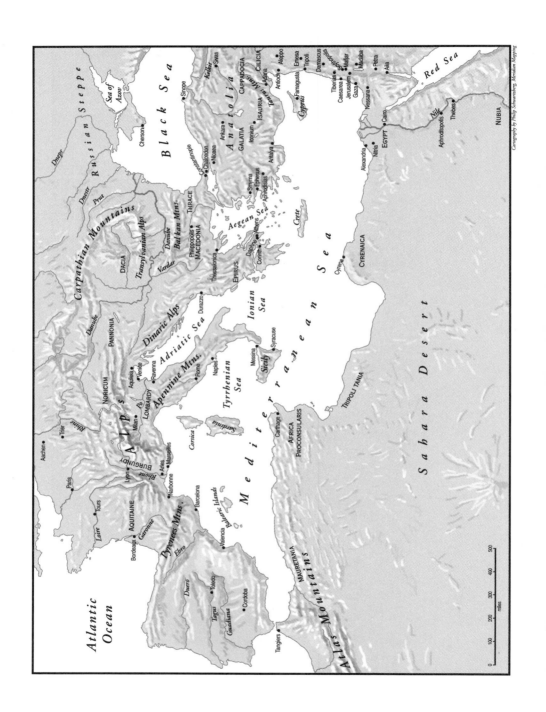

Atlantic
Ocean

Carpathian Mountains

Russian Steppe

Sea of Azov

Black Sea

Dnepr

Dnestr

Prut

Sinope

Cherson

Chalcedon
Constantinople
Nicaea

Anatolia

Kelkit

Sivas

CAPPADOCIA

Ankara

GALATIA

Iconium

CILICIA

ISAURIA

Taurus Mtns.

Smyrna
Ephesus
Aphrodisias

Antalya

Aleppo

Antioch

Emesa

Tripoli

Damascus

Scythopolis
Beifar
Madaba

Petra

Aila

Red Sea

Cyprus

Famagusta

Tiberias

Caesarea

Jerusalem

Gaza

Nessana

Cairo

Nitria

EGYPT

Alexandria

Aphroditopolis

Thebes

Nile

NUBIA

Cartography by Philip Schwartzberg, Meridian Mapping

THRACE

Bal'kan Mtns.

Danube

Transylvanian Alps

DACIA

Vardar

Philippopolis
MACEDONIA

Thessalonica

Aegean Sea

Athens

Crete

EPIRUS

Daphne
Corinth

Durazzo

Dinaric Alps

Adriatic Sea

Ionian Sea

Pannonia

NORICUM

Danube

Apennine Mtns.

Aquileia

Venice

Po

Ravenna

Rome

Naples

Messina

Syracuse

Sicily

Tyrrhenian Sea

Sardinia

Corsica

LOMBARDY

Milan

ALPS

BURGUNDY

Rhine

Aachen

Trier

Paris

Lyon

Arles

Marseilles

Narbonne

Loire

Tours

AQUITAINE

Garonne

Bordeaux

Pyrenees Mtns.

Barcelona

Ebro

Valencia

Balearic Islands

Duero

Toledo

Tagus

Guadiana

Cordoba

Tangiers

MAURETANIA

Atlas Mountains

AFRICA
PROCONSULARIS

Carthage

TRIPOLITANIA

Cyrene

CYRENAICA

Mediterranean Sea

Sahara Desert

0   100   200   300   400   500
          miles

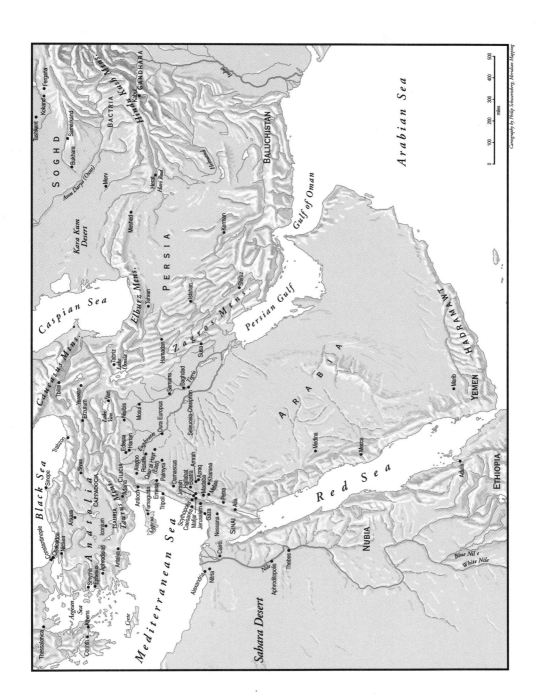

Arabian Sea

Gulf of Oman

BALUCHISTAN

GANDHARA

Kabul

Hindu Kush Mtns.

BACTRIA

Kara Kum Desert

Tashkent • Kokand • Fergana

S O G H D

Samarkand

Bukhara •

Merv •

Anu Darya (Oxus)

Herat •

Hari Rud

Meshed •

P E R S I A

Kerman •

Shiraz •

Isfahan •

Tehran •

Elburz Mtns.

Caspian Sea

Tabriz •

Lake Urmia

Hamadan •

Zagros Mtns.

Susa •

Persian Gulf

A R A B I A

H A D R A M A W T

Marib •

YEMEN

Adulis •

ETHIOPIA

Blue Nile

White Nile

NUBIA

Red Sea

Mecca •

Medina •

Caucasus Mtns.

Tbilisi •

Erzurum •

Yerevan •

Lake Van

Van •

Nisibis •

Mosul •

Dura Europus •

Samarra •

Baghdad •

Ctesiphon •

Seleucia-Ctesiphon •

Trabzon •

Sinope •

Black Sea

Constantinople •

Chalcedon •

Nicaea •

Ankara •

Iconium •

CAPPADOCIA

Sivas •

A n a t o l i a

Taurus Mtns.

ISAURIA

CILICIA

Melitene •

Edessa •

Harran •

Aleppo •

Rusafa •

Qasr al Hayr (East)

Palmyra •

Euphrates

Antioch •

Famagusta •

Cyprus

Emesa •

Damascus •

Tripoli •

Jerash •

Hallabat •

Bustra • Azraq •

Amman •

Madaba • Kharana •

Petra •

Aila •

SINAI

Thessalonica •

Aegean Sea

Athens •

Corinth •

Crete

Smyrna •

Ephesus •

Aphrodisias •

Antalya •

Scythopolis •

Caesarea •

Mafjar •

Jerusalem •

Gaza •

Nessana •

Cairo •

Nile

Aphroditopolis •

Thebes •

Alexandria •

Nitria •

Mediterranean Sea

Sahara Desert

miles

0 100 200 300 400 500

Interpreting Late Antiquity

Remaking the Past

Averil Cameron

In his poem on the war against Count Gildo in North Africa, the late 4th century Latin poet Claudian depicts Roma, the personification of the city, as aged and unkempt, "feeble her voice, slow her step, her eyes deep buried. Her cheeks were sunken and hunger had wasted her limbs. Scarce can her weak shoulders support her unpolished shield. Her ill-fitting helmet shows her grey hairs and the spear she carries is a mass of rust."[1] His contemporary Quintus Aurelius Symmachus depicted Rome in similar guise, pleading with the emperor for toleration for pagans, while the Christian poet Prudentius reversed the trope and portrayed Roma rejuvenated by Christianity.

There was no nostalgia for the past here. Romantic ruins and decayed grandeur held no magic for this generation; indeed, Emperor Constantius II, who visited Rome in 357, and the historian Ammianus Marcellinus, who was at work on his Latin history there in the 380s, were as overcome by Rome's present majesty as by her great past.[2] Not for men such as these the self-conscious lament for past greatness or the fascination with antique decline familiar to us from Edward Gibbon's *History of the Decline and Fall of the Roman Empire,* or from 18th century pictures such as Fuseli's *The Artist Moved by the Grandeur of Ancient Ruins* (1778–1779), which shows a seated figure mourning beside the colossal hand and foot that remain from the monumental statue of Constantine the Great set up after his victory over Maxentius and his entry into Rome.[3] By the 7th and 8th centuries, Constantine the Great had passed from history into orthodox sainthood, his chief function in Byzantine legend being his commemoration with his mother Helena as the founder of Constantinople and finder of the True Cross; in the west, Rome laid claim to his Christian identity by means of the legend of his baptism by Pope Sylvester.[4] This is no romanticizing of the past, but rather its practical adaptation to the needs of the present. If the men and women of late antiquity did not romanticize the past, nor were they conscious of a sense of modernity. Rather, they wished devoutly to connect with a past which they still saw as part of their own experience and their own world. This could easily lead to incongruity in modern eyes; but it puzzles us far more than it did contemporaries to find, for example, fragments of classical masonry or sculpture built in to new constructions which we tend to find inferior.[5] The past was very real to the men and women of late antiquity: as they saw it, it had not so much to be remade as to be reasserted.

The past was so real that it was the subject of intense competition. For Eusebius of Caesarea (d. 339), the apologist of Constantine the Great, and for other Christian writers, it had above all to be wrested from the grip of pagans. According to Eusebius, the great oracles, the sources of ancient knowledge, were silent and the pagan shrines the home only of "dead idols." So much for centuries of tradition. But in fact the most prestigious oracular shrines were far from dead, and Eusebius's views were set out in direct challenge to the recent arguments of the great Neoplatonic philosopher and scholar Porphyry, expressed in his work *On Philosophy from Oracles*, which demonstrated through a collection of oracles that oriental, Jewish, and indeed Christian divine revelation had all been encompassed in the sayings of the gods.[6] Just as crucial for Eusebius, the greatest biblical scholar of his generation, was the question of the date of Moses; his Christian conception of history required a progression from the Mosaic law, through the development of Greek philosophy, represented above all by Plato, toward the attainment of the *pax Augusta* which alone provided the necessary setting for the coming of Christ and the spread of Christianity. Eusebius had set out these ideas most fully in his *Preparation for the Gospel,* an apologetic positioning of Christian revelation in the context of world history. Here too Porphyry, also the author of *Against the Christians,* a dangerously influential attack on Christianity (Emperor Constantine later ordered copies to be burnt), was Eusebius's chief target.

The *Preparation* asserted the primacy of Moses over Plato, the Jewish law over Greek philosophy, more particularly in its contemporary Neoplatonic manifestation in the teachings of Porphyry. In the *Life of Constantine,* a panegyrical defense of the emperor, Eusebius went much further than he had done in book nine of the *Ecclesiastical History* in presenting Constantine himself as the new Moses, bringing his people from the slavery of persecution and paganism to the new dispensation of Christianity, and—as Eusebius also claimed in the *Oration* he wrote for Constantine's thirtieth anniversary in 335–36—establishing a Christian kingdom on earth that was a true likeness of God's kingdom in heaven. In the heat of victory the emperor had made Porphyry the subject of public condemnation, but even so Eusebius's optimistic assertions were far from convincing pagan intellectuals. As so often, the optimism publicly expressed by both sides betrays the intense anxiety which was privately felt. Just one among many revealing indications of that is the scornful portrayal of Constantine by Julian, the son of his half-brother and a convert from Christianity to paganism, in Julian's *Caesares;* far from being the triumphant new Moses of Eusebius, Julian's Constantine is a pitiful suppliant in heaven unable to find a god willing to befriend him.

The need to claim the past for one's own in no way diminished. A curious work by Epiphanius, bishop of Salamis (Constantia) in Cyprus, known as the *Panarion* or "Medicine Chest" (376 C.E.), presents a catalogue of heresies start- ing with a chronological survey of religious belief in world history, from the Bible to Christian heresy. There are two schemes: in one, heresy was preceded by the sins of adultery, rebellion, and idolatry, which originated from the Fall, while in the other, four great periods of heresy succeeded each other from Adam onward: barbarism, Scythian superstition, Hellenism, and Judaism. Epiphanius's catalogue is not of course a history, but rather a formalist treatise, in which, indeed, the number of heresies is explicitly made to fit the eighty concubines in the Song of Songs (6:8). It is an odd work to modern eyes. Yet Epiphanius was a leading controversialist of his generation, and the work an- swered to burning contemporary concerns.[7]

The *Panarion* also displays the difficulty which Christian scholars experi- enced in their attempts to deal with biblical texts. The later 4th century saw a series of such efforts, focusing on the accounts of creation in the Book of Genesis. Basil of Caesarea composed a *Hexaemeron*, a series of sermons on the six days of creation. Their purpose was, in the words of a recent writer, to present a "complete cosmology," which would give "an account of humanity's place in that world, and of humanity's destiny."[8] For Christians, the two aims were inseparable, for Christianity saw itself as a religion grounded in history; consequently, not just the Scriptures but the whole of history had to be ex- pounded in Christian terms. This rereading of history also implied human psychology; it called forth from Basil a "translucent overlay of different planes of perception: the self, the world and the drama of God's action."[9] But a detailed exegesis of Genesis was also required. Augustine attempted to expound its meaning in several of his major works, including the *Confessions* and the *City of God*.[10] He also composed twelve books of commentary on its literal meaning, the *De Genesi ad litteram* (from 401 C.E.). Then as now, others gave the text a fundamentalist interpretation, and Augustine too wrote with an eye to the Neoplatonist view that the world was uncreated. The debate on creation between Christians and Neoplatonists was still continuing in the 6th century, when the Alexandrian John Philoponus wrote a work in which he argued against the views of Proclus on the subject, and a mysterious Cosmas Indico- pleustes, "the sailor to India," composed a prose *Christian Topography* arguing against Aristotle for a flat earth with the damned below and heaven above; illustrations from the 9th century and later indicate that Cosmas's work in- cluded pictures of this hierarchical arrangement, which took the Ark of the Covenant as their model.[11] Augustine's approach to creation and to time was of course more sophisticated: Plato's *Timaeus*, with its account of creation, was a work read by both Christians and Neoplatonists and offered Augustine some possibility of a middle ground. Yet God must be seen to have created the world.

The Scriptures, above all Genesis, provided more than a guide to the history of the world and a template for anthropological understanding. The advent of sin and its effects in history pervade Augustine's *City of God,* and this consid- eration of sin led him and others to ask a whole variety of further questions about the past, for instance whether angels existed before the creation of the world.[12] Especially in the late 4th century, Genesis also became the fundamental text for expounding male and female relations, the "tunics of skins" of Gen. 3:21 a token for some interpreters of the fact that human sexuality followed only after and as a consequence of the Fall.[13] But as human history, and human anthropology, were thus mapped onto the biblical story of Paradise lost, so the present was offered as a series of reenactments of Scriptural history, Constantine as Moses, holy men and women as Job. Scripture provided both a past and a living present. Even the conservative genre of imperial panegyric eventually wove images from the Hebrew Bible into its texture, and the victories of Heraclius over the Persians in the early 7th century led to his being hailed in poetry and depicted in visual art as the new David.[14] Heraclius is likened also to Elijah and Moses, and his court poet, George of Pisidia, also returned to the theme of the creation as an image of imperial renewal in a long poem also known as the *Hexaemeron,* written soon after Heraclius's victory over the Persians in 628 and his restoration of the True Cross to Jerusalem in 630.[15]

The Scriptures, then, presented both an opportunity and a challenge in late antiquity. They provided vocabulary, imagery, and subject matter for poets; models for holy men and women; and ways of understanding humanity and the world. But they required exegesis, and this could be difficult and risky. Sometimes "saving the text" resulted in interpretations which now seem fanciful and undisciplined in the extreme. But no one in late antiquity would have understood the post 19th century view of the story of the creation and Fall as "profound religious myths, illuminating our human situation."[16]

It was not only Christians in late antiquity who were remaking their past or using mythology in order to do so. The same inventive Epiphanius, author of the *Panarion,* gives us some information about a cult of Kore's giving birth to Aion ("time") in late 4th century Alexandria.[17] Aion is known at an earlier date from an inscription at Eleusis, a relief at Aphrodisias and a cosmological mosaic at Mérida in Spain, and from the 4th century from mosaics at New Paphos in Cyprus. But by the 4th century, in Egypt at least, Aion had taken on the new role of god of the mysteries, sprung from a virgin birth. In the Cyprus mosaic he is associated with the myth of Cassiopeia, in a composition including the infancy of Dionysus, themes also found at Apamea.[18] Domestic textiles surviving from Egypt show the popularity of mythological and especially Dionysiac themes as decoration even into the Islamic period. Paganism in late antiquity, especially of the more intellectual kind, was vigorous and productive, and knew how to take its cue from Christianity. It was not only Christians, for instance, who made pilgrimages: Neoplatonists, too, sought for origins, and went looking for sacred springs and streams in remote places.[19]

One way of shaping and making sense of the past in accordance with contemporary ideas was, paradoxically, via the routes of prophecy, eschatology, and millennialism. Again, one is confronted by a powerful sense of rivalry and competition. An industry grew up in oracles: in the 3rd century, the thirteenth Sibylline Oracle (the very name lent an aura of antiquity and mystery) interpreted the wars and invasions in the east in that period in oracular terms,[20] while the so-called Chaldaean Oracles popularized by Iamblichus claimed to convey messages from the soul of Plato himself. The net was cast wide: a late 5th century collection of oracular utterances known today as the Tübingen Theosophy survives as part of a Christian polemical work, and corresponds in some part with a famous inscription from the city of Oenoanda in Lycia.[21] Though oracles by their essence were anonymous, no less a person than the Emperor Constantine cited the Sibylline Oracles and Virgil's Fourth Eclogue to Christian purpose in his *Oration to the Saints*.[22] Even as late as the 7th century a collection of pagan oracles was circulating in Syria.

The appeal to tradition was another way of staking a claim in the past. Church fathers like Basil of Caesarea sought authority in the notion of an unbroken tradition handed down since the early days of the church. More recent tradition could be held to lie in councils, above all those recognized as ecumenical. By the 6th and 7th century, lists of councils, with their canons, had become a standard way of claiming authority in doctrinal matters. John Scholasticus and Eutychius, rival patriarchs of Constantinople in the late 6th century, drew up competing lists of conciliar decisions to support their opposing positions. During the period of the iconoclast controversy in Byzantium, from 726 to 843, the nature and meaning of "tradition" were vigorously debated; icons were held by their defenders to represent "unwritten tradition," which, it was claimed, had equal authority with the written tradition of Scriptures, the Fathers, and the councils. Like the drafting of their acts, the identification of authoritative councils was also a matter of contest; the iconoclasts held their own Council at Hieria in 754, the proceedings of which have survived only in the long quotations contained for the purpose of refutation in the Acts of the (iconophile) Second Council of Nicaea of 787.[23] After the ending of iconoclasm, the visual depiction of the ecumenical councils in Byzantine churches was one of the ways of asserting the triumph of tradition and authority which was how the iconophiles saw their victory.[24]

But citation of councils was only one of the means by which competing groups within the church had sought to claim the authority of the past. Handbooks, lists of approved citations from Scripture or from the Fathers, commentaries on the Scriptures are only a few of the methods they used.[25] Once the church had gone down the route of trying to define the nature of God in formulas that must be generally agreed, the inevitable result was intense competition and rivalry, in which every participant and every group resorted separately to the authority of tradition. The ultimate futility of the search can be seen in the progressive appeal to God as mystery, beyond human knowing;[26] nevertheless, neither the attempt nor the appeal to authority was abandoned. Not only Christians appealed to tradition. Proclus and other Neoplatonists saw Plato as offering a kind of sacred text.[27] Reading Plato constituted true spiritual life; the dialogues contained the truth about the gods, and this knowledge was handed down by the succession of heads of the Academy, the Platonic school *par excellence*. A program of Neoplatonic studies presented the dialogues in progression of difficulty. And the succession of heads of the Academy was accompanied by appeals to divine inspiration, as with Proclus, whom Marinus depicts as the recipient of signs that he should take on the mantle and preserve the heritage of Athena in her own city of Athens.[28]

Athens shared with all other cities in late antiquity a changing urban environment. It had suffered from Herul attack in the 3rd century, was probably sacked by Alaric in 395–96, and was to undergo invasion again by the Slavs and Avars who raided Greece at the end of the 6th century.[29] But church building came late to Athens, and even in the early 5th century a substantial amount of secular building and restoration took place, which according to a recent excavator "respected the traditional character of the city."[30] It included restoration of the Library of Hadrian and the so-called Palace of the Giants, probably in fact a large villa; additions to the Theater of Dionysus; and restorations of a sundial, the so-called House of Proclus, and several other villas and private and public baths. A late Roman villa at Cenchreae, the port of Corinth, was adorned in the 4th century with representations of antique philosophers, like the seven Sages at Apamea in Syria in the same period. The Empress Eudocia, whose husband was Theodosius II, was an Athenian, said to be the daughter of a sophist and a Christian convert; she had pretensions to classical learning (she wrote rather bad poetry), presented herself as a patron of building in the Holy Land, and may have provided the incentive for some of this 5th century building in Athens.[31]

No doubt Athens was a special case; nevertheless, the majority of city-dwellers in late antiquity still lived among manifestations of the past in the built and visual environment. The porticoed houses of the rich in late antiquity continued in use into the 6th century, even though the stones of the forum might be used without embarrassment for church-building. In Carthage, the Vandal aristocracy on the eve of the Byzantine reconquest by Belisarius in the 530s prided itself on the culture it had taken over from its Roman subjects; passable Latin epigrams celebrated the houses and lifestyle of the Vandal nobles, and the circus remained in use into the Byzantine period. In what is now Jordan, the 6th century was a period of economic vitality, and some Christian communities were still commissioning fine Hellenizing mosaics late into the 8th. But in Constantinople the fire which accompanied the so-called Nika revolt in 532 destroyed not only the original Great Church but also the classical statuary which had adorned the Baths of Zeuxippus and the Senate House. An Egyptian poet, Christodorus of Coptus, had written a long (416 lines) Greek hexameter poem in praise of the Zeuxippus statues.[32] The *spina* around which the chariots raced in the Hippodrome continued to display some of the most famous statues of antiquity, including the reclining Herakles of Lysippus, until they were looted in the Fourth Crusade. But already by the 8th century the city had shrunk to a shadow of its former self, and the remaining classical statuary was only half-understood, or indeed the object of superstitious fear by reason of its pagan associations.[33] By now there was little sound secular education to be had, even in the capital; fascination with the past had replaced actual knowledge, just as the historical Constantine had given way to the Constantine of legend, the saintly founder of Christian Constantinople.

This legendary past was embellished in the imagination in a variety of ways.

An exotic growth of story steadily came to overlay the historical record. Unsatisfactory gaps in the Gospel record were filled in by an abundant mass of apocryphal detail: the infancy of the Virgin and her Dormition and Assumption into heaven, Christ's descent into Hades, the journeyings of the apostles and their contests with pagan disputants like Simon Magus, or the exploits of Thecla, the virgin follower of St. Paul—as vivid and real a model as any real-life person for late antique Christian women like Macrina, the sister of Basil of Caesarea and Gregory of Nyssa. The powerful but apocryphal idea of the finding of the True Cross by Constantine's mother Helena gave rise to a tangle of further stories, among them the entirely legendary tale of the baptism of Constantine by Sylvester, the bishop of Rome.[34] The legends of Constantine lead us, perhaps, into a more recognizably medieval atmosphere, but the apocryphal stories came into being early, and some of them had immense popularity during late antiquity. From the 5th and 6th centuries onward, in particular, the very abundance of their versions and translations indicates how widespread was their influence. Some of their themes were taken into visual art, especially the scenes from the life of the Virgin and the typically Byzantine portrayal of the Resurrection ("Anastasis"), with Christ throwing open the gates of Hell, bringing up Adam, surrounded by the figures of the dead being raised, with the keys and chains of Hell scattered around. Greek homilies, many of them preserved without the name of the author, developed these scenes in dramatic dialogues between Pilate and the Jews, or Hades and Satan, and in the 6th century Romanos, the great poet and deacon of Hagia Sophia, wove similar dialogues between Mary and the Archangel into the texture of his elaborate *kontakia* for performance in the Great Church.[35] The past was open to the poetic and the religious imagination. Even as more severe and scholastic authors were attempting to control the past by marshalling conciliar decisions, or, as John of Damascus did in the 8th century, listing the forms of orthodox belief in a comprehensive synthesis, a flowering of legend, homiletic, and poetry covered the bare bones of Scripture with human detail and unbridled embellishment.

In such a context, and under the influence of a powerful desire for local heroes and heroines, it was easy to conjure up new martyrs to add to the historical record. Many of these were claimed as victims of the Great Persecution under Diocletian or the earlier 3rd century persecutions. Among them were the Forty Martyrs of Sebasteia in the Pontos—according to Basil of Caesarea, whose homily is the earliest testimony, all of them soldiers who froze to death for their Christian faith when they were condemned to stand naked all night in an icy lake; the story was to become so popular that it became one of the commonest motifs in Byzantine art.[36] In the late 4th century the Spanish poet Prudentius composed the *Peristephanon,* a collection of Latin hymns in Horatian style and meter, in which he celebrated the local female martyr Eulalia; he was not the only Latin author to experiment with hymns, but his are the most accomplished to survive, and earned him the description "the Christian Virgil and Horace" from the classical scholar Bentley.[37] Other martyrs appear for the first time in Prudentius's collection, including Emeterius and Chelidonius, the Eighteen Martyrs of Saragossa and St. Cassian of Imola, a schoolteacher killed by his own pupils; Lawrence and Vincent, on the other hand, were already popular saints when Prudentius wrote about them. Lawrence was the subject of inscriptions put up by Pope Damasus and of an account by Ambrose of Milan, even if the "Acta" of the saint are themselves later, and Vincent was the subject of five sermons by Augustine. Yet another category is that of the early fictional or apocryphal figures like Thecla, subject of the late 2nd century *Acts of Paul and Thecla,* who acquire shrines and increasingly elaborate legends; Thecla's shrine at Seleucia in Isauria (Meriemlik in southern Turkey) was one of the largest of such complexes, with extensive hostel accommodation for visitors. It was visited and described by Egeria on her journey in the 380s, and the large basilica was rebuilt on a grand scale by the Emperor Zeno in the 5th century. The Greek *Life and Miracles of Thecla,* also of the 5th century, was therefore an understandable and desirable addition to the available materials about the saint.[38]

By these means, the past became populated with heroic figures capable of marvelous deeds. The "invention" (quite literally, "finding") of relics of such saints, whether for a new church or as the focal point of a town or a shrine, was simply another way of connecting with the saints of the past, of rendering the past more real. In the 6th century a pilgrim to the Holy Land from Piacenza recorded that when he came to Cana in Galilee, he reclined on the very couch where Jesus had attended the famous wedding; he then did what so many others have done since in other such places—he carved on it the names of his family.[39] The bones of martyrs, eagerly transported across the empire, conveyed the same exciting feeling of closeness to the past. Constantine had to make do with being placed in his mausoleum at Constantinople surrounded by twelve empty sarcophagi representing the apostles, but his son Constantius managed to find the bones of Timothy, Luke, and Andrew and bring them to the capital.[40] Likewise Ambrose of Milan immediately appropriated for the city's basilica the relics of SS. Gervasius and Protasius conveniently found in a different shrine nearby. Peter Brown has written of the sense of closeness, and the link with the past, which Paulinus of Nola experienced through the honors he paid to St. Felix.[41] Relics provided a sense of supernatural protection in the present; but they also linked the present and the past.

The most prestigious of relics, but also the most elusive, were those associated with Christ himself. Constantinople claimed Mary's girdle and her robe, Ephesus her last dwelling place. In the late 6th century the pilgrim from Piacenza saw a cloth at Memphis in Egypt which bore the features of Christ, and in the 7th century Arculf, another western pilgrim, saw his burial cloth in Jerusalem.[42] Eusebius in the early 4th century already knew that the city of Edessa in northern Mesopotamia boasted of a letter written by Jesus to King Abgar, and Egeria saw it when she visited Edessa in the 380s. But a written document was not enough: a miraculous image was also produced, impressed directly from Christ's face onto a cloth, and thus "not made by human hands."[43] Other such images existed in the late 6th century, but this one had a longer history. By the 8th century it was known in the west, and it was cited during iconoclasm as proof that pictures had divine approval, and that they represented the unwritten but authentic tradition to be set beside the written one of the Scriptures and the Fathers. The culmination of the story came in 944, when the Edessan image itself, now known as the "Mandylion," was brought to Constantinople and solemnly ensconced in the imperial palace chapel. It was destined to become the model for reproductions of the Holy Face of Christ in Byzantine and later churches even up to the present century. But significantly, reproductions were not enough; a new narrative of origins was produced, which combined a variety of early stories about how the image had come into being and been found and preserved at Edessa.[44] Once again the past was retold to fit the present.

Religious images—icons, mosaics, frescoes, or works in other media—also retold the past. Their authority was challenged by the iconoclasts in favor of the Eucharist and the symbol of the Cross. But iconoclasm did not last, and its end (represented by the iconophiles as a major victory) was an endorsement of the truth claims of religious narrative art. For even though the formal cycles characteristic of later Byzantine figural church decoration were by no means yet established,[45] nevertheless, icons were held not merely to symbolize but actually to reveal the truth, and as such to make plain the sacred past.[46] They revealed it as much as did the councils, the Scriptures, and tradition; and in so doing they affirmed orthodox belief.[47] The past was not only rewritten, it was revealed in pictures.

The physical remains of the sacred past were also sought elsewhere, above all in what is tellingly referred to as "the Holy Land."[48] The late 4th century pilgrim Egeria traveled to the east, book in hand; the Bible provided the text and the guidebook. But she also found human guides ready to point out what she should see. On her first sighting of Mt. Sinai, she was told by her guides, she should say a prayer; in this valley the children of Israel made their golden calf, and waited for Moses to come down from the mountain. There were already holy men living in cells around a church at the foot of the mountain, who could show the way, and a little church on the very top, where Egeria and her party listened to the reading of the story of Moses from the Bible and received communion.[49] The Burning Bush was growing in "a very pretty garden" in front of a church, much as today it grows beside the *katholikon* of the Monastery of St. Catherine, and Egeria was shown the spot where Moses unloosed his sandals, again with a reading of the appropriate passage in Exodus. This pattern was repeated as the journey continued, and Egeria's own account is full of her close knowledge of the Hebrew Bible and her enthusiasm to fit what she saw to the biblical text. On the way to Mt. Nebo, Egeria identifies the plain where the children of Israel wept for Moses, where Joshua the son of Nun was filled with the spirit of wisdom when Moses died, and "where Moses wrote the Book of Deuteronomy" and blessed all the Israelites individually before he died.

Egeria may not have possessed the highest level of culture, to judge from her style of writing, but she was an enthusiast. She already had copies at home of the letter sent by Abgar of Edessa to Jesus and the latter's reply, when she was given further copies by the local bishop; nor was she anyone's fool, noticing at once that the new text was not only preferable, as coming from Edessa itself, but was in fact longer.[50] The praise given to Egeria in a letter to fellow monks by a certain Galician monk called Valerius in the 7th century is entirely justified. He describes her approach to the task before her very well: "First with great industry she perused all the books of the Old and New Testaments, and discovered all their descriptions of the wonders of the world; and its regions, provinces, cities, mountains and deserts. Then in eager haste (though it was to take many years) she set out with God's help to explore them."

By Egeria's day the idea of a Christian Holy Land was well established; Jerome, Paula, Melania the Elder, and other prominent persons went there to found monastic communities and live in proximity to the holy places. It had not always been so. Another of Eusebius's works, the *Onomasticon*, paved the way for the identification of Scriptural sites. But it was Constantine who invented the notion of Christian archaeology in the Holy Land with the excavation of the sites of Golgotha and the tomb of Christ. The aim was to go down below the Hadrianic levels of Aelia Capitolina and reveal the city as it had been in the time of Christ. The workmen demolished a pagan temple built on the spot, and the emperor ordered all the rubble and stones to be cleared away from the site, and for the site to be excavated to a great depth. Then, "as stage by stage the underground was exposed, at last against all expectation the revered and all-hallowed Martyrion of the Savior's resurrection was itself revealed, and the cave, the holy of holies, took on the appearance of a representation of the Saviour's return to life."[51] Even Eusebius's contorted prose, and the many difficulties surrounding this account, cannot hide the sense of excitement in the writing. This piece of excavation was followed by others: the Church of the Nativity at Bethlehem and a church on the Mount of Olives were both built over and around caves, and there was a further church at Mamre, where Abraham met with the angels. In due course the building of the Holy Sepulcher complex (which was also described in detail by Egeria) produced the greatest relic of all, the True Cross, soon to be joined by such objects as the *titulus* (inscription) from the cross of Christ, the crosses of the two thieves, the crown of thorns, the sponge, and the lance used to pierce Jesus's side.[52] Pilgrimage took off in the 4th century, and Egeria was one among many who sought to make the sites of sacred history their own.[53] The emotion with which these holy places became vested can be experienced nowhere more profoundly than in the laments after the loss of Jerusalem to the Persians in 614 composed by Sophronius, monk of St. Theodosius and future patriarch of the city; or in the heartfelt sermon written on his first Christmas by the same Sophronius after he became patriarch in 634, when he found Bethlehem, the place of Christ's birth, in the hands of "Saracens" and out of reach of his flock.[54] In late antiquity the Christian Holy Land was won and lost, reclaimed by Constantine and his mother in the 320s and lost first to the Persians and then to the Arabs in the 7th century. Both sets of events required extraordinary feats of historical reorientation.

The Sassanians had their own annals of the dynasty.[55] And when Muhammad received his revelations they included long disquisitions on the past of the

peoples of the Book, the descent from Abraham, and the line of prophets of
whom Muhammad was the final example and culmination. Like Christianity,
Islam found a way of incorporating the Hebrew Bible to its own advantage.
Jesus, too, was recognized as a prophet; he could perform miracles, and his
mother was honored as a virgin, but he did not die on the cross, and certainly
was not God incarnate. Muhammad's task was to correct history as well as to
fulfill it by announcing the final revelation. The debt of Islam to Judaism and to
Christianity is profound, but it did not continue those religions so much as
reinterpret them. The process took some time; in the meantime the religious
culture of the Middle East presented the appearance of a patchwork of interpretations and memories by three religions with a shared past (which is not to
discount either the surviving traces of paganism or the different varieties of
Christianity). One technique employed in the Qur'ān, as in the Bible, was
genealogy: the genealogy of Mary, for example, was a theme shared in Muslim
scholarship and in the Christian-Jewish debates,[56] and the descent of the children of Israel became a major issue. In the west, too, genealogy was a powerful
tool in the formation of a Gothic history and Gothic self-understanding.[57] The
writers of Gothic history created a historical past and a written history for the
Goths out of materials which included the existing social memory.[58]

Those who sought to understand history from within the context of the
Roman empire faced different, though often related, problems. In his *Histories
against the Pagans,* Orosius tried to make sense of the fact that disaster could
strike an apparently Christian empire by placing the sack of Rome by Alaric in
410 in a long context of disasters which had happened before the *tempora
christiana.* Augustine's view expressed in the *City of God* was more complex
and more profound, but not essentially different: Rome before Christianity had
been fundamentally flawed, the missing element a proper respect for God.
Augustine was less interested here to absorb Old Testament history into his
own long view than to wrestle with the Roman, non-Christian past, and to ask
wherein lay Rome's greatness; the answer he came up with was not encouraging. But Augustine was hardly typical; for most, the past represented by the
Hebrew Bible was indeed gradually incorporated into general historical understanding.

Some writers, indeed, were resistant, and went on composing secular histories without recourse to the Scriptures or to sacred time. As late as the 6th
century it was still possible to write in this way, taking studious care to preserve
conventions set a thousand years before. But the task became more difficult,
and the attempt was eventually abandoned. In the late 4th century Ammianus
Marcellinus was the author of a Latin history which in its sweep and sheer
energy rivals any of the works of the classical historians, and he was followed
by a line of historians writing in Greek, of whom Procopius of Caesarea was the
best and the last. But there was no Byzantine narrative history of the Arab
conquests, and the Persian wars of Heraclius have to be pieced together from
poetic and religiously inspired sources.[59] In late antiquity, and even through to
the late Byzantine period, the yearly calendar with its representations of the
months and seasons continued to carry a heavy traditional symbolism; a mosaic

from the Villa of the Falconer at Argos of around 500 displays a cycle of
months with their attributes that can be paralleled in manuscript illustration as
late as the Empire of Trebizond in the 14th century.[60] But already the more
explicitly pagan elements of earlier imagery of the months had given place to
the more neutral theme of the labors of the months, and the familiar symbolism
of the seasons had long been adapted to a Christian purpose. In his Latin
panegyric on the accession of Justin II (565 C.E.), Corippus applies to the
Hippodrome the symbolism of the annually revolving seasons and the sun god
with his four-horse chariot. He adds the cautious reminder that "when the
maker of the sun decided to let himself be seen beneath the sun, and when God
took the shape of humankind from a virgin, then the games of the sun were
abolished, and honors and games were offered to the Roman emperors, and the
pleasant amusements of the circus to New Rome";[61] but the disclaimer licenses
him to associate the accession of the new emperor with the rising of the sun and
the perpetual renewal of the phoenix, another symbol of renovatio that had
been appropriated for Christian use since the 4th century, when the image was
applied to Constantine by Eusebius.

Historical time, that is, linear time, was by and large transformed into religious time. Augustine struggled to understand time; "What is time? Who can
explain this easily and briefly? Who can comprehend this even in thought so as
to articulate the answer in words?"[62] He was sure, though, that it must have
begun with creation. So were the writers of the chronicles, who now self-
confidently began to take as their starting point nothing less than the creation
of the world. If a chronicle did not begin with creation, it was only because it
was a continuation of an earlier one which did; thus Marcellinus the comes,
writing in Latin in 6th century Constantinople, begins by recalling the wonderful work by Eusebius which covered the period from the creation of the world
to Emperor Constantine, and its Latin continuation by Jerome up to the time of
Emperor Valens (d. 378).[63] The date of creation was a matter of dispute, being
variously counted as 5500, 5508, or (by Eusebius and Jerome) 5200 B.C.E., but
the point was to continue the tradition of harmonizing scriptural events with
Greek and Roman history, and for the more recent period to weave together
secular and religious material. Marcellinus took official lists, such as lists of
consuls, and material that apparently came from city annals of Constantinople,
and expanded it with the aid of a limited range of other authorities.[64] His
chronicle was continued in turn by another author, just as he had consciously
continued that of Jerome. But the chroniclers' perception also pointed to the
future: linear time implied not only the beginning but also the end of the world.
The Second Coming would be preceded by the rule of Antichrist and the end of
things; history could be divided according to the prophecy of the four successive
kingdoms contained in the Book of Daniel, and the last things could be expected at a date which would allow an interpretation of the history of the world
as corresponding in millennial terms to the six days of creation.[65] Speculation as
to exactly when and how this would occur varied. It intensified as the year
which might notionally represent 6000 years since creation approached, and
particularly so in the context of the wars against the Persians and then against

the Arabs. As always, the actual date was successively adjusted to accommodate the world's stubborn refusal to end. The claim that Jewish prophecy had in truth been fulfilled in Christianity was reiterated with more and more urgency, both in written texts and in visual art; Jews are shown as routed, and Christian imagery to have appropriated and subsumed that of the Tabernacle. (It was a small step, given this scenario, for iconophile art and texts to represent the iconoclasts in the guise of Jews.)[66]

In Islam, which inherited the linear conception of history, the progression was that of revelation. Previous prophets, of whom Jesus was one, had served to prepare the way for the final revelation and for Muhammad, the final prophet; the peoples of the Book had their place in history, and were worthy of respect—certainly they were to be placed far above pagans and idolaters—but their revelation was at best partial and therefore inferior. The shadow of impending judgment extended to all.

Faced with so powerfully coherent a view, historians found it hard to maintain a secular approach to the past. Christians found various ways in which to exert a claim over the classical culture which long remained the main staple of education for the elite. Indeed, among the 7th century liturgical and documentary papyri found in the remote outpost of Nessana on the Egyptian border are texts of Virgil. Attempts to come to terms with this literary heritage included Christian experiments with classical form, among which one of the quainter attempts is the Christian "cento" on creation and the life of Jesus, which was put together by an upper-class woman called Proba in the 4th century from lines taken from Virgil's *Aeneid;* portrayed in the vocabulary and persona of *pius Aeneas,* this is a heroicized Jesus who would fail to convince most Christians. Corippus's use of the Virgilian model for his eight-book hexameter poem on the campaigns of John Troglita in North Africa in the 540s was somewhat more appropriate. Others also tried the experiment of putting Christian material into classical dress: the Greek paraphrase of the Gospel according to John by the learned 5th century poet Nonnus was one example, and in Latin, biblical epic became a respectable genre. Claudian, another major Latin poet of the late 4th century, and an Egyptian, like so many of the poets of the period, was the author of a short poem on the Savior, but preferred to keep Christian themes and vocabulary out of his major works, choosing even in his eulogy of Serena, the pious wife of Stilicho, to draw instead on the conventional apparatus of classical mythology.[67] Generations of Christians struggled to reconcile the literary culture they had learned with their Christian faith. Many of their accommodations were facile. But others, like Tertullian in the 2nd century, who had asked, "What had Athens to do with Jerusalem?" or Augustine in the 5th, who was still wrestling with the question, saw the issue in bleaker terms; Augustine's answer, in the *City of God,* was long in coming and gloomy in its message. His "great and arduous work"[68] devoted ten of its twenty-two books to the demonstration that the literary and philosophical culture of Augustine's youth, to which he had given his best efforts and his loyalties, must finally be rejected. "Your" Virgil, the Virgil of the pagans, is contrasted with "our" Scriptures, and the edifice of Platonism, which Augustine recognizes as having come nearest to that of Christianity, is seen to be, in Peter Brown's words, "a magnificent failure."[69]

But even a rejected pagan past could be put to use. A work that proved to be fundamental in providing the model for subsequent saints' lives, the *Life of Antony* (d. 356) by Athanasius, makes much of its hero's rejection of worldly education and sophisticated learning; Antony's speech to pagans, as well as his response to the receipt of an imperial letter, are meant to teach the superiority of faith and holiness over learning and secular authority.[70] Yet the text itself deployed literary models borrowed from pagan lives, and pointed the way for virtually all subsequent hagiographic literature to base itself on the categories of the classical encomium. The Christian holy man or woman described in hagiographic literature was henceforth presented in the mode prescribed for the classical writers of encomia by the rhetorical handbooks.[71]

Nor were emperors exempt from this treatment; it was applied to Constantine by Eusebius, and continued to provide the basic categories of the qualities of the Christian emperor.[72] Till late in the Byzantine period, emperors were judged and their reigns interpreted in the light of expectations derived from the twin sources of the traditional Roman imperial virtues and the Christian framework, onto which the former had been grafted by Eusebius and his successors. Inevitably emperors themselves also accepted these categories, and presented themselves in their official pronouncements and writings simultaneously as heirs to the Romans and as pious Christian *basileis*.[73] In what was surely one of the greatest achievements of late antiquity, Justinian brought about the codification of the whole of existing Roman law, and legislated how law was to be taught and the legal profession recruited henceforth. His preambles present him in the guise of restorer, his work of codification as a *renovatio*. But his reign was fraught with ambiguities. While in the works of Procopius we find both praise and condemnation, John Lydus, a contemporary and a conservative, saw the emperor as a restorer, and placed the blame on his ministers when things went wrong; the contradictions led Edward Gibbon to the negative verdict that Justinian's proclaimed restoration of Roman law was no such thing.[74] Gibbon's final verdict on Justinian as lawmaker reads: "the government of Justinian united the evils of liberty and servitude; and the Romans were oppressed at the same time by the multiplicity of their laws and the arbitrary will of their master." John Lydus complained of the decline of Latin in his day, and indeed Justinian's own laws were commonly issued in Greek. But while Greek did indeed take the place of Latin in official use from the reign of Heraclius (610–641), emperors continued to see themselves as following in the Roman tradition, and Byzantines called themselves by the name "Romans" for centuries.

It would be wrong, however, to suggest uniformity. Gregory of Tours, the historian of the Franks, begins his history by asserting his own Christian faith and doctrinal correctness; part of the proof of that probity is, "for the sake of those who are losing hope as they see the end of the world coming nearer and nearer," to explain in chronicle fashion the history of the world since creation.[75] His predecessors in this enterprise are named as Eusebius, Jerome, Orosius, and Victorius. Signs, portents, and wonders articulate Gregory's work and point to

the approaching end, and the bloody history of the Merovingian dynasty marks
the "beginning of our sorrows," when internal strife and disorder were destroying the Frankish people and the kingdom.[76] The work ends with a computation
of the years that have elapsed since the creation: 5792,[77] perilously close to the
6000 after which the world would end. Gregory precedes this computation
with a list of all the bishops of Tours, and of his own works.

Yet life in Merovingian Gaul also preserved some of the qualities of the elite
lifestyle of the late Roman upper class, and a courtly piety developed among
women in royal circles and elsewhere. Gregory's friend and contemporary, the
poet Venantius Fortunatus, who ended his life as bishop of Tours, conducted a
delicate literary friendship with Queen Radegund and the ladies of the convent
at Poitiers, punctuated by elegant poems and gifts of fruit and delicacies.[78]
Despite the praise of the Byzantine historian Agathias, when he wrote about the
Franks in the late 6th century,[79] the Merovingian royal dynasty was prone to
plots and violence; nevertheless, it created a kingdom in which, for all Gregory
of Tours's complaints about the decline of the liberal arts, the court and the
administration continued until the later 7th century to act as a focus and
stimulus for the kind of social and governmental literacy familiar from the later
Roman empire.[80] Even in the 7th century, it was still possible at times to think
of a united Mediterranean, linked by common ties of religion and learning.
Greek culture, in the persons of monks and ecclesiastics, spread to Italy and
Sicily; there was a series of Greek popes; and Archbishop Theodore of Canterbury, himself from the east, founded a scriptorium for the copying of Greek
texts and was a participant in the theological disputes which occupied the
minds of 7th century eastern churchmen.[81]

The project of remaking the past during late antiquity demanded great imagi-
native effort and ingenuity. Successive generations of Christians struggled either
to weave together the strands of their classical and their biblical inheritance or
to assert the primacy of the latter over the former. Their attitudes toward Jews
sharpened; the Hebrew Bible, and especially the prophets, were now to be read
as foretelling Christianity, the Tabernacle and the Mosaic law as superseded by
the new dispensation. Already in the 4th century Eusebius had portrayed Constantine, the new Moses, as building a tabernacle for himself while on campaign, and in the 8th century Bede in his Northumbrian monastery composed
three homilies and three works of biblical exegesis on the themes of the Tabernacle and the Temple. The Temple, the cherubim, the Ark, and manna were all
read as prototypes of Christian religious images, proof against any suspicion
that the latter might be the cause of idolatry. Dealing with the classical past
presented other problems: it could be approached on the level of literary culture, attacked as false and demonic for its pagan associations, or neutralized by
being absorbed into the Christian chronological framework which started with
creation and placed world history in successive phases thereafter. Islam marked
the past as different, as the "age of ignorance" for the idolatrous pagan past, or
as containing only partial, if legitimate, revelation in the cases of Judaism and
Christianity. Moreover, the past was assigned a meaning and a purpose; it
pointed the way toward full revelation, which in turn pointed toward the end of

the world. Much effort and labor went into this remaking of the past: first the scholarly labor of commentary and chronicle and, especially from the 6th century onward, encyclopedic labor which sought to define a total and comprehensive definition of Christian knowledge; and second the labor of imagination, which filled every gap in the record with a rich texture of story and legend.

The sheer energy of late antiquity is breathtaking. Every inch of the past received attention, and many topics and many texts were the subject of volumes of exegesis and comment. Nor were texts enough: the story was told, and thus its truth fixed, in pictures and other forms of visual art. It was this very exuberance and invention which the reforming iconoclasts attempted unsuccessfully to curb.

We see in late antiquity a mass of experimentation, new ways being tried and new adjustments made. The process of myth-making and development of new identities inevitably implied the shaping of the past according to current preoccupations. Like the medieval west, Byzantium was also engaged in this process. Byzantine society has often been seen as static and unchanging, "theocratic" and without the possibility of dissent. But all recent research demonstrates that this was far from the case in practice: we have been taken in by the Byzantines themselves, who liked to emphasize their own traditionalism. Both east and west continued to engage in the reshaping of the past. The contemporary sense of the approaching end of the world lent itself to infinite procrastination and renegotiation as the projected day came closer.[82] The early medieval west was characterized by diversity, not uniformity.[83] The final collapse of iconoclasm gave rise in the east to a burst of artistic and cultural activity, from manuscript decoration to literary works. In both east and west, state and church, the two poles of authority, were in constant tension with each other.[84] Conversion continued to be a main preoccupation in both east and west. Faced by a huge loss of territory, including Jerusalem and the Holy Land, Byzantium turned its attention to the peoples of the north, peoples like the Slavs and the Bulgars who were still pagan. The outcome of the struggle between church and state was as yet uncertain; and within the diminished empire of the 8th century the relation of the present to the past was still a topic of tension and struggle. During late antiquity the past had been remade, but it had been remade in many different ways, and the effort continued.

Notes

1. Claudian, *De bello Gildonico* 1.21–25, Loeb trans.; see Alan Cameron, *Claudian* (Oxford, 1970), 365–366.
2. Ammianus Marcellinus, 16.10.1ff.; see John Matthews, *The Roman Empire of Ammianus* (London, 1989).
3. See David Lowenthal, *The Past Is a Foreign Country* (Cambridge, 1955), 155.
4. Some of the legends of Constantine are translated in S. C. Lieu, *From Constantine to Julian: Pagan and Byzantine Views. A Source History* (London, 1996).
5. The difficult question of an apparently changing aesthetic sensitivity is the subject

of an interesting discussion by Jas Elsner, *Art and the Roman Viewer: The Transformation of Art from the Pagan World to Christianity* (Cambridge, Eng., 1995).

6. For a major discussion of Eusebius's apologetic work and his biblical scholarship see T. D. Barnes, *Constantine and Eusebius* (Cambridge, Mass., 1981). Contrary to Eusebius's claims, oracular shrines were in full function in the reign of Constantine and after, and were supported by many other forms of pagan divination: see R. Lane Fox, *Pagans and Christians in the Mediterranean World from the Second Century A.D. to the Conversion of Constantine* (Harmondsworth, 1986); P. Athanassiadi, "Dreams, Theurgy, and Freelance Divination: The Testimony of Iamblichus," *Journal of Roman Studies* 83 (1993): 114–130; "Persecution and Response in Late Paganism: The Evidence of Damascius," *Journal of Hellenic Studies* 113 (1993): 1–29.

7. See Elizabeth A. Clark, *The Origenist Controversy: The Cultural Construction of an Early Christian Debate* (Princeton, 1992).

8. Philip Rousseau, *Basil of Caesarea* (Berkeley, 1994), 320.

9. Ibid., 325.

10. *Confessions* 11–12; *De civ.Dei* 11.

11. See Herbert Kessler, "Gazing at the Future: The *Parousia* Miniature in Vatican gr. 699," in Christopher Moss and Katherine Kiefer, eds., *Byzantine East, Latin West: Art-Historical Studies in Honor of Kurt Weitzmann* (Princeton, 1996), 365–371. Kessler describes the miniature in question (fol. 89r) as "one of the earliest representations of the Last Judgment" (365).

12. *De civ.Dei* 11.32.

13. See Elaine Pagels, *Adam, Eve, and the Serpent* (New York and London, 1988); Peter Brown, *The Body and Society: Men, Women, and Sexual Renunciation in Early Christianity* (New York, 1988).

14. *Exp. Pers.* 2.2.113; for the Heraclian "David plates," part of a silver treasure found on Cyprus at the site of the Byzantine town of Lambousa, see K. Weitzmann, *The Age of Spirituality: Late Antique and Early Christian Art, Third to Seventh Century* (New York, 1979), nos. 425–433.

15. *PG* 92.1161–1754; see Mary Whitby, "The Devil in Disguise: The End of George of Pisidia's *Hexaemeron* Reconsidered," *Journal of Hellenic Studies* 115 (1995): 115–129; "A New Image for a New Age: George of Pisidia on the Emperor Heraclius," in E. Dabrowa, ed., *The Roman and Byzantine Army in the Near East* (Cracow, 1994), 197–225.

16. John Hick, in John Hick, ed., *The Myth of God Incarnate* (London, 1977), 184.

17. *Panarion* 51.22.10; see G. W. Bowersock, *Hellenism in Late Antiquity* (Cambridge, Eng., 1990), 22–28.

18. See Bowersock, *Hellenism*, 49–52.

19. See M. Tardieu, *Les paysages reliques: Routes et haltes syriennes d'Isidore à Simplicius* (Louvain and Paris, 1990).

20. See David S. Potter, *Prophecy and History in the Crisis of the Roman Empire: A Historical Commentary on the Thirteenth Sibylline Oracle* (Oxford, 1990).

21. Potter, *Prophecy*, 351–355, and see also Stephen Mitchell, *Anatolia: Land, Men, and Gods in Asia Minor II. The Rise of the Church* (Oxford, 1993), 43–44, in the context of a very interesting discussion of the linked developments in pagan, Christian, and Jewish theology.

22. *Or.* 18–21.

23. For the uses (and sometimes the fabrication) of texts at these councils see P. Van den Ven, "La patristique et l'hagiographie au concile de Nicée en 787," *Byzantion* 25–27 (1955–1957): 325–362; and see Cyril Mango, "The Availability of Books in the Byzantine Empire, A.D. 750–850," in *Byzantine Books and Bookmen* (Washington, D.C., 1975), 29–45.

24. Councils in visual art: C. Walter, "Le souvenir du IIᵉ Concile de Nicée dans

l'iconographie byzantine," in F. Boespflug and N. Lossky, eds., *Nicée II, 787–1987: Douze siècles d'images religieuses* (Paris, 1987), 163–183.

25. Averil Cameron, "Texts as Weapons: Polemic in the Byzantine Dark Ages," in Alan K. Bowman and Greg Woolf, eds., *Literacy and Power in the Ancient World* (Cambridge, 1994), 198–215; "Ascetic Closure and the End of Antiquity," in Vincent L. Wimbush and Richard Valantasis, eds., *Asceticism* (New York, 1995), 147–161.

26. See Frances Young in Hick, ed., *The Myth of God Incarnate*, 13–47, 28–29; for the expression of Christianity in terms of mystery and paradox, which pulled against the totalizing thrust of theological discourse, see Averil Cameron, *Christianity and the Rhetoric of Empire* (Berkeley, 1991), chap. 5.

27. Proclus, *Platonic Theology* 1.4.

28. Marinus, *Vit.Procli* 10.

29. See Paavo Castrén, ed., *Post-Herulian Athens* (Helsinki, 1994) (for Alaric see p. 9); Alison Frantz, *The Athenian Agora XXIV: Late Antiquity, A.D. 267–700* (Princeton, 1988), 93.

30. Ibid., 9.

31. Socrates, *Hist.eccl.* 7.21; see Julia Burman, in Castrén, *Post-Herulian Athens,* 63–87; Alan Cameron, "The Empress and the Poet: Paganism and Politics at the Court of Theodosius II," in John J. Winkler and Gordon Williams, eds., *Later Greek Literature* (Cambridge, 1982), 217–289.

32. *Anth.Pal.* II.

33. Gilbert Dagron, *Constantinople imaginaire: Étude sur le recueil du Patria* (Paris, 1984); Averil Cameron and Judith Herrin et al., eds., *Constantinople in the Eighth Century: The Parastaseis Syntomoi Chronikai* (Leiden, 1984); Cyril Mango, "Antique Statuary and the Byzantine Beholder," *Dumbarton Oaks Papers* 17 (1963): 53–75; Liz James, "'Pray Not To Fall into Temptation and Be on Your Guard': Pagan Statues in Christian Constantinople," *Gesta* 35.1 (1996): 12–20.

34. See Lieu, *From Constantine to Julian,* 27.

35. Anna Kartsonis, *Anastasis: The Making of an Image* (Princeton, 1986). Dramatic dialogues: Averil Cameron, "Disputations, Polemical Literature, and the Formation of Opinion in the Early Byzantine Period," in G. J. Reinink and H. L. J. Vanstiphout, eds., *Dispute Poems and Dialogues in the Ancient and Mediaeval Near East* (Leuven, 1991), 91–108.

36. Henry Maguire, *Art and Eloquence in Byzantium* (Princeton, 1981), 36–42; Basil, *PG* 31.508–540.

37. Anne-Marie Palmer, *Prudentius on the Martyrs* (Oxford, 1989), 98.

38. Gilbert Dagron, ed., *Vie et miracles de Sainte Thècle* (Brussels, 1978); F. Hild and H. Hellenkemper, *Kilikien und Isaurien* (Vienna, 1990), 441–443; S. Hill, *The Early Byzantine Churches of Cilicia and Isauria* (Aldershot, 1966), 208–234.

39. *Itin.Anton.* 4.

40. See Cyril Mango, "Constantine's Mausoleum and the Translation of Relics," *Byzantinische Zeitschrift* 83 (1990): 51–62, repr. in Mango, *Studies on Constantinople* (Aldershot, 1993), V, with Addendum.

41. Peter Brown, *The Cult of the Saints* (Chicago, 1981), 53–57; cf. 36–39 on Ambrose.

42. See E. Kitzinger, "The Cult of Images before Iconoclasm," *Dumbarton Oaks Papers* 8 (1954): 85–150; Memphis: *Itin.Anton.* 4: *pallium linteum in quo est effigies Salvatoris.*

43. See Averil Cameron, "The History of the Image of Edessa: The Telling of a Story," *Okeanos: Essays Presented to I. Ševčenko* (Cambridge, Mass., 1983), 80–94; the first reference to the image as "not made by human hands" is in the *Ecclesiastical History* of Evagrius Scholasticus, written in the 590s (*Hist.eccl.* 4.27).

44. *Narratio de imagine edessena, PG* 113: 421–454.

45. Liz James, "Monks, Monastic Art, the Sanctoral Cycle, and the Middle Byzantine Church," in Margaret Mullett and Anthony Kirby, eds., *The Theotokos Evergetis and Eleventh-Century Monasticism* (Belfast, 1994), 162–175.

46. This is the argument of Hans Belting, *Likeness and Presence: A History of the Image before the Era of Art* (Chicago, 1994).

47. The bibliography is large: see especially J.-M. Sansterre, "La parole, le texte et l'image selon les auteurs byzantins des époques iconoclastes et posticonoclaste," in *Testo e Immagine nell'alto medioevo, 15–21 aprile 1993* (Spoleto, 1994), 197–243.

48. On the development of the idea of the Christian "Holy Land," see Robert L. Wilken, *The Land Called Holy: Palestine in Christian History and Thought* (New Haven, 1992).

49. John Wilkinson, trans., *Egeria's Travels,* rev. ed. (Warminster, 1981), 96, 105, 117, 175.

50. The process is vividly described in book 3 of Eusebius's *Life of Constantine;* for the history of the site and scholarly investigation to date see the comprehensive account by Martin Biddle, "The Tomb of Christ: Sources, Methods, and a New Approach," in Kenneth Painter, ed., *"Churches Built in Ancient Times": Recent Studies in Early Christian Archaeology* (London, 1994), 73–147.

51. *Vit.Const.* 3.28.

52. Three crosses and the nails: Socrates, *Hist.eccl.* 1.17 (5th century).

53. See in particular E. D. Hunt, *Holy Land Pilgrimage in the Later Roman Empire A.D. 312–460* (Oxford, 1982); R. Ousterhout, ed., *The Blessings of Pilgrimage* (Urbana, Ill., 1990).

54. Ed. H. Usener, "Das Weihnachtspredigt des Sophronios," *Rheinisches Museum für Philologie,* n.s. 41 (1886): 500–516.

55. Discussion of this *Book of the Lords,* traces of which survive in the later Persian *Shāhnāma* of Firdausi and Arabic chronicle of al-Tabarī: Zeev Rubin, "The reforms of Khusro Anūshirwān," in Averil Cameron, ed., *The Byzantine and Early Islamic Near East I: States, Resources, and Armies* (Princeton, 1995), 227–297. In the late 6th century Agathias claims to have drawn on these *Annals* in the sections of his *History* where he recounts the history of the Sassanians (*Hist.* 2.23–27; 4.24–30; cf. 2.27.4–8; 4.30.2–5).

56. See Averil Cameron, "Byzantines and Jews: Recent Work on Early Byzantium," *Byzantine and Modern Greek Studies* 20 (1996).

57. See Peter Heather, "Cassiodorus and the Rise of the Amals: Genealogy and the Goths under Hun Domination," *Journal of Roman Studies* 79 (1989): 103–128.

58. For the historians, see Walter Goffart, *The Narrators of Barbarian History (A.D. 550–800): Jordanes, Gregory of Tours, Bede, and Paul the Deacon* (Princeton, 1988); James Fentress and Chris Wickham, *Social Memory* (Oxford, 1992), contains a chapter on the medieval west (144–172).

59. See Michael Whitby, "Greek Historical Writing after Procopius: Variety and Vitality," in Averil Cameron and Lawrence I. Conrad, eds., *The Byzantine and Early Islamic Near East I: Problems in the Literary Source Material* (Princeton, 1992), 25–80.

60. See G. Åkerström-Hougen, *The Calendar and Hunting Mosaics of the Villa of the Falconer in Argos: A Study in Early Byzantine Iconography* (Stockholm, 1974), esp. 83–85.

61. Corippus, *Iust.* 1.340–44.

62. *Confessions* 11.17, trans. Chadwick.

63. Marcellinus, *Chron., praef.*

64. See Brian Croke, *The Chronicle of Marcellinus: Translation and Commentary* (Sydney, 1995); another well-known (Greek) 6th century chronicle is that of John Malalas, for which see the translation by Elizabeth Jeffreys, Michael Jeffreys, and Roger Scott et al., *The Chronicle of John Malalas* (Melbourne, 1986), and Elizabeth Jeffreys et al., eds., *Studies in John Malalas* (Sydney, 1990).

65. See Paul Magdalino, "The History of the Future and Its Uses: Prophecy, Policy, and Propaganda," in Roderick Beaton and Charlotte Roueché, eds., *The Making of Byzantine History: Studies Dedicated to Donald M. Nicol* (Aldershot, 1993), 3–34.

66. See Averil Cameron, "Byzantines and Jews."

67. *Carm.min.* 32. De Salvatore, ed. J. B. Hall., cf. 30, Laus Serenae.

68. *De civ.Dei* I, *praef.*, 8.

69. Peter Brown, *Augustine of Hippo* (London, 1967), 306–307.

70. Athanasius, *Vit.Ant.* 74–80, 81.

71. See Cameron, *Christianity and the Rhetoric of Empire,* chaps. 2 and 3.

72. From the surviving collection of twelve Latin imperial panegyrics, several deal with Constantine and their content, and the categories they apply are closely paralleled in Eusebius's Greek *Vita Constantiniana:* see C. E. V. Nixon and Barbara Saylor Rogers, eds., *In Praise of Later Roman Emperors: The Panegyrici Latini* (Berkeley, 1994).

73. The combination persisted: see Margaret Mullett, "The Imperial Vocabulary of Alexios I Komnenos," in Margaret Mullett and Dion Smythe, eds., *Alexios I Komnenos: Papers* (Belfast, 1996), 359–397. One of Eusebius's most influential successors was Agapetos the deacon, author of a "Mirror for Princes" in the 6th century (*PG* 86.1, 1163–1186): see P. Henry III, "A Mirror for Justinian: The *Ekthesis* of Agapetus Diaconus," *Greek, Roman, and Byzantine Studies* 8 (1967): 281–308.

74. *Renovatio:* see Michael Maas, "Roman History and Christian Ideology in Justinianic Reform Legislation," *Dumbarton Oaks Papers* 40 (1986): 17–31; John Lydus on Justinian: cf. *Mag.* 2.28; 3.69; see Michael Maas, *John Lydus and the Roman Past* (London, 1992), esp. chap. 6. Edward Gibbon, *History of the Decline and Fall of the Roman Empire,* ed. J. B. Bury, IV (London, 1901), chap. 44.

75. *Hist.* 1, *praef.* (trans. Thorpe).

76. *Hist.* 5, *praef.*

77. *Hist.* 10.31.

78. Peter Brown, *The Rise of Western Christendom: Triumph and Diversity (A.D. 200–1000)* (Oxford, 1996), 151–153.

79. Agathias, *Hist.* 1.2–5; II.14.8–14.

80. *Hist.* 1, *praef.;* cf. Ian Wood, "Administration, Law, and Culture in Merovingian Gaul," in Rosamond McKitterick, ed., *The Uses of Literacy in Mediaeval Europe* (Cambridge, 1990), 63–81; Ian Wood, *The Merovingian Kingdoms 450–751* (London, 1994).

81. Michael Lapidge, ed., *Archbishop Theodore: Commemorative Studies on His Life and Influence* (Cambridge, 1995); Jane Stevenson, *The Laterculus Malalianus and the School of Archbishop Theodore* (Cambridge, 1995); Bernard Bischoff and Michael Lapidge, *Biblical Commentaries from the Canterbury School of Theodore and Hadrian* (Cambridge, 1994).

82. See Magdalino, "The History of the Future."

83. See Brown, *Rise of Western Christendom,* Part II: "Divergent Legacies: A.D. 500–750."

84. See Gilbert Dagron, *Empereur et prêtre: Étude sur le "césaropapisme" byzantin* (Paris, 1996).

Sacred Landscapes

Béatrice Caseau

In 201, when the newly arrived Roman legionaries decided to build a military camp at Gholaia (Bu Njem, Libya), in the province of Tripolitania, their first move was to consecrate the place to divine beings. Their immediate concern was to conciliate the deity presiding over that precise spot, the genius of Gholaia.[1] The Romans, although they brought their own deities with them, did not want to vex local gods ruling this part of the universe. They installed their own gods inside the camp, along with the genius of Gholaia. Around the camp, the Romans also built or maintained a circle of temples dedicated to romanized African gods—such as Jupiter Hammon, overseer of caravan routes—acknowledging the competence and power of these gods. Indeed, in the Roman mind, it was the duty of human beings to honor and not to offend those divine beings who had some power over a region.

This sacralization of the land could be undone either through an elaborate ritual of deconsecration or, more violently, through desecration. After the departure of the Roman legion from Gholaia around 260, the local inhabitants, now freed from Roman domination, took their revenge on the gods of the invaders. They carefully desecrated the religious spaces inside the Roman camp and destroyed the cult statues. This gesture was meant to prove the weakness of the Roman gods, already demonstrated by the retreat of the army. It was also a gesture of fear. By destroying the cult statues of Victory and Fortune, these people were making sure that the goddesses would not have any means of harming them.

This episode of consecration and desecration of a Roman camp in the 3rd century reveals two possible attitudes toward divine beings: one encompassing and accumulative, that seeks the protection of and attempts to avoid the wrath of all sorts of divine beings; the other a deliberate choice of one or more deities accompanied by the rejection of all others. The Roman legion had chosen the syncretistic attitude by incorporating African gods into their Roman pantheon.

The local inhabitants of Gholaia chose the second option. Their iconoclasm was selective: they continued to worship Jupiter Hammon in the temple built by the Romans into the 4th and 5th centuries, but rejected those goddesses whose cult had been organized inside the camp for Roman legionaries. Their iconoclasm was directed against foreign deities whose cult was closely connected to the military domination by their former Roman rulers.

The phenomenon of sacralization includes the dedication of something or somebody to a divine being. Space, in particular, can be transformed into or revealed as a place of interaction between human beings and gods. Dedicating a space to a deity creates a nodal point of communication, ensuring the benevolence of that divine being over a region or over a group of persons. Not only space and objects but also time can become sacred, through the organization of a religious calendar. People also can be consecrated to a divine being. The rituals of sacralization range from public and solemn ceremonies, such as the dedication of a city, to small private offerings, like the burning of incense.

The notion of desacralization is more complex: it encompasses both the return of sacred things to a profane use, such as the secularization of religious buildings, and desecration, that is, a violent breach of the rules of behavior toward sacred things or persons. Defilement of shrines, sacrilege, and willful destruction fall in this category.

In the late antique period we can watch the processes of sacralization and desacralization as different religions came into contact and competed with each other. By altering the spatial and temporal rhythms of a community, sacralization also profoundly affected many other aspects of life and thus made cohabitation between different religious groups difficult. Defining sacredness in each religion required the setting of the boundaries of licit and illicit behavior, as well as restricting access to some categories of persons. What was impure for one religion was not for another; what was considered impious by some was perceived as pious by others. Episodes of public religious persecution and private religious violence were recorded during this long period of time. Religious communities desecrated sacred buildings or cult objects belonging to competing religious groups. Civil authorities often preferred one specific religion and wished to restrict the public display of other less favored religions. If the Roman and Sassanian empires could not control individual minds, they could nevertheless persecute religious communities and control their religious buildings. More than once, Roman authorities ordered the confiscation or the destruction of Christian religious buildings and sacred books.

At the same time, on the eastern border of the Roman empire the Sassanians, who had made Zoroastrianism the official religion of their empire, were also persecuting the Christian minority within their borders—especially members of the Sassanian aristocracy who converted to this faith, known to be the favored religion of their powerful Roman neighbor. When Christianity became the official religion in the Roman empire, the pagan forms of sacralization were gradually outlawed by church and state authorities. Pagan religious buildings and objects were desacralized and sometimes desecrated, while the land and the people were undergoing a new Christian sacralization. The intense sacralization of space during the centuries that saw the establishment of numerous pagan cults was superseded by the no less intense sacralization of space by Christianity.

Despite thriving economies in many provinces of the Roman world, members of a religious community no longer sought to impress by building secular public structures as their ancestors had done; instead, from the 4th to the 6th century money was poured into constructing churches and synagogues. In some regions, such as Palestine, it is possible to follow the spread of two competing religious groups, the Jews and the Christians, as they built splendid synagogues and churches that shared many similar architectural features.[2] The transformation of the Roman empire into a Christian state eventually led to restricted freedom for Jews and non-orthodox Christians. Although Judaism was a legal cult, Jewish proselytism and the building of new synagogues or the adornment of old ones were forbidden by law during the 5th century. This legal restriction on constructing religious buildings was also imposed by Islamic authorities on Jews, Christians, and Zoroastrians when the Muslim Arabs came to rule the Middle East. Under their influence, Christian, Jewish, and Zoroastrian sacred sites slowly vanished during the Middle Ages, to be replaced by shining new mosques, which are now the landmarks of Islamic cities.

Religious buildings attested to the vitality of a community and its right to practice its religion and publicize its cult. This is why they were targeted by imperial authorities who wished to control the religious affiliation of the population they ruled. By taking a journey through the late antique landscape, from the 3rd to the 8th century, it is possible to visualize the effects of sacralization and desacralization at different times. How did the religious buildings of the different communities fit into the fabric of ancient cities? How did they relate to existing religious buildings? Was the sacralization of a space valid only for a specific religious community, or could it be recaptured by another?

The competition for converts as well as for highly visible or conveniently located sacred spaces can be tracked in the conversion of buildings from one religion to another. Monumental new shrines were erected next to the derelict religious buildings of an ancient cult. Avoidance of ancient religious centers and the deliberate creation of new sanctuaries, located far away, was another tactic. The shift in religious preferences of the people and of the rulers over this long period of time, resulting in successive waves of sacralization and desacralization, should not be isolated from other relevant factors. Economic and demographic changes such as the decline of urban life, the loss of population after the plague of the 6th century, and catastrophes—natural and manmade, earthquakes and wars—transformed the sacred landscape.

A visitor to the Roman world at the end of the 3rd century would have been overwhelmed by the presence of temples, altars, and images of gods and goddesses. Whether in town or in the countryside, shrines consecrated to the gods were ubiquitous. They were often the first visible buildings of a distant city, gleaming on top of an acropolis. In any new city, reports Libanius (*Oration* 30.5), shrines were the first buildings erected, immediately after the walls. Splendid entrances to majestic temples opened on the main streets. Statues of gods and goddesses, adorned with garlands and fragrant with the offerings of incense, were to be found in numerous parts of the cities: they embellished not only temples, but crossroads, theaters, baths, and forums.

The gods were offered sacrifices in exchange for their benevolence and protection of the city or the house. In each house, space was devoted to propitiating the deities of the household. Often this was a simple patch of earth, while shrines, or even miniature temples, adorned more opulent houses.[3] Inhabited space was religiously consecrated space in a broader sense: prescribed religious rites modeled after the mythical foundation of Rome set the limits of each Roman city, consecrating the inner space of the city to the gods. When the city of Constantinople was established, in 324, the new limits of the city, three times bigger than Byzantium, were duly consecrated following the traditional rites of inauguration.

A stroll in the countryside would also reveal an intense sacralization of space. Cities were surrounded by temples, fields were limited by consecrated "boundary marks," and major estates had rural shrines where peasants thanked the deities for the harvest by offering them first fruits, flowers, and incense. Numbers of these *sacella,* little sacred spots in the countryside, were donated by wealthy landlords, along with a statue of a divinity and an altar for the offerings.

The sacralization of the landscape proceeded either from a sense of the numinous in natural spots or from a deliberate attempt to attract the benevolence of the deities. Some places were felt to have been elected by the gods and goddesses, who made them holy. Seneca evokes this source of sacralization in a letter to a friend: "If you have ever come on a dense wood of ancient trees that have risen to an exceptional height, shutting out all sight of the sky with one thick screen of branches upon another, the loftiness of the forest, the seclusion of the spot, your sense of wonderment at finding so deep and unbroken a gloom out of doors, will persuade you of the presence of a deity" (Seneca, *Letters* 41.5, trans. R. Campbell). Sites of natural beauty such as springs, hills, caves, and groves were often seen as numinous.[4] A sacred geography was thus created, grounded in the mythology of the deities' birthplaces, travels, and adventures. To honor the gods and goddesses in these locations, offerings were deposited and enclosures, altars, and temples were built. Some expanded into major sanctuaries such as those at Delphi or Aegae. Others remained natural holy spots, where food offerings or votive ribbons tied to a tree indicated that this was a place of worship.

A space could also be made sacred through the deliberate dedication of a piece of land to a deity. To propitiate specific gods, Roman magistrates and generals vowed to build temples to them.[5] The ritual of dedication transferred land to the deities, but only the ritual of *consecratio,* performed on public land in the name of the *populus,* transformed this dedicated land into a *res sacra,* a public sacred space where violent or damaging behavior would be a sacrilege (*sacrilegium*). Damage done to private shrines was not considered a sacrilege, yet they were to be approached with respect, for the sake of piety. They too were dedicated to the gods and therefore sacralized. Thus the Romans distinguished two different types of religious spaces: one closely connected to the state, where sacrifices funded by the state were offered for the prosperity of the Roman people, and one private, where sacrifices were offered in the name and with the money of private persons or groups of persons. The Roman empire officially approved and sponsored a number of cults which were celebrated at public festivals. Yet the pontiffs, state priests responsible for imperially sponsored cults, also supervised private cults, ruled by the *ius divinum*. The emperor, as *pontifex maximus,* was at the top of the priestly hierarchy. His duty was to preside over official religious ceremonies and to offer sacrifices for the sake of the empire. He also supervised the temples and authorized and patronized the erection of new shrines and the restoration or embellishment of old ones. Wherever he went, he was expected to offer sacrifices to the gods. When the city of Alexandria heard of Caracalla's impending arrival in 215, large public sacrifices were organized for his reception: "All kinds of musical instruments were set up everywhere and produced a variety of sounds. Clouds of perfume and incense of all sorts presented a sweet odor at the city gates. As soon as Antoninus entered the city with his whole army, he went up to the temple, where he made a large number of sacrifices and laid quantities of incense on the altars" (Herodian 4.8.7–8, trans. C. R. Whittaker).

Rather than imagining a homogenous pagan world before Christianization, we should picture flourishing cultic centers, the loci of major festivals, as well as a number of more or less deserted shrines left to decay.[6] While some cults were popular at the end of the 3rd century, others had lost their appeal and declined. The maintenance of religious buildings relied on public money for public and civic cults and on generous worshipers for private cults, but cities as well as private donors could decide which temples they preferred to restore, embellish, or build anew. The Mithraea, for example, were private religious buildings. Although Mithraea were still being maintained in some areas in the 4th century, their often decayed state in Gaul, Germany, and Britain reveals both the crisis that struck these regions in the 3rd century and the slow decline of Mithraism.[7]

Sacralization was not therefore a continuous phenomenon everywhere. It tended to be cumulative, creating holy spaces that remained holy even if the buildings were left in decay. Yet even this sacralization could fade away if no one cared to maintain the sacred enclosure any longer. It is therefore important to keep in mind the very real diversity in status and success of the numerous cults in the late antique Roman world.

Common features in the buildings and in the rituals of sacrifice nevertheless gave some unity to the pagan cultic centers of the late Roman world. Cities had undergone drastic changes during the High Empire: from Gaul to Arabia, lavish temples to Jupiter or Zeus, to Rome, and to the imperial cult were built on prominent sites in the provincial cities. They added a Roman aspect to cities that already had a long history. At Jerash (Gerasa), for example, the major Hellenistic cultic center disappeared when it was rebuilt into monumental Roman temples dedicated to Zeus.[8] Throughout the Roman empire, local cults were maintained following an *interpretatio romana,* while oriental cults were introduced to Rome and the western provinces.[9] The addition of new cults and festivals to the city of Rome can be traced by comparing 1st century religious calendars with that of 354, which records the state-supported public festivals celebrated at Rome.[10] Those festivals, which included processions, sacrifices, and banquets as well as games and spectacles, were major social events.[11] The numerous new festivals reveal the vitality and flexibility of late antique paganism.[12] Yet this flexibility had limits. Although in general Roman rulers confirmed the existing privileges of an ancient sanctuary when they conquered a region, and also welcomed numerous oriental cults into Rome, not every new cult was legally recognized.[13] After the expulsion of Christians from the synagogues, Christianity no longer enjoyed the legal protection that was granted to Judaism as a *religio licita*. Starting with Nero in 64 C.E., Roman emperors began to persecute the devotees of this new cult. The simple fact of professing Christianity could lead to death, if one were denounced to the Roman authorities, as the rescript of Emperor Trajan to Pliny the Younger reveals. Another religious group, the Manichees, disciples of Mani (216–276), a man from Persia who claimed to be an apostle of Jesus, was also persecuted for introducing into the Roman empire a "superstitious doctrine" based on principles opposed to those of the Romans' ancient religion.[14] The standard punishment for individuals who were denounced as belonging to either group and who refused to renounce their religion was capital punishment and confiscation of their goods.

Religion in the pagan Roman world had a civic and consensual dimension. The religious skyline of cities was very often dominated by the imperial cult. Some participation in civic cults was mandatory to preserve the *pax deorum* and to show political loyalty to the Roman rulers. The latter took on a renewed importance with the political crisis of the 3rd century. In 250, Emperor Decius ordered a general sacrifice for his sake. Those who could not produce the *libellus* proving that they had offered the sacrifice were thrown into jail. The sacralization of imperial power, already well established through the temples devoted to the imperial cult, found a renewed expression in the sacralization of living emperors under the tetrarchs. Diocletian and his colleagues considered themselves *dis geniti* and *deorum creatores,* to whom *adoratio* should be offered. In pagan houses as well as in temples of the imperial cult, the *genius* of the emperor was to be honored for the *natalis Caesaris,* birthday of the emperor; for the *natalis imperii,* anniversary of his accession to power; and for the health of the imperial family, at the *vota publica* each year, and at the *vota quinquennalia.* The tetrarchs resented Christians' refusal to offer sacrifices for the emperors. After isolated cases of Christian soldiers who were martyred for their refusal to offer a sacrifice, a general persecution was launched against the Christians in 303. Their churches were to be destroyed, their leaders arrested, their sacred books burned, and their sacred vessels confiscated. In 304, when a general sacrifice was ordered, those who refused to perform it were to be put to death or condemned to the mines. It was the longest and the most destructive of the persecutions against the Christians. It was enforced with such efficacy in the east, and so thoroughly destroyed Christian meeting places, that we hardly know anything about their style and characteristics. What most enraged the emperors and their officials was the Christians' belief that contact with pagan sacrifices was polluting. In 308 Maximinus Daia, to punish the quite numerous Christian population, ordered food sold in the markets to be sprinkled with libations or blood from the sacrifices.[15] A petition against the Christians addressed to the emperors by the provincial assembly of Lycia-Pamphylia in 312 reveals that pagans felt threatened by their refusal to participate in pagan festivals, including those of the imperial cult: "all should take part in the worship of the gods your kinsmen on behalf of your eternal and imperishable kingship. Such an action [forcing Christians to participate] will be most beneficial to all your people, as is obvious."[16]

Even when they were not deliberately persecuted, those who wanted to avoid contact with what they considered a reprehensible cult found it difficult to avoid its observances, because sacrifices were offered not only on altars inside the temple's precincts but also in private houses and in public spaces. Jews and Christians shared the same aversion to pagan sacrifices, based on strict biblical prohibition against taking part in them. Treatises were written to help Jews and Christians sort out licit from polluting contact with the pagan way of life. At stake was their participation in the social life of the Roman world. One of the arguments that Tertullian, a 3rd century African Christian, developed to forbid the marriage of a Christian woman with a pagan concerns the intense sacralization of pagan life: "The maiden of God lives with foreign *lares*; in their midst, she will be tormented by the vapor of incense each time the demons are honored, each solemn festivity in honor of the emperors, each beginning of the year, each beginning of the month" (*Ad uxorem*, 6.1). Even an invitation to a banquet in a pagan house meant that a Christian would be exposed to sacrifices. Banquets included prayers and offerings to the gods, in particular to the protective deities of the household, the *lares*. The church authorities frowned on any involvement of Christians in pagan religious festivals. Some gestures, such as the exchange of gifts with neighbors and patrons for the religious festival of the Kalends, or the running in the streets of Rome for the *Lupercalia,* were seen by many Christians as traditional activities rather than participation in pagan worship, and bishops had a hard time trying to enforce a complete withdrawal from these social aspects of pagan festivals.[17] The bishops' criticism of the theater is also linked to the traditional association of spectacles with pagan festivals and with the lewdness of some of the mime and pantomime performances.[18]

Jewish sources such as the Mishnah or Talmudic treatises *Avodah Zarah* reveal that the same kind of questions were raised by the Jewish rabbis. Was it an act of idolatry to go to the theater or to the baths, both places where statues of the gods were often presented with sacrifices? The answer attributed to the Jewish patriarch Gamaliel asserts that it is an act of idolatry to go to the theater if sacrifices take place there; otherwise it is just foolishness (Rosefta 2.5–6). It is not an act of idolatry to go to the baths of the Gentiles as long as the statues displayed there—that of Aphrodite often stood at the entrance—are simply meant to adorn the place (Mishnah, *Avodah Zarah* 3.4).

One of the last echoes of this debate could still be heard in the preaching of Jacob of Serugh, an early 6th century bishop in Syria. He complains about the theater as a place where the stories of the gods are publicized and some forms of sacrifice are still performed: "[the actor] mimes the stories of the gods, and burns perfumes at the plays, in order that he may do great honor to tales which are true for him. If this is not so, why then does he burn incense at that time to the Fortune of anything? All this pertains to paganism."[19]

Even if pious Christians avoided public spectacles and all forms of festivities tinged with pagan rites, the risk of pollution by contact with sacrificial offerings was still significant for anyone mixing with pagans on an everyday basis. In a letter to Augustine, Publicola reveals how difficult it still was in 398 for a pious Christian to avoid all contact with pagan sacrality. He voices his concern by asking the bishop: "Is it lawful for a Christian to use wheat or beans from the threshing-floor, wine or oil from the press, if, with his knowledge, some part of what has been taken thence was offered in sacrifice to a false god? . . . May a Christian drink at a fountain or well into which anything from a sacrifice has been cast? . . . May a Christian use baths in places in which sacrifice is offered to images?" Publicola had reason to be concerned, for the meat found at the butcher's could very well come from sacrifices offered to the gods, and the food at the market could come from temple estates. Images of the gods in public buildings did receive garlands and fragrant offerings from worshipers.

This fear of pollution and prohibition against participating in idolatrous sacrifices had far-reaching consequences. It not only condemned a religion and the way of life that accompanied it, but it also required the complete desacralization of a world. Maximus, bishop of Turin in the early 5th century, preached that Christian landowners should desacralize everything on their property: "Idolatry is a great evil. It pollutes those who practice it. It pollutes the inhabitants of the region. It pollutes those who look on. The peasant's offering defiles the lord of the land. He cannot not be polluted when he eats food gathered by sacrilegious hands, brought forth by earth stained with blood, stored in foul barns . . . There is nothing free from evil where everything is steeped in evil."[20]

Yet it is possible to find numerous examples of peaceful cohabitation without much religious concern. One also finds acknowledgment by Christians that works of art produced for pagan cults or inspired by mythology possessed beauty. And the continued value of an education based on classical pagan authors was widely recognized. Yet the ruins of despoiled theaters, not to mention defaced temples, attest to the quite thorough desacralization of the pagan Roman empire in the 5th and 6th centuries.[21] Starting with the Roman state, desacralization spread to pagan religious monuments and cultic objects and, at the same time, to cities, where inhumation of the dead took place inside the consecrated boundaries.

Because the approval of the gods was necessary for any acts involving the community, prescribed rituals were followed in dutifully giving to the gods the offerings and prayers that they were entitled to receive. Sacrifices and festivals were paid for by public funds because they were offered for the benefit of the entire community. The emperor, as *pontifex maximus,* was designated to offer sacrifices for the sake of the empire. At the local level, magistrates assumed religious responsibilities. If they were Christians, they were caught between their civic duty to perform sacrifices for the sake of the community and their religion's proscription. When Christians were still a minority in the town councils, Christian magistrates could find someone to replace them to perform the sacrifices, but who could replace a Christian emperor?

Although he is depicted as offering a sacrifice on the arch dedicated to him by the Senate in Rome, Constantine, the first emperor to adopt Christianity, shied away from performing the sacrifices traditionally offered on the Capitoline. If we are to believe Zosimus, who wrote in the 6th century with a definite hostility toward Christianity, Constantine agreed to participate in the festivities to placate his soldiers, but nevertheless refused to perform the sacrifices (*Hist.eccl.* 2.29.5). With the exception of Julian, all the following emperors were also Christians, whose religious affiliation led them first to withdraw their participation from state-funded sacrifices. Then, as the population in the empire became increasingly Christian, the emperors ordered the end of all sacrifices.

The strict interdiction of all pagan sacrifices at the end of the 4th century, which sapped the consensual and public aspect of the Roman religion and desacralized the Roman state, followed a series of intermediate steps.[22] In 325, a small city in Phrygia, Orcistus, was granted a dispensation from taxes used to fund civic pagan cults. In 333, Constantine authorized the inhabitants of a group of towns in Umbria to build a temple of the Gens Flavia, with the restriction that the building "should not be polluted by the deceits of any contagious superstition"—which means he agreed to an imperial cult only if no sacrifices were performed.[23] By the middle of the century, orders were given to close the temples and sacrifices were forbidden,[24] though these laws suffered numerous exceptions and were not enforced everywhere.[25] In February 391, a law addressed to the praetorian prefect, Albinus, specified: "No person shall pollute himself with sacrificial animals; no person shall slaughter an innocent victim; no person shall approach the shrines, shall wander through the temples" (*C.Th.* 16.10.10). The prohibition was extended the following year to domestic and rural cults, forbidding burning incense, lighting candles in honor of the *lares,* hanging garlands on sacred trees, and making offerings on improvised turf altars (*C.Th.* 16.10.12). This was the official end of public as well as private forms of pagan sacrifices.[26]

One of these measures in particular was symbolic of the deliberate desacralization of the state: the removal of the altar to Victory placed in the Roman Senate. If there was a place where religious piety and the fate of the republic had been combined, and where the juridical-religious system of the Roman world had been created, it was the Senate in Rome. Senators offered incense and libations on the altar of Victory. On their accession, emperors took an oath of loyalty on it. Removing this altar was a symbolically charged gesture, a rupture with the pagan understanding that the virtuous piety of the Romans toward the gods had entitled them to conquer an empire. This altar of Victory,

removed under Constantius in 357, was restored, perhaps by Julian, and remained in the Curia until the emperor Gratian ordered its removal in 382. The
plea of a group of pagan senators led by Symmachus has come down to us in
the form of a *relatio*, a petition, addressed to the emperor. Symmachus mov-
ingly referred to the "religious institutions that had served the state well for so
long," to the love of tradition and to the powerful symbol of Victory, at a time
when the Goths were a real threat to the empire. For Symmachus and his
friends, no prosperity or protection would be granted by the gods if they did
not receive sacrifices funded by public taxes. The measures taken by Gratian
completely cut out the public funding of pagan ceremonies. He even ordered the
imperial treasury to confiscate properties bequeathed to the priesthoods and to
the temples. Gratian's decree that "public funding was denied to a religion no
longer that of the state" was the crux of the problem. Shall our seat of government be no longer holy? exclaimed Symmachus in dismay. Symmachus was
drawing the emperor's attention toward a very real change. The Curia had lost
its sacrality for many of the senators who were Christians and who protested
against Symmachus's petition to the emperor. It is easy for us, knowing the
outcome, to assume that Symmachus was wasting his time. The worried letter
from Ambrose to the emperor proves that this assumption would be wrong. Yet
Symmachus, aware of the idolatrous implications of sacrifices for the Christians
and of their revulsion for them, himself proposed desacralization of the statue
of Victory: "If she cannot be honored as a god, at least let her name be honored."[27] This is precisely what happened. The statue remained in the Curia as a
secular symbol of the state, held in honor but no longer offered sacrifices.

The desacralization of the Roman state and the conviction that sacrifices
were a source of pollution led the Christian emperors to order the closing of the
temples. It was the only way to make sure that the interdiction of pagan sacrifices would be respected. Yet the temples were significant structures in the
cities, often occupying the most prominent sites. Leaving them as deserted shells
was impractical. The legislation concerning the fate of these buildings left room
for very diverse treatments of both the temples and their contents. Some temples were desacralized by the removal of their cultic statue, then closed and left
to decay. Others received a harsher treatment: they were not only desacralized
but desecrated. Many temples, damaged either by natural causes or by human
action, were used as stone quarries, their *spolia* adorning other buildings, including churches. Finally, some temples, usually after a time of desacralization
and abandonment, came back into use either as secular buildings or as Christian churches.

The first cases of desacralization of temples may have occurred early in the
4th century, sponsored by *curiales* (town councilmen) in cities where the majority of the population was already Christian.[28] Town councils and provincial
magistrates could indeed decide what to do with public religious buildings,
such as whether to repair them. Failing to repair old or damaged temples
amounted to de facto condemnation of the buildings. Yet until the end of the
4th century, and apart from rural and private temples, the destruction of temples was carried out under imperial orders, in accordance with legal procedure.

Official consent of the governor and the emperor was required to deconsecrate and remove public temples.[29] As *pontifex maximus,* the emperor had the right to direct the removal as well as the construction of a temple.

Constantine used that power after the defeat of Licinius. He ordered the confiscation of precious objects from the temples in the east and the destruction of specific sanctuaries. Some of the temples Constantine chose to destroy were located on biblical sites, especially those associated with the life of Christ. Other temples were destroyed because they were offensive to new standards of morality, like the temple of Aphrodite at Aphaca in Phoenicia where ritual prostitution was practiced, or because they were a locus of anti-Christian polemics and had encouraged the previous emperors to persecute the Christians.[30] The temple at Aegeae in Cilicia falls in this last category. Dedicated to the "Savior god" of healing Aesculapius, who was perceived as a dangerous competitor of Christ, its fame had been publicized in the *Life of Apollonius of Tyana.* A pagan wonder-worker, Apollonius shared many features with Christ, including a godlike ability to resurrect the dead, and he had been exalted as superior to Christ during the great persecution. The destruction of the building ordered by Constantine did not eradicate the cult, but the faithful in search of a cure had to leave without the traditional night's stay in the temple. A priest was still present under the reign of Julian, and is reported to have asked the apostate emperor to order the restitution of the columns of the temple, which the Christians had removed to build a church.[31]

The complete demolition of the Roman temple which stood on the supposed site of Christ's crucifixion and tomb in Jerusalem is linked to the emerging interest in all the places where Christ had set foot.[32] In that case, not only was the temple razed but the stones and even the soil, perceived as defiled by the pagan sacrifices, were removed, until "the most holy cave," identified as the hallowed place where the resurrection had taken place, appeared. Constantine ordered that the place be purified and that a "house of prayer worthy of God" be built on "a scale of rich and imperial costliness."[33] Along with a church on the supposed site of the nativity at Bethlehem and a church on the Mount of Olives commemorating Christ's ascension, the Church of the Holy Sepulcher, for which no expense was spared by Constantine, contributed to the creation of the Holy Land.[34] These edifices also supported new notions of the inherent holiness of places and objects touched by Christ—a holiness made palpable by miracles, as the identification of the True Cross by its miraculous healing powers made plain.[35]

As these examples show, the destruction of temples ordered by Constantine, though very sporadic, was still precise in its targets. It did not entail a general destruction of temples, yet it created a precedent. At the end of the 4th century and even more in the 5th century, the destruction of temples, sometimes in the hands of imperial authorities, sometimes totally out of their hands, became so common as to worry those who wished to preserve the monumentality of the Roman cities.[36]

Legislation on this matter was not consistent. Emperors authorized the destruction of rural temples devoid of artistic value, especially if the work could be done without causing turmoil (*C.Th.* 16.10.16; 399). They also allowed stones from the destroyed buildings to be quarried, especially for use in building roads, bridges, or city walls (*C.Th.* 15.1.36; 397), but they repeatedly tried to curb the destruction and spoliation of sound public monuments in cities. The imperial edicts distinguished among temples, altars, and idols. City temples had to be protected against vandalism and unauthorized looting, for they contributed to the monumentality of the cities and could be turned to secular use. But their altars had to be destroyed because they had been defiled with sacrifices. The idols could be desacralized unless they were still openly worshiped. In that case, they too should be destroyed. This last clause is very interesting. It is likely that violent desecration of temples, with destruction of the statues or of the temple itself, happened mainly in places where a strong pagan party organized resistance in the face of the imperial edicts and a growing Christian community. The combination of zealous missionary bishops preaching against idolatry and a social order still dominated by pagans often led to violent clashes around pagan statues or temples.

Determined bishops like Porphyry of Gaza asked for edicts authorizing the demolition of specific temples and the deposition of idols.[37] When Porphyry arrived as the new bishop of Gaza in 395, the Christian community was a minority kept at bay by the pagan-dominated town council. It may have counted less than 300 souls, relative to an estimated population of 15,000 to 20,000 pagans and Jews. The church of Gaza was also rather poor, with only one basilica inside the city and two churches located outside the city walls. Bishop Porphyry was determined to change that situation, and he used his connections at Constantinople to win the emperor to his cause. He first sent one of his deacons to gain the support of the bishop, John Chrysostom, who helped him obtain an audience with Eutropius, one of the influential eunuchs at the court. The deacon triumphantly returned in 398 with an imperial edict ordering the closing of the temples at Gaza. To obtain the more problematic permission to destroy the famous temple of Marnas, Porphyry himself went to the capital. He gained the confidence of Empress Eudocia, and although Emperor Arcadius pointed out that the city was duly paying its taxes and should not be disturbed, in 402 Porphyry finally brought back an imperial edict not only allowing the destruction of the temples of Gaza by imperial troops but also endowing the church of Gaza. To further humiliate the pagans, he used the precious slabs of marble taken from the temple as pavement for the street now leading to the church named after its main donor, Empress Eudocia. Mark the Deacon points to the deliberate defiling of the marble slabs, placing them where they would be trodden upon by men, women, and animals.

Temple destruction was a costly process that required manpower, so the only temples that were completely razed were those on which the army worked. The vast majority of temples were probably left to decay.[38] Sacred caves, springs, and trees, which could not be destroyed, remained the last refuge for pagan piety, a fact attested by medieval church councils.[39] Private missions were sometimes organized to destroy temples in a specific region, but in the face of so many temples, their effect was rather negligible, in spite of the assertion by

Libanius that the countryside around Antioch had lost its soul through the destruction of rural shrines stormed by Christian monks (*Oration* 30.9). Theodoret, bishop of Cyrrhus, records the organization of an expedition against some Phoenician temples by John Chrysostom: "John got together certain monks who were fired with divine zeal, armed them with imperial edicts and dispatched them against the idols' shrines. The money which was acquired to pay the craftsmen and their assistants who were engaged in the work of destruction was not taken by John from imperial resources, but he persuaded certain wealthy and faithful women to make liberal contributions, pointing out to them how great would be the blessing their generosity would win" (*Hist.eccl.* 5.29). Temple bashing had become a meritorious act.[40] Episodes of temple destruction or idol-smashing became an expected element in male saints' careers. Such activities were even projected back onto the martyrs of the early church, who in later accounts of their lives were shown smashing idols or burning pagan sacred books. It is possible to demonstrate that monks and bishops with a monastic background, fired with a mission to fight demons, could have a stronger inclination toward temple destruction than others.[41] Yet the desacralization of the pagan religious buildings and the ending of idol worship was applauded by the vast majority of bishops and monks. A council of African bishops held in Carthage in 419 agreed to ask the emperors to order the destruction of idols and of remaining temples. The shrines and altars which had once sacralized the land were now scorned as polluting the earth, and the statues of the deities worshiped there became the first target of that mopping-up operation.

Many pagans believed that the statues of the gods rendered the deities present in the minds of those who passed by. They were more than art objects, even if they could be recognized and valued for their beauty and grace: they were portents of the sacred, potentially inhabited by the deities they represented. Christians often shared the pagan belief that deities inhabited their sculptured images, a belief that pagan priests sometimes reinforced through hidden mechanisms which made these statues move.[42] Yet, for Christians, the deities living in the statues were now identified with demons.[43] Some Christians even viewed idols as dangerous objects, in which devils lay in waiting, willing and able to harm pious Christians.[44]

When, around 480, a group of Christians discovered a hidden pagan shrine filled with idols at Menouthis, not far from Alexandria, stories circulated that the profanation of their statues would be punished by the offended deities and that the Christians who had agreed to guard the sanctuary during the night would not be alive the next day (Zacharias Scholasticus, *Life of Severus*). Christian monks settling in an abandoned pagan enclosure expected the demonic pagan deity to give them trouble. For example, after finding a buried bronze idol during the construction of Benedict of Nursia's monastery on the hill dedicated to Apollo at Monte Cassino, around 530, the monks were so scared that they attributed the collapse of a wall that killed a young monk to the action of the disturbed demon (Gregory the Great, *Dialogues* 2.10.1–2). An episode in the *Life* of the patriarch Eutychius illustrates that even flat images could be dangerous: the vengeful Artemis bites a poor mosaicist who had been paid to remove the image of the goddess and replace it with a Christian motif when the room of a house was transformed into a chapel.[45]

For many Christians influenced by these beliefs, the safest action regarding the statues was their utter destruction. The belief that deities could act through their representations explains the thoroughgoing mutilation of many statues or bas-reliefs. Rufinus of Aquileia describes the Alexandrian Christians' efforts to be as thorough as possible in their destruction of images of Sarapis after the main cult statue located in the famous temple had been chopped up and the parts publicly burned in different parts of the city. The images of Sarapis and other deities omnipresent on walls, doorposts, and windows of private houses were effaced throughout the city.[46] Archaeological traces of this iconoclastic behavior have been found in the Allat temple at Palmyra and in the Mithraea of Saarebourg, Macwiller, and Koenigshofen, to cite just a few examples from different regions. At Palmyra, the head of the goddess Allat-Athena was knocked off the torso, the facial features were then scrupulously obliterated, and the statue was ultimately hacked into pieces which were discovered scattered on the floor of the temple.[47] In the Mithraea, cultic reliefs had been hammered into hundreds of pieces.[48] Such actions were not necessarily the work of a minority of overzealous monks, or of fearful uneducated Christians. When Justinian ordered the transformation of the Isis temple into a Christian church, precautions were taken to exorcise the place. The temple's treasures of gold and silver were carried away to be melted down at Constantinople, while the images of the deities were carefully scratched and chiseled away (this work was done by the army). The sign of the cross and exorcistic inscriptions were carved on the lintel and the columns to protect the building: on the north pylon, one of the crosses was positioned to obliterate the goddess's head.[49] Those among the Christians who destroyed pagan statues believed that the biblical exhortations ordering the children of Israel to throw down idols and reduce them into dust (Deut. 7:5) were meant to guide them in dealing with pagan cult statues.

Yet another attitude toward pagan statues also came to be adopted by Christians, one of appreciation for the artistic value of the statues and their adornment of gardens, villas, and public spaces. Constantine epitomizes the complex attitude of many late antique Christians toward pagan shrines and works of art.[50] He was the first emperor inclined toward Christianity to order both the complete destruction of some pagan temples and the collection of beautiful pagan statues to adorn his capital, Constantinople. Eusebius of Caesarea, in the *Life of Constantine,* found it difficult to reconcile the two attitudes in the same person: he attempted to assert that Constantine had collected those sculptures for the purpose of ridicule. Yet the destruction of specific temples to promote Christianity and fill up the imperial treasury was not irreconcilable with the collection of secularized statues chosen for their size and beauty. Displayed in the public spaces of the new city bearing his name, these masterpieces proclaimed his imperial glory and power to the world. For him, as later for Constantius (*C.Th.* 16.10.3), the traditions that celebrated the grandeur of Rome should be preserved, for they also celebrated the might of Rome's emperors.

Masterpieces of statuary and monumental temples should be preserved—in a desacralized form—for the enjoyment of Roman Christians, who had a different understanding of history from their pagan ancestors but shared their civic pride.

This civic pride is revealed in the inscriptions that some *curiales* put up after transferring statues from the desacralized temples to open public spaces. They were proud of the beauty of their cities and wished not only to preserve it but also to contribute to it.[51] For them as for the Christian poet Prudentius, the statues, once desacralized, were perfectly harmless and enhanced the monumental centers of the cities (Prudentius, *Peristephanon* 2.481–484; *Contra Symmachum* 499–505)

Some well-connected Christians even took the opportunity offered by the desacralization of the temples to gather important art collections for themselves. In the 5th century, under the reign of Theodosius II, at a time when Christianity was dominant at the court of the emperor, a member of that court had masterpieces imported from different sanctuaries that had been officially closed. He could not have collected the Phidian statue of Zeus from Olympia, a statue of Aphrodite from Cnidos, and other valuable works of art without the full consent and help of the emperor.[52] The mosaics discovered in numerous villas dating from that period also reveal a taste for mythological subjects; the presence of pagan deities did not seem in the least to bother their Christian owners.[53] It is possible that this relaxed attitude toward pagan art was a privilege of the well-to-do. In a rather poor villa outside the walls of Antioch, a collection of figures of emperors and deities, mostly replicas of well-known statues, was found buried.[54] Many ancient statues were discovered piled up in wells or in pits, which indicates that some statues had either become an embarrassment for the owners or were in need of protection from zealous Christians.

In a Roman house at Carthage, the entrance to an underground room was concealed under early 5th century mosaics. In that room, behind a hastily constructed wall, archaeologists were surprised to find a collection of cult statues. Beautiful marble images of Venus, Jupiter, and Demeter had been carefully hidden in that remote room, possibly awaiting the return of better times. Jean-Charles Picard has suggested that Caecilius Honoratus, the owner of the house at that time, had gathered these objects not only to save them from iconoclasts but also to sacralize his house and attract to himself and his family the beneficial powers of the divine beings.[55] In Athens, on the other hand, some statues were buried in humiliating fashion, such as one found face-down under the threshold of a late antique house. The house, once owned by an amateur of pagan art or a person inclined toward pagan cults, was occupied by devout Christians at the time of the burial.[56]

Christian attitudes toward pagan cult statues and spaces were very diverse during this period. The violent and destructive behavior of the Egyptian abbot Shenoute of Athribis/Atripe (ca. 335–451) becomes understandable in a world where Christians feared demons. If we are to believe Shenoute's biographer, the abbot dreamed of freeing the world from demonic powers by searching temples and private homes for idols to smash. The protective or admiring attitude toward the same sort of image held by a wealthy *curialis*, ready to follow in the footsteps of his fathers and adorn a public building with the statues, is also perfectly understandable in its context. Indifference and disdainful abandonment of pagan cultic spaces and objects were also common. Each of these attitudes contributed to the eventual desacralization of the pagan world. Religious motives evidently played a major role in the action against pagan temples and idols, yet they do not alone account for the destruction of temples. Tense relationships between the two main religious communities (as in Gaza), a sense of pollution, or the fear that the beauty of a temple could entice Christians to take part in sacrifices (as in Baalbek) could lead to destructive behavior, as could the very profane desire of ambitious magistrates to avail themselves of cheap and beautiful building material in order to place their name on a new building (as in Rome). A new world was created with the ruins of the old one. Religious change was accompanied by a wider change in the perception and use of space.

Even with their temples closed and their religious festivals partially secularized, cities remained religiously consecrated ground. One consequence of this dedication of inhabited space to the gods was the prohibition against burying the dead inside the city walls. Christians had developed a different attitude than pagans and Jews toward the dead. Their martyrs' dead bodies, far from being perceived as polluting, were approached with veneration, for the saints were deemed to be alive and present at God's side, interceding for the faithful who placed their trust in them. Such ideas were horrendous to pagans and Jews (not to mention Zoroastrians), who considered that contact with the dead created impurity that barred one from performing religious duties. Rather than an obstacle to sacrality, the dead bodies of the saints were considered by Christians a locus of sacrality and became the most common means of making space sacred.

This new attitude required a shift of attitude toward the dead that happened only gradually. St. Thecla would not hear of having bodies buried in her shrine. Some Christians, such as Gregory of Nyssa in the 4th century, did not approve of the disinterment of dead bodies presumed to belong to saints. During the reign of Julian tensions were caused by Christians' religious attitude toward the dead. Julian's edict on funerals, in 363, ordered that burial rites take place at night, "for the persons happening upon a funeral are filled frequently with disgust, supposing a bad omen; for others proceeding to the temples, it is not meet and right to enter until they have washed from themselves the pollution. It is not proper after such a sight to approach the gods, who are the cause of life and are, of all things, most unfavorably disposed toward dissolution."[57] Christian funerary processions had become a nuisance for the polytheists who wanted to worship in their temples. In a rich suburb of Antioch, at Daphne, an incident caused by the attention Christians paid to their holy dead powerfully reveals the difficult cohabitation of Christians and pagans. It was claimed that the oracle of the temple of Apollo had ceased to speak because the god was repulsed by the presence of the remains of St. Babylas buried nearby. Julian, in an effort to please the priests, ordered the removal of the saint's sarcophagus from that area of the temple.

Christians were often suspected of not respecting the religious dedication of urban space. Pagans justly feared that Christians would unlawfully bury martyrs inside their churches. Some complaints must have reached the emperors because, in 381, a law promulgated by Gratian, Valentinian II, and Theodosius I tried to curb this development: "All bodies that are contained in urns or sarcophagi and are kept above the ground shall be carried and placed outside the city, that they may present an example of humanity and leave the homes of the citizens their sanctity." Although written by Christian emperors, the law reminded everyone that Roman cities still sat upon religiously consecrated ground that was not to be polluted by the dead, and that burial of bodies was not allowed in the shrines of the martyrs. The law ultimately did not stop this practice, but it did make it possible for pagan believers to defend the religious purity of their cities for a short time. Such conflicts between Christians and pagans over sacred ground are still in evidence at the end of the 4th century. Around 396, in the city of Gaza, a riot started when some pagans thought that Christians were bringing a dead body into the city.

This was a battle the pagans were to lose: from the 5th century onward, the dead began to make their triumphal entrance into the cities. It started with saints, the "very special dead," who were formally installed in churches located inside the city walls during the 4th century.[58] It then continued with the remains of privileged Christians, such as clerics and generous patrons of the churches, who wished to be buried close to the saints. Finally the tombs of ordinary Christians slowly but steadily appeared inside the cities.

The Christian lack of respect for this fundamental element of pagan sacralization is well illustrated by the case of Constantinople. Although the new capital had probably received formal pagan rites at its foundation in 324, its new walls included former cemeteries. They were covered with earth and the rule requiring the dead to be buried outside the city was still enforced during the 4th century. Yet, as the walls were extended under Theodosius II, burial of the dead outside the city walls became more expensive and the space between the two walls was used for burial. By that time the city had closed and desacralized its temples and become a Christian city. It was now a metropolis not in the least concerned with the pollution brought by dead bodies and it gladly welcomed corporeal relics into city churches. An ivory plaque of the 5th or 6th century, now in Trier, depicts a procession of relics triumphantly carried by the bishop while censers are swinging on their passage. The whole community gathered to celebrate this coming of heavenly patronage in the city.[59] The presence of the saints' bodies was considered a blessing and a protection for the city.

In about a century, a total revolution had happened. That which had defiled the space in the eyes of pagans sacralized it in the eyes of Christians. Prudentius, at the dawn of the 5th century, could write about Rome's famous relics of Paul and Peter: "Tiber separates the bones of the two and both its banks are consecrated as it flows between the hallowed tombs" (*Peristephanon* 12.29, trans.

H. J. Thompson). For Christians, Rome was made sacred by its famous martyrs. Cities less favored with local martyrs "invited" saints to reside with the Christian community. Bishops such as Gaudentius of Brescia or Vitricius of Rouen gathered relics as they journeyed to communities more richly endowed with saints than their own. The practice of moving and parceling out the remains of the saints became very common. As a result, a city as unfavored with local saints as Rouen in 396 could boast: "our habitation is now among a legion of Saints and the renowned powers of the Heavens."[60]

A visitor to the Roman world in the 380s would still have been impressed by the temples of the pagan world. He would have found the monumental city center quite intact and would have searched in vain for Christian buildings in the midst of pagan temples. The city had been offered Christian basilicas by the generous Constantine, yet they were not to be seen near the Fora, nor on the Capitoline or Palatine hills.

Arriving at Ephesus, by sea or by road, he would have been impressed by the huge pagan religious complexes, and by the bathhouses and other public monuments which gave character to the cities of the east. In Ephesus at that time the churches were very much in the shadow of these impressive buildings. Returning half a century later by sea, he would have noted major changes. The huge baths and the gymnasium complex on the harbor were still dominant, and the biggest church in the city was very tiny next to them, but the largest temple— probably the Olympeum, built in honor of Hadrian, that had proudly shone on top of the hill facing the sea—had been pulled down, its stones ground and burned for lime. No longer would he have found the temples of Domitian or Isis, for they had been destroyed and their stones reused elsewhere. On the site of what may have been a Sarapeum now stood a church. Temples damaged by earthquakes had not been repaired but rather had been used as stone quarries. Similarly, the slightly earthquake-damaged statues of Artemis were no longer visible: they had been carefully buried underground. A church council organized in Ephesus in 441 to defend the title of Mary as Theotokos, Mother of God, was held in a large church dedicated to her, possibly built into the southern portico of the now destroyed Olympeum. On a hill overlooking the road leading to the city, an impressive Christian basilica dedicated to St. John dominated the landscape. Down the hill, the world-renowned temple of Artemis lay closed and abandoned. Had this visitor journeyed to the city in the 380s and again in the 440s, he would have felt like one of the Seven Sleepers of Ephesus, who woke from their slumbers to walk in a city they could hardly recognize.

The stories of Rome and of Ephesus are not uncommon. About twenty churches have been identified in Ephesus, and in each case that excavation has reached the level before the construction of the church, a public building or a temple has been found. This is the major difference with Rome. Numerous churches were built in Rome in the course of the 4th and 5th centuries, yet the city did not transform its temples or public buildings into churches. Only in the late 6th century do we hear of a chapel built in the imperial palace on the

Palatine. In the early 7th century we know of a public temple, the Pantheon, that was transformed into a church with due imperial authorization. The difference between the two cities reveals the growing power of the bishops of Ephesus, who were able to control the town council and use public sites for their religious buildings. In Rome, the resistance of a pagan aristocracy, along with the symbolic aura of most public buildings of the Roman Fora, kept the powerful church of Rome from having much effect on the central areas of the city. By the 6th century, the Christianization of space was accomplished. In the depiction of cities, churches were landmarks as important as city walls and porticoed streets, as the 6th century mosaic depicting the Holy Land discovered in a church at Madaba attests.

The late 5th and the 6th centuries were a time of intense church building.[61] In Palestine and Arabia, for example, over 350 churches have been discovered, most of them built during the 6th century. Bishops, who had gained a leading position in the town councils, often chose to spend money on building or beautifying churches. As a result, Jerash had 15 churches; Caesarea, 10.[62] Attention shifted from civil buildings to private and religious buildings. Private individuals built oratories, and small communities gathered money to erect or adorn new churches. Umm al-Jîmal, a big village, but still only a village, had 15 churches, mostly private oratories large enough to welcome only the local residents.[63] Money was also poured into monastic complexes and other religious buildings or objects, as the beautiful ecclesiastical silver treasures discovered in the region reveal.[64] In Justinian's time, the emperor, the bishops, and the wealthy citizens shared the same enthusiasm for religious buildings.

In Syria and Palestine, most cities went through intense rebuilding. Social and judicial activities shifted to sites untrammeled by pagan cult associations. Sections of the cities were deliberately abandoned, in particular those linked to pagan shrines. New active city centers emerged, often around the bishop's cathedral. The erections of churches, *xenodochia* (inns), and monasteries Christianized the cityscape. By the 6th century, in many of the prosperous cities of Syria, churches competed in size and splendor with former temples.

In Apamea, for example, the cathedral complex grew to cover 12,000 square meters. The city had chosen to move away from the area of the major temples. Around 384 the majestic temple of Zeus Belios was first desecrated and damaged, possibly by an expedition against it organized by Bishop Marcellus. This partial destruction was followed by a more insulting desecration: it was used as a dump in the 5th century. During the 6th century this ignominious treatment was followed by sealing off access to the abandoned sanctuary. The road leading from the *cardo* (main transverse street) to the temple and the once-thriving agora was blocked by latrines.[65]

In Jerash, the temples were partially reused. The city had two major cultic centers, one devoted to Zeus, the other to Artemis. At the end of the 5th century, the temple of Zeus was partially demolished and its stones used to adorn nearby churches. The vaulted corridors of its lower terrace were transformed into Christian shrines and dwellings, possibly for a monastic community.[66] The temple of Artemis, once a splendid monument, also served as a quarry. One of the frieze blocks from the temple embellished the door of the Theodore church, dated to 496. Church building reached its peak at the time when whole sections of the pagan city were destroyed or abandoned. Building materials ranging from ordinary stones to beautiful colored marbles were accessible and cheap. The 6th century church of Bishop Isaiah was built with columns taken from the *decumanus,* whose northern part went out of use in the 5th century.[67] A new geography of the sacred, composed of numerous Christian sanctuaries—from simple chapels to imposing basilicas—was emerging in a transformed city landscape.

The Christian sacralization of space was not as old as Christianity itself. For the first two or three centuries, Christians met in private houses, which were not sacred buildings. Christianity emerged in Jewish circles and drew its religious life from Jewish traditions. The first disciples of Christ used to pray every day in the Temple of Jerusalem until its destruction by the Romans in 70 C.E. Ejected from the Jewish synagogues, they set up their own religious meeting places on the model of the synagogues.

Before the year 70, the Jews had two types of religious buildings: the Temple at Jerusalem and the synagogues. The synagogues were houses of the congregation, where prayer, learning, and communal social events took place. They were not buildings dedicated to God, in that God did not live in them in the way that a pagan deity lived in his or her temple. Not being sacred in itself, a synagogue could be sold or moved to another location when necessary, although during late antiquity Jewish synagogues recaptured some of the Temple's sacrality.[68] The one sacred place where the *shekhinah,* the divine presence, always resided was the Holy of Holies in the Temple of Jerusalem. (At least this was true for the first Temple; and it was argued about for the Herodian Temple.) It was in the Temple that sacrifices were offered to God. Although their Temple had been defiled and replaced by a pagan temple, the Jews never lost the sense of the sacrality of the Temple platform on Mount Moriah. They repeatedly attempted to have the Temple rebuilt, at first under Julian, who granted them permission to do so, and then under the Persian occupation in the early 7th century. For Christians, the destruction of the Temple was the fulfillment of a prophecy and the visible proof of God's displeasure with the Jews for rejecting Christ. It mattered to Christians that the Temple area be left unoccupied. As a result, they did not try to build a church on the Temple platform, though they very probably used the stones of the Roman temple for their own building purposes in the 4th century. In 638, when the Arabs arrived in Jerusalem, they found the platform filled with stones and rubbish.

For Christians, the Temple had been replaced by Christ, and its sacrifices by spiritual worship. They no longer had an official sacred space. The Jerusalem community had dispersed to Pella and elsewhere in the Roman world. Although Christians believed Jerusalem would be the place of the *parousia,* the second coming, there is no indication that Christians chose to consider Jerusalem a sacred place during the first four centuries of Christianity. The location of their religious buildings, like the synagogues', depended on the opportune donation of a house or part of a house for the needs of the community. The only excavated example of a group of rooms obviously remodeled to suit the needs of the Christian community is the so-called house-church at Dura-Europos, abandoned after the city's destruction by the Sassanians in 256.[69] This house, located not far from the city walls, was in the same street as a synagogue and a Mithraeum. During the 3rd century, two rooms located at the back of the house, away from the entrance, were transformed and used only for religious ceremonies.

At one point, probably in the 3rd century, the development of Christian communities began to require the erection of specific buildings for worship, vast enough to welcome the faithful. The first Christian basilicas were built on sites that were not in themselves sacred, but had been determined by the donation of land by converts. This rule still applied in the later centuries: donations of land were the most common origin of churches. From the discourse of the early Christian apologists, very insistent on the fact that God cannot be circumscribed in a space and that Christians are very different from pagans in respect to temples and altars, we can deduce that the Christians were not interested in creating sacred spaces, let alone a sacred geography.[70] Indeed, if the Christian communities adopted a model for their religious spaces, it was that of synagogues rather than pagan temples. Like synagogues, early churches were houses of the congregation rather than houses of God, but they were religious buildings, already called basilicas during the persecution of Diocletian.[71] These churches owned movable goods, such as precious vessels and books that they had to surrender during persecutions.[72]

The reluctance that Christians felt at having to give up vessels used for the Eucharist to the Roman magistrates is an indication that some form of sacralization was taking place in the pre-Constantinian basilicas. The vessel used for the Eucharist was no longer used also for profane purposes. The table around which Christians shared *agapē* had become an altar, even if it was a portable one. The location of the church was not sacred, but the celebration of the Eucharist sacralized the church. It was a place of theophany, where decent and respectful behavior was expected.

Until the 6th century the celebration of the Eucharist was the only thing required to dedicate a church. The Christian ceremony of the Eucharist was surrounded with solemnity and splendor, as the long list of objects donated to adorn the altars of the Roman churches founded by Constantine attests. Nothing was spared to beautify the area of the church where Christ made himself available in the bread and the wine: magnificent candelabra holding a myriad of oil lamps, standing censers perfuming the sanctuary, colored marbles, and shimmering mosaics all contributed to attract attention toward the altar. The organization of space inside the basilicas also reveals that there was a gradual increase in sacredness from the door to the sanctuary. The sacred rites of the Eucharist were open only to fully baptized Christians. The catechumens were kept at the back of the church, along with the penitents, and escorted to the doors after the sermon. The sanctuary was reserved for clerics, while the rest of the faithful shared the nave.

The long-lasting defensiveness of Christian apologists against sacred spaces of a pagan kind was still echoed in the 4th and early 5th centuries. Christianity sacralized people, not objects: the true dwelling place of God was the heart of the baptized Christian, not his or her church, and holiness resided in the whole community of Christians rather than in the stones permeated with their prayers (Augustine, *Sermon* 337). Yet the belief that God had sent his son to walk on this earth and the theological debates about the nature of Christ made physical traces of his incarnation and humanity all the more important. The sacralization of the Holy Land transformed the sacred geography of Christianity from one of a relative uniformity, where God could be worshiped anywhere and the sacrifice of the Eucharist could be shared by Christians all over the world, to one incorporating the notion of privileged holy space and of local sanctity.

Persecutions greatly contributed to the creation of a specific Christian way to sacralize space. They deprived Christians of their religious buildings and killed many of the faithful, leaving Christian communities to express their faith through the mourning of their dead at the tombs of their martyrs. Many of the Christians' gestures and attitudes toward the martyrs were similar to those offered by the pagans to their dead. But they differed with the pagans in imagining for their martyrs an eternal bliss in the company of God, and an eternal loving concern for the Christians left behind. The welcoming of the saints to heaven gave the martyrs a privileged position as intercessors. Brothers and sisters in humanity, they also belonged to the court of God and could intercede for the faithful.

Early in the 4th century, around 305, the church of Cirta had a house in the *area martyrum* that it used for its meetings.[73] This is an early attestation of construction linked to the tombs of the martyrs, which created numerous basilicas around Roman cities.[74] In Rome, Constantine provided funds to build magnificent basilicas in honor of the most prominent Christian martyrs, Paul and Peter. During the 4th and 5th centuries, other basilicas were built in the different cemeteries where the martyrs rested in peace. By engraving poems near the tombs of fifteen unknown saints whose days were added to the church festal calendar, Pope Damasus created a wreath of oratories around the city, defining an *urbs sacra* surrounded by martyrs.[75]

The two springs of holiness, the Eucharist and the martyrs, were from now on combined to create a specifically Christian way of sacralizing space and time. In the 4th century, the location of the *martyria* was dictated by the location of the tombs, but the habit of disinterring the saints gave many other areas a chance to enjoy the protection and blessings of relics. The saints were distributed or sold in bits and pieces until only the dust collecting on their tombs and reliquaries was left to sell.[76] Relics make sacredness transportable, as even tiny fragments could protect their owners and link them to the inhabitants of paradise. Caution had to be exerted by church authorities before welcoming the cult of a new saint. Martin of Tours stopped a group of Christians from offering veneration at a tomb which was, according to Martin, that of a brigand, not of a saint. Sure signs of sanctity such as the smell of sweet perfume emanating from an opened tomb or miracles that contact with saintly relics produced were now dutifully recorded in books of miracles or saints' lives to justify the ecclesiastical recognition of a cult.

A fundamental idea in the cult of martyrs was that holiness was contagious. The sweet perfume coming from St. Stephen's sarcophagus had healing powers, for it came from paradise. Because Stephen was in heaven and yet still in contact with his body, the healing perfume of divinity emanated from his bones.[77] This holy contagion could be extended: in Syria, reliquaries were made with holes allowing oil to be poured on the holy bones, which was gathered at the other end to produce blessings for the pilgrims.[78] Most of the time, contact with just the place was enough to invoke the power of relics; even the fragrant oil that was burned before the tombs of saints became invested with holiness and was carried away by pilgrims in *ampullae*.[79] The success of a shrine can be established by the number of its *ampullae* distributed through the Roman world.

Celebrations of the discovery of relics and their processions filled up the Christian festal calendar as they did Christian chapels. Both time and space were made sacred through the idea that the saints are particularly available when and where they are honored. Many of the miracles performed by St. Martin at Tours happened during his festivals. It is clearly in the interest of Bishop Gregory of Tours to publicize such events in order to attract pilgrims to the shrine of St. Martin. The *virtus* and goodwill of the saint are localized in time as well as in space: Martin was believed more likely to hear the prayers of the faithful near his tomb at the date of his festival.

Bishop Perpetuus (458/9–488/9) also understood the power of festivals for gathering Christian pilgrims, mostly from neighboring regions, in the city of Tours, around the bishop. For the pilgrims Perpetuus had a basilica rebuilt in honor of St. Martin. A new festival was created celebrating the dedication of the new church. The date, July 4, conveniently occurred during a month with no festival, far from the other festival in honor of St. Martin, November 11. Both festivals were major events: pilgrims came two to three days before and stayed one or two days after the festival. As the holiness of the tomb had spread to the building and the immediate area, so the holiness of the saint's festival also spread to the days before and after.[80]

These practices changed the notion of space for Christians. As they traveled to the shrines of the saints, they created a sacred geography. The location of churches where the saints were buried went from being neutral to being sacred. There was nothing cosmically determined about this sacredness. It was acquired through contact, linked to the saint's relics and to the consecration of the Host on the altar. A removal of reliquaries and altars could desacralize a church and the site on which it was built. Contrary to pagan natural holy sites, and with the exception of the sites linked to Christ's life, Christian sacred geography was movable.[81]

Christian sacrality also became dispersed and private. Innumerable fragments of the remains of the saints circulated widely, often in the possession of individual owners. Images of the saints sold to the faithful were invested with the protective power of the saints, as the stories in hagiographies make plain.[82] By performing miracles, icons proved that they were not mere images but were the resting place of the saints. This dispersion of sacrality, now movable and portable, and no longer confined to the altar or to the churches, allowed a very individualistic approach to the sacred. From the major monastic sanctuaries such as that of the two saints known as Simeon Stylites or that of St. Menas, relics and icons could be bought to protect persons and houses. This privatization of the sacred created inequalities. While the powerful or well-connected, such as Queen Radegund in Poitiers or Bishop John the Almsgiver in Alexandria, could avail themselves of a piece of the Holy Cross, the less fortunate had to hope that less prestigious relics or images would still offer some protection. The protection saints were deemed to grant to the faithful and the resources they could bring to churches explains why they began to be transported from their original resting places. The first centuries of the Middle Ages saw an increase in the traffic of relics. It became a standard practice both in the west and in Byzantium to deposit relics before dedicating a new church. As precious relics were bought, exchanged, or even stolen, the sacred geography of the Christian world was constantly being redefined.[83]

The increasing attention devoted to relics and the belief in their power to protect the faithful explain the shock felt by the Christian world when the holy city of Jerusalem and the relic of the Cross were captured by the Persians in 614.[84] The conquest by the Persians of the eastern provinces of the Byzantine empire led not only to the destruction of numerous cities but also to a spiritual crisis among Byzantine Christians. Stories circulated relating the desecration of the churches of the Holy Land, the massacres of Christians, and the cruelty of the Jews. How could God let fire-worshipers defeat the Christians? Had he abandoned the Holy Land to Zoroastrian Persians and to their Jewish allies to punish the Christians for their sins? The Monophysites and the Chalcedonians believed that the theological error of the opposite camp had attracted onto them the wrath of God. They did not question the power of the saints. Heraclius had an icon of the Virgin attached to the mast of the ship that took him from Carthage to Constantinople to conquer the imperial title. When in 626 Avars and Persians besieged the city of Constantinople, the patriarch Sergius had icons of the Virgin mounted on the doors of the city and carried in processions on the walls, in the hope that they would create an invisible protective barrier against the enemy. The eventual retreat of the enemies was ascribed to the active protection of the city by the Virgin. By the early 630s, Emperor Heraclius had reconquered the lost lands and negotiated the return of the relic of the Cross to Byzantine hands. This victorious return of the Byzantines in Syria and the Holy Land, accompanied by theological compromises to unify the Christians and forced baptism of the Jews, was short-lived, for in 634 Muslim Arabs invaded Syria. The army of this new religious group overpowered the Byzantine and Sassanian rulers of the Middle East, and came to control a vast region populated mostly by Christians, Jews, and Zoroastrians. Muslims were only a tiny minority, but as rulers they transformed the religious life of the communities under their power.

In Arabia, the Prophet Muhammad treated the pagans, Jews, and Christians he encountered differently. Pagans were offered a choice of death or conversion to Islam. The pagan Arabs had created *ḥaram* territories, areas in which the neighboring tribes agreed that no blood should be shed, no trees cut, no farming done. These areas also provided a right of asylum. Mecca in the 6th century was very much a pagan stronghold, with a temple where idols were worshiped. The takeover of that shrine by Muhammad in 630 and his destruction of the numerous idols inside the temple combines a Judeo-Christian aversion for idols with a wish for the continuity of an important Arabic sacred space. Muhammad kept not only the sanctuary and the black stone, but also the rules of behavior which prevailed around sacred spaces in pre-Islamic Arabia. This continuity was justified by the reconstruction of the history of the holy site as having been originally built by Abraham, a true worshiper of the one God, and later misused by polytheists until the Prophet reestablished monotheism.[85]

Christians and Jews had a special status because the Prophet recognized their religions as revealed by God. If they did not want to convert, they usually could keep their life in exchange for tribute. At Medina, however, the Prophet had encountered the resistance of three Jewish tribes. He offered the choice of conversion or exile to two of the tribes, conversion or death to the other.[86] After each conquest, relations with the non-Muslims were regulated by negotiated agreements. At the oasis of Khaybar, after the victory of the Prophet, the Jews were allowed to keep their lives and their land, but would have to hand over one-half of their produce to the Muslims. For the Christians of Najran, settlement included the payment of a tribute by the Christians, who were also to welcome the Prophet's representatives and provide them with supplies in time of war. They could otherwise practice their religion and run their own affairs. This arrangement was abrogated when Caliph ʿUmar ibn al-Khattāb (634–644) ordered the expulsion of Christians and Jews from the Arab peninsula.

Under ʿUmar's reign, Syria, Palestine, Mesopotamia, western Iran, and Egypt came under Muslim rule. As Palestinian and Syrian cities opened their gates or were conquered, treaties were concluded which secured the life and property of the citizens, as well as their right to keep some if not all of their religious buildings, in exchange for taxes and services. The Muslims were mostly interested in the wealth of these regions and many Christians belonging to the Monophysite and Nestorian churches found that the change of rulers also meant the end of persecution.

In the conquest of the Sassanian empire, the Muslim armies came in contact with Zoroastrians. The Sassanian rulers had followed a form of Zoroastrianism closely associated with their structures of power.[87] They worshiped in fire temples.[88] In Mesopotamia, the Muslims took over the Sassanian state's properties, including the fire temples, which they desacralized. The disappearance of the main fire temples did not mean the end of the religion, whose cult continued domestically. Yet the religion did lose its main centers of worship and its public festivals.[89] Eventually Zoroastrianism came to be identified with the third religion recognized in the Qur'ān. As a result, the status of Zoroastrians became quite similar to that of Jews or Christians.[90]

As the Muslims settled in the conquered lands, they started to assert their religious presence through the building of mosques where the male Muslims gathered for prayer. Instruction and legal functions also took place in mosques.[91] Unlike churches, mosques were not consecrated buildings. Indeed, at first they were not always buildings. Early mosques, such as those dated to the end of the 7th century or the early 8th century discovered in the Negev, were simple stone enclosures, often located on a hilltop, facing south toward Mecca and adorned with a protruding prayer niche, the *miḥrāb*. These mosques served nearby settlements and accompanied the dispersal of Arab tribes.[92]

These mosques consisted mainly of a hall to allow as many persons to gather as necessary, yet the space was not randomly organized. Even in very early mosques, the *qibla*—the direction of Mecca—gave an orientation to the enclosure. This sacred direction was soon marked by the *miḥrāb*. Sometimes a simple niche, sometimes surrounded by columns and richly adorned, the *miḥrāb* gave a focus to the prayer inside the mosques. It was eventually invested with sacrality. The process of sacralization started for mosques as it had for churches and synagogues. Rules of behavior that were at first mainly dictated by common sense, such as the removal of shoes or the prohibition of spitting, became charged with religious meaning. They were marks of respect for God and by extension for the place where prayers were offered to him. Three major sanctuaries, Muslim *ḥaram*, are mentioned in the Qur'ān: Mecca, Medina, and what has been identified as Jerusalem. These were the historical holy places of Islam, sacralized by the Prophet. As the navel of the earth, Mecca added a cosmological sanctity, akin to that of Jerusalem, to its historical role in the Prophet's life. The sacralization of these holy places progressed with time, as stories proved their holiness. Sanctity could also arise in other Muslim cities: Damascus was revealed to be the place where the house of Noah stood before the flood, and Aleppo was identified as a site visited by Abraham.[93]

In newly founded cities such as Basra, Kufa, or Fustat, the mosque was set up in the center of the city, but in ancient Byzantine or Sassanian cities the Muslims had to find a place for their mosques in already built cities. The location of these new religious buildings was in part determined by the availability of space, as well as by a wish to secure a central and convenient location for the rulers' religion. Like the Christians in the late 4th century, the Muslims could avoid the monuments of the old religions and build anew; or they could try to capture some of the attraction of the old shrines by building their mosques next to them. Or they could take over the holy places of the old religions and eventually replace their buildings.

When the Muslim armies arrived in Palestine and in Syria, they must have been overwhelmed by the number and splendor of Christian churches, and to a lesser extent of Jewish synagogues.[94] Churches glittering with marbles and mosaics caught the eye in cities as well as in villages. In the countryside monastic sites dotted the landscape, some with huge complexes such as Qalat Seman, some with very simple dwellings such as the hermits' caves of the Judean desert. A traveler such as Arculf, who came from Gaul to the Holy Land and Constantinople in 670, commented admiringly on the beautiful churches that he was able to visit along his pilgrimage route. He is the first pilgrim from the lands of the former western empire to report a mosque in Jerusalem. The building, which he appropriately called a house of prayers, did not impress him. Like many other mosques in that region, it was a very simple and unadorned structure built on open ground. In the conquered lands, early mosques were usually new and very simple buildings, easily distinguished from pagan temples, Jewish synagogues, and Christian churches.[95] Muslim authorities were concerned about the effect such beautiful buildings could have on their flock.

Early Muslims did not hesitate to visit and even pray in Christian churches.[96] Some Christian saints' shrines in particular attracted them. The shrine of St. Sergius at Resafa-Sergiopolis was an important pilgrimage center, which received numerous donations from Muslims that made possible the erection of beautiful churches in the city. St. Sergius had even received gifts from the Sassanian Zoroastrian king Khosro II, in thanksgiving for the child his Christian wife had prayed to the saint for. The cult of St. Sergius was particularly popular among the Ghassanids, an Arab tribe converted to Christianity in the 4th century, whose princes had established their residence in Resafa. They may have been connected with the erection in the 7th century of a mosque attached to the Christian cathedral, with the hope of benefiting from the cult of St. Sergius by attracting pilgrims to the mosque and to the new religion. The mosque was built north of the cathedral in the pilgrims' courtyard. Two passageways were built between the courtyard, now reduced in size but still in use, and the mosque, creating an architectural unity between the two religious spaces. Thilo Ulbert, in charge of the excavations at Resafa, explains the choice of this location by the enduring veneration of St. Sergius among the nomads of the region.[97] The mosque was built with the stones of a nearby Christian basilica dating from the 6th century and apparently destroyed by an earthquake before its final dedication. If the presence of the mosque next to the Christian basilica can be interpreted as a sign of the tolerance of early Umayyads for Christianity, it also shows a wish to occupy a religious site very much in favor among the local Arab population with a prestigious building belonging to the new religion.

In the Negev, the location of some early mosques indicates a wish to supersede the stele cult as well as Christianity. At Shivta, for example, the building of the mosque blocked a road which led from the village to a Christian church. The curved *miḥrāb* was built so close to the Christian baptistery as to bar one of its entrances.[98] Such competition is also clearly at play in the decision of the Umayyad caliph ʿAbd al-Malik to build the Dome of the Rock on the Temple Mount higher than the Anastasis church, and to take over the church of St. John the Baptist in Damascus.[99]

In the 4th century Damascus was called the true city of the god (Julian, *Ep.*

24), for it worshiped Jupiter in splendid ceremonies staged by a temple renowned for its wealth and beauty, on the site of a shrine dating back to the Iron
Age—in fact the biggest temple that is known in Syria. The temple was protected and separated from the city by two walls. The first contained a wide area
inside which a market, the property of the temple, developed. The second wall
surrounded the most sacred area, where only purified visitors could enter, and
contained the altar and the temple itself. Its central location and its market
made of the Jupiter temple a focus of city life. To cross the city from east to
west, one had to go through the temple market. Although the site of the temple
was very ancient, some of the temple walls were still under construction until
the 3rd century. An extension of the market was built in the first half of the 4th
century with temple funds. When the temple was closed along with the other
pagan temples, at the end of the 4th century under the reign of Theodosius I, its
site was very quickly transformed by Christians. The temple was destroyed and
its stones were probably used to build a Christian basilica on a different site
inside the *temenos* (sacred enclosure).[100] The Christian community of Damascus had lost two churches, burned by Jews during the reign of Julian if we
accept Ambrose of Milan's testimony. This community, then, very certainly
wished to assert itself with the support of the imperial authorities. What better
way to do that than to occupy this central area of the city? The Christian
cathedral was an impressive building. It was built on the south wall of the
temenos and used its door, now Christianized with an invocation to the Trinity,
as the main entrance. It deliberately turned its back on the desecrated temple
courtyard where sacrifices had taken place.

It is only during the 5th century, when the memory of the sacrifices had begun
to wane, that the cathedral was rebuilt to open onto the courtyard. The Christian basilica was dedicated to St. John the Baptist, whose relics had been dispersed under the reign of Julian. Once again the brief episode of Julian's reign
and its religious turmoil seem to have played a major role in the self-assertion of
the Christian community in Damascus. At the dawn of the 7th century, the city
of Damascus was taken twice by the Arabs. The first time, in 634, a treaty
granted the citizens their life, property, and churches. But after the Byzantine
defeat at Yarmuk in 636, the city was taken again and the conditions of the
Muslim rulers were less favorable to the Christians. One tradition reports that
only fourteen of the forty-two churches remained at the disposal of the Christian community.[101] The Muslim conquerors also decided that the central area
where the temple had been and where the Christian basilica now stood in
splendor should be the site for their mosque. A mosque was built in the courtyard of the *temenos,* which Arculf saw around 670.[102] Another ancient tradition, possibly influenced by the situation in cities such as Homs, reports that the
Christian church was divided into two buildings with different doors. The
Christians kept only the western part of the building and lost the altar area. The
eastern part was desacralized as a Christian church and transformed into a
mosque with direct communication to the palace of the governor.

Finally, the sharing of the religious heart of the city was no longer admitted by the Muslim rulers who had made Damascus their capital. In 705 Caliph al-Walīd decided to evict the Christians. A new splendid mosque was to be built in this area and the remains of the previous religions erased.[103] The antique square towers were transformed into minarets. Oleg Grabar has noted that minarets were first built in Christian cities and were absent from mosques of the major Iraqi cities. Their function was not only to call the Muslims to prayer but also to assert the victorious presence of Islam in the center of Christian cities.[104] So, in Damascus, competition for a highly visible and central spot of the city led to a succession of religions inside the same sacred area, marked each time by the physical elimination of previous sacred buildings whose stones were often simply reused. The place retained its continuous sacrality. The right of asylum that the temple had probably enjoyed under the Seleucids was granted to the same area of the *temenos* in the 5th century, possibly at the time of the extension of the church. Under Muslim rule, this area held the ancient right of asylum under the name of Djairoun, in which *jer* means to be the guest of the God. Ibn Baṭṭūṭa saw men who lived in the shadow of the mosque, never leaving the enclosure and constantly praying.[105] In his *Cosmography* written around 1300, the compiler Dimishqi marveled at what was for him a sanctuary of four thousand years. The mosque, he noted, was originally a temple to Jupiter. He even added an episode to that long story: the Jews had transformed Jupiter's temple into a prayer house before the Christians changed it into a church and the Muslims into a mosque. Dimishqi had no doubt that he could in that place, and in that building, recapture the religious history of the human race and assert the one true religion that finally overcame the others, Islam.

Like rivers that create currents when they meet the sea, the religions in competition in the Roman and Persian worlds altered the societies they encountered. In regions like Syria and Palestine the currents were the strongest. First the sounds and perfumes of pagan processions had filled the streets of Syrian cities; then the music of Christian hymns and the odor of incense sanctified the urban space as Christians went in procession from one sanctuary to another; finally their voices were silenced by the chanting of the muezzin calling the Muslims to prayer from the minarets which dominated the ancient cities.

These two major religious changes within five centuries took different forms. Pagan sanctuaries were officially closed and their rites forbidden by Christian authorities of late Rome, while when the Muslims came to power they allowed Christians and Jews to practice their religions as long as they were silent and discreet. Yet Christians were often not allowed to repair their religious buildings, let alone build new ones, after the 8th century. The effect of these two religious shifts on the landscape can therefore be compared. With each new wave, religious buildings, once sacred sites visited by the faithful, collapsed in decay, while others were created to sacralize the land and the life of the faithful in a new manner. The Syrian and Palestinian landscape is dotted with ruins of abandoned temples, churches, and synagogues. Other religious buildings were officially desacralized and used for profane purposes. Still others were considered highly charged holy places and were transformed from temples to churches to mosques, such as in Damascus.

The 8th century was a turning point in the relationship between the Muslims and the *dhimmīs* (subject peoples). In Palestine, churches show traces of deliberate destruction of mosaics, particularly human and animal figures. We know that ʿUmar II (d. 720) had ordered that representations of crosses be destroyed.[106] Caliph Yazid II (720–724) ordered the destruction of statues, according to an Arab source of the 10th century, and of Christian images representing living creatures, if we follow Byzantine sources.[107] A study of the damaged mosaics suggests that they were destroyed not by violent Muslims intruders, but most probably by Christians themselves.[108] Whether this attitude was the result of Islamic pressure or arose from an inner and independent conviction that the representation of human and animal figures was ungodly remains an open and debatable question.[109] This period was marked by a tightening of the rules concerning the *dhimmīs*. A ruling of ʿUmar II (717–720) excluded non-Muslims from government administration unless they were willing to convert. The family of John of Damascus had been involved with tax collecting for many generations, under Persian, Byzantine, and now Muslim rulers. When he heard of the new ruling, John resigned and became a monk at St. Sabas in Palestine. This unfavorable evolution of the status of the *dhimmīs*, protected yet second-class citizens, clearly appears in the writings of the "Abbasid jurists," where numerous prohibitions, including restrictions on religious freedom and other new vexations, are noted.[110] No new churches or synagogues were to be erected, no proselytizing or public ceremonies were allowed. Authorization was required for the restoration of damaged religious buildings. Whether or not the prohibitions and vexations were enforced depended on the policies of the caliphs or the local emirs.

Archaeological evidence shows that until the middle of the 8th century Christians in Palestine still built or embellished churches. The same mosaicists worked for the Christian community in churches and for the new rulers in palaces.[111] Compared with the desacralization of pagan temples in the course of the 4th and 5th centuries, the desacralization of churches and synagogues was not caused primarily by the conversion of the population to the new religion— the evidence for massive conversion to Islam is rather later[112]—nor was it imposed by Umayyad caliphs or by violent actions on the part of individual Muslims. The abandonment of religious buildings, which is very noticeable throughout these regions in the course of the 7th and the 8th centuries, was due to a combination of causes, human (such as invasions, mostly the Persian invasion) and natural (such as earthquakes). Most likely the depopulation and impoverishment of the congregations explain why buildings were not repaired.[113] The same desacralization of Christian buildings happened in regions where no earthquakes damaged the churches. In Egypt, the taxes that the *dhimmīs* had to pay to the Muslim state eventually led to a real impoverishment of the Christian communities. At Philae, the Isis temple transformed into a Christian shrine under Justinian had remained a simple chapel, for the Christian community had other churches, notably a cathedral, also at Philae. Only after the Arabic invasion did the declining Christian community adopt the sturdy temple as its regular church, which probably indicates a lack of means or authorization to repair its other churches.[114]

Earthquakes in the Middle East, such as the terrible one of 746/7, caused the destruction of many buildings, among them numerous churches which were never rebuilt. One example reveals how an earthquake could follow a period of declining means combined with a gradual loss of respect to wipe out a magnificent church. The most majestic church in Pella, probably the cathedral, was built around 400 with columns and stones from a monumental temple.[115] The church was erected in the busy civic center of Pella, a prominent site in the city, highly visible to travelers coming from the Jordan valley. The building was refurbished in the 6th century. It was restored after the departure of the Persians in the early 7th century, and its final embellishments were a new monumental entrance, consisting of a majestic staircase and a large arch, along with new apartments for the clergy. The staircase enhanced the grandeur of the entrance to the building and served as a stage for solemn processions of the Christian community. Yet little more than a century later the atrium was being used to stable animals—as the discovery of the bones of camels who died in the earthquake of 747 reveals. In the city conquered by the Muslims in 635, the Christian community had lost its prosperity as well as its political power. After the earthquakes of 658–660, the grand portal was sealed. At that time, Christian processions were forbidden and Christians were allowed to practice their cult only inside their churches, as discreetly as possible. The loss of respect for the sacred building by a growing non-Christian population is attested by the fate of the other church entrances; during this time they were either sealed or reduced in size, probably to prevent animals from wandering into the atrium and the sanctuary. Finally, after the 717 earthquake, the partially collapsed church must have been deconsecrated and its interior furnishings, including the altar, removed. The fallen stones, tiles, and marble paving were taken away to repair other buildings. The rest of the church collapsed during the earthquake of 747, which destroyed most of the city of Pella. The fate of the once magnificent church of Pella was shared by many churches, synagogues, and Zoroastrian temples located in Muslim lands.

In the Byzantine world, it is also possible to see the 8th century as a turning point. As the Byzantine empire was still in shock from the amputation of its richest provinces, Egypt and Syria, as well as that of the nearby province of Illyricum, the Byzantine population turned its attention to saints, who seemed to be the only powers able to protect them. They did not consider the emergence of Islam, which they believed was only another Christian heresy, to be the cause of their empire's defeat. Rather, they assumed that the shrinking of the empire resulted from their own sins. Particularly under scrutiny were the remaining "pagan" or idolatrous practices, which could have angered God.[116] In 692, the Trullan Synod denounced a number of them. In the early 8th century, voices were raised by bishops in Asia Minor against the veneration of icons. Yet it was the deliberate policy of two emperors, Leo III (717–741) and Constantine V (741–775), who wanted to focus all energy on the figure of the emperor in order to save the empire, which created the destructive iconoclast movement.[117] The intense sacralization of painted images, which focused attention away from the altar and the Eucharist, was suddenly condemned as idolatry, opening a debate concerning the *locus* of the sacred. This reaction against the dispersal of Christian sacrality was combined with a political agenda of centralization of powers: Leo III replaced the image of Christ on coins with his own portrait. In 730 he ordered the destruction of all icons in the Byzantine empire. Only crosses were allowed, because they were symbols rather than images. By 787, when Empress Irene decided to restore the veneration of icons, a different Byzantine empire had emerged. Whole regions had seen their urban centers destroyed or depopulated.[118] Moreover, the late antique ceremonial modes of sacralizing space and time had changed to more discreet and inward-looking forms. Instead of huge basilicas with atria where large processions took place, the Byzantines now built more centripetal churches on a modest scale. In the new liturgies, processional movements were reduced to symbolic steps inside the churches.[119]

In the west, the 8th century is marked by the rise of the Carolingian rulers in Francia, changes in the political geography in many other countries, and the threat of the Islamic empire, which reached Spain and Sicily either through raiding or through conquest. Yet from a religious point of view, there was overall continuity from the 5th to the 8th century. The church domesticated the landscape through an intense sacralization of the land. In Rome, the number of churches, monasteries, and religious institutions rose to some 200 around 800 C.E., in a city whose population had sharply declined since the 4th century.[120] Churches large and small, hermits' cells and imposing monasteries, holy wells and monumental crosses studded the inhabited landscape. Kings maintained the tradition of church patronage in urban centers in order to demonstrate their public standing above other aristocratic families. In Metz, church building depended on the royal patronage of the Merovingian kings of Austrasia after they chose the city as their major urban base after 560. Six known churches, possibly fifteen in all, were built on their order. By 700 the citizens of Metz could hear the psalms sung in thirty churches or so.[121]

These numbers, however, conceal the deep transformation that occurred in early medieval kingdoms. Organized around their kings and their aristocracies, these Christian societies invested mostly in private religious buildings and in family monasteries set up on their lands. As the urban population diminished, some suburban sanctuaries were slowly abandoned. Even in Rome, a city marked by the continuity of its sacred spaces, the insecurity caused by Saracen raids led to the removal of relics from the catacombs in the 8th century and a withdrawal of religious activity from the once thriving cemeterial basilicas. Finally, as the sacred geography of the former Roman provinces adapted to the new medieval societies, the religious conquest of new lands started. East of the

Rhine and north of the Danube there were still pagans to convert, pagan shrines to desecrate, and new Christian sanctuaries to consecrate with perfumed oil and incense.

Notes

1. René Rebuffat, "Divinités de l'oued Kebir (Tripolitaine)," in Attilio Mastino, *L'Africa romana: Atti del VII convegno di studio* (Sassari, 1990), 119–159. An inscription on an altar records the consecration of the camp to the local genius (150).

2. Michael Avi-Yonah, "The Mosaic of Mopsuestia—Church or Synagogue?" in Lee I. Levine, ed., *Ancient Synagogues Revealed* (Jerusalem, 1981), 186–190.

3. David G. Orr, "Roman Domestic Religion: The Evidence of the Household Shrines," *ANRW* 16.2.1557–1591; J. T. Baker, *Living and Working with the Gods: Studies of Evidence for Private Religion and Its Material Environment in the City of Ostia (100–500 AD)* (Amsterdam, 1994).

4. Henri Fugier, *Recherches sur l'expression du sacré dans la langue latine* (Paris, 1963), 71–88.

5. E. M. Orlin, *Temples, Religion and Politics in the Roman Republic* (Leiden, 1997).

6. Susan E. Alcock, "Minding the Gap in Hellenistic and Roman Greece," in Susan E. Alcock and Robin Osborne, eds., *Placing the Gods: Sanctuaries and Sacred Space in Ancient Greece* (Oxford, 1994), 247–261.

7. Eberhard Sauer, *The End of Paganism in the North-Western Provinces of the Roman Empire: The Example of the Mithras Cult* (London, 1996).

8. Fawzi Zayadine, ed., *Jerash Archaeological Project (1981–1983)* (Amman, 1986).

9. Martin Henig and A. C. King, *Pagan Gods and Shrines of the Roman Empire* (Oxford, 1986); Françoise Dunand, *Le culte d'Isis dans le bassin oriental de la Méditerranée*, vol. 2 (Leiden, 1973); Robert Turcan, *The Cults of the Roman Empire* (Oxford, 1996).

10. Such a comparison is offered for *ludi* and festivals in Michele R. Salzman, *On Roman Time: The Codex-Calendar of 354 and the Rhythms of Urban Life in Late Antiquity* (Berkeley, 1990), 121–125.

11. Wonderful descriptions of the colorful and lively processions can be read in Greek novels; see B. P. Reardon, ed., *Collected Ancient Greek Novels* (Berkeley, 1989). On the imperial cult festivals, see Simon R. F. Price, *Rituals and Power: The Roman Imperial Cult in Asia Minor* (Cambridge, Eng., 1984).

12. J. H. W. G. Liebeschuetz, *Continuity and Change in Roman Religion* (Oxford, 1979).

13. K. J. Rigsby, *Asylia: Territorial Inviolability in the Hellenistic World* (Berkeley, 1996).

14. S. N. C. Lieu, *Manichaeism in the Later Roman Empire and Medieval China: A Historical Survey* (Manchester, 1985).

15. Eusebius, *Hist.eccl.* 9.5.

16. *CIL* 3.12132, trans. in Simon R. F. Price, *Rituals and Power: The Roman Imperial Cult in Asia Minor* (Cambridge, Eng., 1984), 124.

17. Gelasius, *Lettre contre les Lupercales et dix-huit messes du sacramentaire léonien* (Paris, 1959); Augustine, *Sermon Dolbeau 26*, in François Dolbeau, ed., *Vingt-Six Sermons au peuple d'Afrique* (Paris, 1996), 345–417.

18. O. Pasquato, *Gli spettacoli in S. Giovanni Crisostomo: Paganesimo e cristianesimo ad Antiochia e Costantinopoli nel IV secolo* (Rome, 1976); Timothy Barnes,

"Christians and the Theater," in W. J. Slater, ed., *Roman Theater and Society*, E. Togo Salmon Papers 1 (Ann Arbor, 1996), 161–180; Richard Lim, "Consensus and Dissensus on Public Spectacles in Early Byzantium," in L. Garland, ed., *Conformity and Non-Conformity in Byzantium, Byzantinische Forschungen* 24 (1997): 159–179.

19. C. Moss, "Jacob of Serugh's Homilies on the Spectacles," in *Le Museon* 48 (1935): 87–112, trans. at 106.

20. Maximus of Turin, *Sermon* 107, trans. in J. N. Hillgarth, *Christianity and Paganism, 350–750: The Conversion of Western Europe* (Philadelphia, 1986), 55.

21. Dietrich Claude, *Die byzantinische Stadt im 6. Jahrhundert* (Munich, 1969), 74–76.

22. A number of the texts relevant to the ending of pagan cults can be found in English translation in Brian Croke and Jill Harries, *Religious Conflict in Fourth-Century Rome: A Documentary Study* (Sydney, 1982). See also Pierre Chuvin, *A Chronicle of the Last Pagans* (Cambridge, Mass., 1990). For a very different view of Constantine's policy toward pagans, see Timothy D. Barnes, *Constantine and Eusebius* (Cambridge, Mass., 1981).

23. Jean Gascou, "Le rescrit d'Hispellum," in *Mélanges de l'Ecole française de Rome* 79 (1967): 609–659.

24. C.Th. 16.10.4 [346; 354; 356]; 16.10.6 [Feb. 356]: death penalty for anyone performing a sacrifice.

25. C.Th. 16.10.8 [Nov. 382] to the Dux of Osroëne: "We decree that the temple shall be continually open . . . In order that this temple may be seen by the assemblages of the city and by frequent crowds, Your Experience shall preserve all celebrations of festivities . . . but in such a way that the performance of sacrifices forbidden therein may not be supposed to be permitted under the pretext of such access to the temple" (trans. Pharr). In 357, during his visit to Rome, Emperor Constantius consecrated a temple to Apollo (*CIL* 6.45 = Dessau 3222). At the end of the 4th century, but before 391, altars to the gods were restored in Sardis and sacrifices offered by a "vicar of Asia" and a "governor of Lydia" (Pierre Chuvin, *Chronicle of the Last Pagans*, 48). On restoration of temples in the west at the end of the 4th century, see H. Bloch, "The Pagan Revival in the West at the End of the Fourth Century," in Arnaldo Momigliano, ed., *The Conflict between Paganism and Christianity in the Fourth Century* (Oxford, 1963), 193–218; André Chastagnol, "La restauration du temple d'Isis au Portus Romae sous le règne de Gratien," in *Hommage à Marcel Renard* (Brussels, 1969), 135–144, repr. in *L'Italie et l'Afrique au Bas-Empire, Scripta Varia* (Lille, 1987); Claude Lepelley, *Les cités de l'Afrique romaine au Bas Empire* (Paris, 1979), 347–351.

26. It was obviously very difficult to enforce the closing of the temples and even more the suppression of sacrifices, especially those made in the privacy of an individual's house; for an archaeological record of private sacrifices, see Arja Karivieri, "The 'House of Proclus' on the Southern Slope of the Acropolis: A Contribution," in Paavo Castren, ed., *Post Herulian Athens: Aspects of Life and Culture in Athens, A.D. 267–529* (Helsinki, 1994), 115–139. Certain cults were hard to kill. In 417, Isiac cults were still being honored in Gaul (Rutilius Namatianus, 1.371–376). Individuals worshiping and sacrificing to the goddess are still attested in the late 6th century: see Michel Tardieu, *Les paysages reliques: Routes et haltes syriennes d'Isidore à Simplicius* (Louvain, 1990); Glen W. Bowersock, *Hellenism in Late Antiquity* (Ann Arbor, 1990). However, sacrifice was now conducted in private in clandestine temples or secret chambers: see Zacharias Scholasticus, *Life of Severus*, ed. and trans. M. A. Kugener, *PO* 2: 20–35.

27. Symmachus, *Relatio* 3, in R. Barrow, *Prefect and Emperor: The Relationes of Symmachus A.D. 384* (Oxford, 1973).

28. Stephen Mitchell, *Anatolia: Land, Men and Gods in Asia Minor*, vol. 2: *The Rise of the Church* (Oxford, 1993).

29. In the year 112, Pliny the Younger, then a governor, wrote to Emperor Trajan concerning a temple obstructing the building of the new forum in Nicomedia. He had religious scruples about authorizing its removal. Trajan answered directing him to remove the temple to another site (Pliny, *Ep.* 10, 50).

30. Robin Lane Fox, *Pagans and Christians* (New York, 1989), 671–672.

31. Louis Robert, "De Cilicie à Messine et à Plymouth avec deux inscriptions grecques errantes," in *Journal des Savants* (1973): 161–211; see esp. 185–192.

32. The notion of physical contact is crucial for understanding the creation of holy places and eventually of the Holy Land, an idea expressed quite literally by Eusebius in a sentence explaining the construction of a shrine on the Mount of Olives, which he identified as the place where the Ascension took place: "There stood in truth . . . the feet of our Lord and Savior, Himself the Word of God" (*Demonstratio evangelica* 6.18.23). On this new notion, see Peter W. L. Walker, *Holy City, Holy Places? Christian Attitudes to Jerusalem and the Holy Land in the Fourth Century* (Oxford, 1990), 206.

33. Eusebius, *Vit.Const.* 3.28–29.

34. Robert L. Wilken, *The Land Called Holy: Palestine in Christian History and Thought* (New Haven, 1992); Francis E. Peters, *Jerusalem: The Holy City in the Eyes of Chroniclers, Visitors, Pilgrims, and Prophets from the Days of Abraham to the Beginnings of Modern Times* (Princeton, 1985); Hagith Sivan, "Pilgrimage, Monasticism, and the Emergence of Christian Palestine in the 4th Century," in Robert Ousterhout, ed., *The Blessings of Pilgrimage* (Chicago, 1990), 54–65.

35. Jan W. Drijvers, *Helena Augusta: The Mother of Constantine the Great and the Legends of Her Finding of the True Cross* (Leiden, 1992); A. Frolow, *La relique de la vraie croi: Recherches sur le développement d'un culte* (Paris, 1961).

36. Claude Lepelley, "The Survival and Fall of the Classical City in Late Roman Africa," in John Rich, ed., *The City in Late Antiquity* (London, 1992), 50–76; Cristina La Rocca, "Public Buildings and Urban Change in Northern Italy in the Early Mediaeval Period," ibid., 161–180.

37. Henri Grégoire and M. A. Kugener, ed. and trans., *Marc Le Diacre: Vie de Porphyre évêque de Gaza* (Paris, 1930). On Gaza, see Frank Trombley, *Hellenic Religion and Christianization, c. 370–529,* vol. 1 (Leiden, 1993); Carol A. M. Glucker, *The City of Gaza in the Roman and Byzantine Periods* (Oxford, 1987); Raymond Van Dam, "From Paganism to Christianity at Late Antique Gaza," in *Viator* 16 (1985): 1–20; Garth Fowden, "Bishops and Temples in the Eastern Roman Empire A.D. 320–435," *Journal of Theological Studies,* n.s. 29.1 (April 1978): 53–78.

38. For Greece: Jean-Marie Spieser, "La christianisation des sanctuaires païens en Grèce," in *Neue Forschungen in Griechischen Heiligtümern,* ed. U. Jantzen (Tübingen, 1976), 309–320. Highly charged parts of a temple could be deliberately attacked, like the *aduton* in the temple of Apollo at Delphi: see Vincent Déroche, "Delphes: La christianisation d'un sanctuaire païen," in *Actes du XIe congrès international d'archéologie chrétienne,* vol. 3 (Rome, 1989), 2713–23. For central Gaul, see Bailey Young, "Que restait-il de l'ancien paysage religieux à l'époque de Grégoire de Tours?" in Nancy Gauthier and Henri Galinié, eds., *Grégoire de Tours et l'espace gaulois,* Suppl. 13 to *Revue archéologique du centre de la France* (1997).

39. Canons of the Trullan Synod in 692.

40. Compare with the early church: T. C. G. Thornton, "The Destruction of Idols: Sinful or Meritorious?" *Journal of Theological Studies,* n.s. 37 (1986): 121–124.

41. W. H. C. Frend, "Monks and the End of Greco-Roman Paganism," in *L'intolleranza cristiana nei confronti dei pagani,* in P. F. Beatrice, ed., *Cristianesimo nella storia* 11:3 (1990): 469–484. On Libanius's accusations of widespread destruction of rural temples at the hand of monks, see François Paschoud, "L'intolérance chrétienne vue et jugée par les païens," ibid., 27–54, and Peter Brown, *Authority and the Sacred* (Cambridge, Eng., 1995): 545–577.

42. Françoise Thélamon, "Destruction du paganisme et construction du Royaume de Dieu d'après Rufin et Augustin," in *Cristianesimo nella storia* 11:3 (1990): 523–544.

43. Sabina MacCormack, "Loca Sancta: The Organization of Sacred Topography in Late Antiquity," in Ousterhout, *The Blessings of Pilgrimage*, 14; for the identification of pagan gods with demons, see Jean-Marie Vermander, "La polémique des Apologistes latins contre les dieux du paganisme," *Recherches Augustiniennes* 17 (1982): 3–128.

44. Even in 8th century Constantinople, extraordinary stories circulated about the antique pagan statues' malevolence toward Christians: see *Constantinople in the Early Eighth Century: The Parastaseis syntomoi chronikai,* ed. Averil Cameron and Judith Herrin in conjunction with Alan Cameron, Robin Cormack, and Charlotte Roueché (Leiden, 1984); Gilbert Dagron, *Constantinople imaginaire: Etudes sur le recueil des "Patria"* (Paris, 1984).

45. Eustratios, *Life of Eutychius* 53, PG 86.2333D, cited in Cyril Mango, "L'attitude byzantine à l'égard des antiquités gréco-romaines," in *Byzance et les images,* ed. Jannic Durand (Paris, 1994), 97–120.

46. Rufinus, *Ecclesiastical History,* 2.29; Françoise Thélamon, *Païens et Chrétiens au IVe siècle: L'apport de l'Histoire ecclésiastique de Rufin d'Aquilée* (Paris, 1981), 267; Christopher Haas, *Alexandria in Late Antiquity: Topography and Social Conflict* (Baltimore, 1997), 159–169.

47. Barbara Gassowska, "Maternus Cynegius, praefectus Praetorio Orientis and the Destruction of the Allat Temple in Palmyra," in *Archeologia* 33 (1982): 114–115.

48. Robert Turcan, *Mithra et le Mithraicisme* (Paris, 1993), 119.

49. The temple, located in the south of Egypt, had remained open long after the official closing of pagan temples, to placate the tumultuous pagan Blemmyes who came to worship Isis in that sanctuary; see Roger S. Bagnall, *Egypt in Late Antiquity* (Princeton, 1993), 147 and 251. The peace treaty being broken, Justinian ordered the closing of the temple and its transformation into a church; see Pierre Nautin, "La conversion du temple de Philae en église chrétienne," in *Cahiers Archéologiques* 17 (1967): 1–43.

50. Helen Saradi-Mendelovici, "Christian Attitudes toward Pagan Monuments in Late Antiquity and Their Legacy in Later Byzantine Centuries," in *Dumbarton Oaks Papers* 44 (1990): 47–59.

51. Claude Lepelley, "Le Musée des statues divines: La volonté de sauvegarder le patrimoine artistique païen à l'époque théodosienne," *Cahiers archéologiques* 42 (1994): 5–15.

52. Marlia Mundell Mango, "Art Collecting in Byzantium," *Etudes balkaniques* 2 (1995): 137–160.

53. Michele Piccirillo, *Mosaics of Jordan* (Amman, 1993); Katherine Dunbabin, *Mosaics of Roman North Africa: Studies in Iconography and Patronage* (Oxford, 1978); R. Wilson, *Piazza Armerina* (Austin, 1983).

54. Dericksen M. Brinkerhoff, *A Collection of Sculpture in Classical and Early Christian Antioch* (New York, 1970).

55. Jean-Charles Picard, *La Carthage de Saint Augustin* (Paris, 1965), 98–107.

56. Jean-Pierre Sodini, "L'habitat urbain en Grèce à la veille des invasions," in *Villes et peuplement dans l'Illyricum protobyzantin* (Rome, 1984), 341–397.

57. Allan C. Johnson, Paul R. Coleman-Norton, and Frank Card Bourne, eds., *Ancient Roman Statutes* (Austin, 1961), 249–250.

58. Peter Brown, *The Cult of the Saints: Its Rise and Function in Latin Christianity* (Chicago, 1981).

59. Kenneth G. Holum, "The Trier Ivory, Adventus Ceremonial and the Relics of Saint Stephen," *Dumbarton Oaks Papers* 33 (1979): 113–133. The author interprets the scene as the welcoming of the relics of St. Stephen by Empress Pulcheria in 421. For another interpretation, see S. Spain, "The Translation of Relics Ivory, Trier," *Dumbarton Oaks Papers* 31 (1977): 279–304.

60. Vitricius of Rouen, *De laude Sanctorum* 1, PL 20.433A, cited in Hillgarth, *Christianity and Paganism,* 23.

61. Neil Christie and Simon T. Loseby, *Towns in Transition: Urban Evolution in Late Antiquity and the Early Middle Ages* (Aldershot, 1996).

62. Alan Walmsley, "Byzantine Palestine and Arabia: Urban Prosperity in Late Antiquity," ibid., 126–158.

63. Bert de Vries, "Jordan's Churches: Their Urban Context in Late Antiquity," *Biblical Archaeologist* 51 (1988): 222–226.

64. Hugh Kennedy, "The Last Century of Byzantine Syria," *Byzantinische Forschungen* 10 (1985): 141–183.

65. Jean-Charles Balty, paper delivered at a conference on Apamea at the École Normale Supérieure, May 21, 1996. A publication on the temple is forthcoming.

66. Jacques Seigne, "Jerash: Le sanctuaire de Zeus et ses abords," *Contribution française à l'Archéologie Jordanienne* (Amman, 1989), 40–48.

67. Fawzi Zayadine, "The Jerash Project for Excavation and Restoration: A Synopsis with Special Reference to the Work of the Department of Antiquities," in *Jerash Archaeological Project, 1981–1983,* ed. F. Zayadine (Amman, 1986), 11–12.

68. Steven Fine, "From Meeting House to Sacred Realm: Holiness and the Ancient Synagogue," in Fine, ed., *Sacred Realm: The Emergence of the Synagogue in the Ancient World* (New York and Oxford, 1996); Joan R. Branham, "Vicarious Sacrality: Temple Space in Ancient Synagogues," in D. Urman and Paul V. M. Flesher, eds., *Ancient Synagogues: A Historical Analysis and Archaeological Discovery* (Leiden, 1995), 319–346.

69. Annabel J. Wharton, *Refiguring the Post Classical City: Dura Europos, Jerash, Jerusalem and Ravenna* (Cambridge, Eng., 1995).

70. *C.Cels.* 8.17–20; Origen, *The Letter of Barnabas,* 16; Joan E. Taylor, *Christians and the Holy Places: The Myth of Jewish-Christian Origins* (Oxford, 1993); Robert Markus, "How on Earth Could Places Become Holy? Origins of the Christian Idea of Holy Places," *Journal of Early Christian Studies* 2:3 (1994): 257–271.

71. In the *Acta purgationis Felicis Abthugnitani,* a pagan *duumvir,* coming back to his city in 303, reports the destruction of two Christian basilicas at Furnos and Zama (*Acta purgationis Felicis Abthugnitani,* ed. C. Ziwsa, CSEL 26, 199).

72. In a city such as Carthage, the church's treasure consisted of gold and silver vessels (*Optatus Milevitani* 1.17, ed. C. Ziwsa, CSEL 26, 19).

73. Bishop Silvanus was elected there; see Yvette Duval, *Auprès des saints, corps et ame: L'inhumation "ad sanctos" dans la chrétienté d'Orient et d'Occident du IIIe au VIIe siècle* (Paris, 1988), 54.

74. Michel-Yves Perrin, "Le nouveau style missionnaire: La conquête de l'espace et du temps," in Jean-Marie Mayeur et al., eds., *Histoire du christianisme des origines à nos jours* (Paris, 1995), 584–621; André Grabar, *Martyrium: Recherches sur le culte des reliques et l'art chrétien* (Paris, 1943–1946).

75. Charles Pietri, "Le temps de la semaine à Rome et dans l'Italie," in *Le temps chrétien de la fin de l'Antiquité au Moyen Age, IIIe–XIIIe siècles* (Paris, 1984), 63–81.

76. E. D. Hunt, "The Traffic in Relics: Some Late Roman Evidence," in S. Hackel, *The Byzantine Saint* (Birmingham, 1981), 171–179.

77. *Epistula Luciani,* 2, PL 41.809; commented on in Brown, *Cults of the Saints,* 91–92.

78. Pauline Donceel-Voûte, *Les pavements des églises byzantines de Syrie et du Liban: Décor, archéologie et liturgie* (Louvain-La-Neuve, 1988), 534; Gary Vikan, *Byzantine Pilgrimage Art* (Washington, D.C., 1982).

79. In Monza, the cathedral owns a collection of these *ampullae,* which contained oils that had burned in front of sixty different tombs of martyrs buried in Rome. See André Grabar, *Ampoules de Terre Sainte* (Paris, 1958); Nicole Herrmann-Mascard, *Les reliques des saints: Formation coutumière d'un droit* (Paris, 1975), 47–48.

80. Luce Pietri, "Calendrier liturgique et temps vécu: L'exemple de Tours au VIe siècle," in *Le Temps Chrétien,* 129–141.

81. Church councils and civil legislation tried to enforce the notion of the irrevocability of church dedication. Once sacralized, a space could not be used for profane purposes.

82. Hans Belting, *Likeness and Presence: A History of the Image before the Era of Art,* trans. Edmund Jephcott (Chicago, 1994).

83. Patrick Geary, *Furta Sacra: Theft of Relics in the Central Middle Ages* (Princeton, 1990).

84. Bernard Flusin, *Saint Anastase le Perse et l'histoire de la Palestine au début du VIIe siècle* (Paris, 1992).

85. Francis E. Peters, *The Hajj: The Muslim Pilgrimage to Mecca and the Holy Places* (Princeton, 1994).

86. Bernard Lewis, *The Jews of Islam* (Princeton, 1984).

87. Carol Bier, "Piety and Power in Early Sasanian Art," in Eiko Matsushima, ed., *Official Cult and Popular Religion in the Ancient Near East* (Heidelberg, 1993).

88. Mary Boyce, *A History of Zoroastrianism,* vol. 3 (Leiden, 1991); Klaus Schippmann, *Die iranischen Feuerheiligtümer* (Berlin, 1971); Paul Bernard, "Le temple du dieu Oxus à Takht-i Sangin en Bactriane: Temple du feu ou pas?" in *Studia Iranica* 23 (1994): 81–121.

89. Michael Morony, *Iraq after the Muslim Conquest* (Princeton, 1984), 121; Eshan Yarshater, *The Cambridge History of Iran,* vol. 3 (Cambridge, 1983).

90. Jamsheed K. Choksy, "Zoroastrians in Muslim Iran: Selected Problems of Coexistence and Interaction during the Early Medieval Period," *Iranian Studies* 20 (1987): 17–30, and "Conflict, Coexistence, and Cooperation: Muslims and Zoroastrians in Eastern Iran during the Medieval Period," *The Muslim World* 80 (1990): 213–233.

91. Annemarie Schimmel, *Deciphering the Signs of God: A Phenomenological Approach to Islam* (Albany, 1994).

92. G. Avni, "Early Mosques in the Negev Highlands: New Archaeological Evidence on Islamic Penetration of Southern Palestine," *Bulletin of the American Schools of Oriental Research* 294 (1994): 83–100.

93. Gustave E. von Grunebaum, "The Sacred Character of Islamic Cities," in *Islam and Medieval Hellenism: Social and Cultural Perspectives* (London, 1976).

94. Oleg Grabar, *The Formation of Islamic Art* (New Haven, 1973; rev. ed. 1987).

95. Oleg Grabar, "La grande mosquée de Damas et les origines architecturales de la Mosquée," in *Synthronon: Art et Archéologie de la fin de l'Antiquité et du Moyen Age* (Paris, 1968), 107–114, at 108; Geoffrey King, C. J. Lenzen, and Gary O. Rollefson, "Survey of Byzantine and Islamic Sites of Jordan: Second Season Report, 1981," *Annual of the Department of Antiquities* 27 (1983): 399–405; Antonio Almagro, "Building Patterns in Umayyad Architecture in Jordan," in Muna Zaghloul et al., eds., *Studies in the History and Archaeology of Jordan IV* (Amman and Lyon, 1992), 351–356.

96. Suliman Bashear, "Qibla Musharriqa and Early Muslim Prayer in Churches," *The Muslim World* 81 (1991): 268–282.

97. Thilo Ulbert, "Resafa-Sergiupolis: Archäologische Forschungen in der Nordsyrischen Pilgerstadt," in *Syrien von den Aposteln zu den Kalifen,* ed. E. M. Ruprechtsberger (Linz, 1993), 112–127.

98. G. Avni, "Early Mosques," 83–100.

99. Oleg Grabar, *The Shape of the Holy: Early Islamic Jerusalem* (Princeton, 1996).

100. Michel Gawlikowski, "Les temples de Syrie à l'époque hellénistique et romaine," in *Archéologie et histoire de la Syrie, 2: La Syrie de l'époque achéménide à l'avènement de l'Islam,* ed. Jean-Marie Dentzer and Winfried Orthmann (Saarbrücken, 1989), 334.

101. Joseph Nasrallah, "De la cathédrale de Damas à la mosquée Omayyade," in *La*

Syrie de Byzance à l'Islam, VIIe–VIIIe siècles, ed. Pierre Canivet and Jean-Paul Rey-Coquais (Damascus, 1992).

102. Lucien Golvin, *Essai sur l'architecture religieuse musulmane, 2: L'art religieux des Umayyades de Syrie* (Paris, 1971).

103. Oleg Grabar, "La grande mosquée de Damas et les origines architecturales de la Mosquée," in *Synthronon: Art et Archéologie de la fin de l'Antiquité et du Moyen Age* (Paris, 1968), 107–114.

104. Oleg Grabar, "Islam and Byzantium," *Dumbarton Oaks Papers* 18 (1964): 74.

105. René Dussaud, "Le temple de Jupiter Damascénien et ses transformations aux époques chrétienne et musulmane," *Syria* 3 (1922): 219–250.

106. Abu Yusuf Ya'qub, *Le livre de l'impôt foncier,* tr. E. Fagnan (Paris, 1921), 196.

107. Texts gathered by André Grabar, *L'iconoclasme byzantin: Le dossier archéologique* (Paris, 1984), 128–129.

108. Robert Schick, *The Christian Communities of Palestine from Byzantine to Islamic Rule: A Historical and Archaeological Study* (Princeton, 1995).

109. G. R. D. King, "Islam, Iconoclasm, and the Declaration of Doctrine," *Bulletin of the School of Oriental and African Studies* 48 (1985): 267–277.

110. Anne-Marie Eddé et al., *Communautés chrétiennes en Pays d'Islam du début du VIIe siècle au milieu du XIe siècle* (Paris, 1997).

111. Michele Piccirillo, "The Umayyad Churches of Jordan," *Annual of the Department of Antiquities of Jordan* 28 (1994): 333–341.

112. Richard W. Bulliet, *Conversion to Islam in the Medieval Period* (Cambridge, Eng., 1979).

113. When the Muslims arrived in cities such as Hama, they found empty houses, the result of depopulation as well as desertion in face of the enemy; see Hugh Kennedy, "The Last Century of Byzantine Syria: A Reinterpretation," *Byzantinische Forschungen* 10 (1985): 141–183. The decline of the population and of the general prosperity in the second half of the 6th century, notably after the plague, is a matter of discussion: see Mark Whittow, "Ruling the Late Roman and Early Byzantine City: A Continuous History," *Past and Present* 129 (1990): 3–29.

114. Nautin, "La conversion du temple de Philae."

115. Robert H. Smith and Leslie P. Day, *Pella of the Decapolis, vol. 2, Final Report on the College of Wooster Excavations in Area IX, The Civic Complex, 1979–1985* (Wooster, Ohio, 1989).

116. Patricia Crone, "Islam, Judeo-Christianity and Byzantine Iconoclasm," *Jerusalem Studies in Arabic and Islam* 2 (1980): 59–95.

117. Gilbert Dagron, "Le christianisme byzantin du VIIe au milieu du XIe siècle," in *Histoire du Christianisme des origines à nos jours,* ed. Jean-Marie Mayeur et al., vol. 4: *Evêques, moines et empereurs (610–1054),* ed. Gilbert Dagron et al. (Paris, 1993).

118. For an evaluation of the destruction of early Christian basilicas and of the few new buildings in the 7th and 8th centuries, see Cyril Mango, *Byzantine Architecture* (London, 1979).

119. Robert F. Taft, *The Byzantine Rite: A Short History* (Collegeville, Minn., 1992); Thomas F. Mathews, *The Early Churches of Constantinople: Architecture and Liturgy* (University Park, Pa., 1971); Natalia B. Tetariatnikov, *The Liturgical Planning of Byzantine Churches in Cappadocia* (Rome, 1996).

120. Louis Reekmans, "L'implantation monumentale chrétienne dans le paysage urbain de Rome de 300 à 850," *Actes du XIe Congrès international d'archéologie chrétienne* 2 (1989): 861–915.

121. Guy Halsall, "Towns, Societies and Ideas: The Not-so-strange Case of Late Roman and Early Merovingian Metz," in Christie and Loseby, *Towns in Transition,* 235–261.

Philosophical Tradition and the Self

Henry Chadwick

Neither classical Greek nor Latin had a word meaning "self" approximating the senses in which that term has come to be used in philosophical discussions since the time of Descartes in the 17th century. Nevertheless there were discussions especially in late antiquity which anticipate propositions heard in more recent times, and the Neoplatonists in particular explored ways and means of investigating the subject, not least because they had an interest in restating the mind-body problem in terms of a Platonic dualism. They wanted to put distance between Platonism (received by them as authoritative truth) and both the materialist accounts of the soul characteristic of Stoicism and the Aristotelian middle position that the soul which gives life and form to the physical body cannot be thought of as existing apart from it and having sovereign independence, though it is not a physical substance.

In late antiquity the logical works of Aristotle's *Organon* were read, and in Alexander of Aphrodisias in Caria, about 200, the master found a learned and very intelligent advocate whose writings on the subject were known to the Neoplatonists. In the interest of showing Aristotle to be in harmony with Plato, they produced voluminous commentaries on his logic, metaphysics, and ethics. Nevertheless Aristotle was largely a philosopher's philosopher, read by an educated elite, but not widely or popularly studied. Nemesius, the cultivated and widely read bishop of Emesa at the end of the 4th century, admired Aristotle's achievements.

Stoicism found influential expositors in Epictetus and Emperor Marcus Aurelius. Galen recorded attending good lectures by a disciple of a Stoic named Philopator. Philopator's book arguing that belief in fate was compatible with free will left Nemesius unimpressed. In the Latin-speaking world Seneca, in the Greek world Epictetus, enjoyed considerable popularity and influence. Writing in 248, Origen observed that Plato's dialogues were not found to be easy reading and that the discourses of Epictetus (written up by his disciple and admirer

Arrian) were much more likely to be read and enjoyed. Stoic logic and ethics long remained influential in a way that the school's physics and metaphysics did not. Yet while in the early Roman empire of the 1st and 2nd centuries Stoic teachers ranked high in the popularity stakes, from the 3rd century onward Platonism became more and more dominant. In the Latin west of the second half of the 4th century, the legacy of Plotinus teaching in Rome and of Porphyry living in Sicily ensured that the new lease of life given to Platonic studies by Plotinus created a widespread Platonizing culture no less general than in the Greek east. Moreover, that educated Christians in Rome or Alexandria found much in the Platonic tradition with which they felt a deep sympathy helped to underpin their generalized assumption that Platonic ideas provided a good background for an appropriate way of life. This Christian sympathy was not welcome to the pagan tradition, within which part of the popularity of Platonism came from its potential to provide an alternative and rival to the rising power of Christianity. Just as within the boundaries of the church the most intense controversies were between those who stood closest to each other, so also Christians such as Gregory of Nyssa or Augustine of Hippo could be particularly sharp in their negativity toward pagan philosophers—and vice versa. But the understanding of the mind-body problem on both sides of this kind of divide was really remarkably similar.

Accordingly the modern reader looking for a coherent account of the self in the writers of this period of antiquity needs to be willing to make some mental adjustment. The ancients were not students of neuroscience and did not comprehend the extremely intricate workings of the brain. They had long known the mind to be all-important in the human constitution, and acutely argued about freedom, responsibility, deliberation, intention, conscience, even consciousness.

One must not forget that although they had read neither Descartes nor Foucault they nevertheless had something to say. Embryonic elements of the theme of the self can be traced in classical authors. The dominance of Platonism among both Christian and non-Christian provided a milieu in which the soul or mind (nous) or self became a major topic with wide areas of agreement and common terminology. One pervasively influential text was the First Alcibiades of Plato in which, starting from the Delphic recommendation "Know thyself," the real nature of man is defined as the soul's making use of the body as an instrument (and therefore secondary). The knowing of oneself is the very first principle of philosophy, the self-understanding which determines a person's way of life, and is therefore also the ultimate ground of religious awareness. It is a widely diffused axiom that the purified soul is a mirror image of the divine, found for example in the apostle Paul (2 Cor. 3:18) or the Sentences of Sextus (450) in the 2nd century. The apostle's aspiration was to know the divine "as he himself is known" (1 Cor. 13:12). In the Coptic Gospel of Thomas III the world is declared by Jesus to be unworthy of the person who achieves self-discovery, and through self-knowledge comes repose (anapausis). Realizing oneself to be one of the elect is the gnostic message giving meaning and dignity to an otherwise dull and probably miserable existence. There are ethical consequences. In

Poimandres, first tract in the corpus of Hermetic writings, this self-recognition entails awareness that the sexual drive is the cause of death (*CH* 1.18), and thereby the soul's elevation is weighed down. Bodily sensation has to be left behind (*CH* 13.10).

Porphyry, biographer and editor of Plotinus, began the *Life* of his master with the famous sentence that Plotinus always seemed ashamed of being in the body. His concern was with the soul which, true to Plato, he saw as being midway between the inferior flesh and the superior incorporeal mind. Moral choices are therefore decisions whether to follow the higher reason or lower bodily appetite. The self (for which Plotinus uses the word *autos*) therefore has levels and power of movement. But the true self is divine and the body no more than its temporary instrument (IV 7.1.20ff.). Naturally the union of soul with body makes for interaction between them. When ashamed we blush, when terrified we go white with fear. Conversely there are pressures which the body can put upon the soul, drawing it downward toward material satisfactions. But the soul's true home is in that higher realm which is not governed by the determinism of fate. Self-knowledge is synonymous with the soul's being identical in being *(homoousios)* with mind (IV 4.28.56; IV 7.10.19). Thereby salvation is the divinizing of the soul, a mystical union comparable to the merging of two torches (I 6.9.18ff.) "in the measure possible to the human soul" (2.9.9.45ff.). The route by which one returns to true being is self-knowledge (VI 5.7), and is a restoration of the unity from which the soul has fallen into multiplicity and has been torn apart in a "scattering" (VI 6.1.5). As the soul moves toward the good, it recovers freedom, which is a liberation from the constraints of the body (VI 8.6–7). Plotinus noted explicitly that in his doctrine of the soul's retaining its divine nature "undescended" he was departing from the normal view of the Platonic schools (IV 8.8.1). Origen (*Prin.* 3.4) shows that the idea was not new with Plotinus.

Iamblichus came to think Plotinus mistaken to suppose that a higher part of the soul does not descend to the body; the entire soul is responsible (Proclus, *In Tim.* 3.334.3–8). It retains choice, and descent is not to a determinist world. Plotinus's language was felt by some among his Neoplatonist successors to have offered a brilliant interpretation of Plato's *Parmenides,* taking the three hypotheses of that dialogue to speak of the One, *nous,* and soul, but nevertheless to have bequeathed some difficult problems. Iamblichus, contemporary with Emperor Constantine the Great, thought the language about the relation between *nous* and soul to be confused and confusing: Was it correct to say that the soul becomes "identical in being" with *nous,* and if so, does that imply that in *nous* itself there are higher and lower levels? It seemed easier to hold that soul is in principle distinct from *nous* and on an inferior level of being. Then again, the Plotinian soul comes from and rises to such exalted heights as to force the questions how and why it could ever have descended to occupy the body, and how it could make gravely mistaken moral decisions so as to sin. Iamblichus's critique of Plotinus on these points does not survive independently of Proclus's summary in his commentary on Plato's *Timaeus* (3.231.245, and especially 333f. Diehl) and a fragment of Iamblichus "On the Soul" preserved in Stobaeus

(1.365–66 Wachsmuth). Proclus warmly concurred with Iamblichus that it must be impossible to assert that "our soul" can be placed on an equality with the gods, identical in being *(homoousios)* with divine souls and on the same level with mind and indeed the One itself, leaving the lower world wholly behind it and by virtue of the union becoming "established." Plotinus's notion that at least the higher part of the human soul remains in the sphere of the noetic realm is impossible to reconcile with the sin and wretchedness of the human condition. It could even be questioned whether the human soul has inherent immortality.

In Plotinus's doctrine of the soul it was important for him to affirm an intimate original link between soul and *nous.* He had to say that *nous* is the sun but soul is the sunlight. Above all, this connection with the *nous* was not destroyed or lost when soul became embodied (IV 3.11–12). For as fire and air remain what they are without the mixture changing their natures, so also is the presence of soul to the body (IV 3.22), and hence Plato was correct in *Timaeus* (36d–e) when he put the body in the soul, not the soul in the body.

In the Platonic tradition there was a tenacious belief that the body is a drag and a hindrance. It penetrated the Wisdom of Solomon that "the perishable body weighs down the soul" (9:15). In *Phaedo* (65a, 66c) the body's unremitting need for food, the diseases which beset it, passions, desires, and fears, the body's love of money "which causes all wars," all add up to a major distraction from philosophical thinking. Plato anticipated the Neoplatonists here in writing of the need for the soul to "collect and bring itself together" from the separate parts of the body (67c).

Plotinus had no hesitation in labeling the body as an evil on the ground of its materiality, whereas the incorporeal soul is free of evil (I 8.4.1ff.). The temporal successiveness of bodily existence—"one thing after another"—created by our physical needs and external circumstances "drags the soul in all directions" (IV 4.17). In the *Republic* (10.603c–d) Plato observed that human beings can hold contradictory opinions at the same time, and that the strife is not merely between one person and another, but within the same person's mind.

Plotinus and the Neoplatonists did not doubt that in the soul or self there is a continuity which makes possible the act of remembering. At the same time, if asked whether this self is multiple or a single entity in a constant state, the answer would certainly have been that amid the distractions of this present physical life, with all the materialist suggestions coming to the soul from the body, the soul's experience is one of alarming multiplicity, and that coherence or unity is the goal to which the study of philosophy can help to guide. In *Phaedo* 78c Plato had based an argument for immortality on the axiom that the nature of the soul is to be a single entity, and that entities composed of a diversity of elements eventually disintegrate and come to destruction; they cannot then be eternal. The argument recurs in the tenth book of the *Republic* (609–610).

Plotinus's answer to the problems of multiplicity and radical diversity in the concerns of the soul is to declare that the soul needs to turn in on itself. Among the complexity of forces pulling the soul in different directions (IV 4.36.9), the soul which has descended from a higher realm rediscovers itself by a return. The self needs to get back to the dynamic source of its being and so to move from an inferior actuality to a higher potentiality. The "true self" is what at its best the soul aspires to be. And that means to return to what it once was, before the body beset and besieged it with distractions. It is, however, axiomatic for Plotinus that if the soul's prayer is answered, that is not a special intervention of universal providence but explicable on the principle of "cosmic sympathy." The soul should not ask for help or grace from higher realms. The calling is to rediscover the presence of the divine already present within the soul.

A century after Plotinus's time the pagan writer Eunapius commented that this philosopher was very hard to comprehend. The language of Plotinus is often sufficiently obscure to have a discouraging effect on would-be readers. It becomes more comprehensible when placed in its historical setting in the mid 3rd century. It should be added that gratitude to his clever biographer and editor Porphyry (who in the view of Eunapius had done much to bring light into dark places) is modified by his bizarre rearrangement of the order of Plotinus's discourses. He was capable of splitting up discourses, sometimes even in the middle of a sentence, and arranged the text into six groups of nine chapters each (hence the entirely non-Plotinian title *Enneads*). Porphyry lived in an age when it could readily be taken for granted that aesthetic or philosophical truth had ultimately a numerological basis. Six was a perfect number.[1] At least it is clear that Aristotle's sharp criticisms of Plato found in Plotinus an eloquent challenger. Aristotle's negative criticism of the Platonic doctrine of the soul began from the utter rejection of the notion that a higher element wholly independent of the body constitutes everything of significance about a human being.

In the 2nd century Aristotle's critique of Plato had been restated and gravely debated. Its force is apparent both in the strenuousness of Plotinus's answers and in those areas where he found it necessary to compromise with so acute a philosophic mind. Plotinus was committed to the defense and restatement of the Platonic system, and could not countenance the dangerous commonsense opinion that the definition of human being must include the body. For him the self is surely more than meets the eye when one contemplates a living man or woman.

Plotinus was able to concede that in an important sense an empirical description of a human being includes both body and soul, soul being the living vitality with powers of choice, deliberation, inward discomfort at the memory of wrong choices, and often awkward emotional experiences of fear, grief, desire, envy, and jealousy. But Plotinus demanded recognition of a higher self, an intellect or *nous* which is no physical thing at all, and is even to be distinguished from the psychological experiences of a human subject. The ordinary embodied soul has powers, some of which are exalted and admirable, others inferior. But all such powers are to be described as the soul's possessions rather than its being. It has them and uses them. Beyond and above them, however, lies something which is more than the skills acquired by a good liberal education. This is the true self.

Being sure that Plato was in essentials right and that if and when his words need correction one should not draw attention to that fact,[2] Plotinus affirmed that the soul has a heavenly and indeed divine origin, but has fallen to be incarcerated in the material body. Nevertheless something crucially important in its transcendent condition has survived, an "undescended" soul which shares in the eternity and immutability of the divine, very different from the time-conditioned existence of the composite empirical being that walks and talks, eats and sleeps, loves and hates, and is ravaged by despair and anguish as successive hopes are dashed.

This higher soul is untroubled by any tie to bodily life. In *Theaetetus* (176a–b) Plato had spoken of flight or escape from this earthly habitat, where we are troubled by pain and seduced by pleasure. Plotinus was surrounded by gnostics, even in his own lecture room, and was vehemently resistant to suggestions that this visible material order was the consequence of some super- or pre-cosmic smudge on the part of an incompetent creator. Some gnostics coupled incompetence with malevolence. His anger against gnostic estimates of the cosmos moved him to his most powerful and eloquent statement, in 2.9. The material body deserves to be properly cared for and not rubbished. The composite human being should regard it with a certain detachment. Plotinus uses the paradoxical analogy of an actor who plays his part but, in his view wisely, does not become totally engrossed with it and identified with his theatrical role (III 2.15–18). However, the body is to the soul a necessary and useful instrument—like a lyre. A good man knows himself to be other than his body and is at any time free to abandon it (I 4.16.17–29). The cultivation of detachment makes possible a gradual purification which is also an awakening of the soul to its true destiny.

Plotinus discusses but is never totally clear about the relationship between the soul that uses the body as tool and the higher soul which aspires to union with the universal soul, which is the third primary hypostasis of the entire cosmic order. What he is perfectly certain about is that mind is not a physical thing, and accounts of it which make it physical end curiously by leaving the mental processes out of the story. He was sure there is something mental about the mind.

The empirical composite human being continually experiences not only fear, desire, pain, grief, and envy but also the relentless sensations of change, destroying any sense of self-sufficiency. How seldom people find satisfaction when they obtain their desires. By contrast the higher soul is self-sufficient and "remains what it always is" (I 12.25). The higher soul and the inferior reflection of it tied to the body are related in the way that in Platonism the intelligible and sensible worlds are related. So the undescended soul is truer in its being. "Intellect transcends us"; everywhere it is one and the same, and each of us has the whole of it (I 1.8.3). Accordingly, the most exalted powers of the composite soul-and-body are a reflection or image of the higher ideal self, which is happily free of all the ills that flesh is heir to and sheds its light upon the lower soul (I 1.10.11). This ideal or true self is the god within, and to wake up to this degree of self-realization is to achieve some identity with the divine, even if the experience of mystical union is never, in this life, more than transient. The embodied soul is in a median position between body and mind *(nous)*, and its destiny is decided by whichever of the two it turns toward. Plotinus (and the Neoplatonic tradition generally) therefore thought of the body as a cause of differentiation and division, while the soul's potential for union with *nous* led to a restoration of unity.

A problem in Plotinus's language is apparent, namely that although he uses strong terms to distinguish soul from *nous,* the characteristics and functions of the two overlap. In part this difficulty interconnects with the wider question how far a concept of individuality can fit Platonic ideas or forms. The Neoplatonists speak as if all souls participate in one common soulness, and separateness or individuality is entirely a matter of body. Providentially (Nemesius and others say), faces are distinct to prevent confusion. But do all differences lie in accidents rather than substance?

Since Celsus in the late 2nd century Platonist critics of Christianity had particularly objected to the notion that after death the souls of the redeemed enjoy union with a resurrected body, a retention of individuality which contradicts any idea of the soul's being absorbed into a greater and amorphous whole or into some kind of Nirvana. The Neoplatonists found themselves divided by speculation about the individuality of souls hereafter. Damascius understood Numenius of Apamea (mid 2nd century) to hold that immortality and participation in the intelligible world extend from the rational soul to the animate body. A less than lucid paragraph in Plotinus (IV 7.14) concludes with the proposition that "nothing of reality perishes." It was widely held among the Neoplatonists that after death the soul possesses a "vehicle," which in the view of (e.g.) Syrianus must be more than temporary and therefore is everlasting. Porphyry himself ascribed immortality only to the rational soul, but denied that this entailed the destruction of the soul's vehicle and irrational functions. So runs the report of Damascius in his commentary on *Phaedo.* The Christians who discuss these problems feared Platonic language about the inherent immortality of the soul because it was inextricably associated with belief in reincarnation and that, in turn, with belief in the eternity of the cosmos, whereas they understood the creation and the end of the world to be unrepeatable, not part of a fatalistic cycle of repetition. On the other hand, Christians could find a sympathetic chord struck in Plotinus's doctrine (V 1.1.6f.) that the initial fall of souls was an act of audacious self-assertion, delighting in the exercise of independence.

Plotinus saw two routes by which the soul is enabled to ascend. The first is to contemplate the world accessible to the five bodily senses and to realize both its beauty and its impermanence. In this process the soul can discern a higher realm belonging to the world-soul, serene and untroubled. The second route is by an interior contemplation leading to the awareness that the higher, indeed eternal world is already present within the truest and deepest self. This process of interior contemplation is also one of moral purification because the body's concerns are being set aside. And this setting aside of the physical means great restraint in food and drink and other bodily pleasures, with complete abstinence from sexual activity.

Porphyry's *Life of Plotinus* depicts not only the sage's ascetic austerity but also his contact with the supernatural. During the six years of Porphyry's study with him, Plotinus had four experiences of ecstatic elevation to "a condition of good feeling," or joy, in union with the highest—admittedly transient, but for those moments liberated from passion and even from being a separate individual mind (VI 7.35.42–45), beyond time and space. The experience is like the melting down which separates gold from the dross (I 6.5.53). Plotinus's language here and in several other passages bequeathed a vocabulary for describing what later writers would call mystical union or beatific vision. Already in Plotinus it is called union with the One (also God), or vision. Following Plato's *Symposium,* he can use strongly erotic terms for his ecstatic experience. To touch the supreme good is a source of joy beyond the power of human words. This vision is on no account to be thought of as physical. God is everywhere because he is nowhere. In the *Enneads* the journey to this union ("not by carriage or ship," a phrase which captured Augustine's imagination) entails a gradual transformation of one's being and is achieved by stages, but ends in an ultimate bliss portrayed in the exalted imagery of earthly love; only there is no notion of the Absolute's reciprocating.

Plotinus was both a schoolman committed to expounding an authoritative Plato and also, like Aristotle, an investigator of difficulties *(aporiai)*. His solutions were not necessarily watertight and consistent, especially on such speculative issues as the relationship between the soul qua third hypostasis after the One, and *nous,* the world-soul mentioned in Plato, and the share that individual souls might have in either or both. Plotinus III 9.1, containing a disconnected series of notes, could easily leave a reader bewildered on the question whether or not the divine Creator is *nous* or soul.

There were other problems on which Platonists were divided among themselves, particularly the destiny of the human soul after this life. Would there be reincarnation and, if so, could it really be true, as Platonic dialogues suggested, that the rational soul could be reincarnated in animal bodies? or should Platonic language be glossed to have a demythologized sense, for instance that evil persons will be reincarnated as humans who behave like pigs or indeed other more fearsome creatures? In *City of God* (10.30) Augustine understood Porphyry to be decisively against the notion that the rational soul is capable of being reincarnated in irrational animals. Texts of Porphyry himself (e.g., on vegetarianism, *De abstinentia* 2.31f.) are hesitant. He either committed himself to no such denial or he simply contradicted himself.

Another debate was whether language about Hades and punishment hereafter should be taken literally or figuratively. Plato certainly regarded the myths of Hades as incorporating truth. The 2nd century Platonist Celsus mocked Christian talk of hell, but disowned the least intention to cast doubt on the judgment of the dead. Porphyry too was decisive for realism and literalism (e.g., *Sententiae* 29), hesitating only about the location of Hades. Porphyry held to the permanent return of the soul to its divine home (Augustine, *City of God* 10.30); Plotinus thought the highest part of the soul could not again fall. Iamblichus thought a fall was possible, but did not in fact occur. Damascius judged it impossible for a soul to remain forever either in the world of intellect or, unredeemed, in Tartarus, the destiny of the apparently incurable. For all in Hades there would be purification. Expounding *Phaedo* 114b–c, Damascius concluded that sinless and godly souls have tenuous spiritual bodies hereafter, the philosophic have luminous bodies at a higher level, while those purified return bodiless to the supramundane region.

By unremitting industry Porphyry was to become among the most influential of 3rd century writers. In the retrospect of the mid 6th century, Simplicius (*In cat.* p. 2.5 Kalbfleisch) called him "the person responsible for all our good things." He regarded himself as Plotinus's best pupil, not only author of Plotinus's *Life* and (three decades after Plotinus's death) editor of his discourses, but also a singularly clear-headed expositor of Aristotle's logical works. A Platonist who thought most of Aristotle to be correct, he became an influential advocate of the conciliatory opinion that, with one or two exceptions such as the reality of universals, Plato and Aristotle could be massaged to speak with a single voice on all essentials. His motives in presenting this last thesis were likely to have included the need to rebuff arguments from Skeptical or Christian sources that the disagreements among the warring philosophical schools of the past altogether discredited any claims they might have to provide reliable guidance. At one stage of his life he was considerably interested in Christianity but the diversities in the Bible persuaded him that allegorists such as Origen were unjustifiably embalming embarrassing texts with explanatory unction. On the eve of the Great Persecution of the church in 303 he composed a sharply negative critique of the Christian Bible. Among the numerous Christian authors mobilized to reply to him, Eusebius, the learned bishop of Palestinian Caesarea, was moved to give quotations of his works a fairly prominent place in his "Preparation of the Gospel," the main thesis of which was that he could find in pagan philosophers themselves witnesses to the truths of faith.

Porphyry did not consider Christians mistaken to think divine power had given holy books to help souls to salvation. Their error was to use the wrong inspired books. The oracles that for Porphyry truly revealed the divine way of salvation were either those of Apollo or the Chaldaean Oracles composed in the pagan interest late in the 2nd century. A special work on "The Philosophy To Be Derived from Oracles," written before he came under Plotinus's spell, developed the theme of the guidance these inspired texts can give for the soul's health and for the purification of the self.

Porphyry's concern to present Plotinus's teaching to a wide public led him to produce a little book of "Pointers toward the Intelligibles" *(Sententiae)*, beginning with terse maxims on the superiority of mental concepts to physical facts but going on to include quite long statements of high spirituality and ethics. The argument is repetitive; Porphyry evidently did not expect his readers to grasp the inferiority of the material world unless he said it many times. The debt to Plotinus is very large. One paragraph (32) outlines the frugal ascetic way of self-purification on the path to union with the ground of our being: the irrational passions have to be suppressed, pleasure is to be forgone, with the proviso that it is allowable as a natural concomitant of wholly necessary acts.

Food and drink may be allowed to the extent necessary for good health, but sexual activity is unnecessary and disallowed (except that there is no responsibility in conscience for seminal emissions in sleep).

The *Life* of Plotinus portrays an elderly man practicing intense mental concentration and deliberate abstinence from meat and baths, and reducing hours of sleep by taking little food. In spirit he was already living in the divine realm, and was the recipient of special illumination and inspiration. His discourses came from the gods; he "loved the god with all his soul" (23). He had a firm belief that he was under the direction of a guardian *daimon* ("daemon," 10 and 22), and had inward power to frustrate the black magic deployed against him by a professional rival (10). When speaking, his face was radiant with light (13.5–7). He was endowed with second sight and could discern the hidden thoughts of those he met, enabling him to realize that Porphyry was on the verge of committing suicide (11).

The first sentence on Plotinus's sense of shame at being in a physical body is more than an observation about Plotinus's psychology or inhibitions about sex. For Porphyry it is a basic principle of a sound doctrine of the soul that "everything physical is to be fled from," *omne corpus fugiendum* in Augustine's lapidary version (*City of God* 10.29 and often). Augustine observes further that in Porphyry's eyes this basic principle of Platonic spirituality was the central ground on which Christian estimates of the body-soul relationship are to be rejected. Augustine himself was nevertheless clear that "we ascend to God not in body but by a likeness to him which is incorporeal" (9.18). Porphyry's personal belief surprised him by being so very close to his own. But Augustine found him—and was glad to find him—hopelessly inconsistent, juxtaposing beliefs that no doubt came to him by authority, as he understood it, but could not really be reconciled. Above all, his continual genuflections to the Chaldaean Oracles (10.32) and his defense of theurgy and the traditional rites of the old gods (e.g., *De abstinentia* 2.33–34) did not easily go with his affirmations that the way of ascent for the soul to union with *nous* is by philosophical reflection, not by theurgy, which he judged incapable of purifying the "intellectual soul" (*City of God* 10.27).

Despite the ascetic model of his hero Plotinus, in his sixties Porphyry married. His eye had fallen upon a well-to-do widow, Marcella, encumbered with children but a strong admirer of his considerable learning. A late and not very trustworthy text says that she was Jewish and came from Palestinian Caesarea. Soon after the wedding Porphyry was called away on a long journey "by the affairs of the Greeks," a phrase suggesting that he was consulted about the persecution of the church unleashed early in 303. He was extremely well informed about the Christian Bible, and the same untrustworthy text says that at one time he had been associated with the Christian church, which is not at all impossible. The biography of Plotinus can be read as a veiled attack on the history of Jesus in the gospels. His wife looked to him as her guide in "the way of salvation," and to assist her spiritual progress during his unhappy absence he wrote her a striking letter of considerable length which survives in a single manuscript at Milan. His advice took the form of a chain of religious and moral aphorisms, some Epicurean, but the majority Neopythagorean, these latter also attested in other collections. One of these Pythagorean maxims runs, "The real ego is not this tangible person accessible to the senses, but that which is furthest removed from the body, without color and shape, untouchable by hands, capable of being grasped only by the mind *(dianoia)*." Marcella's true teacher is within herself, and by concentrating on inward purity she will find Porphyry himself close to her day and night as in continence she gathers her disintegrated and distracted self. She should reckon that every good act has God for its author; evil acts we do ourselves and God is not responsible.

The Pythagorean aphorisms contained warnings that "it is impossible for one person to love both God and bodily pleasure or money" (14). Marcella should be reserved, not uttering even the truth about God to people corrupted by mere opinion. Indeed to be giving honor to God the sage does not need to break silence. God is pleased by works of devotion, not by sacrifices and participation in cults, whose worshipers may be very evil people. Nevertheless "the greatest fruit of piety is to honor God in accordance with ancestral customs," at the same time remembering that "God's temple is the mind within you," and that the four essentials are faith, truth, love, and hope (24). The quartet of virtues echoes the Chaldaean Oracles, on which Porphyry wrote a lost commentary.

The aphorisms which Porphyry found congenial for his wife's edification were also highly estimated by a Christian who about the end of the 2nd century made an adaptation of the collection for use in the church. The "Sentences of Sextus" became immensely popular among Christians, as Origen in 248 expressly testified, and the Latin translation by Rufinus of Aquileia enjoyed a large circulation. The collection was a Christianizing of an originally Neopythagorean text. Sextus wanted a believer (his word to replace "sage") to realize the noble dignity to which he or she is called. In the hierarchy of the cosmos the believer is next to God. Only by this realization can the Delphic command "Know thyself" be fulfilled. The mind within is the mirror of God, and so the soul is to be "ever with God." Bodily appetites may be satisfied only to the extent necessary to maintain health, which is the meaning of Jesus's saying that one should render to the world the things of the world, while the soul renders to God the things that are God's. But the body is the door of temptation. A man and his wife should compete to see which of them can most suppress the sexual impulse. Castration would be better than sexual incontinence. Meat-eating is allowable, but vegetarianism is more congruous with the higher life. Private property is incompatible with the ideal of universal brotherhood in the one family of God. Love of money is a snare; the desire to possess was never yet quenched by acquisition. Indispensable to the good life is almsgiving to the destitute and to orphans. The dignity of the true self depends on the practicalities of the moral life.

Porphyry's letter to Marcella is so close in spirit to the kind of Christian spirituality found in Clement of Alexandria and later ascetic texts that it is no wonder to find later pagan Neoplatonists regarding his writings with mixed feelings. In correspondence with Iamblichus he put a series of awkward questions about polytheistic ritual. Following a lead given by the Chaldaean

Oracles, Iamblichus and others in the Neoplatonic tradition fused Plotinus's highly philosophical path, bringing the self to realize God within the mind, with a zealous justification of the rites for the old gods, under the name of theurgy. The term *theourgia* is ambivalent in meaning, signifying both human rites to persuade (or according to the Chaldaean Oracles to compel) the gods, and also the willing cooperation of the gods in bringing about certain effects. Insofar as the rites are understood to compel divine powers, theurgy is hard to distinguish from magic—white in polytheistic eyes, black in the view of monotheists. Theurgy depended for its credibility on the general ancient belief that between the various constituent parts of the cosmos there is a hidden sympathy. The argument could be used by a disbeliever in astrology to explain why the forecasts of some horoscopes turn out to be correct (Augustine, *Confessions* 4.3.5).

Porphyry's defense of theurgy was embarrassed. Iamblichus, who settled at Apamea in Syria, had no hesitations or blushes. Iamblichus's defense of theurgy coheres with his generally more pessimistic estimate of the capacities of the human soul as compared with Plotinus's and Porphyry's. Whereas his predecessors wrote as if the soul possessed innate powers to rise to union with *nous* or even the One, Iamblichus took a more somber view, and therefore thought fragile souls needed propping up with old cultic rites.

In the *Republic* (10.600b) Plato had written of the Pythagorean life as a known frugal lifestyle. Iamblichus wrote an impressive, repetitive work on this way of living, insisting on Pythagorean respect for the traditional rites in the temples, with the correct white vestments and the right images. "The fruit of piety is faith in the gods" (148). With this goes an austere way of life which reads as conscious rivalry to incipient Christian monasticism. Requirements are little food or sleep, no meat or wine, contempt for money or fame, control of the opposing powers within the body (69, 229), chastisements to check self-indulgence and greed, and property held in community (168, 257). There are Pythagorean hermits in the desert (253). The rule on sex is that a woman who has slept with her husband can go to temples the same day, but never if she has slept with someone else (55, 132). A procreative intention is also indispensable (210). It is presupposed that the majority of adherents to the old religion are women (54–56). The goal is purification of *nous* and soul together (68–70). In the 2nd century Lucian observed that Pythagoreans were generally regarded as superhuman (*Vit.Auct.* 2).

The notion that formulas and rites and amulets could compel the gods seemed very difficult to Porphyry in his questions to Iamblichus. Nevertheless he could concede that theurgy could bring some degree of purification to the soul, even if it could not actually achieve a return to God. Augustine (*City of God* 10.9) thought Porphyry wavered between superstition and philosophy, granting with embarrassment that a kind of magic, though without influence on the *nous* of intelligible realities, does something for the inferior soul, putting it into a prepared state for angelic and divine visions; but he goes on to say that the spirit powers influenced by these rites are inferior daemons inhabiting the lower air. Even Porphyry thought it strange that the rites of the gods needed herbs or stones, special forms of words and gestures, and celestial observations of the configurations of the stars. Iamblichus, who was certainly much impressed by the Egyptian hermetic tradition, seemed to Porphyry to have gone altogether too Egyptian.

To Iamblichus, on the other hand, Porphyry was capable of expounding Platonic dialogues in a sense which was neither Platonic nor true and manifested barbarian arrogance—this last phrase, Emperor Julian's and Iamblichus's label for Christianity, suggests that he regarded Porphyry as influenced by Christian notions and terminology.[3] His skeptical questions were playing the Christians' game for them (*De mysteriis* 10.2). There are also places where Iamblichus judged Porphyry's doctrine of the soul to be unrealistically exalted and his doctrine of inferior deities and daemons too pessimistic and perhaps akin to gnosticism. Proclus's commentary on *Timaeus* frequently records Iamblichus's criticisms of Porphyry, some of which reflect the judgment that Porphyry was too detached toward religious practice. For pagans like Eunapius, Iamblichus was supreme as a holy man, able to work miracles to call up spirits from the vasty deep, credited with powers of levitation (which he modestly disowned). Marinus's funerary panegyric on Proclus (d. 485) is no less rich in anecdotes of his hero's powers as a thaumaturge. Damascius once marked a clear line between the philosophers Plotinus and Porphyry and the "hieratics," Iamblichus and Proclus.

No Neoplatonist was so prolific in writing as Proclus, who, after studying in Alexandria, became head of the richly endowed academy in Athens. His commentaries on Plato's *Timaeus, Republic, Cratylus*, and *First Alcibiades* contain major restatements of the general Neoplatonic theses. In his large but unfinished six-book "Platonic Theology" he especially set out the theological exegesis of the *Parmenides*.

Proclus's commentary on the *First Alcibiades* (edited by L. G. Westerink, 1954; English trans. by William O'Neill, 1965) expounds the dialogue as a proper introduction to all Platonic dialogues and indeed to philosophy generally. He presupposes that in between Plato and Plotinus philosophers did not get many things right. The exchanges between Socrates and Alcibiades are treated as an elaborate allegory of the role of higher reason in moderating and healing the soul of an amiable but highly undisciplined person of considerable influence. Plato's dialogue meditates on the Delphic command "Know thyself." The primary task of philosophy is to make such self-knowledge possible. Throughout the commentary Proclus's discussion revolves around the question, What is the true self? On the one hand the mind's experience is marked by multiplicity, pulled in many diverse and contradictory directions and finding concentration hopelessly problematic as attention is captured by irrational pleasures and bodily appetites (245f.). Time for reflection on philosophy needs to be set free from the tugs of many loves (44f.—a phrase strikingly reminiscent of Augustine in the garden at Milan, *Confessions* 8.11.26). The soul, as in Plato and Plotinus, is in a middle position between mind and body (116, 226). The body exerts a downward pressure on the soul and would bring the soul to "the region of dissimilarity" (Plato, *Politicus* 273d, cited by Plotinus I 8.13.15f. and Augustine, *Confessions* 7.10.16).

Nevertheless, the soul's choices, which determine who we are, are freely made (144) and capable of being trained into good habits (224f.). The soul is self-moved. Irrational decisions result from the emotions, rooted in the world of matter (233), responsible for the incoherence and disconnectedness of experience (57), tearing us apart like the Titans (104). Each human individual has a restraining guardian daemon, one of a semi-divine order of spirits in six ranks watching over the souls as they descend and ascend (71ff.), but this daemon is not to be identified with the rational soul (73).

Proclus rejects both those who think the soul part of the physical organism and those who claim that soul is part of divine being (226). The ascending soul has the capacity to be united with higher intellect or *nous*. Therefore the physical body is no more than the instrument being used by the soul (73), and only a strong dualism of soul and body can underpin the belief that it is never right to pursue private advantage at the expense of what is just (294, 315), or can justify the courageous confidence that death is no evil (332).

The soul's upward ascent begins from a freely chosen decision to contemplate itself (17). It is axiomatic that while the first mover or *nous* is unmoved and physical entities are moved by external pressures, the soul in its intermediate existence is self-moved and so has the power to revert to itself. Soul is incorporeal and in principle independent of the body. The key to ascent is the power of self-consciousness. When the self authentically knows itself, it also sees the divine (20) and enters into a relationship of love (51).

The priestly rituals or theurgy of the traditional gods are means of elevating the soul to the level of and to union with *nous*. For Proclus, Iamblichus was right about theurgy. Its power is greater than all human knowledge attained by philosophical thinking (*Theol. Plat.* 1.25), able not only to thrill the ascending soul but also to be a means of divination. Cosmic sympathy pervading the realm of nature explains how what appears as (white) magic can assist the soul to be one with the highest. Syrianus of Alexandria and Proclus his pupil appear to have retained usage of the term "theurgy" for a transcendent mental experience in which, on the far side of the rituals of the old gods, the mind is carried up to an ecstatic knowledge of God.[4] Iamblichus in *On the Mysteries* had written of divine epiphanies and visions granted through theurgy (2.9, 3.6).

Proclus was saddened by the negative attitudes of the "atheists," i.e. the Christians, who in his time had become a majority. They denied the very existence of the gods. Yet they said things marked by moderation and even divine inspiration (*In Alcib.* 264). This last concession is remarkable when one considers in Proclus's writings a number of veiled allusions to the Christians indicating ice-cold hatred for them. In his eyes they were a cultural and intellectual Black Death. But then the Christians made no secret of their belief that whatever merits there were in Neoplatonic religious philosophy (which might be deemed considerable), theurgy with the old rites was black rather than white magic, an invocation of spirits which, as one could see in the pages of Porphyry, were essentially inferior and malevolent, longing for their nostrils to be titillated by the blood and smoke of animal sacrifices, and needing to be placated if they were not to make life unpleasant.

Iamblichus's criticism of Porphyry's doctrine of the soul centered on the vulnerable notion that the true self is always constant and unchanging by virtue of its participation in the higher realm of divine entities. This, however, bequeathed a problem for his successors: If the soul is mutable and changeable, in what sense can it be said to remain the same throughout its existence? Can the soul undergo substantial changes and still retain its identity? The issue troubled Damascius, the last head of the Platonic Academy at Athens. During his tenure Justinian discontinued its large endowments, in part perhaps because of its militantly anti-Christian stance (529), in part because, after an undistinguished period of mediocre successors to Proclus after his death in 485, the Athenian school began to enjoy a dangerous revival led by Damascius and Simplicius. The closing of the school did not bring Neoplatonist teaching to an end. Damascius and Simplicius temporarily traveled to the Persian court, but soon found it better to return to the eastern Roman empire (exactly where is not known) and to continue working much more privately.

Damascius judged it necessary to grant that the soul can undergo considerable changes in its moral and spiritual life. Soul is not to be thought of as serene and secure, always gifted with divine illumination. For soul is not an order of being that remains ever attentive to the will of the gods without a touch of neglect or satiety. Soul is capable of going down a long way into the inferior realm of matter and the flux of "becoming," of the passions and inferior daemons. In a somber estimate of the depravity to which soul is vulnerable, Damascius can say that the very being of the soul is altered when matter and the daemonic spirits get a hold. And yet identity remains because free choice makes soul responsible for its actions. Damascius felt harassed by Justinian's Christianity. Nevertheless his estimate of human nature was remarkably close to the kind of language found in Augustine of Hippo or in some passages of Cyril of Alexandria.

The Platonic account of the relationship between soul and body and the dominance of Platonism generally among educated people of both east and west in late antiquity created problems for the Christians. They were committed to belief that the human body was made by the supreme Creator and, whatever problems it might cause, must be good. At the same time the Christians were also disinclined to think that the soul or *psyche* in its natural state, at least since Adam's Fall, was readily capable of knowing its Maker as it should. The natural order needed elevation by divine grace. The apostle Paul spoke of *psyche* as being on a lower level than spirit or *pneuma* (1 Cor. 2:14). *Psyche* is the natural order of creation but flawed by human sinfulness; *pneuma* is the point at which humanity can touch the divine. And in 1 Cor. 15:44 the *psyche* can rise to the level of *pneuma* in the life to come. To remain at the level of natural creation is not necessarily a permanent condition.

Third century Alexandria produced in Origen a commentator and theologian who was highly competent in his grasp of the classical Greek philosophers. There are Stoic and Epicurean doctrines which first become intelligible when his discussions of them are considered. He knew his Plato intimately. He built on foundations already outlined by two predecessors, Philo and Clement. Philo understood the two accounts of creation in Genesis 1 and 2 to signify that the first and primary creation was spiritual, the second earthly and bodily. So there is an inferior soul giving vitality to the body, as to animals or plants, and a higher soul which is divine and has pride of place in the divine plan. (Paul in 1 Cor. 15:46 opposes the interpretations that the spiritual creation preceded the physical.) In Philo, as mind ascends to God it comes to see the body to be an evil, presumably by comparison (*Leg. Alleg.* 3.71). The fall of souls began when they became sated with the divine goodness (*Heres* 240) so that they neglected to love God. Some souls fell further than others (*Gig.* 12). To know oneself is to realize one's weakness and dependence on God (*Spec. Leg.* 1.263ff. and 293). God gives the soul illumination and grace, drawing souls up toward Being (*Plant.* 21). No ascent is possible without divine aid (*Migr.* 170f.). A real self-knowledge is self-despair (*Somn.* 1.60), a realization of the nothingness of created thoughts in comparison with the transcendent uncreated mind (*Congr. erud.* 107). But deep self-knowledge is impossible for the individual soul (*Leg. Alleg.* 1.91). Because mind has the capacity to know something of God it is necessarily incorporeal (*Somn.* 1.30f.). But all things human, including the soul, are unstable and mutable (*Somn.* 1.192).

Most of these themes recur in Origen, who particularly took over the idea of degrees or levels of soul both in descent and in possible ascent. The notion that souls fell in consequence of satiety he found congenial. That souls fell varying distances from heaven helped to explain the diversity of humanity. Though all human beings have mind, soul, and body, the quality of each individual differs (*Or.* 24.2). The human soul, being in God's image, possessing powers of reasoning, memory, imagination, and reception of impressions from the five senses, differs in kind from the soul or life principle in animals (*C.Cels.* 4.83). Therefore it cannot be true that all souls have the same "form" *(eidos),* a universal soulness in which all living things and angels share.

Origen thought it would be very difficult to maintain the goodness of divine providence unless free choices lay at the ultimate root of evil in the cosmos. The widely differing lot of human beings, where some live on fertile land in a kind climate while others do not, could be explained as the consequence of mistakes and sins in an existence prior to incorporation in this body of flesh (*Prin.* 2.9.3–6). Leviticus 17:14 (which says the soul or life principle is blood) ensured that Philo and Origen both knew of materialist conceptions of the soul, reinforced by Stoicism.

In the second book of his commentary on the Song of Songs, Origen gives a list of questions concerning the soul: Is it corporeal or incorporeal? composite or simple? created or uncreated? transmitted to the embryo with the physical sperm or independently from some external power? If the latter, is the soul given to the body *ad hunc* or *ad hanc* at the moment of conception? Or is it already in a divine storehouse ready to be supplied to a body when needed? Can it be reincarnated? Are all rational souls of the same *ousia* (being)? Do angels and human beings, both endowed with free will, share the same kind of soul? Or is promotion to angelic status a gift of divine grace transcending the created and natural order? Can a soul which has once acquired a state of virtue lose it?

(Parallels to this list in *C.Cels.* 4.30 and in Seneca, *Ep.* 88.34, suggest that there was a standard list of questions in philosophical schools.) In Origen's commentary on St. John there is a catalog of problems about reincarnation (6.14).

Origen's main polemical target in almost all his work was the predestinarianism of the 2nd century (and later) gnostic sects. They appealed to biblical texts, such as Paul in Romans 9:16–21 or Exodus 4:21 on God hardening Pharaoh's heart, and held that the saved and the lost are determined from the beginning, so that free human choices play no part in the path to either heaven or hell. Both Clement of Alexandria and Origen declared against these views, and this argument on behalf of freedom became a dominant theme for both writers. The third book of Origen's *De principiis* presented the case for free choice and against the view that external impressions received through the body's senses can overwhelm individual judgment. A chaste celibate confronted by a beautiful woman in undress inviting him to bed may find it impossible not to be stirred, but he still retains a rational power of decision enabling refusal both possible and responsible. Human beings are not automata, deterred from acts only by some external cause or consideration. In practice, moreover, education and discipline can change even the most uncontrolled and uncivilized people so that, after conversion, they surpass in gentleness the most courteous folk. Contrariwise, entirely respectable individuals in middle life can suddenly kick over the traces to live disordered and immoral lives. Their behavior reflects their personal decisions. Such unpredictable changes constitute for Origen strong evidence for human responsibility and undetermined choice. And this choice is not simply a physical reflex. The decision is made by the mind, not by the body.

Platonic influence is evident in the conviction, common to both Origen and the pagan opponent of Christianity, Celsus, that God, being incorporeal, can be known only by the mind. Mind is no mere epiphenomenon of matter (*Prin.* 1.1.7), a notion which is assumed by simple people who imagine God to possess physical characteristics—an old man with a long beard. The mind, being made in God's image (or, as the Platonists would say, having a kinship with God), is so constituted as to look toward the divine. Admittedly mind is hindered and rendered dull by contact with the body: "sea sickness makes the mind less vigorous" (*Prin.* 1.1.5). Nevertheless the ability of the brain to cope with arguments of extreme subtlety and to remember words and events of the past surely points to incorporeality.

Like pagan Platonists, Origen thought the soul midway between flesh and spirit, capable of ascending to be united with and even transformed into spirit (e.g., Commentary on Romans 1:5, or on John 32:18). It also has the capacity to be united with soggy materiality. Nevertheless, like Plotinus, Origen held that every soul has a guardian, a *paidagogos,* which is commonly called the conscience. This is an inner judgment, combining awareness of an action done or a word spoken with a sensation of pain at the memory, but also in certain cases vindicating the act or the word when others are critical. The martyr was called to be true to his integrity. Origen was skeptical of the notion that conscience is a separate and substantial organ (Commentary on Romans 2:9).

Everyone who goes against his conscience "kindles his own fire" (*Prin.* 2.10.4).
"Outer darkness" is a condition of the soul, not a place (2.10.8). A "longing for
reality" is implanted in us (11.4), and paradise will be a school in which holy
people will learn the answer to many questions which baffle them in this life
(11.5).

The majority of Origen's writings consisted of biblical exposition, either in
the form of homilies preached to congregations in Caesarea (Palestine), whither
he moved after difficulties with the bishop of Alexandria, or full-scale commentaries, all of which were too voluminous to survive intact. Scribes become
exhausted. His understanding of human nature is therefore distributed over a
wide area. But in the early work *On First Principles* and the late reply to the
pagan Platonist Celsus a consistent picture emerges. He was passionately committed to defending the goodness of God manifest in providential care and the
freedom of the rational being (angelic or human). "Take away freedom from
moral virtue and you destroy its essence." Divine care is unendingly patient,
and has a perspective far longer than "the fifty years or so of this life." Against
the gnostic estimate of the total earthliness and irredeemability of lost humanity, Origen asserts that "a totally depraved being could not be censured, only
pitied as a poor unfortunate" (*In Ev.Joh.* 20.28.254). The entire process of
human existence is a gradual education, and the miseries of human life are part
of that operation, to prevent our being too comfortable and forgetting about
higher things. Therefore Origen regarded as gnostic the idea that any fallen
being endowed with rationality and freedom is beyond redemption, even including Satan. Like a wise tiller of the land, God is not in a hurry, and what
seems difficult or impossible will simply require longer time. "Love never fails,"
wrote the apostle, and Origen thought it a fundamental principle, even if the
retention of freedom as a permanent endowment of all rational beings must
carry the corollary that they may choose to fall once again.

Augustine's critical comment was that Origen's concept of human destiny
was "endless real misery punctuated by short periods of illusory happiness"
(*City of God* 12.20). At a time of religious crisis while residing in Milan,
Augustine was given by an anti-Christian pagan "books of the Platonists" in
Latin translation (almost certainly pieces of Plotinus and Porphyry). Plotinus's
account of providence and evil convinced him. Neoplatonism brought to him
the doctrine of the body as instrument of the soul, as taught in the Platonic
Alcibiades. At the same time Bishop Ambrose of Milan was preaching eloquent
sermons, of which he admired the oratory but went on to be impressed by
the content. Ambrose found congenial matter in Plotinus and Porphyry and
had a command of Greek greater than Augustine had acquired. Ambrose's
discourse on the life of the patriarch Isaac was both Christian and Neoplatonic.
The philosophical dialogues written by Augustine at Cassiciacum during the
months between his conversion and baptism are also indebted to Porphyry and
Plotinus, not least in the express conviction that the true self is the soul, to
which the body is a distraction and at best secondary.

It remained Augustine's conviction that "our bodies are not what we are"

(*Vera relig.* 89). The doctrine that the body is the instrument of the soul occurs a few times, but principally with the emphasis that when we do wrong the fault lies not in the body but in the soul which uses it. Augustine liked triads, and for describing the fragility of goodness especially cited 1 John 2:16, "the lust of the flesh, the lust of the eyes, the pride of life." The primal sin of the soul is pride, which impels the soul to play at being God (*Mor.* 1.12.20). The early writings of Augustine restate the notion, found in Philo and Origen, that humanity in Adam was originally created spiritual—that is, with a tenuous body of light such as the spirits in heaven possess—but this state was lost at the Fall. More mature texts affirm the positive qualities of the body as intended by the divine Creator. Sexual differentiation is in the body, not in the soul. Augustine insists that in mind and soul male and female are equal in the human race. The biological function of women as childbearers gives them a private and domestic role which has to be socially secondary to that of their husbands. Augustine knew of strong-minded women who wholly dominated their husbands (*Gen. c. Manich.* 2.29.). On the other hand more than one text speaks of women as possessing far deeper feelings about sexual partnership than many men are capable of achieving, and the tendency to have superficial and brief affairs is described as "a common male disease" (*Adult.conjug.* 1.6). Against exegetes of 1 Cor. 11:5–7 (such as Ambrosiaster), Augustine devoted some part of his argument in *De Trinitate* (12.7.9f.) to opposing the notion that women are not in the image of God as men are. His doctrine that the image of God is entirely in the mind made that conclusion natural and inevitable.

Controversy with the Manichees (with whom he had been associated for a decade) ensured that Augustine affirmed the positive value and beauty of the human body, and was not inclined to think it a merely accidental or secondary element in the constitution of the human person. In oblique criticism of his elder contemporary Jerome he wrote a work of protest against the disparagement of marriage and its physicality. The early Augustine could echo Porphyry's advice that for the higher life "one must escape from the body." The mature Augustine could readily say that in the limitations of this present physical life there are hindrances, "ignorance and difficulty," where the latter term tends to mean the emotion of desire. But like Origen he did not believe that even a powerful sexual impulse was irresistible. That the human body was recalcitrant was evident, especially in the fact that the sexual impulse is not rational. But the fallen state of humanity is one of both body and soul together, not simply of body. And in sexuality the body manifests its fallenness by wanting sexual pleasure when the mind knows it cannot be, or in not wanting it when the rational mind knows that it would be appropriate (*Nupt. et Concup.* 1.6.7) and would have the procreative intention which was deemed essential by ancient moralists, both pagan and Christian. It was never Augustine's intention that posterity should associate sin and sex. In the *Literal Commentary on Genesis* (10.13.23) he wrote scathingly of some who talk "as if the only sins are acts performed with the genital organs."

A problem that much occupied Augustine's anxious attention, and on which he decided not to make up his mind, was how the soul and the body came to be joined together. Porphyry had written a small treatise for a friend named Gaurus on this issue; but for Christian thinkers the matter had special interest and importance because it had a bearing on human responsibility. The Platonist view was that the soul preexists the body, and from a storehouse somewhere a soul comes to animate the embryo. Among Christians Origen not only held to the preexistence of souls but even thought divine providence would be very hard to defend without this doctrine. His critics however associated preexistence with reincarnation, and cordially disliked the fatalistic treadmill which went with this view. Many texts of Augustine, especially in the *Confessions*, use language that comes close to the notion of preexistence of souls, but the associations of the idea prevented him from giving assent. That left two remaining alternatives: traducianism, or the doctrine that the soul is transmitted from the parents with the seed and egg, a view which carried the implication that the soul has material qualities; and creationism, or the doctrine that the soul is created by the omnipotent Creator in response to the conception of the physical embryo. For Stoics traducianism explained why children frequently resemble their parents not only in physical appearance but in character. In his *De Anima* Tertullian provided an eloquent statement of a Christian doctrine of heredity, which for him explained the "fault in origin" *(vitium originis)* that Augustine would name original sin. Augustine conceded that traducianism made it easier to account for the church's practice of baptizing infants, which carried the implication of a stain to be washed away by the sacrament. On the other hand, traducianism sounded very Manichee to orthodox ears, and therefore there emerged a preference for the creationist view, even though it seemed to involve the Creator, or some angel delegated to take care of the matter, in unending fuss, including the provision of newly minted souls for embryos conceived in immoral circumstances. The last point was easily answerable with the consideration that the bastardy of such children in no way added to the personal responsibility that they would come to carry.

Of the three possible hypotheses the doctrine of preexistence carried the most pessimistic implications for human nature, traducianism being less somber. Creationism obviously asserted a clean start for the infant soul, and therefore made "original sin" a more social than individual thing, the child being sinful by becoming a member of the group which manifests egocentricity on a scale far beyond that of individuals.

Augustine's determined agnosticism about the bonding of soul and body showed that he regarded it as a secondary or insoluble question. What was certain to him about the self was the "inward war" that goes on within the individual person. The observation was as old as Plato (*Laws* 626d). Poor wretches, people sin in hope that it will help them out of a difficulty, and then find the situation far worse (*City of God* 14.4). Sin or wrongdoing is ultimately rooted in treating ends as means and means as ends (*Against Faustus* 22.78; again a Platonic echo, *Republic* 443d). The perversity of the heart is visible in the delight taken in performing an act which is known to be forbidden, and if that act is being done by a group of which one is a member, it can seem irresistible. (Hence the adolescent theft of bad pears described in *Confessions* 2.)

So the soul is beset by self-made problems, not merely human transience in a life which is "a race toward death," not merely the ignorance of the right and the good, but an actual resistance to what is right and the will of God when this is known. "Human beings are ambitious for nothing so much as power" (*On St. John* 43.1). Their lust for venting anger is sometimes directed at blameless inanimate objects (*City of God* 14.15). Above all, the fetters of habit bind the soul so that what begins as a free choice becomes necessity (*Confessions* 8, 5, 10). Humanity, social by nature, becomes anti-social by corruption (*City of God* 12.28).

Yet God has mercy and gives grace. The late works of Augustine say that this is given to God's elect. Earlier Augustine can write of a universal intuition in the human heart, brought from potential to actual by God's love and presence within. The innermost self is indistinguishable from this divine presence, "deeply hidden yet most intimately there within" (*Confessions* 1.4.4). So to love God is also to love oneself. "Love is within the mind, and therefore God is nearer than my brother" (*Trin.* 8.8.12).

In his work on the Trinity Augustine expressed reservations about the terminology for the Trinity, traditional in Latin theology since Tertullian—namely three persons, one *substantia*. But the thesis in that work that the persons of the Trinity are relations suggested to him that the term "person" could convey the meaning of a human self defined by relations, and in letter 137.11 this becomes explicit. The Latin word did not previously carry this meaning for the individual constituted of body and soul together. The context was one of mysterious and incomprehensible depth. A frequent theme in Augustine's writings is the unfathomable depth of the human mind, knowing what it does not know it knows, remembering joys and griefs of the past, so that the memory can be described as "the stomach of the mind" (*Confessions* 10.13.20) but never capable of authentic self-understanding. "I do not know what kind of man I am—how much less do you know" (*Sermon* 340A 8). A fundamental mark of the human mind is restlessness, and the overriding theme of the *Confessions* is the incompleteness of humanity, which can find its true self and true rest only in God.

Although the Christians of late antiquity found themselves in much sympathy with the language of the Platonists, the generalization holds good that in the long run they were to take a more positive view of the physical realm of nature, and of the human body in particular. This is evident already in Nemesius of Emesa, *On the Nature of Man,* in which the debt to Porphyry is at least equaled by that to Aristotle. For the upholders of a dualism of soul and body, there was, perhaps is, always an issue in the background: human responsibility. An entirely materialist view of the mind or soul has acute difficulties in maintaining that a human being is actually a moral agent with capacities for deliberation and argument on grounds of reasoning, capable of changes of mind. Birds need feathers to fly. Human beings need brain cells to produce the most baffling of things in consciousness. But in consciousness there are aspirations beyond the material world.

Notes

1. In the 5th century Neoplatonist Proclus, the number nine can carry a heavy weight of symbolism, e.g. in his commentary on *Timaeus* 3.193.17ff., where "ennead" signifies the creator gods. Porphyry was well known to have detected nine distinct hypotheses in the text of Plato's *Parmenides* (Proclus, *Theol.Plato.* 1.10). In Proclus's commentary on *Timaeus* 35b (2.215.20), reporting Iamblichus's views, it is said that "the Ennead has an affinity to the Monad."

2. Augustine (*City of God* 10.30) once allows himself a sentence of gentle mockery at the Neoplatonic reverence for Plato as a sacred text.

3. Julian *Ep.* 89a Bidez-Cumont; Iamblichus on *Timaeus* 47b–d in Proclus, *In Tim.* 153.10 (= frg.16 Dillon with his commentary, p. 282).

4. See Anne Sheppard, "Proclus' Attitude to Theurgy," in *Classical Quarterly* 32 (1982): 212–224.

VARIETIES OF RELIGIOUS COMMUNITY

Garth Fowden

In November or December of the year 408, when Alaric was besieging Rome and its inhabitants were on the brink of cannibalism, certain Etruscan diviners found their way into the city and reported how, by their rituals, they had recently repelled the Goths from the town of Narnia. Pompeianus, the prefect of the city and probably himself a polytheist, sought Bishop Innocent I's leave for the Etruscans to conjure the gods on Rome's behalf. In the words of the historian Zosimus, also a follower of the old religion, Innocent agreed to "put the salvation of the city before his own belief, and authorized them to perform their rites in secret."[1] The Etruscans answered that the traditional rituals must be performed openly and at public expense.[2] The Senate must go as a body to the Capitol, and invoke the gods there and in the marketplaces, if their prayer was to be heard. But nobody dared turn the clock that far back, and the city fathers resorted once more to bargaining with Alaric.

Not all Christians shared Innocent's flexibility—or perhaps they had not found themselves in so tight a corner. In 391 Bishop Theophilus of Alexandria, supported by the imperial authorities, had attacked and destroyed the great temple of Sarapis in the Egyptian metropolis.[3] Sarapis was responsible for the annual flooding of the Nile; and when the flood was delayed, some polytheists angrily demanded they be allowed to sacrifice to their god. The governor appealed to the emperor; and Theodosius I refused, adding that he would sooner the river stopped flowing altogether. We also read that at this time Christians went around chipping off the reliefs of Sarapis that adorned lintels and other parts of private houses throughout the city, and painting crosses in their place. On the one hand we have the worshipers of the old gods, who believed that on their cults depended Egypt's prosperity and indeed the world's, so that all stood to be penalized for the Christians' impiety. On the other hand we have the new Israelites whose dwellings, as in the days of Moses, the vengeful Lord would surely pass over, if only they marked their lintels and doorposts with the appropriate sign.

In both these sets of events we see articulated under duress an ancient sense of community which before Constantine's conversion had rarely needed to make itself explicit. We can sense its presence, though, in certain gravestones of ordinary foreigners buried at Rome that identify them simply by their village or town of origin.[4] The polytheist envisaged his native place as a unique whole defined by geography, climate, history, and the local economy, as well as by the gods who particularly frequented it, ensured its prosperity, and might even assume its name. No part of this identity, a delicate interweaving of divine, natural, and human which was often itself worshiped as a Tychē or Fortuna, could be subtracted or neglected without impairing the harmony and viability of the whole. In times of danger one addressed the gods with a single voice, often according to formulas revealed by an oracle to a representative deputation of leading citizens. Travel abroad might, admittedly, acquaint the member of such a community with exotic gods; yet honor paid them was attended by no sense of abandoning one religious and therefore social system for another. The vocabulary might change, but not the grammar; and even those who sought to explain the distinctive characteristics of particular peoples in terms of the influence of ethnarch-gods saw no religious incompatibility, since all mankind was subject to the king of the gods.[5]

Christians, by contrast, might add to their gravestones a statement of belief, such as a roughly carved cross, which attached them to a universal community of faith while separating them from compatriots who were not Christians.[6] Before the 3rd century this idea of a *religious* community, founded on self-consciously distinctive beliefs about the divine world and what those beliefs implied for conduct of individual and communal life, would have made sense only to certain philosophers, to Jews and those who sympathized with Judaism without having fully accepted it, and to Christians. The members of such a community accepted a more or less defined and internally coherent, and to some extent even written—that is, scriptural—system of belief and practice, and tended to exist in a reactive, mutually defining relationship with other such (theoretically) closed systems, that is, other religious communities. Such coexistence further implied the possibility of abandoning the community of one's birth for another—in other words, the possibility of conversion. Acceptance across broad sections of society of this previously rare type of self-consciousness was among the distinguishing characteristics of the late antique world.[7]

The unselfconsciousness of traditional religion in the Roman empire—what we call "paganism" or "polytheism"—is manifest especially in its lack of a distinctive name for itself. *Thrēskeia, eusebeia,* and *nomos; hieros, hosios,* and *hagios; religio* and *pietas; sacer* and *sanctus:* all these words lack the specific historical reference contained in such terms as "Jew" or "Christian."[8] Relations with the gods were conducted not according to the commandments of a scripture and an

orthodoxy derived from it, but on the basis of traditional behavior—an orthopraxy—reinforced by the ad hoc pronouncements of oracles or sometimes of
sages, men like the 1st century Pythagorean Apollonius of Tyana or Emperor
Julian, or the 5th century Platonist Proclus, who had studied the writings
of ancient authorities and especially the poets, such as Homer and Hesiod.[9]
Even to begin to form a mental picture of this vast, complex world of traditional polytheism, one needed exceptional resources and opportunities. Emperor Caracalla (211–217), for example, probably had a better grasp of the
range of religious life in his day than almost anyone else alive, since he spent
most of his time traveling or campaigning, and was so troubled in both mind
and body that he made a point of visiting the principal oracular and healing
shrines wherever he went.[10] It was Caracalla's mother, Julia Domna, who commissioned from Philostratus a biography of Apollonius of Tyana; but although
the semi-fictional account Philostratus wrote takes its protagonist to holy
places from Cadiz to the Ganges, it offers nothing to hold together the many
gods and rituals Apollonius encountered except the philosopher's own curiosity
and piety.

   In cities there was a greater variety of cultic activity concentrated in one
place, and therefore a higher level of self-consciousness, than in the village. Yet
distinctions between groups of worshipers, and even between associations that
adopted the name of one god or another, tended to reflect personal choice and
ethnic or occupational categories rather than any notion that preference for one
god over another might imply a special way of life.[11] Many worshipers of
Mithras were officials or soldiers; Jupiter Dolichenus, too, appealed to those
with an army background. At Leptis Magna in Tripolitania, the temple of
Sarapis was frequented—to judge from its totally Greek epigraphy—mainly by
merchants and others from the east.[12] The cult association of the Iobacchi at
Athens duly observed the festivals of Dionysus, and even on occasion assembled to hear a "theological" discourse in his honor; but the vivid inscription of
ca. 175, which is our best source, exudes the clubbishness of those who need to
remind themselves they have arrived.[13] Some divinities, like Isis, do seem to
have been exceptionally widely esteemed, but their status was manifested more
by association with other gods than by distinction from them, hence the tendency of Isis to adopt as epithets the names of numerous other goddesses
(polyonymy).[14] If, in the 4th century, certain prominent polytheists liked to
point out that it is natural for humans to pursue truth by many different ways,
this observation was provoked not by tensions among rival groups of core-
ligionists but by the threat from Christianity, which denied the very existence of
the traditional gods.[15] Judaism had struck polytheists as assimilable, because its
austere monotheism did not, on the whole, seek to impose itself on non-Jews by
proselytism.[16] It could, if necessary, be treated as one more ethnic cult.[17] But
Christianity addressed itself to all mankind; and by the time of the Severans
(193–235), the tendency toward dissolution of the traditional sense of local
community that was likely to result from this may have been already apparent.

   In either 212 or 213 Emperor Caracalla issued what has come to be known
as the *Constitutio Antoniniana*, extending Roman citizenship to almost all his

subjects with no distinction on grounds of faith. According to the fragmentary text preserved in a papyrus now at Giessen, Caracalla proclaimed that his motive for taking such a momentous step toward the integration of the empire was a wish to honor the gods and fill their sanctuaries with grateful worshipers.[18] The social model implicit here strongly resembles the traditional Roman civic one, with the whole community expected to come to the gods to give thanks and ensure continued favor: the Etruscan diviners were still demanding the same thing two centuries later. If Caracalla applied this traditional model to the whole empire rather than just the city, he was hardly innovating—official cults of emperors and of Rome had long sought to reinforce such broader loyalties. But Caracalla was perhaps also aware of a growing absenteeism from the temples at the local level, and he may have connected this with the spread of Christianity. Certainly the *Constitutio* sought to reinforce the dwindling Roman sense of community that acknowledged differences of race and much else among the empire's peoples and gods alike, but saw no need for an idea as implicitly divisive as that of rendering God's to God and Caesar's to Caesar, since there could be no way of telling these two spheres apart. Nonetheless, the challenge presented by Christianity had, a century and a half later, become an oppressive everyday reality. Emperor Julian's response was blunt in the extreme: if the citizens of Pessinus wished to enjoy his favor, they should supplicate the Mother of the Gods forthwith, in a single body, *pandēmei*. Otherwise, he might even take measures against them (*Ep.* 84.431d–432a).

Only in the philosophical milieu—of which Julian was a representative—did the polytheist world offer something that resembled the religious communities fostered by scriptural religions. Philosophy was often set down in texts which were carefully preserved and expounded, albeit not normally regarded as above criticism. And to adopt the philosophical life involved a choice—a conversion—which implied a rejection of alternatives and an introduction of distinctions and divisions into the prevailing model of society. Philosophers were perfectly aware of this, and divided about its possible consequences. Stoics insisted that the sage should continue to participate in the civic cults;[19] but the followers of Epicurus, who treated their founder and his literary legacy with unusual reverence, and formed closed circles defined solely in terms of belief, were regarded by outsiders with the suspicion the polytheist world reserved for private or surreptitious religion.[20] The conviction of the rabbis and philosophers, that study makes holy, was nonetheless destined for a long and influential life. In the ecumenical perspective characteristic of learned late polytheists, Porphyry of Tyre (234–ca. 301–305) drew particular attention to the habits of the Egyptian priesthood. Quoting one of its members, Chaeremon, Porphyry underlined how it had formed a caste apart (*De abstinentia* 4.6–8). Its members had lived in highly regulated communities, and had deplored the impiety of those who traveled outside Egypt and exposed themselves to alien ways. They had also been dedicated to science and the knowledge of the gods. Having discovered in their past this religious and almost scriptural community as a model, groups such as the later Platonists, and the Egyptian coteries that composed treatises under the name of Hermes Trismegistus, could adopt what they imagined to have been its conventions in their own lives and discourse. Perhaps this model even served, alongside the example offered by the church, as an impulse for the reforms to the priesthood proposed by the last polytheist emperors, Maximinus Daia and the philosopher Julian.[21]

Not surprisingly, it was under an Egyptian priestly pseudonym, Abammon, that Porphyry's pupil the Syrian Platonist Iamblichus of Apamea (d. ca. 320–325) sat down to write the only surviving account of ancient polytheism as a closed, coherent system. The title *De mysteriis Aegyptiorum*, by which Iamblichus's *Abammonis responsio ad epistolam Porphyri* is now generally known, is an inappropriate Renaissance invention, since Egyptian doctrines are touched on only summarily and toward the end, while the primary subject matter is the whole range of polytheists' experience of the divine. This experience Iamblichus sees as compounded of both thought and action, theology and theurgy. By welding together a sophisticated Platonism and the wide spectrum of traditional cult, including sacrifice, divination, and oracles, Iamblichus aroused opposition among polytheists as well as Christians. And the perfected "theurgists" who had mastered the whole of this sacred science, from healing and rainmaking to the vision of the demiurgic God, were bound to be a tiny elite, deploying skills easily misrepresented.[22] Yet unprejudiced study of the *Abammonis responsio* reveals an understanding of the divine and human worlds as a coherent, interlinked hierarchy (4.2.184; 5.22); while the need for a clear exposition of this vision is underlined by veiled yet hardly ambiguous reference to the propaganda of the "atheist" Christians (3.31.179–180; 10.2). That Iamblichus saw fit to compile this *summa* of polytheist belief and cult implies that he thought there could be a polytheist or, as he put it, theurgical community with an acquired consciousness of distinct identity as well as, of course, an appreciation of the variety of religious practice that was bound to occur within a genuine community with all its necessary range of human types. "One must make available this [material, corporeal] manner of worship to cities and peoples that have not been liberated from participation in generation and from close communion with bodies; otherwise one will fail to obtain either immaterial or material goods. For the former one will (anyway) not be able to receive, while as regards the latter one will not be offering that which is appropriate . . . That which comes to one man with great effort and after a long time, at the culmination of the hieratic art, we should not declare to be common to all men, nor make it immediately the shared possession of novices in theurgy or even of those who are already half-initiated; for these people give a somewhat corporeal character to the practice of piety" (5.15.219–220, 20.228). And along with consciousness of distinct identity, such a community would also acquire a capacity for self-explanation and self-defense. The *Abammonis responsio* is itself, as its correct title makes plain, a polemical work, written to counter certain objections to theurgy raised by none other than Porphyry.

Clearly Iamblichus believed that this theurgical community would be stronger and more likely to survive than if polytheists just went on pretending there was nothing new in their environment, and ignoring the need to articulate themselves. Iamblichus's admirer Julian pushed this idea further when he became emperor, and tried to endow his tradition with some of the features that had contributed to the church's success: a hierarchically organized and well-instructed priestly class, regular liturgy and preaching, an accessible religious literature, and philanthropic ideals and institutions.[23] And Julian too was aware of the need for a name. Iamblichus had called the approach to the gods that underlay the whole tradition "theurgy," studiously preserving polytheism's avoidance of specific historical reference in the vocabulary it used to talk about itself, and implying a refusal to fight on an equal footing with Jews and Christians. Julian abandoned this high ground. By calling worshipers of the gods "Hellenes" and Christians "Galileans," he acknowledged that both sides were at least in the same arena, even if the Christians were an upstart provincial minority.[24] But both Iamblichus's and Julian's solutions were problematic, in that they might too easily be applied to a part rather than the whole. Just as theurgists—the accomplished masters of the tradition, that is—could be seen as a tiny elite, and even encouraged the idea,[25] so too Hellenism was not necessarily what every polytheist wanted to identify with.[26] Polytheism simply did not have a founder, revelation, or scripture of sufficient stature to generate a name that could be applied to the whole tradition—proof, if one is needed, that in the end this was a more than usually "imagined" tradition.

There are modern parallels, in Indonesia for example, to this reactive type of identity imparted by monotheistic and scriptural religions to the adherents of older ways.[27] In order to survive as communities, such traditions necessarily adjust, even at the cost of imposing on themselves a spurious homogeneity and watering down that instinctive understanding of divinity that comes through dwelling together with the gods in a certain place, a precise local knowledge that no distant prophet would or could ever make into a scripture. Survive, though, these local traditions do, and did in late antiquity as well. Seen from one perspective, late antiquity is primarily of interest for its "formation of Christendom"; but it also generated another model, the empire of communities—against authority's better judgment in the Roman sphere, with the connivance of authority in the Sassanian world, and as a matter of policy in the Islamic caliphate. And alongside or in succession to these empires there were also commonwealths, built in part on political but primarily on cultural—that is, religious—foundations.

Increasingly, polytheism survived as a mere remnant, though quite widespread in certain regions, or underground as crypto-polytheism, which might allow small local groups to develop a sharply focused religion-based sense of community in the face of adversity but was not a viable basis for regional structures.[28] Only in the minds of a few intellectuals like Iamblichus or Julian did polytheism as a whole, at all social levels, come to be seen as a religious community. And even intellectuals were in practice more likely to experience the community as a diachronic succession, perhaps involving very few people at any given moment, rather than as a substantial, autonomous social organism. The *Lives of the Philosophers and Sophists* by the rhetor Eunapius of Sardis (ca. 345–ca. 414) is a good example of this approach from the end of the 4th century, and introduces the phenomenon of group biography, which not only bulks large in our evidence for religious communities at this period, but also itself helped define them. The production by both Nicaean Christians and their opponents of a number of such compilations from about the time of Theodosius I onward underlines the success of this emperor and his heirs in confirming Rome's adoption of Christianity, in particular its Nicaean version, as the official religion of the state.

Christianity had, of course, been a religious community long before it became the state religion. In the Acts of the Apostles and the Epistles, its adherents are most frequently referred to without explicit mention of their distinctive faith in Jesus Christ. They are "saints" or "brothers" or "disciples," who follow a "way"; but in Acts we also read how "for a whole year [Barnabus and Paul] met with the Church and taught great numbers of people; and the disciples were first called Christians at Antioch" (11:26). This pregnant passage implies much of what we need to know about Christianity as a religious community.

Especially at this early stage, leaders—here Barnabus and Paul—were the *sine qua non,* since only through their teaching did the congregation, "great numbers of people" consisting entirely of converts, exist at all. Just as Acts is centered on the missionary work of the apostles, so Eusebius's *Ecclesiastical History,* the next most important account of the church's early progress, is built around the "apostolic succession" of bishops who led the major sees and, by fair means or foul, constantly consolidated and widened their territory.[29] On this hierarchy were focused the church's necessary institutions. Its self-organization presupposed a place of assembly, the *ekklēsia.* Here were accommodated all the community's gatherings, especially the liturgy. And during the 4th and 5th centuries there evolved also a distinctive type of Christian art, or rather, a Christianization of late antique art, so that churches came to be adorned with images which, even when they seemed to preserve an earlier idiom, conveyed an unmistakably Christian message for those with eyes to see. In or near the church was a place for administering the sacrament of baptism, without which there was no true membership in the communion of the saints, or hope of salvation. As time went by, provision was also made for the poor and the sick. Indeed, Luke's very next verses (Acts 11:27–30) describe an act of charity, and toward fellow believers not at Antioch but in Palestine, for each *ekklēsia* was but the local manifestation of a wider and potentially universal communion.

We are reminded by the fact that Barnabus and Paul tarried at Antioch "a whole year" how time as well as space was encompassed by the Christian revelation and the community it generated. The revelation itself had of necessity been made within historical time, by God become man. The foundation documents of the faith were therefore, at one level, historical narratives. Then the succession of bishops, generation by generation, reinforced the possibility not only of perpetuating the teaching of the apostles, but also of creating a Christian chronology. On the profoundest level, sanctification of time was effected by the liturgy; by the development, especially during the 4th century, of a daily cycle of offices; and by an ever evolving calendar of festivals.[30] These commemorated the events of Christ's life, his sacrifice upon the Cross—a Pascha calculated never to coincide with its Jewish predecessor[31]—and his closest imitators the martyrs, over whose relics the Eucharist was celebrated in a powerful image of community and continuity.[32] Simultaneously the participant might see reflected the heavenly liturgy, and glimpse the angels gathered around God's throne in eternal praise.[33] The cycle of liturgy, offices, and festivals also offered a means of instruction, which Acts says was the apostles' chief concern at Antioch. In conjunction with homilies and catechisms and reading, the act of worship inculcated knowledge of the Scriptures and of the theology derived from them; and without its Scriptures, Christianity would at an early date have lost direction and been absorbed back into the synagogue. From the Scriptures, the community drew the narrative, belief, and discipline, even the very language that was at the heart of its identity.[34] All that was needed to confirm and proclaim that identity was a name.

Jesus had said he would be present even "where two or three are gathered together"; but it was on the whole felt that size and variety were positive factors in helping a community surmount the obstacles it was bound to encounter. Communities built of only one sort of person—virgins, for instance—were no more than sects, whereas the ship of Christ's church is made of many different woods.[35] Families, though they offered an effective medium for the dissemination of the gospel,[36] might easily be corrupted by heresy if the bishop did not exercise constant supervision.[37] As for numbers, Bishop Cornelius of Rome observed of the heretic Novatian that "this vindicator of the Gospel did not know that there should be one bishop in a catholic church, in which he was not ignorant—for how could he be?—that there are forty-six presbyters, seven deacons, seven subdeacons, forty-two acolytes, fifty-two exorcists, readers and doorkeepers, and above one thousand five hundred widows and persons in distress, all of whom are supported by the grace and loving kindness of the bishop. But not even did this great crowd, so necessary in the Church, and through God's providence abundant in number and multiplying, nor an immense and countless laity, turn him from such a desperate failure and recall him to the Church."[38] Nonetheless, there was an optimum number for even the most energetic bishop's flock. And who would shepherd the bishops themselves? There was no avoiding this issue once Constantine resolved to make the whole empire Christian.

In certain of Constantine's pronouncements preserved by Bishop Eusebius of Caesarea, as well as in Eusebius's own works, it is possible to discern an ideal image of a Christian Roman empire treated as a single religious community.[39] Under one God reigned one emperor, who called himself "bishop of those outside [the Church]"; while the "bishops of those within" were regarded as providing absolute Christian authority, under Christ, each in his own community of course, but a fortiori when deliberating collectively in regional councils or, at Nicaea, in a council designed to represent all Christendom, including the church in Iran.[40] The function of such gatherings was to provide guidance under the authority of Scripture and the Holy Spirit. And they excluded those who felt unable to communicate together in the same sacraments. Acceptance of scriptural and episcopal authority, and participation in the sacraments, defined the Christian community both during the proceedings of the council—a rare, paradigmatic, even, as described by Eusebius, ideal event—and also whenever or wherever else Christians gathered together. But still there was room for interpretation and therefore disagreement. Who would have the final word? Before Constantine, Christian congregations enforced their decisions by excluding those who did not comply. Under Constantine, the church succumbed to the temptation to repress its deviants, and with fatal logic made the emperor God's active representative on earth. With this move, the theoretical preconditions for the conversion of Rome into a single homogeneous religious community had been met.

If the Constantinian model had a decidedly vertical, exclusivist, and repressive aspect to it, reality organized itself, as usual, somewhat more horizontally—or better, perhaps, segmentally. Eunapius's work reveals painful awareness of the Constantinian model and simultaneously demonstrates its failure to eradicate dissent. From the 320s onward, polytheist philosophers were under constant suspicion, especially if their theurgical and in particular divinatory rituals were felt to be inspired by curiosity about the prospects of those in authority; but for Eunapius's readers these men and women were also proof of historical continuity and a living reinforcement, by example, of their doctrine. That such readers existed is guaranteed by the production of later works such as Marinus's biography of Proclus (d. 485) or Damascius's of Isidore (d. before 526), whose length and digressiveness, apparent even in its present fragmentary state, made of it, in effect, another group biography; it seems also to have been called a *Philosophical History*. In these works a polytheist intellectual community comes to life, and thanks to them this community dominates our view of late Greek philosophy and even late Greek religion. It is an urban community dominated by scholars and founded on study of philosophical texts and on the right worship of the gods wherever and whenever possible. From a strictly sociohistorical point of view, it seems apter to describe these groups as circles rather than as a community; yet Eunapius's concentration on them to the exclusion of most of the rest of society (whose fortunes he treated in a separate work, the *History*), his skillful foregrounding of Julian, the only polytheist emperor after Constantine, and his emphasis on the groups' historical continuity as part of a "succession" *(diadochē)* create the comforting illusion of community amid a world of rapid and alienating change.

In the study of late polytheism, illusionism is far from being the prerogative only of late antique writers. A romantic and of course very political school of thought used to hold that ancient polytheism—that of the temples rather than the schools—"survived" under a decent yet not suffocating veiling of Christianity.[41] In the extreme case of crypto-polytheism one might indeed literally turn around an icon of Christ and find Apollo painted on the back.[42] But what more usually happened was that late polytheism went on evolving, often—as in the case of Iamblichus and Julian—under the direct or indirect influence of Christianity, but also itself influencing the practices of ordinary Christians, so that in the resultant local fusions there was much, on both sides, that was passed to posterity, although impure and thoroughly alloyed. In the year 348, for example, according to an Arian historiographer, "a mighty earthquake hit Beirut in Phoenicia, and the larger part of the town collapsed, with the result that a crowd of pagans came into the church and professed Christianity just like us. But some of them then introduced innovations and left, stripping off as it were the conventions of the Church. Dedicating a place of prayer, they there received the crowd, and in all things imitated the Church, resembling us just as closely as the sect of the Samaritans does the Jews, but living like pagans."[43]

And then there was Augustine of Hippo, trying hard to dissuade his flock from holding a drunken festival in honor of one of their martyrs in the very church itself. He even tried to explain to them the historical background to their situation: "When peace was made after many violent persecutions, crowds of pagans were anxious to come over to the Christian name but were hindered by the fact that they were accustomed to spend their feast days with their idols in drunkenness and excessive banqueting, and could not easily abstain from those baneful but long-established pleasures. So our predecessors thought it good to make concessions for the time being to those weaker brethren, and to let them celebrate in honor of the holy martyrs other feast days, in place of those they were giving up, unlike them, at any rate, in profanation, though like them in excess. Now that they were bound together by the name of Christ and submissive to the yoke of his great authority, they must inherit the wholesome rules of sobriety, and these they could not oppose because of their veneration and fear for him whose rules they were. It was now high time, therefore, for such as had not the courage to deny that they were Christians, to begin to live according to the will of Christ, casting behind them, now that they were Christians, the concessions made to induce them to become Christians" (*Ep.* 29, trans. J. H. Baxter).

In these situations, the church was unlikely ever to purge itself thoroughly of the old ways the converts brought; while the theological or, rather, pastoral principle of "economy" that Augustine alludes to in this passage might at times be unashamedly abused, as when Archbishop Theophilus of Alexandria consecrated Synesius bishop of Ptolemais even though, as a philosopher, he refused to entertain the idea that all matter will pass away, and had reservations about the resurrection as conventionally understood.[44] But it was no doubt sincerely believed that the old ways, of the philosophers and the illiterate alike, would not remain entirely untouched by the powerful liturgical and iconographical context in which they were now embedded, and that the new theology would seep, however slowly and anecdotally, into the subconscious of those unruly congregations.

Christians at the beginning had been forced to define themselves by reaction to a polytheist world. In the Christian world of late antiquity polytheists were in a similar position. Some even found the experience stimulating. Adjustments and accommodations were made by both sides. Even so, the influence of the different Christian communities on each other was naturally far more insidious:

at the end of the letter just quoted, Augustine remarks how, even as he spoke to his own flock, "we could hear in the basilica of the [Donatist] heretics how they were celebrating their usual feastings" (*Ep.* 29.11). Opponents and supporters of Nicaea experienced the same proximity. In the eastern empire from 337 until the accession of Theodosius I in 379 (except under Julian and Jovian), opponents of Nicaea carried at any given moment considerable and at times overwhelming weight, and from 354 to 360 in the western empire too. Under Julian, Arians acquitted themselves with distinction, gaining many martyrs. Probably under Theodosius I, when the Arian ascendancy was threatened, these martyrs' *acta* were gathered together into an Arian martyrology, another group biography designed to set a good example, this time to Arian congregations called on to resist Nicaean persecution. Eventually, the triumphant Nicaean church was to adopt these soldiers of Christ as its own, drawing a discreet veil over their Christological shortcomings.[45] Try as the church might to apply legal exclusions to heretics, their communities were interwoven with those of the Nicaean Christians, while their culture was often too closely related to that of the "orthodox" to be distinguishable.

In order to solve precisely this problem of how Christians, or at least their pastors, might tell sound from unsound doctrine, the church generated a variant form of group biography, the catalogue of heresies. Irenaeus and Hippolytus were early exponents of this genre, which was closely related to the combination of philosophical biography and doxography we find in Diogenes Laertius's *Lives and Opinions of Eminent Philosophers.* But the most impressive collection of heresies is to be found in the "medicine chest," the *Panarion,* that Bishop Epiphanius of Salamis was busy stocking up between ca. 375 and ca. 378. Among the more extensive compendia of "research" to have survived from antiquity, the *Panarion* contains historical and biographical information about the heresiarchs and their followers, and summaries and refutations of their teaching. Such works were used for reference and as sources of proof texts during the deliberations of church councils, which proceeded according to the same principle that animated the heresiologists, namely that Christian doctrine was best defined in brief, pregnant statements such as the Nicaean creed or the *De fide* appended to the *Panarion,* and elaborated only when it became necessary to exclude some specific error. As a principle on which to found a universal religious community, this avoidance of the temptation to spell out every last detail, especially in the sphere of the individual's personal knowledge of God, had much to commend it. It compensated somewhat for Christianity's insistence on adherence to credal formulations, however summary, instead of the general gratitude and reverence that Caracalla had thought sufficient for the maintenance of the polytheist empire.

The career of Epiphanius of Salamis illustrates the way that monks were among the most zealous drawers of boundaries (especially against polytheism) and upholders of what they saw as doctrinal rectitude. In the monastic sphere we find in the late 4th and 5th centuries a tremendous interest in the use of group biography in order to define and propagate a communal way of life. The anonymous *History of the Monks in Egypt* (ca. 400) and Palladius's *Lausiac*

History (ca. 419–420) are travelogues and recollections of personal encounters that did much to crystallize the image of the ascetic way of life. The various collections of sayings of the desert fathers, the *Apophthegmata patrum* that were compiled in the later 5th century, tend to a more doxographical or gnomological approach, but still abound in anecdotal biography. They are of special interest because they appear to preserve either the prevalent inside view of the anachoretic community that developed at Nitria, Kellia, and especially Scetis, or at least the views of persons who considered themselves the community's direct heirs.[46]

A wide and flexible range of relationships prevailed among the anchorites in the *Apophthegmata,* who could nevertheless be portrayed as members of a community in the loose sense. The *Lives* of Pachomius, whose writers' anecdotal style suggests an origin in materials similar to the *Apophthegmata,* depict a far more formal, structured style of living together, the cenobitic monastery under the governance of an abbot.[47] In the sense that Pachomius's life (and *Life*) was itself as good as a rule, his monasteries were founded on individual example; but the monk's personal relationship with God was worked out in a strictly corporate context which encouraged members of the community to participate in each other's practical spiritual development. Theological speculation was of little concern in these circles—it might too easily lead to schism, as in the wider church. Instead, Pachomius offered his followers a light. He once told them of a dream in which he had seen brothers wandering lost in a vast, gloomy, pillared hall—apparently one of the temples of the old Egyptian gods. From all sides they could hear voices crying: "See, the light is here!" But it was impossible to work out where the voices were coming from, and eventually they began to despair. Then they beheld a lamp advancing in the dark, and a crowd of men following it. The brothers followed, each holding onto the shoulder of the one in front. Those who let go were lost in the shadows, and all those behind them. But as many as followed steadfastly were able to ascend through a doorway toward the light (*Vita prima S. Pachomii* 102).

The charming simplicity of this vision would have bemused Athanasius. Not that Pachomius was ineffective in the environment he created: the monks became in turn the shock troops of Nicaea. But neither Nicaea's triumph under Theodosius I nor Arianism's retreat to the Germanic successor states in the west (where it was just what was needed to reinforce Gothic identity against the siren song of *romanitas*) prevented the Christological debates that rekindled in the 5th century from bringing about a situation in which the Constantinian paradigm could be imposed only on a much reduced Balkan and Anatolian empire, while the eastern provinces went their own way. The "solution" proposed at the fourth ecumenical council at Chalcedon in 451 was to split the empire into irrevocably hostile communities, and fracture even the monastic world.

From the moment Justin I (518–527) became emperor, it was evident that Constantinople would no longer compromise with Chalcedon's opponents, the

Miaphysites, who emphasized the one incarnate nature of the Word, but only in extreme cases doubted the Savior's consubstantiality with man—against the fourth ecumenical council's insistence on two natures inseparably united (an apparent Dyophysitism that could all too easily be denounced as Nestorianism).[48] Until the 520s, pro- and anti-Chalcedonian factions commonly coexisted, without open rupture, within the same see; but once Justinian was enthroned, the council's opponents took the steps needed to create their own episcopal hierarchy, in order to guarantee ordination of priests to celebrate sacraments free of Chalcedonian pollution. The wide-ranging missionary activities of figures such as Jacob Baradaeus and Simeon of Beth-Arsham simultaneously propagated the anti-Chalcedonian position and maintained contact between far-flung communities; while the frequently repressive response of the Chalcedonian hierarchy and the imperial authorities focused and strengthened allegiances at the local level, which often crystallized around anti-Chalcedonian monastic communities.[49] John of Ephesus, in his *Lives of the Eastern Saints* (ca. 566–568), provided an attractive and inspiring group biography, at least for the Syriac-speaking world. The anti-Chalcedonian churches of Egypt, Syria, and Armenia were aware, despite often bitter disputes among themselves, of a shared faith, and of the desirability of apparent unity. Constantine and Nicaea were their slogans, and they continued to pray for the emperor in Constantinople and for his illumination, because their Roman identity remained strong. Although in the immediate present they were a persecuted and outlawed community, they believed in the restoration of a single Roman Christian church, even if this hope sometimes took on an eschatological tinge.[50] It became increasingly apparent that the Roman empire had entered a phase of semi-permanent credal segmentation. It had become an empire of two main communities, both of them Christian.

But what of Christians outside the empire? Rome's self-identification with the church had created a situation in which Christians beyond the frontiers might be implicated in the empire's political aspirations. For this reason, Christians in Iran were eventually prepared to identify themselves with theological positions that Rome labeled Nestorian, so as to underline their separate identity for the benefit of their Sassanian rulers. And once Rome's own eastern provinces began to dissociate themselves from the imperial church, it was natural for anti-Chalcedonian views to take root in Iranian territory too.[51] Syria-Mesopotamia was geographically a continuum, and the political boundary that ran through it had little cultural significance. In the contested sphere between the two empires, a string of sometimes more, sometimes less independent Christian polities—Armenia, the Ghassanid Arabs, Himyar, Aksum, and Nubia—saw advantage in the emergence of a powerful anti-Chalcedonian community free from Constantinople's supervision. In the vast area between the Taurus and the Arabian Sea, the Zagros and the Mediterranean, there emerged a commonwealth of peoples held together by the distinctive form of Christianity they shared, and by their hankering after a Constantinian paradigm occluded but by no means invalidated by the Christological strife since Nicaea. The force of this Constantinian and Nicaean ideal was such that the commonwealth was clearly east Roman in its orientation, just as its theological culture was essentially Greek. Yet only beyond the Roman frontier, in the polities that perched uneasily between Rome and Iran, or in the Iranian empire itself, could Chalcedon's opponents breathe freely. The Sassanians recognized both them and the majority Nestorian church as official religious communities, with a status inferior to that of official Mazdaism, but comparable to that of the Jewish community.

Sassanian monarchs might marry Christians or Jews, and even display personal interest in the teachings of these religions, but none of them ever converted. They were too dependent on an aristocracy and a priesthood, the magi, at once hereditary and strongly Iranian. Mazdaism itself was very much a religion of Iranians, and was highly conservative, doing without a written version of its scripture, the *Avesta,* until perhaps as late as the 6th century, and preserving markedly polytheist elements even longer.[52] But the magi knew a threat to their social and political position when they saw one. Right at the beginning of the Sassanian period, the Mesopotamian prophet Mani (216–276) had challenged them on their own territory. Manichaeism was a dynamic, polyglot, scriptural dualism of thoroughly universalist aspiration, deeply indebted to both Christianity and Mazdaism.[53] Had it captured the Iranian empire—Shapur I (239/240[241/242?]–270/272) apparently showed some interest—it would surely have become as involved in the exercise of power as the Christian church under Constantine and his heirs.[54] But the magi counterattacked, Mani died in prison, and his followers concentrated their energies on the missions Mani himself had set in motion, so that small Manichaean communities were soon scattered across the Mediterranean world as far as the Atlantic, as well as eastward into Central Asia. But within the Roman and Sassanian empires, the Manichaeans were always feared and repressed. Only to the east of the Sassanian realms did they manage to take firmer root.

As an original religious teacher who wrote his own scriptures rather than leaving the job to disciples, created a structured community, launched organized missions, and thought seriously about the possibility of converting the rulers of this world, Mani was rightly feared. He reminds us more of Muhammad than of Christ. Likewise, it is the Sassanian rather than the Roman empire that presents the clearer precedent for the political arrangements adumbrated in the Qur'ān. Something should be said of Iran's Christians, and of the Jews in both empires, in their own right and in the perspective of Islam.

The Jewish communities in the Roman and Iranian empires were led—sometimes nominally, at other times very actively—by hereditary officials of allegedly Davidic lineage called respectively patriarch and exilarch.[55] But although the imperial authorities appreciated the advantage of having a single Jewish interlocutor, the line of patriarchs died out in 429, while the exilarchate went through difficult times under the later Sassanians. And anyway it was the rabbinical class that took the lead in organizing local communal institutions, encouraged the religious observances without which there could be no living sense of a community and its boundaries, and produced those two bodies of commentary on the Torah, namely the Mishnah and the Talmud, from which we derive most of our knowledge of late antique Judaism, and to which Juda-

ism was thenceforth to look for a touchstone of communal identity. This rabbinical literature adopts a gnomological and occasionally anecdotal format that
reminds one of the *Apophthegmata patrum*—though the subject matter is very
different.[56] Once more we observe that characteristic phenomenon of late antiquity, the formation of a community identity by a class of people either learned
or holy or both, acting in person, of course, but also making themselves known
to much wider circles through gnomology and group biography.

This is not to say that these literary genres excluded the development of
others more discursive in style, such as the vast mass of Christian patristic
literature made up of treatises, commentaries, sermons, letters, and so forth.
But the popularity of gnomological literature and anecdotal biography is especially significant, because it underlines the role of memorization and of a basic
literacy, at least an oral literacy, at all social levels, acting to form a community
around a written tradition, but also around individual exponents of that tradition—the sages. Judaism and Islam in particular, lacking the sacramental dimension of Christianity, were to become communities of students, religions
built on texts in languages that were intrinsically sacred, all the more so for
being incomprehensible even to many of those who learned by rote texts written in them, squatting long hours in childhood, maturity, and old age by the
pillars of synagogue or mosque. At the heart of these communities, a pure
world of signs was—and is—being performed rather than rationally reflected
upon. But the performance, the recitation, reveals a different sort of rational
triumph, that of the spirit-filled man of God over the brute urges which at all
times threaten the community's integrity.[57]

Christianity, too, revered its sages, the apostles and the Fathers of the church.
But until the 4th century, sanctity meant quite simply martyrdom, surrendering
one's life for one's belief in Christ, as Christ himself had suffered for humanity's
redemption. Study had no necessary part in the making of saints, while historical memory of their sacrifice was maintained as much through the liturgy as
through hagiography. But as the church adapted to the world, its literature
came to reflect a more complex relationship. Accordingly, Sassanian Christianity is accessible to us today mainly through two literary genres which are both
eloquent about the formation of community.[58] The so-called *Acts of the Persian
Martyrs* circulated widely west of the frontier as well, and were an important
medium through which Roman Christians became aware of their cousins in
Iran.[59] Most of the martyrs gained their crowns during the four decades of
persecution that ended with Shapur II's death in 379, and their deaths were
presumably caused by the Magians' wish to forestall any repercussions of the
Constantinian revolution east of the Euphrates. In this they were successful,
and the Christian community was ever thereafter careful to underline its loyal-
ism, although its favoring of Antiochene (Nestorian) Christology may have
been a reaction to the spread of Miaphysitism in Iranian territory, as well as an
attempt to mark its distance from the empire of east Rome.

The other main literary—or at least written—legacy of Sassanian Christianity is contained in the proceedings of its ecclesiastical synods. Like the Torah

and its successive layers of interpretation, the canon law formulated at these synods came to cover all civil matters—marriage, property, and inheritance—and not just church business narrowly defined. And like the Jewish exilarch, the *katholikos* or patriarch of the east at Seleucia was made responsible not only for the administration of justice to his fellow religionists (and thus also for their good behavior), but also for the collection of taxes. In effect, the church became a state agency. In this way the community both tightened its own bonds and acquired a secular, administrative identity recognizable to those who had no knowledge of Christian doctrine. That doctrine, meanwhile, as well as being spread through the liturgy, was disseminated within the community through a network of schools that reached down to the village level and taught the Antiochene theology of Theodore of Mopsuestia rendered into Syriac and made accessible to the uneducated through hymns. The monasteries were another major factor in the formation of a Nestorian identity, for the monks were vigorous teachers and proselytizers, and acutely aware of the difference between themselves and the Miaphysites, from whom they distinguished themselves even in their costume and tonsure.

Naturally enough, the community boundaries so sedulously built up and maintained by religious elites were constantly being eroded by the everyday reality of intercourse between ordinary people, especially in commercial contexts. Nonetheless, the compact nature of the Jewish and Christian communities of the Sassanian empire, compared to their counterparts under Rome, did give them a certain innate coherence, which was further sharpened by the unsympathetic Mazdean environment and by the intense competitiveness of the Christian sects. The relatively uncentralized character of the Sassanian state, especially before the reforms of Kavad I (488–496, 499–531) and Khosro I (531–579), likewise favored the development of community identity. And whereas in the Roman empire the Jews were the sole recognized community other than the approved variety of Christianity, the Sassanians recognized Jews, Nestorians, and non-Chalcedonians or Miaphysites, as well as Mazdeans. This coexistence of recognized and scriptural communities not only continued after the Muslim conquest, but also provides the clearest precedent in the pre-Islamic world for the Qur'ān's general principle that "people of the Book" should be tolerated.[60]

Initially, at least, Islam was an *Arabic* monotheism, and the army and state were run by a Muslim Arabian elite, which had no motive either to force the conversion of those whose beliefs were reasonably inoffensive—that is, not polytheistic—or to deny the universality of the Qur'ān's teaching by actively impeding those who wished to join the *'umma* (community) of Islam. Recognition of separate and subordinate communities of non-Muslims, obliged to pay a special tax *(jizya)* in return for protected status *(dhimma)*, turned out to be an ideal device for regulating the large and sophisticated populations that suddenly had fallen under Muslim rule.[61] Unlike Christian Rome, the Islamic empire was prepared to preserve the religious life of any community that had a scripture; while unlike the Sassanian state, the caliphate was committed in principle to this policy, for it had been enjoined by Allah on the Prophet Muhammad.

The approved communities, the "people of the Book" *(ahl al-Kitāb)*, are named in three passages in the Qur'ān (2:63, 5:69–70, 22:18) as the Jews, the Christians, and the Sābi'a. Although the Qur'ān also contains much criticism of these peoples' beliefs, they are distinguished from the polytheists, whose traditions Muhammad knew well and rejected utterly. As a response to major religious communities of the late antique world, and to the problem of how to create a new one that could learn from its predecessors' mistakes, the Qur'ān is a unique document that deserves a more prominent place in the study of late antique religion than has so far been accorded it. To convey in a brief space the way in which the Qur'ān's statements on this subject brought about, in practice, the transition from polytheism to membership in the Islamic empire of communities, we may consider the Sābi'a and a minor but instructive incident that occurred in the year 830.

For Muhammad, it seems that the Sābi'a were a sect of baptizers, probably identical with the Elchasaites of Mesopotamia, the sect into which Mani had been born; but this group was never widely known in the lands of Islam.[62] In the year 830, the Caliph al-Ma'mūn passed through the city of Harran in northern Mesopotamia on his way to campaign against the east Romans, and was struck by the peculiar garb and hairstyle of some of those who came to greet him. In this way he discovered that the city contained a substantial remnant of star worshipers, who probably owed their survival to the sensitive position they occupied between the Roman empire on the one hand and the Iranian empire and later the caliphate on the other. Enraged by the persistence of such a substantial group of idolaters within the caliphate, al-Ma'mūn ordered them to adopt one of the approved religions before he returned from his campaign against the Christian empire.

Although some complied and became Muslims or Christians, others devised the ingenious stratagem of renaming themselves Sābi'a. After all, if nobody else knew who these people were, why not adopt their identity and claim the protection the Qur'ān afforded? In this way the "Sabians" managed to survive for at least another two centuries, and perennially to fascinate Muslim historians and geographers, who describe them as a community with a priesthood, a highly developed calendar of religious observance, and a marked sense of its own history and identity. This fascination was not just antiquarian. Muslims believed that polytheism had once been the religion of all mankind; and these earlier polytheists, too, they naturally called Sābi'a, or Sabians. The first to perceive the error of this belief, and to proclaim the unicity of God, had been Abraham, who had lived under King Nimrod's rule in Babylon before he fled via Harran to Palestine. Eventually, with his son Ishmael, he built the Ka'ba at Mecca.[63] In effect, Abraham had been the first Muslim. The continued existence of a Sabian polytheist community at Harran must have seemed a stunning confirmation of the Qur'ānic story of the origins of monotheism; while the figure of Abraham, the rejected prophet, along with a whole succession of other such "messengers" culled from the pages of the Hebrew Bible and ending with Jesus, son of Mary, provided a firm and universally familiar genealogy for the last and most evolved of all religious communities, the 'umma that Muhammad had brought into being (see, for example, Qur'ān 21).

There was, though, some elasticity regarding "peoples of the Book." In only one of the three Qur'ānic passages in question is Mazdaism alluded to, and even then ambiguously and in direct association with polytheism. Even so, it was tolerated in practice, as a kind of third-class religion.[64] And Islam itself did not for long remain monolithic. The 'umma soon became bitterly divided by struggles between different parties that saw themselves as Muhammad's heirs and could not decide whether inspiration should be regarded as having dried up on the Prophet's death, or as being still available within the community—the fateful divergence, in other words, between Sunnis and Shiites. Only after 'Abd al-Malik reestablished order in the 690s did it become possible to draw tighter the bonds that held the caliphate together, from the Indus to the Atlantic, and to impose a more explicitly Islamic style in place of the earlier imitation of Roman and Sassanian models. And perhaps it was at this point that the classical Islamic 'umma first came clearly into focus, since it is likely that, in the early decades of the new faith's dissemination, amidst the heat and confusion of rapid conquest and internal strife, local loyalties and identities had tended to prevail over any wider vision.[65]

That wider vision was focused in part on the person of the caliph, who held in his hands interdependent religious and politico-military authority, just as the Prophet himself had exercised absolute authority in order to make of the Muslim community an effective brotherhood (Qur'ān 49.11) and a substitute for the traditional clans its members had abandoned. Behind the caliph lay the Qur'ān, other sayings of the Prophet (hadith), and the whole complex of dogma and practice in the context of community that went under the general heading of *sunna*. In daily life, the community's identity and coherence were most clearly expressed not in the marketplace, as in Graeco-Roman cities, but at the place of congregational worship and indeed of judgment, the *masjid;* while the pilgrimage to Mecca, the hajj, imprinted in the mind of every participant the ecumenical dimension of Islam and its sacred history right back to the time of Abraham.[66] Rooted as it was in a world rich in Jewish, Christian, and Mazdean communities and traditions, Islam naturally drew on all of these; but to the cultural continuities thus accepted, a distinctively Muslim tone was always imparted, as one can see already in the Qur'ān's constant emphasis on the fact that Muhammad is called to purge the error of the monotheist and prophetic tradition of the Jews and Christians.

The mid 8th century transition from Umayyad to Abbasid rule, and the loss of Spain, did not weaken the Islamic empire, which attained its greatest glory under the early Abbasid caliphs ruling from the new capital at Baghdad. By al-Ma'mūn's day, though, strains were showing; by the early 10th century the empire was in full dissolution. But the social and cultural foundations of the

Islamic world had by then been firmly laid, and could not be shaken by any degree of political fragmentation. Conversion to Islam was by the 10th century making substantial inroads into the "peoples of the Book."[67] Nevertheless, these communities inherited from late antiquity remained vital contributors to the flexibility, entrepreneurial spirit, and international contacts that characterized the Islamic commonwealth; while the commonwealth became in turn one of the crossroads of the world economic system that began to emerge between the China Sea and the Atlantic by the 11th century and matured in the 13th.[68]

If 10th or 11th century Cairo, for example, seems to us the quintessential example of the classical Islamic city of communities, that is partly because Islam in general accorded a degree of recognition to other religions for which even the Sassanian world had offered only partial precedent, and partly because, as Shiites, the ruling Fatimids favored other minority communities that were also attempting to survive in a Sunni environment.[69] And these communities were often by now beneficiaries of secondary identities accumulated over the centuries, best exemplified by the vast and increasingly systematized commentary literatures they had been producing throughout late antiquity. As well as the Torah, the Jews now had a Mishnah and a Talmud, none of which had been written down much before the year 200; while the Christians had generated an enormous body of theological writing, a luxurious growth that had spilled out from the narrow terraces of Scripture and could now, under Islam, be trained, pruned, and shaped at leisure. Hence John of Damascus's compilation of Christian doctrine, *De fide orthodoxa,* which in precisely 100 chapters covers everything from proof of God's existence to circumcision, in a systematic, accessible fashion that had seemed unnecessary when the church was comfortably enshrined within the all-powerful empire of Christian Rome. To his heirs in the Greek-speaking world John of Damascus bequeathed narrower horizons and a refusal to think constructively about Islam, typified by his supercilious account of Muhammad's life and teaching, the last entry in a catalogue of (again) 100 Christian heresies. But increasingly Christians, especially in John's Chalcedonian or "Melkite" tradition, wrote in Arabic too; and some were clever enough to see that the unrivalled clarity of the Qur'ān's language about God might be used in the service of the gospel as well.[70] In the Islamic world as in the Roman, religious communities derived from the experience of coexistence a sharper understanding of their own identity.

On the life of the Christian communities under Islam, literary sources such as the Arabic *History of the Patriarchs of Alexandria* throw only a partial light, since their concern is with the way in which an elite—in this case, the leadership of the anti-Chalcedonian, Coptic church of Egypt—dealt with the Muslim authorities and conspired to fix succession to the community's highest offices, especially the patriarchal throne.[71] But the contents of the document depository of the synagogue of the Palestinians at Fustat, better known as the Cairo Geniza, have made possible an in-depth portrait of this not especially influential or privileged community's everyday life—a portrait that has been triumphantly drawn by S. D. Goitein in his *A Mediterranean Society: The Jewish Communities of the Arab World As Portrayed in the Documents of the Cairo Geniza.*

Through Goitein's five vast volumes we come to know the Jews of Fustat as *pars pro toto* of the international Jewish community, in a world where long-distance travel was common and law was personal, not territorial: one was free to appeal to leading judges from one's own community even if they were resident in a foreign state. And this right of self-government, exercised within relatively small groupings in which a significant degree of individual participation was feasible (2:57), gave Christians and Jews one privilege denied to the great mass of Muslims, who had little opportunity to express a point of view in the hearing of those who controlled their destiny. There were no ghettoes either: the religious communities of Fustat were at once supraterritorial and closely intermixed, much more so than one would ever guess from literary sources like the *History of the Patriarchs of Alexandria*.

The deepest foundations of personal and communal identity were of course laid at home: "Before taking food or drink of any kind one would say the appropriate benediction, and grace . . . after . . . followed by an Amen by those present, so that the children learned them by listening. For them, opening the mouth for food without opening it first for a benediction would soon become awkward and unusual" (5:352).[72] But it was in the synagogue or church that the community felt itself most truly a community. "A high claim to pride for any Geniza person was his ability to read and recite in public the Torah and the Prophets in their original language—a task to which he had dedicated most of his years in school. The emotion accompanying this performance found its expression in the benedictions said by him before and after the recital, respectively: 'Blessed be you . . . who chose us of all nations and gave us his Torah' and 'who, by giving us a true Torah, planted eternal life within us'" (5:348).

If space allowed, I would say more about the formation of scriptural canons and commentaries, the formulation of liturgies, and the organization of study. These are processes that point to eternity, yet take place within historical time; and their prominence in the formation of religious communities illustrates how those communities' self-consciousness is in significant part historical memory, focused of course on the origin and development of their own distinctive beliefs and practices. Such memory—unlike awareness of eternity, or the need to conform to the annual cycle of the seasons—may be lost. In 1890, the British traveler and archaeologist David Hogarth crossed Lake Egridir in Anatolia to visit "a remnant of fifty Christian families huddle[d] at one end of the island, where is a church served by two priests. No service is held except on the greatest festivals, and then in Turkish, for neither priest nor laity understand a word of Greek. The priests told us that the families became fewer every year; the fathers could teach their children nothing about their ancestral faith, for they knew nothing themselves; the Moslems were 'eating them up'. We had to force the church door, and brush dust and mould from a vellum service-book dated 1492. It was all like nothing so much as a visit to a deathbed."[73]

But while communities die out, their individual members may live on with new identities, and in so doing add in distinctive ways to the community of their adoption. Where there has been a long-term, intimate interpenetration, as in Ottoman Anatolia between Christians and Muslims, this is a relatively natural and easy process; but we have seen that something similar happened even in the more abrupt transition from polytheism to Christianity. In particular, the rapid rise of the cult of saints just as the temples were closing indicates that many communities never fully abandoned a diffused understanding of divinity. Once the trauma of transition had been healed, the same scriptural religions which in urban environments defined themselves in opposition to polytheism and each other turned out to be no less capable than polytheism of responding to the need of simple rural communities for a faith that expressed both their undivided, relatively unselfconscious identity and their awareness of dependence on a natural world whose external manifestations are multiple and seem, at times, contradictory. Just because in other places there were known to be fellow religionists of different hue, or even people who professed other faiths entirely, members of such Christianized or, eventually, Islamized communities did not necessarily feel constrained to relativize everything, or to deny the possibility of expressing man's intuition of the essential oneness and holiness of all creation in a specific, unique, and exclusive religious language. As the anthropologist Juliet du Boulay wrote in her account of a village in Northern Euboea in the 1960s: "Their own religion they consider to be the only correct path to God, for they find on the whole what they hear of non-Christian practices incredible and ludicrous, and what they hear of other denominations of Christianity strange and shocking. Inevitably, therefore, except when they are consciously defining ethnic and cultural differences, their concept of mankind is either an implicit extension of the Christian Orthodox world to cover all humanity of whatever actual faith, or the idea of humanity in general as Christendom, from which non-Christians are unconsciously excluded."[74]

The possible merits of unconscious exclusivism are not much considered in our time. Yet nor was the variety of religious communities—which some see as offering grounds for comparison with modern situations[75]—what most struck late antique observers. Almost all the literary evidence drawn on in this essay is oriented toward a single community or tradition and, whatever that community's debt to others, shows no disinterested curiosity about them, let alone esteem for the inherent merits of variety.[76] The Qur'ān, though it takes an exceptionally considered and generous approach to the religious communities of the late antique world, does so summarily, from the perspective of a revelation at the apex of a long historical development, and addressed to Arabs, in Arabic. Eventually Muslim scholars, most famous among them al-Shahrastānī (d. 1153), applied themselves to wide-ranging descriptions of *al-milal wa'l-niḥal,* that is, revealed faiths on the one hand and human speculations such as philosophy on the other, anticipating in some respects the comparative study of religions. Yet even the broad-minded al-Shahrastānī dealt with his materials from a firmly monotheist, and ultimately Qur'ānic, perspective.[77] Even to educated city-dwellers, accustomed to pluralism, their own community's orthodoxy and coherence were what mattered most.

Notes

1. Zosimus 5.40–41; and compare Sozomen, *Historia ecclesiastica* 9.6.3–6. Apparently both depend on a lost account by Olympiodorus, whose angle is probably reproduced more faithfully by his coreligionist Zosimus.

2. Compare Sextus Pompeius Festus (2nd century), *De significatione verborum*, 284 (Lindsay): "Publica sacra, quae publico sumptu pro populo fiunt."

3. Sozomen, *Historia ecclesiastica* 7.15, 20; Rufinus, *Historia ecclesiastica* 9.29; G. Fowden, *The Egyptian Hermes: A Historical Approach to the Late Pagan Mind* (Cambridge, Eng., 1986; repr. with new preface, Princeton, 1993), 13.

4. *IGUR* 2:478–480. Only a minority of Roman epitaphs of Greek-speaking polytheists state the place of origin; but almost none allude to religious belief: I. Kajanto, *A Study of the Greek Epitaphs of Rome* (Helsinki, 1963), 2, 38.

5. *Myst.* 5.25.236; Julian, *Contra Galilaeos* fr. 21 (Masaracchia).

6. Eusebius, *Vit.Const.* 2.23.2, records how Constantine sent out a letter in two versions, one "to the Churches of God," the other "to the peoples outside, city by city."

7. See also J. North, "The Development of Religious Pluralism," in J. Lieu, J. North, and T. Rajak, eds., *The Jews among Pagans and Christians in the Roman Empire* (London, 1992), 174–193.

8. W. Burkert, *Greek Religion* (Oxford and Cambridge, Mass., 1985), 268–275; J. Irmscher, "Der Terminus *religio* und seine antiken Entsprechungen im philologischen und religionsgeschichtlichen Vergleich," in U. Bianchi, ed., *The Notion of "Religion" in Comparative Research* (Rome, 1994), 63–73.

9. Philostratus, *Vita Apollonii* 4.24; Julian, *Epistulae* 89.300c–302a; Marinus, *Vita Procli* 15, 32.

10. Dio Cassius 77.15.5–7.

11. F. Poland, *Geschichte des griechischen Vereinswesens* (Leipzig, 1909), 5–6, 65, 173–176.

12. M. F. Squarciapino, *Leptis Magna* (Basel, 1966), 117.

13. *IG* 2–3².1368.

14. For example, *P Oxy.* 1380.

15. For example, Symmachus, *Relatio* 3.10; Augustine, *Epistulae* 104.12 (quoting the addressee, Nectarius of Calama).

16. See, recently, E. Will and C. Orrieux, *"Prosélytisme juif"? Histoire d'une erreur* (Paris, 1992); P. van Minnen, "Drei Bemerkungen zur Geschichte des Judentums in der griechisch-römischen Welt," *Zeitschrift für Papyrologie und Epigraphik* 100 (1994): 253–258.

17. Julian, *Contra Galilaeos* frs. 19–20 (Masaracchia).

18. *P Giess.* 40 I; K. Buraselis, *Theia Dōrea* (Athens, 1989), 20–21; P. A. Kuhlmann, *Die Giessener literarischen Papyri und die Caracalla-Erlasse* (Giessen, 1994), 217–239.

19. Marcus Aurelius 5.33, 6.30.

20. Numenius, fr. 24 (des Places); Aelian, fr. 89 (Hercher).

21. Compare, for example, Chaeremon's account with Julian, *Epistulae* 89.302d–303b.

22. Iamblichus, *Myst.* 5.16–18, 10.6.

23. Julian, *Epistulae* 84, 89; Sozomen, *Historia ecclesiastica* 5.16; Sallustius, *De diis et mundo.*

24. Note especially Julian, *Epistulae* 98.400c, applying the term indiscriminately to all the polytheist inhabitants of a town in Syria. Julian's highly political use of names is decried by Gregory of Nazianzus, *Orationes* 4.76.

25. For example, Julian, *Orationes* 8.172d–173a.

26. *Corpus Hermeticum* 16.1–2; Philostratus, *Vita Apollonii* 3.32; Iamblichus, *Myst.* 7.5.259.

27. C. Geertz, *The Interpretation of Cultures* (New York, 1973), 181–189; R. S. Kipp and S. Rodgers, eds., *Indonesian Religions in Transition* (Tucson, 1987).

28. On crypto-polytheism see, for example, Libanius, *Orationes* 30.28; Zacharias Scholasticus, *Vita Severi,* 17–37 (Kugener); Procopius, *Anecdota* 11.32.

29. On the role of episcopal violence in the definition of the community see P. Brown, *Religion and Society in the Age of Saint Augustine* (London, 1972), 326–331; G. Fowden, "Bishops and Temples in the Eastern Roman Empire A.D. 320–435," *Journal of Theological Studies* 29 (1978): 53–78.

30. C. Jones et al., eds., *The Study of Liturgy* (2nd ed., London, 1992), esp. 403–420, 472–484; and cf. R. Taft, *The Liturgy of the Hours in East and West: The Origins of the Divine Office and Its Meaning for Today* (Collegeville, Minn., 1986), 331–334.

31. Eusebius, *Vit.Const.* 3.18.

32. Ambrose, *Epistulae* 22.13. On the role of saints and their relics in the formation of Christian community, see P. Brown, *The Cult of the Saints: Its Rise and Function in Latin Christianity* (Chicago, 1981).

33. John Chrysostom, *De sacerdotio* 6.4 (*PG* 48.681); Palladius, *Historia Lausiaca* 18.25; Cyril of Scythopolis, *Vita Euthymii* 19; Gregory the Great, *Dialogi* 4.60.3; *Liturgy of S. Basil,* in F. E. Brightman, ed., *Liturgies Eastern and Western,* vol. 1 (Oxford, 1896), 312.

34. But see *Apophthegmata patrum* (Greek alphabetical series), in *PG* 65.128c–d, on preferring the language of the (desert) Fathers to the dangerous idiom of the Scriptures.

35. Epiphanius, *Panarion* 61.3.4–8.

36. Sozomen, *Historia ecclesiastica* 5.15.14–17.

37. For example, Leo the Great, *Epistulae* 1.1; and see H. O. Maier, "The Topography of Heresy and Dissent in Late-Fourth-Century Rome," *Historia* 44 (1995): 235–244.

38. Eusebius, *Historia ecclesiastica* 6.43.11–12 (adapted from trans. by J. E. L. Oulton).

39. A. Grillmeier, *Jesus der Christus im Glauben der Kirche,* vol. 1 (3rd ed., Freiburg, 1990), 386–403; G. Fowden, *Empire to Commonwealth: Consequences of Monotheism in Late Antiquity* (Princeton, 1993), 85–97.

40. Eusebius, *Vit.Const.* 4.24; compare 2.23.2, and 1 Cor. 5:12–13 (where it is God who judges those outside).

41. M. Herzfeld, *Ours Once More: Folklore, Ideology, and the Making of Modern Greece* (Austin, 1982), 116–117.

42. John of Ephesus, *Historia ecclesiastica* 3.3.29.

43. "Arian historiographer," J. Bidez and F. Winkelmann, eds., *Philostorgius, Kirchengeschichte* (3rd ed., Berlin, 1981, 202–241) 23.

44. Synesius, *Epistulae* 105. On "economy" as a necessary compensation for the rigidities and tensions of a Christian empire, see G. Dagron, "La règle et l'exception: Analyse de la notion d'économie," in D. Simon, ed., *Religiöse Devianz: Untersuchungen zu sozialen, rechtlichen und theologischen Reaktionen auf religiöse Abweichung im westlichen und östlichen Mittelalter* (Frankfurt am Main, 1990), 1–18.

45. H. C. Brennecke, *Studien zur Geschichte der Homöer der Osten bis zum Ende der homöischen Reichskirche* (Tübingen, 1988), 93–94, 152–157. The martyrology apparently formed part of the work of the "Arian historiographer" (see n. 43). Compare also I. Shahīd, *The Martyrs of Najrān: New Documents* (Brussels, 1971), 200–207, for a similar conversion of anti-Chalcedonian martyrs into Chalcedonians in the 6th century.

46. G. Gould, *The Desert Fathers on Monastic Community* (Oxford, 1993), 1–25.

47. I rely on P. Rousseau's sensitive account, *Pachomius: The Making of a Community in Fourth-Century Egypt* (Berkeley, 1985).

48. W. H. C. Frend, *The Rise of the Monophysite Movement: Chapters in the History*

of the Church in the Fifth and Sixth Centuries (Cambridge, 1972; corrected repr. 1979), 184–254; Fowden, *Empire to Commonwealth*, 100–137 and esp. 124–137, for documentation of the points made in the next two paragraphs. "Miaphysitism" is a less misleading name than "monophysitism," which implicitly excludes the human aspect of Christ's one and undivided nature.

49. A. Palmer, *Monk and Mason on the Tigris Frontier: The Early History of Ṭur ʿAbdin* (Cambridge, 1990), 149–153.

50. As in the national epic of Ethiopia, the *Kebra Nagast*, parts of which appear to go back to the 6th century.

51. M. Morony, *Iraq after the Muslim Conquest* (Princeton, 1984), 372–380; Palmer, *Monk and Mason*, 153–154.

52. Morony, *Iraq*, 280–305.

53. Fowden, *Empire to Commonwealth*, 72–76.

54. Cologne Mani Codex, 134–135, 163–164 (A. Henrichs and L. Koenen, eds., *Der Kölner Mani-Kodex: Über das Werden seines Leibes* [Opladen, 1988], 96, 112); C. E. Römer, *Manis frühe Missionsreisen nach der Kölner Manibiographie* (Opladen, 1994), 154–159.

55. Rome: *C.Th.* 16.8; L. I. Levine, *The Rabbinic Class of Roman Palestine in Late Antiquity* (Jerusalem, 1989); M. Goodman, "Jews and Judaism in the Mediterranean Diaspora in the Late Roman Period: The Limitations of Evidence," *Journal of Mediterranean Studies* 4 (1994): 208–212, 220–221. Babylon: Morony, *Iraq*, 306–331.

56. See the interesting remarks by H. L. Strack and G. Stemberger, *Introduction to the Talmud and Midrash* (Edinburgh, 1991), 66–68.

57. J. Glicken, "Sundanese Islam and the Value of *Hormat*: Control, Obedience, and Social Location in West Java," in Kipp and Rodgers, eds., *Indonesian Religions*, 240–244; B. Anderson, *Imagined Communities: Reflections on the Origin and Spread of Nationalism* (2nd ed., London, 1991), 12–16.

58. J. P. Asmussen, "Christians in Iran," in W. B. Fisher and others, eds., *The Cambridge History of Iran* (Cambridge, 1968–1991), 3:924–948; Morony, *Iraq*, 332–383, 620–632.

59. E. K. Fowden, *The Barbarian Plain: Saint Sergius between Rome and Iran* (Berkeley, 1999), chap. 2.

60. Note Ṭabari, *Taʾrīkh* 1.991 (tr. T. Nöldeke, *Geschichte der Perser und Araber zur Zeit der Sasaniden* [Leiden, 1879], 268), for a succinct statement of this policy attributed to Hormizd IV.

61. C. E. Bosworth, "The Concept of *Dhimma* in Early Islam," in B. Braude and B. Lewis, eds., *Christians and Jews in the Ottoman Empire* (New York, 1982), 1:37–51.

62. T. Fahd, "Sābiʾa," *Encyclopedia of Islam*, 2nd ed., 8:675–677. On the "Sabians" of Harran see D. Chwolsohn, *Die Ssabier und der Ssabismus* (St. Petersburg, 1856); Fowden, *Empire to Commonwealth*, 62–65.

63. H. Schützinger, *Ursprung und Entwicklung der arabischen Abraham-Nimrod-Legende* (Bonn, 1961); R. Firestone, *Journeys in Holy Lands: The Evolution of the Abraham-Ishmael Legends in Islamic Exegesis* (Albany, 1990).

64. Qurʾān 22.18; M. G. Morony, "Madjūs," *Encyclopedia of Islam*, 2nd ed., 5.1110–18; S. D. Goitein, *A Mediterranean Society: The Jewish Communities of the Arab World as Portrayed in the Documents of the Cairo Geniza* (Berkeley, 1967–1993), 5:334.

65. On the ʾumma see Morony, *Iraq*, 431–506; Fowden, *Empire to Commonwealth*, 153–159.

66. Not that one should forget the sanctity of the Roman marketplace (Maximus of Madauros, in Augustine, *Epistulae* 16.1), or the use of the courtyards of large Syrian temples as public squares (*C.Th.* 16.10.8).

67. For recent comment on this complex subject see M. G. Morony, "The Age of

Conversions: A Reassessment," in M. Gervers and R. J. Bikhazi, eds., *Conversion and Continuity: Indigenous Christian Communities in Islamic Lands, Eighth to Eighteenth Centuries* (Toronto, 1990), 135–150.

68. J. L. Abu-Lughod, *Before European Hegemony: The World System* A.D. *1250–1350* (New York, 1989), especially chap. 7, "Cairo's Monopoly under the Slave Sultanate." On the Islamic Commonwealth see Fowden, *Empire to Commonwealth,* 160–168.

69. But Goitein, in *Mediterranean Society,* opines that the Fatimids "excelled in laissez-faire, out of indolence . . . rather than conviction" (2:404–405).

70. S. H. Griffith, "The First Christian *Summa Theologiae* in Arabic: Christian *Kalām* in Ninth-Century Palestine," in Gervers and Bikhazi, eds., *Conversion and Continuity,* 15–31.

71. *History of the Patriarchs of Alexandria,* ed. and trans. B. Evetts, PO 1(2,4), 5(1), 10(5). See also H. Kennedy, "The Melkite Church from the Islamic Conquest to the Crusades: Continuity and Adaptation in the Byzantine Legacy," in *The 17th International Byzantine Congress: Major Papers* (New Rochelle, N.Y., 1986), 325–343.

72. See also J. Assmann, *Das kulturelle Gedächtnis: Schrift, Erinnerung, und politische Identität in frühen Hochkulturen* (Munich, 1992), 16: "In the Seder celebration the child learns to say 'we,' as he becomes part of a history and a memory that creates and constitutes this 'we.' This problem and process is basic to every culture, although seldom so clearly visible."

73. D. G. Hogarth, *A Wandering Scholar in the Levant* (London, 1896), 84.

74. J. du Boulay, *Portrait of a Greek Mountain Village* (Oxford, 1974; corrected repr. Limni, 1994), 42.

75. E.g. Morony, *Iraq,* 524.

76. See also Goitein, *Mediterranean Society,* 2:277.

77. See al-Shahrastānī, *Al-milal wa'l-niḥal,* trans. D. Gimaret, G. Monnot, and J. Jolivet, *Livre des religions et des sectes* (Leuven, 1986–93).

BARBARIANS AND ETHNICITY

Patrick J. Geary

The concept of "barbarian" was an invention of the Graeco-Roman world, projected onto a whole spectrum of peoples living beyond the frontier of the empire. Except for the Persians, whose cultural and political equality the Roman world begrudgingly recognized, Romans perceived all other societies through generalized and stereotypical categories inherited from centuries of Greek and Roman ethnographic writings. Each people's complex of traits, along with geographical boundaries, became the determining factors in Roman ethnic classification.

If barbarians were a Roman invention, ethnogenesis, or ethnic formation and transformation, was emphatically not. Classical systems of territorialization and classification, typical of Roman concerns for precision and order, objectified and externalized the identity of peoples, relegating them to an eternal present. Geographers such as Pliny delighted in combining as many sources as possible, mixing peoples long disappeared with contemporary ethnic groups in his *Natural History*. The result was a sort of law of conservation of peoples: no people ever disappeared, no trait ever changed. At best, a group might acquire a new name and novel, even contradictory customs and characteristics. Moreover, the geographical location of peoples took on increasing importance as Roman contact with barbarians increased. The maps of the Roman world became crowded as their compilers sought to fill their land masses with as many peoples as possible. These peoples, like other natural phenomena, had no real history: they encountered history only when they entered the sphere of the civilized world. Thus the concept of ethnogenesis was alien to the Roman understanding of their neighbors. Typical of the Roman explanation of peoples is this account of the emergence of the Goths: "Now from this island of Scandza, as from a hive of races or a womb of nations, the Goths are said to have come forth long ago under their king, Berig by name. As soon as they disembarked from their ships and set foot on the land, they straightway gave their name to the place" (Jordanes, *Getica*, ed. Mommsen [Berlin, 1882], 60). Thus begins the 6th century account of Gothic origins by the Gotho-Roman Jordanes, writing in the Constantinople of Justinian. The account reflects traditional concepts of Graeco-Roman ethnography more than Gothic oral traditions. The Goths (to Jordanes, equivalent to the Getae) are but one more of the innumerable peoples who emerged from the north in a timeless "long ago" and began their long migration toward Italy and thereby entered the sphere of Roman civilization.

In contrast to this classical image of peoples as static, eternal, and without history, an inscription erected by a Turkic Khagan presents an alternative understanding of the origin of a people: "My father, the khagan, went off with seventeen men. Having heard the news that [he] was marching off, those who were in the towns went up mountains and those who were on mountains came down [from there]; thus they gathered and numbered seventy men. Due to the fact that Heaven granted strength, the soldiers of my father, the khagan, were like wolves, and his enemies were like sheep. Having gone on campaigns forward and backward, he gathered together and collected men; and they all numbered seven hundred men. After they had numbered seven hundred men, [my father, the khagan] organized and ordered the people who had lost their state and their khagan, the people who had turned slaves and servants, the people who had lost the Turkish institutions, in accordance with the rules of my ancestors" (Tariat Tekin, *A Grammar of Orkhon Turkic* [Bloomington, Ind., 1968], 265). In this model of the origin of a people, one sees a new creation brought about through military success: as a war leader is successful, he draws more and more followers to himself, and they become a band and then an army. This critical mass of warriors under a successful commander is converted into a people through the imposition of a legal system. Peoplehood is the end of a political process through which individuals with diverse backgrounds are united by law. So conceived, a people is constitutional, not biological, and yet the very imposition of law makes the opposite appeal: it is the law of the ancestors. The leader projects an antiquity and a genealogy onto this new creation.

In general, three models of barbarian ethnic formation can be discerned among the peoples who came into contact with the late Roman empire. The first and most closely studied is that which took its identity from a leading or royal family. Among the Goths, the Longobards, the Salian Franks, and other successful barbarian peoples, members of a successful family of warriors succeeded in attracting and controlling a following from disparate backgrounds that adhered to the traditions of the family. In such peoples, the legendary origins of the royal family became the legendary origins of the people that coalesced around this "kernel of tradition." These traditions traced the origin of the family or people to some distant, divine ancestor who led the people out of their original territory, won a significant victory over another people or peoples, and went on to find a place within the Roman world. The success of such peoples depended on the ability of their leading family to destroy alternative claimants to leadership and to find a way of grafting onto the fluid barbarian cultural and political tradition Roman institutions of law, polity, and organization. Thus, these barbarian peoples were dependent for their survival on the cooperation and recognition, however grudgingly accorded, of the emperors.

The second model of ethnogenesis drew on traditions of Central Asian steppe peoples for the charismatic leadership and organization necessary to create a people from a diverse following. The primary model for such an ethnic formation was the Huns of Attila, although the Alans, the Avars, and later the Magyars also were steppe empires. These polyethnic confederations were if anything even more inclusive than the first model, being able to draw together groups which maintained much of their traditional linguistic, cultural, and even political organization under the generalship of a small body of steppe commanders. The economic basis of these steppe confederations was semi-nomadic rather than sedentary. Territory and distance played little role in defining their boundaries, although elements of the confederation might practice traditional forms of agriculture and social organization quite different from those of the steppe leadership. Thus the Goths in the kingdom of Attila and the Bulgars in the kingdom of the Avars could not only maintain but even develop their own traditions while remaining firmly attached to the central organization of the empire. The survival of such confederations required constant military successes to an even greater extent than did the first model. A combination of terror and military victory held them together. The death of a leader or his defeat at the hands of another barbarian or Roman army could lead to the rapid disappearance of the mightiest of these empires. Reversals such as that of the Huns following the death of Attila, or of the Avars following Charlemagne's successful penetration of their kingdom in the late 700s, resulted in their rapid and total disappearance. At the same time, the disintegration of these vast steppe confederations generated new and transformed peoples. The Ostrogoths, Gepids, and Longobards emerged from the empire of Attila; and the Bulgars and other Slavic peoples emerged from the ruins of the Avar empire.

The last model, that of decentralized peoples such as the Alamanni, perhaps the Bavarians, and certainly the Slavs, is perhaps the most difficult to understand. In these configurations, whatever traditions may have informed the community were transmitted not by a central royal family but in a more communal form. It is impossible to know to what extent such peoples had any consciousness of communal identity at all. The Alamanni appear in Roman sources from the 3rd century, but no evidence of any collective legends, traditions, or genealogies has survived that would indicate the emergence of a common sense of identity among the Germanic peoples living on the upper Rhine. In the case of the Slavs, some have hypothesized that these peoples were the amalgamation of the Germanic-Sarmatian peasant populations left behind in those regions from which warrior bands and their leaders of the first type departed for the lure of the Roman empire. This may be so, but whenever the Slavs appear in sources, they do so not as peasants but as fierce warriors, loosely organized into short-lived bands. Centralized leadership was not the norm and often came in the form of outside elements, from nearby Germanic peoples such as the Franks, or from Iranian Croats, Turkic Bulgars, or Scandinavian Rus'.

Regardless of the form of ethnogenesis, it must be understood as a continuing process rather than a historical event. Ancient names could and did come to designate very different groups of people. Alternatively, certain groups underwent repeated, profound social, cultural, and political transformations such that they became essentially different peoples even while maintaining venerable names. The only way to understand the varieties of ethnogenesis, then, is to observe the historical transformations of the most significant of these groups across late antiquity.

By the 5th century, Romans and barbarians had learned a great deal about each other, much of it through painful contact and all of it filtered through their own modes of understanding the world. Romans viewed barbarians through the inherited categories of classical ethnography stretching back over four centuries, but also with the more pragmatic eyes of conquerors and adversaries whose faith in Roman superiority had been severely shaken in the last quarter of the 4th century. Barbarians viewed the Roman empire as the home of the great king, as a source of inexhaustible wealth, and frequently as a powerful but treacherous ally. Still, this empire was deemed as essential to the barbarians as it was alien to the Romans. The Visigothic ruler Athaulf was said to have contemplated replacing the empire with his own, but abandoned the idea as a chimera. Four hundred years later another barbarian ruler, Charlemagne, absorbed the empire into his person, having himself acclaimed emperor on Christmas Day, 800.

Romans of the 5th century contemplated the barbarians of their own day from the perspective of almost a millennium of interaction with the barbarian world. These centuries of Roman presence had profoundly influenced the peoples living along the frontiers. Roman policy dictated the creation of client buffer states that could protect the empire from contact with hostile barbarians further afield; provide trading partners for the supply of cattle, raw materials, and slaves; and, increasingly from the 4th century, fill the ranks of the military with mercenary troops. Thus the empire supported friendly chieftains, supplying them with weapons, gold, and grain in order to strengthen the pro-Roman factions within the barbarian world. The effect on not only the barbarians living along the *limes* but also those further away was considerable. Roman economic and political power destabilized the rough balance of power within the barbarian world by enabling pro-Roman chieftains to accumulate wealth and power far in excess of what had been possible previously. These chieftains also gained both military and political experience by serving in the Roman military system with their troops as federates. At the same time, fear of the Romans and their allies drove anti-Roman factions into large, unstable, but occasionally mighty confederations that could inflict considerable damage on Roman interests on both sides of the borders. This had happened in the time of Caesar among the Gauls and at the end of the 1st century among the Britons. In the late 2nd century a broad confederacy known as the Marcomanni tested and temporarily broke the Danubian frontier. In the aftermath of the Marcomannic wars, new barbarian peoples appeared along the Rhine-Danube frontiers in the course of the 3rd century. A loose confederation along the upper Rhine known as simply "the people" (Alamanni) appeared in the early 3rd century and a similar confederation on the lower Rhine, "the free" or "the fierce" (Franci), came to the attention of the Romans a generation later, as did a confederation of Germanic, Sarmatic, and even Roman warriors along the lower Danube under the generalship of the Goth Cniva. Behind these constellations on Rome's borders stood still other groups, such as Saxons beyond the Franks, Burgundians beyond the Alamanni, and Vandals beyond the Goths.

These confederations were in turn composed of small communities of farmers and herders living in villages along rivers, seacoasts, and clearings from the North and Baltic Seas to the Black Sea. Most members of the society were free men and women, organized in nuclear households governed by the husband or father. Status within the village depended on wealth, measured by the size of a family's cattle herd, and military prowess. Some wealthier individuals presided over households that included not only their wife or wives and children, but free dependents and slaves housed in outbuildings around the leader's home.

Households were in turn integrated into the larger kindred group known to scholars as the Sip (German: *Sippe*) or clan. This wider circle of kin included both agnatic and cognatic groups who shared a perception of common descent, reinforced by a special "peace" that made violent conflict within the clan a crime for which no compensation or atonement could be made, by an incest taboo, and possibly by some claims to inheritance. This wider kindred might also form the basis for mutual defense and for pursuit of feuds. However, membership in this larger circle was elastic. It provided the possibility but not the necessity of concerted action since individuals might select from a variety of possible broader kin affiliations depending on circumstances. The nuclear family, not the wider clan, was the primary unit of barbarian society.

Village life was directed by the assembly of free men under the leadership of a headman whose position may have come from a combination of factors including wealth, family influence, and connections with the leadership of the people beyond his village. Binding together this larger entity was a combination of religious, legal, and political traditions that imparted a strong if unstable sense of unity.

Members of a people shared ancestry myths, cultural traditions, a legal system, and leadership. However, all of these were flexible, multiple, and subject to negotiation and even dispute. Ancestry myths took the form of genealogies of heroic figures and their exploits. The founders of these genealogies were divine, and the chain of their descendants did not form a history in the Graeco-Roman sense of a structured narrative of events and their broader significance. Rather, these myths preserved an atemporal and apolitical account of individuals, woven together through ties of kinship and tales of revenge and blood feud, to which many individuals and families could claim ties. Other cultural traditions, too, such as dress, hairstyles, religious practices, weapons, and tactics provided strong bonds but also fluid and adaptable ways of creating unity or claiming difference. Legal traditions were an outgrowth of this religious and cultural identity. In the absence of strong central authority, disputes were regulated through family leaders, village assemblies, and war leaders. Control was exerted to preserve peace or at least to set the rules for feuds to take place in a manner least destructive of the community. Finally, these religious and cultural groups were organized under political leadership, a leadership that underwent profound transformation in the early centuries of contact with Rome.

When the Romans first came into contact with the Celtic and Germanic peoples, these populations were largely governed by hereditary, sacral kings, who embodied the identity of their people by their sacred ancestry. This traditional type of king, termed *Thiudan* (from *thiuda*, "people" in east Germanic languages such as Gothic) or in Celtic languages *rhix*, continued among peoples far from the Roman *limes* in portions of the British Isles, in Scandinavia, and in the Elbe region. In the course of the 1st and 2nd centuries, those living in proximity to the Romans had largely abandoned their archaic sacral kings in favor of warrior leaders who might be selected from old royal families or, as frequently, from successful aristocratic fighters. This change favored the empire, since Rome could more easily influence new leaders emerging from oligarchic factions than heirs of ancient religious authority. These leaders were raised up by their heterogeneous armies and formed the centers around which new traditions of political and religious identity could develop and onto which, in some cases, older notions of sacro-social identity could be grafted. The legitimacy of these leaders (termed *duces, reges, regales* by different Roman sources; *kuning,* that is, leader of the family, in west Germanic languages; or in Gothic *reiks,* borrowed from the Celtic *rhix*) derived ultimately from their ability to lead their armies to victory. A victorious campaign confirmed their right to rule and drew to them an ever growing number of people who accepted and shared in their identity. Thus a charismatic leader could found a new people. In time, the leader and his descendants might identify themselves with an older tradition and claim divine sanction, proven by their fortunes in war, to embody and continue some ancient people. The constitutional integrity of these peoples then was dependent on warfare and conquest—they were armies, although their economies remained dependent on raiding and a combination of animal husbandry and slash-and-burn agriculture. Defeat, at the hand of either the Romans or other barbarians, could mean the end not only of a ruler but of a people, who might be absorbed into another, victorious confederation.

At any given time, therefore, within these broad confederations, a variety of individuals might claim some sort of kingship over portions of the people. The Alamannic confederation that fought the emperor Julian in 357, for example, was led by an uncle and nephew termed "the most outstanding in power before the other kings," five kings of second rank, ten *regales,* and a series of magnates. Although Roman sources termed all of these leaders "Alamanni," they also observed that the Alamanni were composed of such groups as the Bucinobantes, Lentienses, and Juthungi under the leadership of their own kings. These subgroups could be termed *gentes,* implying a social and political constitution, or *pagi,* suggesting that organization was at least in part territorial; or, as in the cases of the Lentienses, both. Similarly the early Franks were composed of groups such as the Chamavi, Chattuarii, Bructeri, and Amsivari, and had numerous *regales* and *duces* who commanded portions of the collectivity and disputed among themselves for primacy. In the late 4th century, for example, the Frankish war leader Arbogast, although in Roman service, used his Roman position to pursue his feud with the Frankish *regales* Marcomer and Sunno in trans-Rhenian territory. Further to the east, the Gothic confederation with its military kingship splintered under Roman pressure. The most eastern portions of the Goths in modern Ukraine accepted the authority of the Amals, a royal family of the new type that nevertheless claimed ancient and divine legitimacy, while among the western Gothic groups numerous *reiks* shared and disputed an oligarchic control.

Warfare, whether large-scale attacks led by the *reiks* or *kuning* or small-scale cattle raids carried out by a few adventurous youths, was central to barbarian life. Warfare within the family was forbidden; within the people it was controlled by the conventions of the feud; but between peoples it was the normal state of affairs. Raiding was a normal way of acquiring wealth and prestige as well as of reestablishing the balance of honor within the community. Successful war leaders gathered around themselves elite groups of young warriors who devoted themselves to their commander in return for arms, protection, and a share of booty. These bands of retainers formed powerful military units that could be invaluable in war, but also, in tendency to fight each other and dispute over spoils, dangerous sources of instability. The following of a successful war leader could grow enormously, as young warriors from surrounding villages and even other peoples joined. In time the warrior band and its dependents could splinter off to create a new people.

For the most part, warfare was directed against neighboring barbarians, and raids and plundering maintained a relative equilibrium within the barbarian world. However, the presence of Roman merchants within this world and of the riches of the empire on its frontiers proved irresistible to barbarian leaders who needed to win glory in battle and to acquire iron, horses, slaves, and gold for their following. For as long as it existed, the empire could serve this purpose in one of two ways, either as the employer of barbarian military bands or as the victim of these same bands.

Until the last quarter of the 4th century, barbarians had found direct assaults on imperial armies less effective than service to them. Barbarian military successes against the empire tended to result from Roman disputes and weaknesses. Barbarian armies were never a match for a competent emperor at the head of his army. Sporadic raiding across the frontier, often carried out by isolated warrior bands, brought severe reprisals, at times through punitive expeditions into the barbarian world accompanied by thorough devastation in the Roman tradition. Large-scale raiding was possible only when the Roman frontier garrisons were withdrawn or weakened by urgent needs elsewhere in the empire. In the 250s, during the darkest hours of the 3rd century crisis for example, the Gothic King Cniva led his mixed confederation into the province of Dacia while Gothic pirates attacked the Black Sea coast from the mouth of the Danube. When legions from along the Rhine were shifted east to deal with internal and external problems, barbarians took the opportunity to raid across the poorly defended frontier. Alamannic bands overran the Roman trans-Rhenian Decumatian territories and Frankish armies advanced deep into Gaul and even Spain. The actual identities of the peoples involved in these raids is difficult to ascertain. Often Roman sources speak of the barbarian inhabitants along the Rhine as simply "Germani." At other times, they tend to identify those on the upper Rhine as Alamanni, those on the lower as Franci, although the extent to which the raiders would have recognized such labels themselves is impossible to determine. Moreover, Romans were aware that other groups such as Burgundians and Vandals and Saxons participated in these raids as well.

However, although neither Dacia nor Decumania was entirely retaken by the empire, Emperor Gallienus (253–268) and his successors decisively defeated the Franks and the Alamanni, and Emperor Aurelian (270–275) crushed Goths in a series of campaigns that splintered their confederation. Raiding continued sporadically, but the frontiers were essentially secure for another century.

For some barbarian armies, defeat meant the destruction of their identity as a cohesive social unit. The devastation caused by barbarian raids into the empire paled in comparison with the wasting and slaughter meted out by Roman armies engaged in expeditions across the Rhine or Danube. A panegyric of the year 310 describes the treatment to which Constantine subjected the Bructeri after a punitive expedition he led against them: the barbarians were trapped in an area of impenetrable forest and swamp, where many were killed, their cattle confiscated, their villages burned, and all of the adults thrown to the beasts in the arena. The children were presumably sold into slavery. In other cases, surviving warriors were forced into the Roman army. These *dediticii* or *laeti,* following a ritual surrender in which they gave up their weapons and threw themselves on the mercy of their Roman conquerors, were spread throughout the empire in small units or settled in depopulated areas to provide military service and restore regions devastated by barbarian attacks and taxpayer flight. One such unit of Franks sent to the shores of the Black Sea managed a heroic escape, commandeering a ship and making their way across the Mediterranean, through the Straits of Gibraltar and ultimately home, but most served out their days in the melting pot of the Roman army.

Defeat also meant major changes for barbarian peoples on the frontiers of the empire not forced into service or sold into slavery. Deprived of the possibility of supporting their political and economic systems through raiding, the defeated barbarian military kings found an alternative in service to the Roman empire. After defeating a Vandal army in 270 Emperor Aurelian concluded a treaty with them as federates of the empire. Similar treaties with Franks and Goths followed before the end of the century. *Foederati* obligated themselves to respect the empire's frontiers, to provide troops to the imperial army, and in some cases to make additional payments in cattle or goods. Barbarian leaders favorable to Rome found that they could reach previously unimaginable heights of power and influence by fighting not against the empire, but for it.

In the course of the 4th century, internal conflict and pressure on the Persian frontier as well as a desire to minimize imperial expenses led to the progressive incorporation of these barbarian leaders and their followings into the Roman military system. Constantine I led the way, not only designating Frankish military units as auxiliary units of the imperial army but also promoting barbarians such as the Frank Bonitus to high military office. Bonitus was the first of a long series of Franks in Roman service. In 355 his son, the thoroughly Romanized Silvanus who was commander of the Roman garrison at Cologne, was proclaimed emperor by his troops. Although Silvanus was quickly assassinated by envoys of Emperor Constantius, subsequent barbarian commanders such as Malarich, Teutomeres, Mallobaudes, Laniogaisus, and Arbogast avoided usurpation but exercised enormous power within the western empire. Ultimately one of these Frankish Roman commanders, Clovis, would eliminate the remnants of the Roman state in Gaul and receive imperial recognition.

For the most part, these Roman generals maintained close ties with the members of their peoples outside the empire. Shortly after Silvanus's assassination, Franks sacked Cologne, possibly in revenge for his murder. Mallobaudes, who participated in Gratian's victory over the Alamanni in 378, was simultaneously termed *comes domesticorum* and *rex Francorum* by the Roman historian Ammianus Marcellinus. Others such as Arbogast used their position within the empire to attack their enemies across the Rhine. Still, their situation was extremely precarious both within the empire and without. Frequently they were the objects of suspicion to their Roman competitors, even though they generally were no less reliable than Romans in high command. At the same time, as Roman officials and as adherents of Roman religion, whether Christian or pagan, they were always targets for anti-Roman factions at home. Assumption of high Roman command generally meant forgoing the possibility of retaining a position at the head of a barbarian people outside of the empire.

Around the Black Sea, the Gothic confederation experienced a similarly ambiguous relationship with the eastern portions of the empire. By the 4th century the more eastern Gothic peoples, the Greuthungs or steppe peoples, had absorbed characteristics of the Scyths. In the western regions, the Tervingi or forest people had come under the greatest direct influence of Rome. Both were sedentary agrarian societies, although in the former the military elite was composed primarily of infantry while in the latter horsemen in the tradition of the ancient Scyths formed the core of the army. In the 4th century, the Tervingian Goths had expanded their lordship over a wide spectrum of peoples with different linguistic, cultic, and cultural traditions.

Settled in agricultural villages and governed by local assemblies of free men, the population of this Gothic confederation was nevertheless subject to the central authority of the oligarchic authority of Gothic military leaders under the authority of a nonroyal judge. In 332 Constantine and the Tervingian judge Ariaric concluded a treaty or *foedus*. Ariaric's son Aoric was raised in Constantinople and the emperor even raised a statue in the city in honor of the judge. Under Ariaric, Aoric, and his son Athanaric, these western Goths became progressively integrated into the Roman imperial system, providing auxiliary troops to the eastern region of the empire. One effect of this closer relationship with the empire was their implication in internal imperial politics. In 365 the usurper Procopius convinced the Tervingians to support him as the representative of the Constantinian dynasty in his opposition to Emperor Valens. After Procopius's execution, Valens launched a brutal punitive attack across the Danube that ended only in 369 with a treaty between Athanaric and the emperor.

Religion was a binding force in the Gothic confederation, but the heterogeneous constitution of the confederation created difficulties in maintaining this religious unity. Christians, large numbers of whom were incorporated into the Gothic world from the Crimea during the time of Cniva, and others who were carried off in trans-Danubian raids, proved the most difficult religious minority to assimilate, both because of the strong exclusivity of their monotheistic faith and because of the importance of Christianity in the political strategies of the Roman empire. Gothic Christians represented the spectrum of Christian beliefs, from orthodox Crimean Goths to the Audian sect that confessed the corporeality of God among the Tervingi, to various Arian or semi-Arian communities in the Gothic Balkans. The most influential Gothic Christian was Ulfila (whose Gothic name means "little wolf"), a third-generation Goth of relatively high social standing whose Christian ancestors had been captured in a raid on Cappadocia sometime in the 260s. In the 330s Ulfila came to Constantinople as part of a delegation, resided in the empire for some time, and in 341 was consecrated "bishop of the Christians in the Getic land" at the council of Antioch and sent to the Balkan Goths. Ulfila's consecration and his mission to the Goths and other peoples in the Gothic confederation were part of an imperial Gothic program, which may have precipitated the first persecution of Gothic Christians in 348 under Aoric and a second beginning in 369 under Athanaric. During the first persecution Ulfila and his followers were exiled to Roman Moesia, where he preached in Gothic, Latin, and Greek to his heterogeneous flock, wrote theological treatises, and translated the Bible into Gothic. Ulfila and his followers attempted to steer a middle course between the Catholic and Arian positions on the nature of the divine persons, a position that inevitably resulted in being labeled Arian by future generations of orthodox believers. In the short run, however, Athanaric's persecution was as ineffective as had been earlier persecutions of Christians by Rome. He succeeded only in badly dividing the Gothic peoples, creating an opportunity seized by the Gothic aristocrat Fritigern, who contacted the Roman emperor Valens and agreed to become an Arian Christian in return for support against Athanaric.

These political and religious tensions between and within the Roman and Gothic worlds were rendered suddenly beside the point by the arrival of the Huns, a steppe nomadic confederation under Central Asian leadership, in the area of the Black Sea in 375. These nomadic riders were like no people seen before by Romans or barbarians: everything from their physical appearance to their pastoral lifestyle to their mode of warfare was foreign and terrible to the old world. The Huns were never, except for the short period of the reign of Attila (444–453), a united, centralized people. Rather, the Huns, commonly referred to as Scyths by Roman sources, were disparate groups of warrior bands sharing a common nomadic culture, a military tradition of mounted raiding, and an extraordinary ability to absorb the peoples they conquered into their confederations. Their startling military success was due to their superb cavalry tactics, their proficiency with short double-reflex bows that allowed them to launch a volley of arrows with deadly accuracy while riding, and their tactical knowledge of the steppes and plains of western Asia and Central Europe that allowed them to appear without warning, inflict tremendous damage, and disappear into the grasslands as quickly as they had come.

Within a generation, these nomadic warrior bands destroyed first the Alans and the Greuthung kingdom and then the Tervingian confederation. With the destruction of the authority of Gothic leadership, constituent groups of the old Gothic confederations had to decide whether to join the Hunnic bands or to petition the emperor to enter and settle in the Roman empire.

The semi-nomadic confederation known as the Huns provided a model for the enormous but fragile steppe confederations such as that of the later Avars. They easily absorbed a vast spectrum of other peoples and profited from their position between the eastern and western halves of the empire, but vanished when their leaders were no longer able to lead them to victories over their victims.

For most of the Goths defeated by the Huns, entering the confederation was an obvious choice. Although a Hunnic core of Central Asians provided central leadership to the Hunnic armies, the peoples they conquered were assimilated with ease. Good warriors, whether of Gothic, Vandal, Frankish, or even Roman origins, could rise rapidly within the Hunnic hierarchy. Even among the central leadership, this polyethnicity was obvious. The Hunnic leader Edika was simultaneously a Hun and a Scirian, and ruled the short-lived Scirian kingdom as king. The greatest of the Hunnic leaders, Attila, bore a Gothic name (or title): Attila means "little father." Gothic, Greek, and Latin were used alongside Hunnic in his court, and among his advisers were not only leaders of various barbarian peoples but even former Greek merchants. For a time the Italian aristocrat Orestes, father of the last Roman emperor in the west, Romulus Augustulus, served the Hunnic king.

To maintain the unity of this heterogeneous Hunnic confederation, its chieftains needed a constant flow of treasure, the principal source of which was the empire. Initially, raids on the Illyrian and Thracian borders of the empire provided the bulk of the booty, supplemented by annual subsidies from the emperors to prevent further incursions; thus the ability to conduct successful military operations was essential for the survival of Hunnic leaders. During the first decades of the Hunnic confederation leadership was shared by members of a royal family, but in 544 Attila eliminated his brother Bleda after Hunnic successes began to abate and unified the Huns under his command. Under Attila annual subsidies from the emperor increased from 350 pounds of gold to 700, and eventually to 2,100, an enormous amount to the barbarians but not a devastating burden on the empire. Theodosius found it easier to pay than to defend against Hunnic raids. In addition to gold, Attila demanded that the empire cease harboring Hunnic refugees and return those who had fled his authority. Those who were returned were impaled or crucified.

After the death of Theodosius in 450, his successor Marcian refused to continue preferential treatment of the Huns. With this source of funding gone, Attila apparently considered himself too weak to extract adequate booty by raiding the eastern empire and turned his attention to the western empire of Valentinian III. He led his armies west in two long raids. The first in 451 reached far into Gaul before being stopped at the battle of the Catalaunian Plains between Troyes and Châlons-sur-Marne. There Attila's army, probably composed primarily of subject Germanic peoples from the western areas of his control—Suebi, Franks, and Burgundians in addition to Gepids, Ostrogoths, and Central Asian Huns—was stopped by an equally heterogeneous army of Goths, Franks, Bretons, Sarmatians, Burgundians, Saxons, Alans, and Romans under the command of the patrician Aetius. The second raid came the following year, when Attila led another army into Italy. Again, in keeping with Hunnic priorities the expedition was primarily undertaken for pillage, not for lasting political objectives, and ended at the gates of Rome when Pope Leo I paid off the Huns, who, weakened by disease and far from their accustomed terrain, were probably all too ready to return to the steppe.

The essential fragility of an empire such as Attila's was demonstrated by its rapid disintegration following his death. Steppe empires built on victory could not endure defeat. A separatist coalition under the leadership of the Gepid Ardaric revolted against Attila's sons. The rebels were victorious and the defeat of Attila's sons led to the splintering of the old confederation and new processes of ethnogenesis. In addition to the Gepid alliance emerged the Rugii, the Sciri, and the Sarmatians along the Danube, and the Ostrogoths, who gathered the remnants of the Greuthungs and entered Roman service as *foederati*. Some of Attila's sons continued to lead splinter groups, some apparently returning to Central Asia, others entering Roman service within the Roman military aristocracy. Within a few generations, they and their followers had become Ostrogoths, Gepids, or Bulgars.

A different fate met those barbarians who fled the Hunnic onslaught in 375. While the majority of the Greuthungs and Alans were absorbed into the new Hunnic confederation, a minority, augmented by deserting Huns, fled toward the *limes*. So too did most of the Tervingi, who abandoned Athanaric's leadership and fled with Fritigern across the Danube. The flight of the Tervingi into the empire set in motion a decisive transformation in the identity of this people. From the Roman perspective, they were but one more barbarian group of *dediticii*, received into the empire and allowed to settle in Thrace, where they were expected to support themselves through agriculture while supplying troops to the military. The reality was that in quality and quantity, the Tervingian refugees' situation was very different from that of earlier *dediticii*. First, these Goths were far more numerous than earlier barbarian bands allowed into the empire, and they overwhelmed the Roman administrative abilities. Second, the Romans did not force them to surrender their arms as was the usual practice. When Roman mistreatment and Gothic hunger pushed the refugees to armed resistance, the result was a series of Gothic victories. Soon the refugee cavalry of the Greuthungs, Alans, and Huns joined the Tervingi, as did Gothic units already in the Roman army, Thracian miners, barbarian slaves, and the poor. The Gothic victories culminated in 378 with the annihilation of the imperial army and the death of Valens at Adrianople.

After Adrianople, Rome could no longer treat the Goths as *dediticii.* In a treaty concluded in 382, the Goths were recognized as a federated people but were allowed to settle between the Danube and the Balkan mountains with their own governors, creating in effect a state within a state. Tax revenues traditionally collected for the support of the military were redirected to the support of the barbarians. In return they were required to provide military support to the empire, but they did so under their own commanders, who were subordinated to Roman generals.

At the same time, the unprecedented success of the Tervingians and their allies led to a fundamental transformation of this disparate band of refugees into the Visigoths, a new people with a new cultural and political identity. The Visigoths quickly adapted the mounted tactics used so effectively by the Greuthungs, Alans, and Huns in the campaigns against Valens, in effect transforming themselves into a highly mobile cavalry on the Scythian model. For the next generation the Visigoths struggled to maintain themselves as a Gothic confederation and simultaneously as a Roman army. Their king Alaric, a member of the royal clan of the Balths, sought recognition and payments at once as ruler of a federated people and as a high-ranking general, or *magister militum,* in imperial service with de facto command of the civilian and military bureaucracies in the regions under his authority. He pursued both of these goals through alternate service to and expeditions against the eastern and western emperors and their imperial barbarian commanders.

Alaric's insistence on his dual role stood in contrast to an older model of imperial barbarian embodied by Stilicho, the supreme military commander in the west and intermittently Alaric's commander, ally, and bitter enemy. Stilicho was of Vandal birth, but he, like pagan Frankish and Alamannic Roman commanders before him, had entirely abandoned his ethnic barbarian ties. He was a Roman citizen, an orthodox Catholic, and operated entirely within the Roman tradition, alternately serving and manipulating both the imperial family (as guardian and later father-in-law of the emperor Honorius) and barbarian federates such as Alaric. Stilicho's path proved fatal when he was unable to maintain the integrity of the Rhone and Danube *limes.* On the last day of the year 406, bands of Vandals, Suebi, and Alans crossed the upper Rhine to ravage Gaul and penetrate as far as Spain unhindered. Around the same time, Gothic bands fleeing the Huns invaded Italy from Pannonia. In spite of Stilicho's ultimate success in defeating the Gothic invaders, these twin disasters played into his enemies' hands. In 408 he was deposed and executed on orders of his son-in-law. Following his death, thousands of other assimilated barbarians living in Italy were likewise slaughtered.

Surviving barbarians in Italy rallied to Alaric, whose dual role as barbarian king and Roman commander offered a more durable model. His efforts to win recognition and payments to support his followers led to his invasion of Italy in 408. Botched negotiations led, after numerous feints, to the capture and pillage of Rome on August 24–26, 410. Although his subsequent attempt to lead his people to the fertile lands of Africa failed and he died in southern Italy, Alaric had established an enduring form of barbarian-Roman polity.

Alaric's successor and brother-in-law Athaulf led the Goths out of Italy and into Gaul. At Narbonne in the year 414 he married Galla Placidia, sister of the emperor Honorius captured in Rome, in the hope of entering the imperial family of Theodosius. The chimera of political advantage through marriage into the imperial family would recur over the next century, with Attila's claims to Honoria, the sister of Valentinian III, and with the marriage between the Vandal pretender Huneric and his hostage Eudocia, Valentinian's daughter. None of these attempts accomplished either peace or parity with the Roman empire.

Athaulf fell to an assassin and after futile attempts first to reenter Italy and then to reach North Africa, his successors accepted a new *foedus* with the mandate to clear Spain of rebel Bagaudae as well as of Vandals and Alans. Following their return to Toulouse in 418, the Visigoths began the form of political and social organization that would characterize their kingdom and those of other federated barbarians, notably the Burgundians and the Ostrogoths.

The barbarians, whatever their ethnic origins, formed a small but powerful military minority within a much larger Roman population. As mounted warriors, they tended to settle in strategic border areas of their territories or in the political capitols. Support of these barbarian armies was provided by the assignment of a portion of traditional tax revenues that had gone to the imperial fisc, thus minimizing the burden of the barbarian occupation on the land-owning Roman aristocracy and keeping these professional warriors free for military service. Collection and distribution of these taxes remained in the hands of the municipal *curiales,* likewise minimizing the effects on the landowning aristocracy that monopolized these offices. At least this seems to have been the arrangement with the Visigoths in 418, the Burgundians in 443, and the Ostrogoths in Italy during the 490s. In some other cases, such as that of a group of Alans settled around Valence in 440, the barbarians were assigned tax debts no longer being collected by imperial officials. Through these tax shares, barbarian kings were able to provide for their followers and keep them from dispersing into the countryside in order to supervise their estates. In the tradition of Alaric, barbarian kings were not only commanders of their people but simultaneously high-ranking Roman officials (*magister militum, patricius,* and so forth), who exercised supreme authority over the civilian administrative system in their territory, effectively governing the two elements of the Roman state that had been separate since the time of Diocletian.

The territorialization of barbarian armies within these terms set into motion a further ethnogenesis. Barbarian kings began the attempt to transform the culturally disparate members of their armies into a unified people with a common law and sense of identity while maintaining their distance from the majority Roman population of their kingdoms. This identity was drawn from vague family traditions reinterpreted and transformed by the new situations in which they found themselves. For the Visigoths, the Balth family provided the center of this tradition. For the Vandals, it was the Hasdings; for the Ostrogoths, the Amals. These royal families projected their imagined past onto the people as a whole, providing a common sense of origin to be shared by the whole of the military elite.

To a lesser extent, barbarian kings likewise used religion to found a common identity. The Gothic royal family, like those of the Vandals, Burgundians, and other peoples, were Arian, and the Arian faith became closely identified with the king and his people. Arianism was neither a proselytizing faith nor a persecuting one. At the most, Arians demanded the use of one or more churches for their worship. Otherwise, orthodox Christianity was not proscribed or persecuted. The exception appears to have been the Vandal kingdom of North Africa, but even here the persecutions and confiscations directed against the orthodox church seemed to have had more to do with confiscation of land and repression of political opponents than doctrinal differences.

Barbarian kings also relied on legal tradition to forge a new identity for their peoples. Nothing is known about barbarian law codes before the Visigothic Code of Euric, which dates from ca. 470–480. Although in general barbarian law codes appear to stand in sharp distinction to Roman law, with their system of tariffs for offenses (Wergeld), the use of oaths, and formal oral procedure, such traditions may not have been much different from local vulgar legal practice in large areas of the west by the 5th century. The laws sought to delineate rights and responsibilities of barbarians and Romans and seem to have been territorial laws, intended to be applied to barbarians and Romans alike, although not to the exclusion of other Roman legal traditions alive in the territories granted to the barbarian armies.

Royal efforts to forge new and enduring ethnic and political identities within these dual kingdoms met with indifferent success. The distinction between the barbarian military and political minority on the one hand and the Roman population on the other remained most sharp in Vandal Africa. The Vandals, unlike most of the other barbarian peoples to create kingdoms within the empire, had done so without benefit of a treaty with the empire and had proceeded to confiscation of property on a wide scale. These confiscations won for them the enduring hatred of aristocratic landowners as well as that of the African orthodox church that had learned political activism during decades of opposition to Donatists. Many of the landowning aristocracy fled or were exiled, as were the Catholic bishops, who returned only in the 520s. Vandal kings eventually won imperial recognition, but even then their rule remained tenuous. Hated and isolated from the rest of the population, the Vandals were easy prey for Justinian's army in 533. Two decisive battles broke the kingdom and the remaining Vandals were deported and dissolved into various federated barbarian armies in the eastern Mediterranean. Within less than a decade, the Vandals had entirely disappeared.

The Ostrogothic kingdom in Italy established by Theoderic the Great in the 490s began with greater prospects but likewise fell to Byzantine reconquest. The Ostrogoths emerged from the ruins of the Hunnic empire as one of the Germanic factions alternatively allying with and fighting against the eastern empire. In 484 Theoderic, who claimed descent from the pre-Hunnic royal Amal family, united a number of these groups under his command and four years later led a polyethnic army into Italy on behalf of the emperor Zeno against Odoacer, a barbarian commander in the tradition of Stilicho who had made himself master of Italy. In 493 Theoderic gained control of the peninsula, eliminated Odoacer, and took over the Roman fiscal and administrative system.

Theoderic sought to transform his heterogeneous, mobile barbarian army into a stable, settled, Gothic people capable of peaceful coexistence within Roman Italy. His goal for his Gothic following was to convince them to adopt *civilitas,* the Roman principles of the rule of law and the traditions of tolerance and consensus in civic society which they were to protect by their military valor. Nevertheless, he intended to maintain Goths and Romans as separate communities, one military, one civilian, living in mutual dependence under his supreme authority. Thus, although Theoderic received the loyal support of Roman administrators and even of the close advisers of Odoacer such as the senator Cassiodorus, like other barbarian kings he sought to strengthen the Gothic element of his rule by appointing his personal agents or *comites* to supervise and intervene throughout the Roman bureaucracy. He likewise privileged the Arian church as the *ecclesia legis Gothorum,* but he saw to it that it remained a minority church which he prohibited from proselytizing among the orthodox majority.

Theoderic's attempt to bring about a new Gothic ethnogenesis failed. The boundaries between Ostrogothic warrior and Roman civilian blurred as many barbarians became landowners sharing the same economic and regional concerns as their Roman neighbors. Their children, educated in the traditions of the Roman elite, grew even further apart from the warrior culture. At the same time, some Romans rose in the ranks of the military and adopted Gothic tradition, even to the extent of learning the Gothic language and marrying Gothic women. In reaction to this loss of Gothic distinctiveness, an anti-Roman reaction set in among a portion of the military concerned about the rapid Romanization of many in their ranks. Tensions mounted following Theoderic's death and culminated in the murder of his daughter Amalasuntha in 535. Justinian took the murder as an excuse to refuse to recognize the legitimacy of the Gothic king Theodehad, Theoderic's nephew, and to invade Italy. Unlike the reconquest of Africa, however, which was accomplished in two battles, the war lasted almost two decades and devastated Italy more profoundly than had all of the barbarian invasions of the previous two centuries. The final result was, however, just as in North Africa: the total disappearance of the Ostrogoths.

In Gaul, the Gothic kingdom of Toulouse and the Burgundian kingdom met similar fates. Both continued to serve as federates, participating for example in the defeat of the Huns in the battle of the Catalaunian Plains. They likewise profited from imperial weakness by expanding their territories. The Goths eventually extended their control north to the Loire and south through Spain, while the Burgundians expanded east until being driven back by the Gepids. Still, the Visigoths remained a small Arian minority and disappeared north of the Pyrenees after a single defeat at the hands of the Franks in 507. Their survival in Spain was due to the intervention of Theoderic, who assisted them in maintaining their independence in Spain. Thereafter they retreated into Spain, where they abandoned their Arianism and thus their separate gentile identity only in 587. The Burgundians rapidly lost any cultural, religious, or genealogical identity they may have had, and by the 6th century "Burgundian" seems to have designated little more than the holder of what had originally been the military allotments first divided among the barbarians.

The type of barbarian polity pioneered by the Visigoths and largely adopted by the Vandals and Ostrogoths—the creation and maintenance of two communities, one orthodox, Roman, and civilian, the other Arian, barbarian, and military, under the unified command of a barbarian king holding an imperial commission—ended in failure. More enduring were the unitary kingdoms created by the Frankish king Clovis as well as by the petty kings of Britain. The reasons for these successes are several. In part, their distance from the core of the Byzantine world meant that by the early 5th century these regions were already considered expendable by the empire, and in the 6th century they lay beyond the reach of Justinian. In part, too, the transformation of Roman civil administration may have been sufficiently advanced that little remained for barbarian kings to absorb: in the case of the Franks, this was only the individual *civitates*; in the case of the Saxons, not even that. Finally, the barbarians themselves were different. Although the Franks and the Saxons initially served as federates of the empire, they had no direct experience of the Mediterranean world of Constantinople or even Italy. They, like the provincial Romans they absorbed, were far removed from the cultural and administrative traditions of a Theoderic or a Cassiodorus. The result was a simpler but in the long run more thorough transformation of these peoples into new social and cultural forms.

In the early 5th century Britain and northern Gaul, long peripheral to the concerns of Ravenna and Constantinople, were forced to look to their own protection and organization. In both areas, old Celtic regional affinities began to take precedence over more recent Roman organization, and new political constellations of Roman, Celtic, and Germanic elements emerged. In Britain, the Roman centralized government ceded to a plethora of small, mutually hostile kingdoms. During the later 5th and 6th centuries, Germanic federates drawn from the Saxons, Frisians, Franks, and other coastal peoples came to dominate many of these kingdoms, particularly in the southwest. Although migration from the coastal regions of the continent was significant, particularly in the 6th century, the frequent appearance of Celtic names in the genealogies of early Anglo-Saxon kingdoms as well as the survival of Christian communities within these kingdoms indicates that the Anglo-Saxon ethnogenesis was the gradual fusion of indigenous populations and new arrivals under the political leadership of families that in time came to regard themselves as descended from mythical Germanic heroes. Indeed most Anglo-Saxon royal genealogies traced their ancestry back to the war god Woden.

Frankish society was the result of a similar fusion that took place in the northern portions of Gaul, those most removed from Mediterranean concern. In the course of the 5th century, a series of rival kingdoms emerged from the ruins of Roman provincial administration, each headed by a warlord or king. Some of these leaders were Frankish kings who commanded largely barbarian units and had ties on both sides of the Rhine. Others were members of the Gallo-Roman aristocracy and drew support from mixed Roman provincial and barbarian armies. Among the former were members of the Merovingian family, who commanded barbarian troops descended from Salian Franks probably settled within the empire in the late 4th century. Ethnic affiliation was much less significant in these constellations than political expediency: the Frankish followers of the Merovingian Childeric, who had grown wealthy and powerful in the service of the empire, temporarily transferred their allegiance to the *magister militum* Aegidius.

Beginning in 486 Childeric's son Clovis expanded his power south and east from his father's kingdom centered around Tournai. He captured Soissons, the administrative center of Belgica Secunda, temporarily dominated the Thuringians, and defeated the Alamanni between 496 and 506. In 507 he defeated and killed the Visigothic king Alaric II and began conquering the Visigothic kingdom north of the Pyrenees. None of his conquests appears to have been based on a commission or treaty with Constantinople, but following his victory over Alaric emissaries of Emperor Anastasius granted him some form of imperial recognition, probably an honorary consulship. He spent his final years, until his death around 511, eliminating other Frankish kings and rival members of his own family who ruled kingdoms in Cologne, Cambrai, and elsewhere.

Ethnogenesis proceeded differently in Clovis's Frankish kingdom from that in Ostrogothic Italy or Visigothic Aquitaine. He did not base his conquests on an imperial mandate nor did he attempt to create the sort of dual society erected by an earlier generation of barbarian kings. Salian Franks had been deeply involved in imperial and regional political struggles in Gaul for generations. Clovis's authority had been recognized by representatives of the Gallo-Roman aristocracy such as Bishop Remigius of Rheims since the death of his father in 486. His absorption of rival power centers caused much less dramatic change than had the conquests of earlier barbarian kings. He certainly took over the remnants of civil administration, but these probably were already in serious decay and in any case did not extend above the level of individual *civitates*.

Moreover, there is little evidence that the Franks had or attempted to create as strong a sense of identity distinct from the Roman population as had Theoderic or other Gothic commanders. Clovis's family apparently claimed some semi-divine descent and counted a minotaur-like beast among its ancestors, but no Frankish genealogical lore could rival the generations of heroes and gods in Gothic tradition. Already in the 6th century Franks may have claimed Trojan ancestry, thus connecting themselves genealogically to their Roman neighbors. Nor were the Franks long separated from their Gallo-Roman neighbors by religion. Prior to the 6th century some Franks had been Christian, whether Arian or orthodox, while others, including Clovis's family, had retained a pagan religious tradition. Clovis probably flirted with the Arianism of his great neighbor Theoderic, but ultimately accepted orthodox baptism, although when in his career this took place remains open to debate.

United by a common religion and a common legend of origin, Clovis's Franks and the Roman provincials of his kingdom found no obstacles to forging a common identity. This they did with considerable rapidity. Within only a few generations, the population north of the Loire had become uniformly Frankish and, although Roman legal traditions persisted in the south and Burgundian and Roman legal status endured in the old Burgundian kingdom conquered by Clovis's sons in the 530s, these differing legal traditions did not constitute the basis for a separate social or political identity. The great strength of the Frankish synthesis was the new creation, within the Roman world, of a unified society that drew without a sense of contradiction on both Roman and barbarian traditions.

As Frankish, Longobard, Anglo-Saxon, and Visigothic kingdoms assimilated surviving Roman political and cultural traditions, they became the center of post-Roman Europe, while new barbarian peoples, most notably the Saxons, Slavs, and Avars, replaced them on the periphery. Ethnic labels remained significant designations within the Romano-barbarian kingdoms, but they designated multiple and at times even contradictory aspects of social and political identity.

In Italy, the Longobards, a heterogeneous amalgam including Gepids, Herulians, Suebs, Alamans, Bulgarians, Saxons, Goths, and Romans who had arrived in Italy in 568 from Pannonia created a weak, decentralized union of rival military units of duchies. The duchies combined traditional military units or *farae* with the Gothic-Roman military and administrative tradition. Religious as well as political divisions ran deep in Longobard Italy: in the 6th century "Longobards" included pagans, Arians, schismatic Christians, and orthodox Christians. Some dukes allied themselves with the Byzantine exarch of Ravenna while others, particularly in the south, remained fiercely autonomous.

In the last decades of the 6th century, however, the constant challenges that the ambitious Longobard armies posed to the Byzantines to the east and the Franks to the west led these two powers to coordinate their attacks on the Longobards. Threatened with annihilation between these two foes, the Longobard dukes restored the monarchy that they had abandoned shortly after their arrival in Italy. This kingship owed much to Gothic precedence, especially in the use of the name Flavius, which sought to connect the new Longobard identity with the imperial Flavian name and tradition, as a claim to universal recognition on the part of all inhabitants of the kingdom. Still, Longobard identity and organization remained porous. The great duchies of Beneventum and Spoleto remained essentially independent of the king throughout the entire history of the Longobard kingdom.

In the course of the 7th century, the Longobard kings solidified their position both externally and internally. They formed marriage alliances with Franks and especially the Bavarians, whose own Agilolfing dukes were closely related to Longobard kings. They strengthened the Arian party within the Longobard kingdom while maintaining a balance between orthodox and "Three Chapter" Christians, a tripartite Christian tradition that ended only around 700. Most important, beginning with Rothari (636–652) Longobard kings published legal codes for their kingdom, codes that enunciated a theory of cooperation between king and people, the former initiating and improving tradition, the latter, through the army and the magnates, accepting the code. The Edict of Rothari (643) also presents a reshaping of a Longobard ethnic myth, centered on the line of Longobard kings. Rothari styles himself the "seventeenth king of the Longobard people," a number meant to assimilate the Longobards to the Romans and the Goths (both Romulus and Theoderic the Great were held to be seventeenth in their lines). The very creation of this claim to an ancient royal history and ethnic identity is proof of the deep assimilation of Gothic and Roman values and identity.

Like the Longobard kingdom, the Frankish world remained divided in fundamental ways through the later 6th and 7th centuries. Core areas of the kingdom—Neustria, Austrasia, and Burgundy—often had their own kings, who drew their legitimacy through descent from Clovis. The peripheral areas of the Frankish kingdom—Aquitaine, Provence, Bavaria, Thuringia, and Frisia—were governed in the name of the Frankish kings by dukes or patricians, often men with central Frankish ties who rapidly integrated themselves into the local power structures.

The Frankish name came to designate the inhabitants of the core territories ruled by the Frankish kings and acquired increasingly a geographical rather than ethnic connotation. Legal codes for the Thuringians, Bavarians, and other peoples within the Frankish realm were essentially regional law codes, modeled on Salic law even while incorporating some local traditions and imposed on peripheral areas of the Frankish realm. In general the vocabulary of ethnic terminology occurs most frequently in the context of military organization, since contingents from different areas were mustered and led by their dukes and counts, the institutional descendants of late Roman military officers.

Merovingian kings of the 7th century, once characterized as incompetent if not mentally deficient, are now recognized to have been nothing of the sort. Still, from the early 7th century, when powerful leaders such as Chlothar II (584–629) and Dagobert I (623–638) could exercise effective control over a unified Frankish kingdom, a gradual decline in royal authority worked to the benefit of regional aristocracies. However, this growth of regionalism was seldom if ever the result of deep ethnic or cultural differences. The leading families in Austria, Neustria, and Burgundy as well as in the peripheral duchies of the Frankish realm were generally themselves descendants of representatives of the Frankish monarchs with both central and regional ties that they used to their own advantage. The struggles between aristocratic factions that eventually led to the rise of the Carolingian dynasty are remarkable for their lack of ethnic overtones, in spite of the attempt by some modern historians to read ethnic conflict into these contests.

In the Visigothic kingdom, the integration of barbarian and Roman populations began with Leovigild (569–586) and his son Reccarid (586–601). Leovigild reunited a much divided Visigothic kingdom and expelled most of the remnants of Byzantine control from the peninsula. Once the orthodox Byzantine presence was eliminated, orthodox Christianity ceased to be the political threat that it had been, and Leovigild began to move his Arian elite toward orthodox Catholicism. His son brought this to completion at the council of Toledo in 589 that followed the conversion of Reccarid himself in 587.

The conversion of the Visigoths had fundamental consequences for the identity of the Visigothic people and kingdom. The Catholic hierarchy and the political and social leadership of the communities they represented became fully integrated into the Gothic state and people. The periodic councils of Toledo that began in the 630s developed into the fundamental institution unifying Visigothic Spain. These councils treated matters of faith, morals, and ritual, as well as politics and administration. Toledo became in time the preeminent metropolitan see of Spain, able both to extend its authority throughout the Spanish church and to define royal legitimacy not in terms of family, as in the case of the Merovingian family, but rather in terms of having received royal unction in the city. The extent of episcopal and royal cooperation in the transformation of the Visigothic kingdom and state was unprecedented in western Europe.

The British isles never knew the kind of unity of people and kingship known on the continent. In Scotland, Ireland, and Wales, as in England, a sense of identity never translated into a political structure. Through the 7th century, southeastern England was closely connected to the cultural and political world of Merovingian Gaul. Political unity was never an issue. At various times petty kings of southeastern England attempted to dominate their neighbors, and in the later 7th century some rulers of Northumbria temporarily managed to enforce some sort of lordship over other kingdoms. However, such claims never amounted to an institutionalized overlordship. The office of a high king, the so-called Bretwalda, is essentially a modern myth. Nevertheless, a *gens Anglorum* was perceived to exist, although it was largely defined by opposition to the British enemies to the west, south, and north. And yet membership in the *gens Anglorum*, through participation in one of the petty Anglo-Saxon kingdoms, was open to people of British and Germanic background alike. Once more, membership in the Anglo-Saxon people was a question of constitution, not simply of inheritance.

Although Roman sources often presented barbarian peoples' ethnic identities as fixed, we have seen that new identities were constantly being established and transformed through contacts with the Romans. The barbarian *gentes* in turn came to play an integral and transformative role in the later Roman empire.

Select Bibliography

Amory, Patrick. *People and Identity in Ostrogothic Italy, 489–554.* Cambridge, Eng., 1997.

——— "Ethnographic Rhetoric, Aristocratic Attitudes and Political Allegiance in Post-Roman Gaul," *Klio* 76 (1994): 438–453.

——— "The Meaning and Purpose of Ethnic Terminology in the Burgundian Law-Codes," *Early Medieval Europe* 2 (1993): 1–28.

——— "Names, Ethnic Identity and Community in Fifth and Sixth-Century Burgundy," *Viator* 25 (1994): 1–30.

Bäuml, Franz H., and Marianna D. Birnbaum. *Attila: The Man and His Image.* Budapest, 1993.

Balsdon, J. P. V. D. *Romans and Aliens.* Chapel Hill, N.C., 1979.

Campbell, James, ed. *The Anglo-Saxons.* London, 1982.

Collins, Roger. *Early Medieval Europe 300–1000.* New York, 1991.

——— *Early Medieval Spain: Unity in Diversity, 400–1000.* London, 1983.

Drinkwater, John, and Hugh Elton, eds. *Fifth-Century Gaul: A Crisis of Identity?* Cambridge, 1992.

Geary, Patrick J. *Before France and Germany: The Creation and Transformation of the Merovingian World.* New York, 1988.

——— "Ethnicity as a Situational Construct in the Early Middle Ages," *Mitteilungen der anthropologischen Gesellschaft in Wien* 113 (1983): 15–26.

Goffart, Walter. *Barbarians and Romans A.D. 418–584: The Techniques of Accommodation.* Princeton, 1980.

——— *The Narrators of Barbarian History (A.D. 550–800): Jordanes, Gregory of Tours, Bede and Paul the Deacon.* Princeton, 1988.

——— *Rome's Fall and After.* London, 1989.

James, Edward. *The Franks.* Oxford, 1988.

Jarnut, J. *Geschichte der Langobarden.* Stuttgart, 1982.

Maenchen-Helfen, Otto. *The World of the Huns.* Berkeley, 1973.

Murray, Alexander C. *Germanic Kinship Structure: Studies in Law and Society in Antiquity and the Early Middle Ages.* Toronto, 1983.

Pohl, Walter. *Die Aawren: Ein Steppenvolk im Mitteleuropa 567–822 n. Chr.* Munich, 1988.

——— "Conceptions of Ethnicity in Early Medieval Studies," *Archaeologia Polona* 29 (1991): 39–49.

——— "Tradition, Ethnogenese und literarische Gestaltung: Eine Zwischenbilanz," in Karl Brunner and Brigitte Merta, eds., *Ethnogenese und Überlieferung: Angewandte Methoden der Frühmittelalterforschung.* Vienna, 1994, 9–26.

——— "Telling the Difference: Signs of Ethnic Identity," in Walter Pohl and Helmut Reimitz, eds., *Strategies of Distinction: The Constitution of Ethnic Communities, 300–800.* Leiden, 1998, 17–69.

Todd, Malcolm. *The Northern Barbarians.* London, 1987.

Wenskus, Reinhard. *Stammesbildung und Verfassung: Das Werden der frühmittelalterlichen Gentes*. Cologne, 1961.

Wolfram, Herwig. *History of the Goths*. Berkeley, 1988.

———— "Gothic History and Historical Ethnography," *Journal of Medieval History* 7 (1981): 309–319.

———— *The Roman Empire and Its Germanic Peoples*. Berkeley, 1997.

Wolfram, Herwig, and Walter Pohl, eds. *Typen der Ethnogenese unter besonderer Berücksichtigung der Bayern*, vol. 1. Vienna, 1990.

Wood, Ian N. *The Merovingian Kingdoms 450–751*. London, 1994.

Zöllner, Erich. *Geschichte der Franken*. Munich, 1970.

WAR AND VIOLENCE

Brent D. Shaw

I know well that war is a great evil—indeed the worst of all evils." So opined
the author of a treatise on strategy written in the reign of Emperor Justinian
(*Peri strat.* 4; Dennis, 1985: 20–21). The sentiments and the judgment were
those of a man of pragmatic battlefield experience, and they evoke the hard
realities of a fighting soldier's life. These bitter words are embedded in the
otherwise cool and technical prose of a military manual, a genre which by the
time of our anonymous author had a millennium-old tradition in the Greek
world. Throughout the Mediterranean and the Near East during late antiquity
this "worst of all evils" was fundamental to the making and unmaking of
political and cultural worlds. The social orders of the time were constituted and
maintained by brute force and compulsion. Yet despite a tradition of historical
writing that placed the conduct of war at the center of its narratives, the
obstacles to a reasoned understanding of war are considerable.

Some of the most daunting problems are posed by the written sources themselves. For the third quarter of the 4th century that is covered by the extant
books of Ammianus Marcellinus, we are reasonably well informed; the same
applies to the middle quarters of the 6th century that are covered by Procopius's
History of the Wars of Justinian. For the period after the Battle of Adrianople
(378) to the early 6th century, however, we are at the mercy of fragments and
summaries preserved by later historians and compilers, none of which permits a
systemic understanding of the nature of war. For the Roman empire, at least
these remnants have survived. For other equally important places and periods
in late antiquity, we face even greater difficulties. As attempts to provide general
analyses of warfare among the illiterate societies of the Eurasian plains north of
the Roman and Sassanid empires have shown, archaeological evidence alone is
no substitute for written sources (Todd, 1992: 162). Although an understanding of social structure and political power in these societies is critical to an
evaluation of the war system of late antiquity, claims about the formation of

proto-states and the development of incipient class structures or political hier-archies based on the mute remains of a few wood huts are both unconvincing and frustrating (Hedeager, 1978, 1988, 1992; Todd, 1992: 65–75). So too, apart from Roman historical sources (mainly Ammianus and Procopius, and later Agathias) little can be said of the military developments and institu-tions of the Sassanid empire. In the Persian case there are no surviving contem-porary literary sources of importance; the basic source materials for a valid reconstruction and analysis of Sassanid military force and practice are surpris-ingly deficient (Schippmann, 1990: 103–106). The much later Arabic sources, such as al-Tabarī, that are used to fill the gap are difficult to interpret, and are often fantastic in their narratives (Howard-Johnston, 1995: 169–180; 211–212). Whereas it is true that some of the first Sassanid monarchs, including Shapur I, provided epigraphical *res gestae* of their reigns that highlighted their military accomplishments, the practice quickly fell into desuetude. With no tradition in which to place them and with very little other indigenous Iranian literary evidence to provide context, evaluations of the information they pro-vide on war are fraught with difficulties.

In the surviving books of the Greek and Roman historians, the focus of their accounts on single dominant narrative characters produces basic distortions. In the historian Ammianus, for example, Julian's campaigns in Gaul in 355–357 are described in considerable detail. But when Julian moves to the eastern Mediterranean, impelled by the demands of civil war, Ammianus leaves Gaul behind. The historian's narrative dutifully follows Julian and his successors eastward. Hence we have a marvelous exposition of the disastrous Persian expedition of 363; a coherent narrative of the cycle of events leading up to the crossing of the lower Danube by groups of Tervingi in 376; and a vivid descrip-tion of the incompetence and chaos leading to the Battle of Adrianople in 378. We therefore happen to be reasonably well informed about the events con-nected with the breach of one riverine frontier of the empire. But in the case of a similar, indeed more serious, breach of the Rhine frontier on that fateful New Year's Eve of 406, all we know, basically, is that it happened. For critical events of the 5th century—the wars connected, for example, with the rise and fall of Alaric or of Attila—we know, and can know, so much less.

Moreover, even in the case of the Roman empire, for which there exists a consistent narrative historical tradition, many of the ancillary primary sources are rather disappointing. Prime among these is the list of civil and military offices of the state *(Notitia Dignitatum)*, which purports to provide complete lists of the principal units of the Roman army along with its command struc-ture (Seeck, 1876; Jones, 1964: 1429–50; Goodburn and Bartholomew, 1976). Apart from the constantly debated problems connected with the document's provenance, composition, and dating (especially of its divergent eastern and western halves), it should provide a good guide to the strategic distribution and organization of the late Roman army. Alas, the Roman army in action as described in narrative prose histories of the late 4th and early 5th centuries is often difficult to connect with the bureaucrat's ideal of the imperial army (Hoff-mann, 1969: 490f.; Liebeschuetz, 1990: 40–41). A quirky 4th century pamphlet entitled "On Warfare" *(De rebus bellicis)* reveals something of the ideology of a reform-minded civilian from the large landowning classes, and reaffirms the commonplace that one of the few places where technological innovations were sought and lauded was in the realm of the devices of war—but not much more (Thompson, 1952; Liebeschuetz, 1994). Vegetius's manual "On the Military" *(De re militari)* would be of great utility were it not that it was written as a picture of how the Roman army used to be (Goffart, 1977; Barnes, 1979; Stelten, 1990; Milner, 1993). The nostalgia signals that the army of Vegetius's own day no longer resembled his model of centralized organization, training, logistics, and command. By contrast, some of the advice found in later Byzantine handbooks on "stratagems" of war (that is, on tactics—not strategy in the modern sense of the word) actually addresses current problems of field combat in the 7th century, and so is more directly useful (Dennis, 1985: 1–2).

Another serious problem is that classical historiography and allied forms of literature had developed canons of reporting violence that were stereotypical and schematic, and that depended on typecast descriptions derived from literary prototypes. These conventions compelled the writer to respect the limits of what was acceptable in the description of violence, even if he was a historian who had been an eyewitness to the events. In modest contravention of these standards, Procopius's reports on the effects of war in peninsular Italy resulting from the battles waged between Gothic and Byzantine forces do sometimes offer a glimpse of the more human sides of war. Of the populace in the regions of Aemilia and Etruria during the warfare of 539 he claims that "many of them as lived in the mountains were reduced to eating loaves made of the acorns of the oak trees, which they ground up like grain. The result of this was that most of the people fell victim to all types of disease . . . It is said that of the Roman farmers in Picenum no less than fifty thousand died from famine, as did a great many more in the region north of the Adriatic" (*Wars* 6.20.18–33). Procopius offers what purport to be eyewitness accounts of women reduced to cannibalism, and scenes of hunger in which people, overcome by starvation, chance upon a patch of grass and rush to pull it out and consume it on the spot. Indeed, it is manifest from Procopius's account that the Byzantine reconquest turned formerly civil areas of the western Mediterranean, especially North Africa and peninsular Italy, into a war zone on the western frontier of the Byzantine state. The eastern Roman military intervention was probably the principal cause of the permanent decline of the city of Rome into a miserable village (Wickham, 1981: 26–29; Cameron, 1985: 193–194) and of the disintegration of the networks of municipal towns that had been the hallmark of a flourishing Roman economy in North Africa (*Wars* 2.58.52; and *Anecdota* 18.1–9; but see Cameron, 1985: 171–172).

In wars of the period, combat was often reduced to brutish hand-to-hand fighting. In his description of the siege of Rome in the year 538, Procopius gives a vivid description of some of the wounds inflicted: "One of the barbarians shot Trajan in the face, above the right eye and not far from the nose. The whole of the iron point penetrated his head and disappeared entirely, although the barb on it was large and very long; but the shaft of the arrow broke off and fell to the ground" (*Wars* 6.5.25–27). In his account of the combat around Rome during the previous year, Procopius offers more reportage of war wounds: a man named Arzes, one of the guards of Belisarius, "was hit by a Gothic archer between the nose and the right eye. The point of the arrow was embedded as far as the back of his neck, but did not penetrate out; the rest of the shaft projected from his face and shook about as he rode his horse" (*Wars* 6.2.15–18). Procopius gives testimony to the aftermath of these brief "fire fights" outside the city walls: "When all the men had returned to the city, they attended to the wounded. In the case of Arzes, although the doctors wanted to draw the weapon out of his face, they were reluctant to do so for some time. They hesitated not because of the eye, which they supposed could not be saved, but for fear lest, by the cutting of membranes and tissues such as are very numerous in the region of the face, they would cause the death of a man who was one of the best in the household of Belisarius" (*Wars* 6.2.25–36). These are just a few of the human costs in one of the seventy or so brief and vicious encounters outside the walls of Rome during the year 537.

These are extraordinary pieces of historical narration, striking because they are not, like most of Procopius's accounts of sieges and set battles, dependent on rhetorical devices and images adopted from earlier historians. Such realism in the description of combat is unusual. When Ammianus offers such reportage, most of his descriptions tend to replay stereotypical scenes and rhetoric (19.2.7–15; 19.8.6–7; 19.9.9: the siege of Amida in 359; 27.2.8; 31.7.14; 31.13.4: Adrianople in 378).

Despite the difficulties posed by the primary evidence, to comprehend the real face of war is very important because many modern-day analyses of war in late antiquity assume that it consisted mainly of one army fighting another—battles of Roman armies against Gothic, German, or Persian forces (Luttwak, 1976; Ferrill, 1986, 1991; Wheeler, 1993). But any full understanding of the actions of armies has to confront the cruel fact that a great deal of the violence consisted of attacks that were deliberately planned to terrorize civilian populations. Time and again, Ammianus reports attacks on indigenous communities across the Rhine and Danube that were not much more than massacres of unarmed civilian populations in their villages and rural farmsteads (Amm.Marc. 17.10. 5–9; 17.13.10–11, 358; 27.5.4; 30.5.13f., 374). Procopius's accounts of the brutalities of war in the Byzantine reconquest of North Africa and Italy are strewn with more violent actions of this type, which were deliberately perpetrated by army commanders and their men (e.g., *Wars* 6.7.25–34; 6.10.1–1; 6.17.1–3; 6.21.38–40). To these planned atrocities must be added the normal pillaging and looting that followed most successful forays—actions that threatened to transform an army from a hierarchically controlled unit under the command of officers to an anarchical mob.

Along with love, its ideological opposite, there is perhaps no human activity that is more insistently dialogical than war. An analysis of war as a total phenomenon therefore entails an understanding of the parties on both sides. The problem is that we are usually well informed about only one of the two parties, the Roman state. The tendency to understand war in late antiquity from a

Roman perspective is also a historiographical tradition, which has been compounded by a pervasive, almost unconscious, desire to share the Roman point
of view (Bury, 1928: 3–4). So the Battle of Adrianople of 378 is a catastrophe;
and the sack of Rome by Alaric in 410 is a political disaster. Similarly, the defeat
of Attila and his Huns on the Catalaunian Plains in 451 is a good thing.
Historians offer endless recipes for how Roman forces could have been better
organized or deployed; few are willing to expend much energy on devising
more successful strategies for Alaric or Attila the Hun. Instead, we are asked to
identify our problems with those of the Roman empire, and to draw from its
grand strategies messages for our own late 20th century military predicaments
(Luttwak, 1976: 2–3; Ferrill, 1986, 1991). A better understanding of how war
functioned for the sum of all persons and societies as they engaged each other in
this particular form of violent behavior is not likely to be enhanced by these
vicarious identifications. To understand war, it is imperative to understand all
war: not only what was done by armies and soldiers, but also what was not
done by them—in fact, what could not be done.

Late antiquity was not an era of any great military revolution. There were
few, if any, strictly technological advances in the practice of war—whether
scythed chariots; heavily armored cavalry, either *cataphractarii* or *clibanarii*
(Eadie, 1967; Bivar, 1972; Speidel, 1984); newfangled *ballistae*, heavier composite bows, or even "Greek fire"—that permanently transformed the nature of
battle in the period (Van Creveld, 1991). The dominant social, economic, and
geographical forces in which warfare was embedded conduced to a basic continuity in the conduct of war itself, even during momentous social and political
transitions (Haldon, 1993). The Parthian and Sassanid states did develop a type
of warfare that was very well adapted to the ecological constraints of their
world—a state-organized type of war that emphasized large numbers of heavy
cavalry, mobility over large open spaces, and the use of long-range strike arch-
ery (Patterson, 1966; Kolias, 1988), whereas classic Mediterranean warfare
was based on massed heavy infantry formations. The repeated confrontation of
these two war cultures naturally produced a degree of adaptation on the part of
either side to the techniques of the other, a movement that is consciously reflected in their military manuals (Dagron, 1993).
   But these adaptations did not constitute a revolution in war technology.
Although there was a certain fascination with innovation in the implements of
war (e.g., Amm.Marc. 21.21.8–9; 28.4; *Wars* 8.11.27, 550), the decisive forces
were those of sheer size, combined with the intensive organization and deploy-
ment permitted by a bureaucratic infrastructure. Thus the Roman state remained throughout this period the major and determinant practitioner of war
in the Mediterranean, with few competitors on any of its frontiers other than
Sassanid Persia. The balance of the evidence supports Hans Delbrück's thesis
that for this type of premodern warfare it was the mobilization of manpower
that mattered in the long run (Delbrück, 1902/1921). From the great to the
small powers, there was a constant pressure to recruit beyond the bounds of

one's own ethnic group or state in order to acquire the manpower needed to
meet or exceed the enemy's.

It has frequently been argued that the Roman empire faced constant recruiting crises, and that the pressures created by a need for military manpower that
could not be met because of a decline in the population of the empire compelled
the late Roman state to recruit more and more barbarians (Boak, 1955; *contra:*
Elton, 1996: 136–151). In the simple terms in which this argument has often
been made, however, it cannot be true. Even if we accept the highest estimates
of military manpower under the aegis of the late Roman state (on the order of
650,000 men), the government never drafted more than 1 percent of the whole
population of the empire. In terms of raw demographic resources, there were
always enough men to provide recruits for Roman armies. There is no need to
postulate an enforced "barbarization" of the Roman army of the 4th century
for these reasons, or indeed a second barbarization of the 6th century Byzantine
army after the great plague of the 540s (Whitby, 1995: 103–106). There were
indeed serious difficulties with recruiting, but the principal causes were social and political, not demographic. It was an established truism that Italians
were resistant to military service in a way that Gauls, for example, were not
(Amm.Marc. 15.12.3, 355–357). The late Roman law codes repeatedly refer to
persons who were willing to mutilate their bodies rather than serve in the
military (C.Th. 7.13.4–5, 367).

The propensity of Roman citizens in Italy to avoid military service is well
attested from the early principate, and was a potential problem even in the
heyday of the Roman republic. The main difference was the response of the late
antique Roman state. Cities and landowners tended to commute their recruiting requirements to cash or gold bullion payments to the state *(aurum tironi-
cum)*. Wealthy landowners made certain that their rural workforces were kept
from the recruiting officer's grasp. Slaves were always banned from army service (except in extreme state crises such as that faced by Rome in 406/7), and
coloni on imperial estates were formally and legally exempted from military
service. The Roman state took the most convenient way out of this reluctance
to serve: it redeployed tax revenues from the center of the empire to pay for the
armed service of men recruited from its peripheries, creating a dangerous circle
of military dependency into which the late Roman state fell (C.Th. 7.13.7,
375). For social, economic, and political reasons, therefore, the real recruiting
base of the empire was rather narrow and regionally specific. In 359 when the
Limigantes asked for permission from Constantius to cross the Danube and to
settle on lands within the empire, the emperor's advisers argued that the reset-
tlement would achieve two objectives. It would provide the emperor with more
child-producing, tribute-paying subjects from whom he could draft soldiers;
and, since "the provincials are happy to contribute gold to save their bodies,"
the emperor would also be able to collect commuted recruiting payments from
them which he could then use for his own purposes (Amm.Marc. 19.11.7). The
advisers of Emperor Valens appealed to the same rationale in support of allowing large numbers of Goths to cross the lower Danube into the empire in 376
(Amm.Marc. 31.4.4–5).

Thus all social orders, whether those of large states like Rome and Persia or those of small segmentary lineage societies such as the Goths or Gepids north of the Danube, tended to recruit polyethnic armies. The "Goths" that crossed the lower Danube in force in 376 incorporated several subethnic groups of Goths (Tervingi, Greuthungi) along with Huns and Alans—a combination of ethnic groups that continued to cooperate after the Battle of Adrianople (Amm.Marc. 31.8.3; 31.16.3). The Sassanid state was no different (Shahbazi, 1986: 497). When Shapur II led his expedition into Mesopotamia in 359, his army included Armenians, Arabs, Albani, Chionitai, Gelani, Segestani, and others (Amm.Marc. 18.6.1; 19.2.3). Sometimes the boundaries of ethnicity and military service were well defined, as in the Roman armies of the high empire, which distinguished between the Roman citizen components of the army and the allied ethnic contingents that constituted at least half of the army's strength. The forces that Belisarius commanded in Italy in the mid-530s included Armenians, Goths, Isaurians, Gepids, Huns, Sklaveni, Antai, Mauri, Thracians, and Iberians (*Wars* 5.5.1–5; 5.27.1–3). The armies that he led in the east in 542 drew recruits from Armenians, Goths, Thracians, Illyrians, Heruls, Vandals, Mauri, and others (*Wars* 2.21.5).

Naturally, various societies of late antiquity policed the connections between social status and military service differently. To the very end, the civil state polities that were part of the Graeco-Roman tradition drew the line at the recruitment of unfree persons (*C.Th.* 7.13.8, 380). Only fearful emergencies justified the breach of this social rule, and even then the propensity was to manumit slaves before enrolling them in the army (*C.Th.* 7.13.6, 406; Whitby, 1995: 83). In contrast, the segmentary lineage societies of northern Europe and the Near East seem regularly to have accepted slave or servile elements as part of their armed forces. This was as true of the Sarmatians along the Danube in the 4th century (Amm.Marc. 17.12.18; 17.13.1; 19.11.1; 29.6.15) as it was of the Heruls who were in the service of Belisarius in the mid 6th century (*Wars* 2.25.27–28). Perhaps more to the point, given later developments in Muslim armies (Crone, 1980; Pipes, 1981), there was also a tradition of slave soldiers in the Ethiopian armies (the kingdom of Aksum) and among peoples across the Red Sea in the Arabian Peninsula (*Wars* 1.20.2).

The other great constraining forces to warfare were limits on communication. All sides, of course, had their paid spies and informants (*Wars* 1.21.11). The problem was that the knowledge obtained by even these professionals was faulty and contradictory (Austin, 1979: 22–40; Lee, 1993; Burns, 1994: 32). Much of the vaunted intelligence apparatus of Rome was provoked more by fears of civil war and potential internal challenges to the emperor's power than by any real outside threats (Austin and Rankov, 1995). Most often, commanders had to deduce what might happen from actual movements of men and supplies, rather than from intelligence reports. Decisions concerning the initiation of war were concentrated in the person of a king and his advisers, who found it difficult to gain any sure knowledge (Amm.Marc. 21.13.4, 361). To the end of late antiquity, therefore, emperors, like Anastasius in the year 503, could send their armies deep into enemy lands without firm knowledge about where the enemy was or what its intentions were (*Wars* 1.8.8–9). Those who did know were usually men on the front line. In the late Roman army this usually meant the generals or *duces* who commanded the different sectors of the imperial frontier, and the frontline soldiers who fed information back to the generals in their field reports (Amm.Marc. 21.7.6–7; 26.6.10–11). In fact, beyond the frontier even wars took place in a no-man's land of the unknown. Distance, difficult terrain, lack of records, illiteracy, and other factors combined to produce a profound ignorance (Heather, 1994). As Ammianus states, reports of major conflicts among the barbarian peoples beyond the northern frontiers of the empire tended to be discounted by the Romans "because wars in those regions are not ordinarily heard of by those living at a distance from them until after they are finished or after the violence has already faded back to quiet" (Amm.Marc. 31.4.3).

These physical restrictions on war meant that actual fighting turned on individual set battles—and the operational units of battle, over the long term, devolved into smaller rather than larger field units: "For all these reasons, battle and war tended to coincide: war properly speaking only began when battle was joined . . . there was a very real sense in which strategy as understood by Clausewitz—namely, that of employing battles in order to forward the aims of war—did not exist, which of course might explain why the term 'strategy' in anything like its modern sense, only entered the English language around 1800" (Van Creveld, 1989: 16–17). Despite their large size, the Sassanid and Roman empires of the period fielded small combat units. The classic legion of the Roman principate, about six thousand men, was reduced to about one thousand men, bringing it close to the standard size for most operational units in the late imperial army. The down-sizing was the result of the practice of permanently removing detachments *(vexillationes)* from their parent legions. The gradual move to smaller operational units of combat was accompanied by an increased premium placed on mobility and a greater importance placed on the cavalry, which became a separate operational branch of the Roman army during this period (Carrié, 1993: 99–103). The Sassanid army also operated with much the same unit scales and a concomitant emphasis on mobility (Shahbazi, 1986: 497–498). The later military development of both states was therefore characterized by forces that became larger overall and more fixed in separate regional armies, but paradoxically came to operate with smaller units that contributed to greater mobility of forces.

The move to smaller operational units and the need to deal with armed threats in geographically limited zones of confrontation meant that what passed for strategy and planning, even in the largest states, were often ad hoc decisions made either by the commander in the field or, given the political dangers of such autonomy, made by him after consultation with the king or the emperor (Millar, 1982). Decision making was therefore highly personalized, and was vested directly in the person of the general or monarch. Indeed, battle capabilities and political power were so inextricably linked with one person that, whether in Rome or Persia, long royal reigns produced, and were reproduced by, military stability. Short reigns, by contrast, were both cause and effect of weakness in war, whether internal or external. The longest reigns, whether Roman (Augustus, Constantine, Justinian) or Persian (Shapur I, Shapur II, Kavad I, Khosro I), were marked by recovery from civil war, the institution of new dynastic regimes, and military reforms that presaged stronger and more stable military states (Rubin, 1995). There is less information on the politics of the frontier ethnic groups of either state, but Theoderic I, king of the Visigoths (418–451), is at least one known case that exemplifies the common pattern.

The close connection between war and political power put constant pressure on monarchs to direct war in person on the field of battle and, indeed, to prove their worth as rulers by showing (most often at the inception of their reigns) success in war. Thus the advent of each new ruler tended to provoke a perceived need to challenge the status quo. So Byzantine emperors of the 5th century, from Anastasius I on, felt compelled to test their greatest enemy's strength, almost as a rite of passage to legitimate their own power (Shahid, 1995). The same is true of the contemporary Sassanid monarchs who, like Bahram V and Yazedgird II in 421–422 and 439, went to war near the beginning of their reigns to strengthen their credentials as kings.

The need for the emperor to be personally close to his troops was provoked more by the threat of internal than external war. One of the more extraordinary documents that exemplify this relationship is a recorded dialogue between Constantine and his soldiers about their terms of employment that is preserved in the late Roman law codes (C.Th. 7.20.2 = C.Just. 12.47.1; 326). The conversation reflects a personal camaraderie that would be rather unusual for the emperor to have had with the humble civilian subjects of his empire. The emperor's presence and active participation in battle were reestablished as part of the Roman imperial system by Marcus Aurelius and the emperors of the 3rd century crisis, and remained true of the empire down to Theodosius. Although the Byzantine state managed to achieve the restoration of a civil state, its monarchs were still under unremitting pressure actively to participate in war. The severe troubles of the early 7th century compelled Heraclius once again to take the field in person at the head of the army.

The constraints on manpower and leadership that were faced by the large states of late antiquity were connected with their transition from conquest states to civil polities. The shift was usually marked by an increasing reluctance to serve on the part of the ordinary citizens of the conquering state, and an increasing professionalization of military service and drawing of recruits from the war zones of the state. The result was a dramatic shift in the war capabilities of the state. The vast citizen and allied levies of the Roman republic formed an enormous recruiting reserve which in turn had produced one of the great and paradoxical secrets of success of the republican state in war: it could lose battles. Indeed, by the standards of almost any ancient state, it could lose on a staggering scale and still return to the field of battle, finally to win the war. The government of the later Roman state was no longer in this enviable position. It ruled an empire that was many times the geographical size and population of peninsular Italy, but commanded armed forces that were not much more than double the size of the manpower reserves of the republic. The state had been

divided into civil and military moieties, such that the former funded but otherwise did not participate in the latter. It was an acceptable compromise of
empire.

Even when conducted by the Roman and Sassanid states that had the greatest
centralized resources at their command, war remained subject to constraints of
topography and climate. Weather imposed seasonal rhythms on war, dictating
periodic campaigning seasons that were followed right to the end of antiquity.
In Gaul and on the Rhine frontier, for example, the war season was signaled
by the beginning of summer (Amm.Marc. 14.10.1; 27.10.6f; 30.5.1; 30.5.14;
30.6.2). These temporal patterns were so well known that they were regularly
presented as part of normal tactical advice. When Valentinian was contemplat-
ing attacking the Alamanni in the autumn of 374, his advisers warned that he
should hold back until the beginning of spring, noting that "the roads, hardened with frost, where neither any grass grew that would serve as fodder nor
anything else that would be of use to the army, could not be penetrated"
(Amm.Marc. 30.3.3). The cycle of Roman war on this frontier, with its annual
forays to the Rhine, the *pax* conveniently "agreed to" just in time by cringing
and repentant barbarians, and the following retreat to winter quarters, can be
seen as a process determined by the harsh winter conditions in these lands. The
regular cycle from a winter retreat from war to a summer campaigning season
was compelled no less upon Persian monarchs (Amm.Marc. 19.9.1: beginning
of October; 20.7; 21.6.7; 27.12.18; 30.2.16). Sometimes these responses to
natural conditions were translated into traditional cultural prohibitions, such
as the time around the spring equinox when Saracens entered a two-month-
long sacred period during which they refused to undertake raids against their
enemies (*Wars* 2.16.18).

With the arrival of inclement autumn weather, the armed forces of the Roman state regularly retired to winter quarters where stored supplies could be
guaranteed. The external peoples along the northern frontiers, however, sometimes found themselves facing midwinter subsistence crises that drove them
to enter the developed regions of the empire. So in midwinter 365–66, the
Alamanni crossed the Rhine in large numbers on the day after New Year's
(Amm.Marc. 27.1.1); the Lentienses crossed the frozen Rhine for similar reasons in mid-February of 378 (Amm.Marc. 31.10.4). The crossing of the Rhine
by German ethnic groups on New Year's Eve of 406 dramatically replayed these
same patterns. So too, on the eastern frontier between Persia and Rome, in the
year 536, compelled by several dry seasons that left nomadic herds without
pasture, a large number of Arabs led by the phylarch al-Mundhir attacked
settlements in the agricultural zone of Euphratensis (Marcell. Com. *Chron.*
2.105; see also Shahid, 1995: 194–196). At least some of the Hephthalite
attacks into the northern frontier zone of Sassanid Persia in the late 4th and
early 5th century were provoked by famine (Thompson, 1996: 35). Climate
variations also hampered the movement of armies. When Theodosius transferred troops from Gaul to deal with the Firmus rebellion in North Africa in
372, his soldiers, accustomed to the colder climates of the north, found it very
difficult to adjust to the scorching heat of the high plains of central Algeria

(Amm.Marc. 29.5.7). The Roman troops besieging Theodosiopolis in 541 fell severely ill with fevers. The explanation proffered for their sickness was that the land was very hot and dry, not the type of climate to which troops brought in from Thrace were accustomed (*Wars* 2.19.31–32). Such impediments could be partly cultural as well; the local German troops recruited by Julian in Gaul in the mid-350s made it a condition of their enlistment that they would never be transferred beyond the Alps (Amm.Marc. 20.4.4; 20.8.7; 8.15.360).

Cultural, climatic, and topographical factors combined to fix limits to warfare, frontiers that could not be altered even by the most strenuous combat. Kings and monarchs tended to adjust their war frontiers to existing ecological ones (Whittaker, 1994: 86–97). Excessive long-term costs caused Diocletian to withdraw the Roman army from regions below the first cataract on the Nile and to attempt to establish a new frontier near Elephantine and the temples of Philae (*Wars* 1.19.28–30). But the classic instance is the war frontier between the late Roman and Persian states in the Near East. Persian monarchs, including Shapur II (340s–350s) and Khosro I (540s), sometimes managed to stage military forays and raids on a massive scale into the fertile zone along the Mediterranean that was under Roman or Byzantine aegis. Similarly, Roman emperors, from Julian (363) to Heraclius (622–630), staged large-scale raids that struck deep into Persian territory along the Tigris and Euphrates. But neither side was ever able to achieve a permanent change in the frontier. Individual cities and forts, especially those in the confrontation zone of Mesopotamia, might change hands for periods of time; but the regional strategic situation remained fundamentally unaltered by the practice of war. From the mid 6th century onward, when recurrent episodes of protracted war erupted—with the concomitant tremendous cost of property and toll in human life, especially in the first decades of the 7th century—cultural and ecological frontiers still determined the limits of battle. It has been noted that "the blood spilled in the warfare between the two states brought as little real gain to the one side or the other as the few meters of land gained at terrible cost in the trench warfare of the First World War" (Frye 1983: 139).

Perhaps the greatest permanent constraint on war in late antiquity, however, is not visible in the surviving records because it is simply not recognized in this period. The fundamental breakthrough that powered the military revolution in early modern Europe was fiscal; the opening of the resources of trading companies, banks, and other institutions of credit enabled nation-states to amortize the expenses of war, both men and equipment. The financing of armies and war in late antiquity, by contrast, was brittle and inflexible, constrained by fixed ceilings of expenditure that were crudely linked to the limits of the tributary system of the state. It was more probable that the entire fiscal, currency, and tribute-collecting system of the ancient state would have to change under the pressure of war, rather than that war would provoke any revolution in modes of banking (Carrié, 1995). The relationship between state, fiscal instruments, and economy was a brutal zero-sum game. There were no private fiscal institutions with massive surplus monies to invest in the high-risk venture of war. The one institution in late antiquity that possessed hoarded wealth on the requisite scale, the church, did provide such a loan on one occasion. Emperor Heraclius, facing a desperate situation in 622, is reported to have taken the hoarded resources of "pious houses" *(euagoi oikoi)* as just such a war "loan" (Theophanes, *Chron.* a.m. 6113). It was a singular occurrence that did not bear repetition, much less developed an institutional linkage between high finance and war (Jones, 1964: 316; Haldon, 1990: 225; Treadgold, 1995: 205–206). The cold fact is that the exorbitant costs of war had to be recouped by the seizure of property, including the stored wealth of sacred institutions. The massive confiscation of pagan temple treasure enabled Constantine to coin enough gold to pay his soldiers' donatives. In presenting his seizure as a loan, Heraclius was being more polite, proper, and pious. Sometimes costs could be recouped during the political purges that followed bouts of civil war, but the usual compulsion was to find another war whose booty would pay for the one just waged.

There are various calculations that estimate the size of the armed forces of the high empire at about 400,000–450,000 men (MacMullen, 1980). The army of the later empire was larger, but certainly not quadruple that of the principate, as is sometimes claimed based on misreading a famous passage in Lactantius (*De mort.pers.* 7.2). Reasonable guesses are that the size of the later Roman army had risen to about half again the size of the army of the high empire—that is, to about 600,000–650,000 men. The army was therefore by far the largest organization of the Roman state, dwarfing its civil administration and any other corporate body before the advent of the Christian church. It was also the most costly. Rough estimates of what this cost might have been are based on what is presumed to be the single largest item: the soldiers' wages, rewards, and benefits. It is generally agreed that by the early 3rd century this amount rose to about a billion sesterces per annum in a state budget with total revenues of about a billion and a half sesterces per annum, or something on the order of three-quarters of the annual budget of the Roman state (MacMullen, 1984; Duncan-Jones, 1994: 45, and chap. 3; see also Ferrill, 1991: 37). Although wages were never paid out in full (a good part of a soldier's pay was docked for various expenses), whatever allowance is made for their reduction must have been more than compensated for by the state's expenditures for weaponry and fixed defensive fortifications. Military expenditures for the late Roman and Byzantine states remained at a similarly high level of about three-quarters of the total state budget (Treadgold, 1995: 166–167, 195–197). These modern calculations are confirmed by the anonymous 6th century author of the manual *On Strategy,* who states bluntly that soldiers' wages alone consumed most of the annual public revenues of the Byzantine state (*Peri strat.* 2.18–21; Dennis, 1985: 12–13). Since the military budget was by far the single largest item in the annual disbursement of the state's assets, it follows that the military was the state-driven force that had the greatest effect on the economy of the Mediterranean world. It is most important to remember that the largest proportion of this military expenditure was directed (or redistributed) to the periphery of the empire, indeed mainly to the war zones on the frontiers where most of the military establishment was located.

When Libanius announced that money constituted "the sinews of war," therefore, he was part of a long tradition that consistently recognized the importance of the tributary infrastructure of the state to the conduct of war (Libanius, *Or.* 46; cf. Cicero, *Phil.* 5.2.5, harking back to Thucydides 1.83.2). The observation raises a second point: that the regular annual receipts (tribute) required for the armed forces of the state were almost at the limit of what the fiscal-political system could bear. (This is not strictly measurable for late antiquity, but reasonable estimates can be provided for the principate, where better data are available.) Therefore, mobilizing the state's military forces to active war, either internal or external, quickly exhausted the liquid cash reserves stored in the imperial treasury. The great surpluses that Antoninus Pius had amassed (675 million denarii, or 2.7 billion sesterces) were soon expended on the northern wars of Marcus Aurelius, who according to legend was reduced to selling his wife's furniture, crockery, and clothing at auction in the Roman forum to meet state expenses (Historia Augusta, *Marc. Aurel.* 17.4). The same pressures also weighed on the Byzantine state. By 457 Emperor Marcian had hoarded a large peacetime surplus (7.2 million nomismata), but almost all of it was run through in paying for Leo I's disastrous expedition against the Vandals in 468 (Treadgold, 1995: 193–194). It was therefore predictable that the vicious cycle of civil conflicts that rent the empire through the mid 3rd century would bankrupt the Roman state and severely undermine its currency. Indeed, it has been argued that fiscal pressures of the military and war expenditures caused the substantial alteration of the fiscal apparatus of the late Roman state under Diocletian and his successors (Jones, 1964: 42–68; Carrié, 1986: 462–469). The anonymous late 4th century pamphleteer who urged basic reforms on the state noted that "it is because of vast expenditures on the army that . . . the whole mechanism of tax collection is collapsing" (*De rebus bellicis*, 5.1).

The development of war in the Mediterranean and Near East was also determined by political preconditions. The most immediate political factor was the presence of the two great states: the Roman empire, centered on the Mediterranean, and the Sassanid empire, centered on Mesopotamia and the Iranian plateau. The Roman empire was a relatively centralized, quasi-bureaucratic patronal imperial state. The Sassanid empire, on the other hand, was a relatively decentralized, quasi-segmentary ethnic or feudal state, but one whose ruling elite commanded complex bureaucratic capabilities (Widengren, 1976; Shahbazi, 1986: 494–495, 497–498; Schippmann, 1990; Howard-Johnston, 1995: 212–226). When it comes to the technical means by which these states supported war, however, the best narrative source materials tend to fail. The infrastructure of the conduct of war, so critical to its success or failure, is imperfectly known even for the Roman state. There is enough evidence to show that the Roman state increasingly assumed the responsibility by its own arms manufactories *(fabricae)* for the provision of armor and heavy weaponry from its arsenals (Bishop, 1985; James, 1988; Ferrill, 1991: 51–54). How and by what means the Sassanid state coped with these same problems is still largely unknown, although there seems to have been a developmental pattern similar to that of the Romans, was marked by the army reforms instituted by Khosro I

(531–579) to create a more professional standing force equipped by the resources of the central state (Rubin, 1995; Howard-Johnston, 1995: 211–220).
Although state-based logistics were an important advantage in the conduct of
war, we know so little about this critical infrastructure that we cannot be sure
when and how it began to fragment into purely local and isolated means of
supply (Haldon, 1990: 220–232; Ferrill, 1991: 27–29; Bachrach, 1993; Kaegi,
1993; Treadgold, 1995: 179–184). State systems of logistics were technically
far superior at the supply of large numbers of mobile troops. Armed ethnic
groups in conflict with the state, unless they could become parasitic on the
existing state systems, very quickly encountered the limits imposed by the exi-
gencies of supply. Gothic forces besieging the city of Rome in 538 were reduced
from many tens of thousands of men to a few by famine and disease (*Wars*
6.6.1). The invasion of a large armed force of Franks that entered Italy in
540 ground to a halt when a third of them perished from starvation (*Wars*
6.25.16–18).

   The convergence of cultural and environmental constraints with the physical
settings in which wars were actually contested produced different types of
combat. Take, for example, the peculiar form of static war characterized by
armed assaults on heavily fortified urban centers. Siege warfare arose when
there was a clearly defined frontier between relatively balanced opposing forces
and when large and heavily fortified urban centers were present in the frontier
zone. The classic case of late antiquity was the land frontier between the Roman and Sassanid states. Where the two empires converged the Syrian desert
formed a large arch-like interstitial space. North of this arid zone, in the great
plain between the upper Tigris and Euphrates rivers, where more permanent
and extensive human settlement was possible, the two empires confronted each
other directly along a shared land frontier. The principal objective of war in this
frontier zone was the wealth stored in the treasuries of the heavily fortified cities
that studded the plain. The presence of urban centers that dominated the countryside, the emergence of a line of direct permanent engagement, and the relative stability and balance of the forces on either side combined to produce a
classic zone of siege warfare. But siege frontiers were just as characteristic of
internal wars: a city like Aquileia that was located on the borderland between
the two halves of the empire was besieged (unsuccessfully) many times
(Amm.Marc. 21.12.1: 361). As ecological, political, and military conditions
altered to produce new frontiers of permanent engagement, siege warfare became characteristic of regions, like the Italian peninsula during the 6th century,
where it had not previously been dominant. Therefore, the determinant characteristic of this type of warfare is the manner in which geopolitical factors
dictated the location of siege warfare, rather than the technical tactical details
of individual sieges.

   Both the narrative accounts of actual sieges and the technical advice on how
to besiege a city offered in military manuals like that of Vegetius (*Mil.* 4)
describe a highly routinized kind of conflict that seems to have been imposed
on both the besiegers and the besieged by the limitations of this type of warfare. Heavily walled urban centers were very expensive to attack (Amm.Marc.

21.13.2). Siege technology was therefore almost entirely under the command of the large states that had the requisite resources to support it. Smaller ethnic peoples, such as those along the northern flank of the Roman empire, were known not to have siege capabilities (Amm.Marc. 19.6.12: Quadi and Sarmatians; 31.6.4; 31.8.1; 31.15.1: Goths; Procopius, *Aed.* 2.9.4–5: "Saracens"). But even when the large states could afford to subvent this costly form of war, its limitations immediately became apparent. Usually the besieging forces first made a tremendous display of power, a parade of armed might by which they hoped to frighten the besieged into submission. If this ploy failed, it was usually followed by a parlay in which the besiegers attempted to negotiate the surrender of the city on equitable terms by a mixture of threats and offers of security and safe-conduct. If these moves failed, the besiegers then moved to the next step: simultaneous attacks directed at the full circuit of the city's walls. The hope was to find a weak spot or to effect a surrender by demonstrating the seriousness of the besiegers' intentions. If this failed, the attackers finally moved to the most serious and costly step—the assemblage of heavy siege equipment and the beginning of large-scale mining operations. Through all of this, the siege had its own temporal rhythms, which tended to be both seasonal and quotidian, with the darkness of each night imposing a cessation of hostilities (Amm.Marc. 19.9.1; 20.7 at Amida; 20.11.20 and 24 at Bezabde; *Wars* 5.25.8–11: Belisarius at Rome, 536).

Because it was also subject to environmental impediments, combat on the high seas has justifiably been allotted a rather small role in histories of warfare in late antiquity. Naval warfare remained peripheral not only for the great land-centered power of Sassanid Persia, but even for the Mediterranean-centered states of Rome and Byzantium (Jones, 1964: 610; Treadgold, 1995: 72–76, 173–177). This is not to say that these powers did not have ships, or in certain periods large collections of boats, oarsmen, and marines that served as naval forces. But the basic historical truth remains that the states and powers of the time were land-based and the decisive types of war were firmly terrestrial. Ethnic groups that did not otherwise have the technical resources of the larger states, such as the Goths in the mid 3rd century, could seize ships to use for raiding or more often simply for transportation (Whittaker, 1994: 194–195). But the usual, if not exclusive, function of seaborne power transporting land-based forces, whether those of large states, as in the case of the Byzantine fleets that shipped forces to North Africa in 468 and again in 534, or of ethnic-based powers, as with the boats used by the Vandals to cross the Straits of Gibraltar to North Africa in 429. Because the great majority of the potential protagonists, whether the ethnic armed groups along the Rhine and Danube, the Hephthalite Huns and Turkic groups of the Eurasian steppe, or the large state powers of Rome and Persia, were land-based powers, almost all combat was necessarily based on infantry and cavalry forces. Control of seas, rivers, or lakes remained important, but mainly for logistical reasons: the most convenient mode of transporting large stores of supplies and large numbers of men was by water (*Wars* 6.7.17; 6.24.13–16). Similarly, denying sea and riverine transport and supply to your enemy was tactically important (Höckman, 1986). But such imperatives never generated a decisive naval warfare, and the strategists of the period reflected this fact in the modest space they allotted to the tactics of seaborne fighting. For instance, Vegetius devoted only a truly exiguous portion of his whole manual to it (*Mil.* 4.31–33); and the classic Byzantine manuals have nothing on the subject (Dennis, 1985).

The purposes of wars varied according to the different social structures that sustained them. The large states fought external wars to maintain the territorial integrity of the state, whereas internal wars were waged to acquire the total resources of the state's territories. The myriad ethnic groups these large states confronted principally fought to dominate other groups and to compel surrender of their personal resources (Pohl, 1980: 244–246; Isaac 1992: 394–401). It is perhaps easy to underestimate the significance of payments that could be described as tribute. For all social groups outside the realm of state structures, war tributes were part of what Aristotle, centuries earlier, had specified as perfectly valid means of economic subsistence. In illiterate and institutionless societies, whose leadership had constantly to be reinforced by military success and material redistribution, this parasitic economy had considerable impact. When Valamir the Scythian broke the treaty and began ravaging Roman lands and towns in 459–461, it was to ensure that Roman envoys would guarantee the payment of 300 pounds of gold each year. In his own words, Valamir claimed that he had been compelled to war out of sheer necessity—because of the hardships suffered by his people (Priscos, frg. 37 Blockley). In the protection racket that was instituted by both state and ethnic forms of violence, these payoffs could be variously portrayed as an immoral extortion, as wages for armed service, or as a tribute (taxation) justly owed to the state (Blockley, 1992: 149–150). The large-scale payments made by the Roman and Byzantine states to the Huns and Hephthalites could be seen, from the state's perspective, simply as the continuation of war by other means (Gordon, 1949; Blockley, 1985; Iluk, 1985; Thompson, 1996: 211–218, 268). The more such fiscal instruments were institutionalized, the more the cycle of dependency on them was confirmed, and the more their stoppage made a return to violence the only economic alternative. Attila blamed the outbreak of war in 441 on the nonpayment of tribute by Theodosius II (Thompson, 1996: 281); Antalas, the African chieftain, went into armed revolt in 543–44 when the Byzantine commander Solomon stopped the usual imperial payments (*Wars* 4.21.17). The linkage between this type of economic dependency and war did not apply just to ethnic groups, however: major wars with Persia were directly provoked by the refusal of Justin II to pay reverse tribute (Menander, frg. 19.1; 12.7; 9.3; Rubin, 1986a; Isaac, 1992: 129–132). Perhaps the most serious consequences of ending tribute payments of this sort were the estoppages that provoked the Arab invasions in the early 630s (Theophanes, *Chron.* a.m. 6123, de Boor, 335f.; Donner, 1981: 115–117; Kaegi, 1992: 89–91; Isaac, 1992: 131–132).

From these basic structural constraints, let us turn to the principal diachronic developments that produced patterns of warfare in late antiquity. The best analytical point of departure is to follow the paradigm of the Roman empire, which remains the most completely documented case. The first great expansion of the Roman state over the Mediterranean was marked by a long cycle of warfare that lasted from about the mid 4th to the mid 1st century B.C.E. The Roman army fought increasingly successful and violent wars, mainly in the heartlands of the Mediterranean Basin. By the end of this period, the great threat to the Roman state was not external but rather internal. Within the Roman state the linkages between political institutions and armed force were inadequate to contain the consequences of state violence. Unresolved political and structural problems threatened to unravel the great success of its violent unification of the Mediterranean. The last century of the republican state was marked by a cycle of civil wars that brought an end to its system of government. The Augustan restoration stabilized the imperial military system by reconfiguring the political institutions to make them concordant with a centralized autocracy and by refashioning and redeploying the central army (Goldsworthy, 1996). These Augustan remedies provided a means for managing the internal threats of war and its effects; with two striking exceptions, they produced a long-term peace in the core areas of the empire. But they simultaneously contributed to a new form of state-driven violence which produced many of the new problems that were to haunt the conduct of war in the Late Roman state.

The Augustan system began with a general relocation of military forces to the land borders of the empire. The legionary and auxiliary units of the army were located at naturally occurring boundaries, either along rivers (the Rhine and the Danube on the northern frontier) or along road systems that ran between the desert and cultivated lands (in Syria and Palestine in the east, and in North Africa to the south). Permanent army bases were located where they could be supplied along dependable networks of communication. Augustus also professionalized armed service. The republican ideal of the citizen who was bound by duty to fight on behalf of his community continued to be mooted, but the need to stabilize the relationship between soldier and state was recognized by making military service a paid occupation, even a well-paid one. This physical and social refashioning of the Roman army effectively demilitarized the center of the empire, and thereby permanently separated the civilian core of the empire from its militarized periphery. Causally linked to this polarization of soldier and civilian was the increasing disinclination to military service of the great majority of men in the empire who did not happen to reside in the frontier provinces. Despite rewards offered to new volunteers, the state still had to resort, rather frequently, to conscription and "press gang" tactics in order to fill the ranks of the army (Jones, 1964: 615–619; Brunt, 1974; Haldon, 1979; Whitby, 1995; Elton, 1996: 128–150, 135–136). The location of most of the army camps along the frontiers of the empire and the rejection of military service by the center made recruiting increasingly provincial. The critical fact is that army recruiting was firmly rooted not just in the frontier provinces, but specifically in the war zones along the periphery of the empire. Indeed, the main bulk of all men recruited to the army was drawn increasingly from the northern frontier zones of the empire.

By implementing measures such as these, the Augustan restoration resolved one of the persistent problems of the late republic: the threat of the army and civil war to the state. By exporting its armed problems to the periphery of the empire and keeping them there, the new order effectively stripped the center of the empire of any substantial military force that might threaten the internal stability of the state. By thus disarming the core of the empire, however, Augustus and his successors, who had to sustain this new military system, simultaneously created a new condition of violence that was to become increasingly difficult to control—a permanent armed frontier around the outer periphery of the empire. Armies and their commanders might no longer emerge from violent conflicts in Italy and the center of the Mediterranean to threaten the state, but the new secret of empire, more insidious than Tacitus imagined, was that civil and military power could not be so easily detached from each other and maintained in discrete sectors. It was not so much that Roman emperors could be created outside Rome, but rather that both the political power and indeed the center of the state itself would gravitate inexorably to its heavily armed periphery. In a long-term geopolitical trend, the newly militarized imperial periphery provoked the concentration of capital cities, military supply factories, and even state mints in regions close to the frontier (Christol, 1977; Carrié, 1986: 463–465; Hollard, 1995; James, 1988).

Along the new post-Augustan frontiers of the Roman empire, the dialectical relationship between local army garrisons and external threats produced border areas of two broad categories: war zones and civil zones. In a war zone the state deployed a significant proportion of its military force in the expectation that major external wars would be fought in the region. On the civil frontier, the armed forces were principally involved in the maintenance of local order—in various forms of policing, quelling local banditry, and controlling minor rural insurgencies and occasional spates of ethnic and urban violence (Isaac, 1992: 161–218, 269–310). The war zones of the Roman empire extended along the length of the Rhine and Danube, and along the eastern face of the empire in a line from Armenia in the north to the frontiers of Syria and Mesopotamia, where Roman forces directly confronted those of Sassanid Persia. The frontier of the whole southern face of the empire—from modern-day Morocco in the west through Egypt in the east, and farther east to regions encompassing the southern areas of Palestine that faced on the Syrian Desert—was a more pacific frontier, where the civil core of the state extended almost to its natural boundaries (Isaac, 1992: 112–118, 138–140, 198–218). Military policing by the Roman state primarily involved advanced observation and control, with "tentacles" extended, like sensitive antennae, into the desert itself—the so-called *praetenturae* found on both the North African and Arabian desert frontiers (Kennedy and MacAdam, 1985; Speidel, 1987; MacAdam, 1989). The basic determinants in the creation of the two types of frontier were ecological; geopolitical forces established their respective war zones. This was just as true for the internal wars as it was for external wars.

The Roman empire was the largest, wealthiest, and most coherent state structure that dominated the Mediterranean and Near East. Recurring internal wars would therefore become the single most important military factor in the whole *oikoumenē*. And since the military establishment was the most expensive item in the state budget, the fiscal effects of civil wars were especially traumatic because they would tend to be recouped from the internal system itself. The shoring up of loyalties among the soldiers in such circumstances, against the internal competition for their resources, cost the state considerably. The dramatic civil war that preceded the 3rd century crisis, the war waged among Septimius Severus, Clodius Albinus, and Pescennius Niger in 192–93, consumed immense resources. Septimius Severus, once he became emperor, had to recover the costs from the resources of his political opponents by conducting a purge of wealthy senatorial and equestrian landowners and by appropriating their wealth for the state (indeed, the *res privata* came to rival the *patrimonium* of the emperor in size and importance). Almost every episode of internal warfare exacted an additional toll of accusation and persecution, invariably connected to the confiscation of the wealth of the landowners who had supported the losing party. Constantine, Constantius, and Magnus Maximus all recovered the costs of civil war in this manner (Jones, 1964: 158f.). Julian staged a purge of the adherents of Constantius (Amm.Marc. 22.3.1–12, 361). Procopius had to activate the services of men skilled in raising money in the cities of Asia Minor in order to support his war efforts (Amm.Marc. 26.8.14, 365); but his conqueror Valens initiated a general slaughter of Procopius's supporters in order to acquire their wealth to pay for the war (Amm.Marc. 26.10.9, 365).

The cycle of civil wars that began to afflict the Roman state during the half-century following the late 230s signaled the breakdown of the "Akzeptanz-System" at the heart of the Augustan restoration (Flaig, 1992). These internal wars also exacted a much greater toll on its resources and its leaders— only one of the fourteen emperors who died violently during this period did so in battle against the external enemies of the empire—than did the barbarian incursions which they did so much to encourage (Carrié, 1993: 93–94). It is a reasonable estimate that at least one-third of the 4th century was consumed by internal wars of one part of the Roman state against another. For a large number of the years that remained, the politics of emperors and armies were determined in no small part by a considerable fear of potential or impending civil conflict. Because of the military resources the Roman state had at its command (much greater than those of the next largest state in the region and vastly superior to those of the various ethnic groups around its frontiers), internal wars within the Roman state had a profound effect on war in general. But the repercussive effects of wars within the empire tended to focus on specific points in the imperial landscape. Fundamental geographical forces encouraged the grouping of the lands west of the Adriatic into one region and those east of the Adriatic into another. This geopolitical fact was recognized by the reforms of Diocletian that divided the empire into eastern and western halves and formally divided the fiscal and military resources of the empire between the rulers of the east and the west. The region of Illyricum and the adjacent mountainous lands between the great Danube bend and the Adriatic coast, located on the midpoint of this division, became the most important internal war frontier of the empire. The collected forces of the eastern half of the empire were regularly pitted against those of the western half along the middle Danube.

The reforms of the Roman central state under Diocletian and Constantine were Augustan in nature. They were new, but stereotypical, answers to the social, economic, political, and military problems caused by repeated fissioning of the empire into its geopolitical components and by the relapse into repeated bouts of civil war. The modular structure of the tetrarchy, with a hierarchy of powers nested one within the other, was meant to countervail the threat of civil war while at the same time answering to the need to have several concurrent emperors in command of armed forces close to the different frontiers of the empire. The "solution" of the Tetrarchy, however, only tended to exacerbate the problems of civil conflict, which resurfaced with ferocity among the successors of Constantine. The creation of mobile field armies (comitatus) during the period was provoked less by the need to do battle with external enemies of the state than it was by the overwhelming pressure for each emperor and subemperor to have his own military forces directly under his command to protect himself from internal threats (Jones, 1964, 97–100; Hoffmann, 1969–70: 131–140; Ferrill, 1986: 47; Carrié, 1993: 124–125).

As the new realities forced a breakdown of the old consensus, any legitimate power player became a potential ruler. Losers were labeled usurpers or tyrants, while winners became emperors. This ex post facto labeling makes it difficult to deduce from the surviving data valid conceptions of usurpation and legitimacy (Flaig, 1997). The new facts of political life caused decisions made by emperors and their subordinates to be overshadowed by a pervasive fear of civil war that repeatedly entered into their calculations (Amm.Marc. 14.7). Emperors such as Constantius might be renowned as warriors, but in his case it was for his good fortune in fighting civil wars rather than external ones (Amm.Marc. 14.11.8, 354). Roman soldiers decided whether to follow him and to obey his orders based on their experience of earlier battles, which convinced them that Constantius had good fortune in fighting internal wars but bad luck when it came to external ones (Amm.Marc. 14.10.16; 21.15.1). It was a reputation of which Constantius was aware and in which he himself firmly believed (Amm.Marc. 21.13.7). He constantly weighed the threats and problems connected with civil war against wars that he might be compelled (or wish) to wage with external enemies. The preparations for war were just as rigorous in either case (Amm.Marc. 20.9.3, 360; 21.6.6, 361; 21.7.1; 21.13.1–2). The same calculations also had to be made by Constantius's opponent, the future emperor Julian. He had reason to fear Constantius's known record of winning civil wars, and he made sure to acquire the services of Arbitrio, an army officer well known for his extensive prior success in civil wars (Amm.Marc. 21.13.16, 361).

Civil wars were often more threatening because they pitted well-trained and well-equipped Roman armies against each other. Almost invariably this parity of power caused a rush to acquire new manpower reserves that would make the difference in the final confrontation, and a haste to settle the matter in a set battle before one's opponent could marshal more recruits. The additional manpower was always to be found among the so-called barbarians. The civil war that pitted Constantine against Maxentius provoked Constantine to draft large numbers of Franks and Alamanni. The civil war of Licinius against Constantine impelled the former to draft large numbers of Goths into his service. The civil war of Constantius against Magnentius compelled the latter to recruit Saxons and Franks to bolster his forces (Julian, *Or.* 1.34c–d). Constantine himself drafted heavily from frontier ethnic groups to create the first mobile strike force, or *comitatus,* of the Roman army (Zosimus, *Hist.eccl.* 1.15; Hoffmann, 1969–70: 130–141, 169–173; Liebeschuetz, 1990: 7).

Civil wars were also the main cause of the systematic recruiting of barbarians along the northern frontiers into the Roman army. Constantius invited barbarians (probably more Franks and Saxons) to cross into the empire and attack his rival Magnentius from the rear. The same recruitment of barbarians characterized the civil wars between Julian and Constantius; and between Procopius and Valens, in which Procopius, relying on personal connections to Constantine's family, recruited from the Goths. And it remained true of the great civil wars that Emperor Theodosius fought, first against Magnus Maximus (387) and then against Eugenius (392–394), in which he recruited on a large scale from Alans, Arabs, Goths, Huns, Iberians, and Isaurians (Pacatus, *Pan.Lat.* 12.32.3–4; 32.3–5; 33.4–5; Liebeschuetz, 1990: 30). These wars were characterized by the same large-scale recruiting of frontier ethnic groups, including Goths (Socrates, *Hist.eccl.* 5.25; Zosimus 4.45.3, 4.57.2), Huns (John of Antioch, frg. 87), and Franks (Orosius, *Adv.Pag.* 7.35.11–12; Rufinus 11.33). Almost every leader in a civil war castigated his opponent for recruiting barbarians, but then did it himself. Julian criticized Constantine, but recruited in the same region and indeed from the same ethnic groups. Magnus Maximus paraded an avowed hostility to Germans, but nonetheless recruited them in large numbers (Ambrose, *Ep.* 24.8). Not only did each contestant in civil war recruit from his own frontier peoples, but he also followed the common practice of inducing ethnic groups on his opponent's frontier to attack his rival from the rear. So Magnus Maximus accused Bauto of inciting "barbarians" to invade his territory (Ambrose, *Ep.* 24.4.6–8).

From the 3rd century crisis onward, therefore, civil wars were the single most important determinant of war for the Roman empire and for war in the Mediterranean and Near East in general. The great internal conflicts within the Roman state compelled contestants to draw on the manpower reserves of ethnic groups along and beyond the frontiers of the empire. This embroiled ethnic groups in a war economy and in recurrent cycles of war from which they could not easily escape. The effects of external recruiting for these internal wars were geographically specific. Only along the Rhine and Danube were found the permanently structurally fragmented social and political orders and the high population levels that both enticed and impelled the leaders in Rome's internal wars to the systematic recruitment of these populations. One important long-term consequence of the interlocking and interdependence of Roman and ethnic warfare on the northern face of the empire was the destabilization of a frontier that was already fragmented along ethnic lines. Then again, the systematic involvement of ethnic groups along the Rhine and Danube in this internal war oriented them permanently toward military service in the Roman state. Like a magnetic force, the rewards of the military tended to attract ethnic groups from ever farther afield to the line of the Rhine and Danube (Pohl, 1994: 75). War service, in which most of them were well experienced, was one of the very few useful things that they could offer to an empire that had the resources to pay.

The permanent involvement of ethnic groups along the northern frontiers in the internal wars of the Roman state affected the late Roman military command structure. In the long series of civil wars that began in the late 230s, which had only a temporary respite with Constantine's victory in 324, the significance of armed ethnic groups to the total manpower of Roman armies increased dramatically. This factor, along with the concentration of operational units of the Roman army in the war zones of the empire's periphery, led to the high command positions in the Roman state of experienced military men whose careers were made by service on these frontiers. It cannot surprise that the same Rhine-Danube war zone that regularly produced Roman emperors from Maximinus Thrax (reputedly the first emperor actually to fight personally in combat) onward also produced the empire's military elite of high-ranking army officers. This was the logical result of the military reforms instituted by Augustus. The permanent location of the army along the periphery of the empire and the heavy recruiting of soldiers from the northern war zone to a professional army created a military with its own frontier war economy, culture, and ideology. The constant exchanges and confrontations in military matters alone, such as weaponry and types of combat, produced a convergence of tactics and modes of operation (Kunow, 1986; Traina, 1986–87; Dagron, 1993: 279–280).

It was only a matter of time before the soldiers who shared this military culture would enforce not only their own regional interests but also their conviction that only professional soldiers were fit to command. The increasing exclusion of senators from high commands in the Roman army, traditionally ascribed to a single act by Emperor Gallienus, was the natural preference of armed forces that favored a local and professional command over a distant and amateur civil aristocracy (Carrié, 1993: 88–90). Bauto the Frank, who served Constantine, and his son Silvanus, who later fought for Magnentius, were both examples of men advanced in status by Romans in the context of civil wars; by the end of the 4th century a considerable proportion of the highest commands in the Roman army (*magistri militum*) were consistently held by such men (Waas, 1971: 10–14; Elton, 1996: 147–151). The separation of military and civilian into distinct spheres formalized the alienation of the two parts of the state from each other, with malign consequences for both sides. When Alaric brought the culture of the frontier to the gates of Rome in 409, the civil aristocracy and the Senate arrogantly rebuffed his requests—an arrogance betraying paralyzing ignorance of what sort of men they had created on the frontiers of their own empire.

The increased dependence on ethnic recruits and the rise of frontier men to high-level army commands have been rather misleadingly characterized as the "barbarization" of the Roman army, the malign effects of which have probably been exaggerated (Elton, 1996: 128–154). Its significance lies instead in the consequences of the dynamic relationships between Roman armed forces and frontier peoples. The patterns of behavior created by this system of war must seriously modify traditional claims that the empire was invaded by northern barbarians. Instead, the original historical sources are replete with repeated solicitations of northern ethnic groups and their leaders to enter the service of a given emperor or pretender in order to serve that leader's interests. The presence of large armed polyethnic bands within the frontiers of the empire cannot be blamed in any simple fashion on barbarian invasions. There was not a single leader of such a large-scale ethnic armed force, from Alaric to Attila, who had not been invited into the empire for the purpose of armed service (Heather, 1991: 193–213; Liebeschuetz, 1990: 48–85). This peculiar dynamic prevailed only on the northern frontier of the Roman empire because this frontier alone harbored large populations whose fragmentary and small-scale social units exposed them so readily to exploitation by the superior resources of the Roman state. The pattern persisted to the bitter end in the west: when in the late 560s Narses, the Byzantine commander (exarch) in Italy, fell into conflict with the eastern emperor Justin, he invited the Longobards into the peninsula (*Hist.Lang.* 2.5; Christie, 1991; 1995: 60–62). He had centuries of precedent before him.

In the dominant explanations of the historical causes of war in late antiquity, internal wars within the great states have not generally been assigned a leading place in the hierarchy. Even though they have been the object of some criticism, hypotheses on the nature of war in late antiquity are still governed by variations on what might be called the domino theory of causation (Goffart, 1980: 3–39; 1989). The domino explanation is committed to the "fact" that there were large-scale wanderings of peoples across the Eurasian steppe and western European plains, and that these movements were impelled by forces endogenous to the economies of the barbarian peoples (Todd, 1992: 55). These developments produced overpopulation and allied economic pressures that compelled the barbarians regularly to seek new lands for settlement (Demougeot, 1969–1979; Musset, 1975; Heather, 1996, chap. 2). As one northern people moved violently into its neighbor's territory, there was a "push on" effect that eventually forced the peoples closest to the northern frontiers of the Roman empire to move against the empire itself. A simple reading of a text in Ammianus Marcellinus (31.2.1) finds in it the paradigm of such a chain of causation: the Huns attack their neighbors, the Alans and Goths, thereby causing the last-named people to "flood" across the Danube in 376 (Ferrill, 1986: 59; Burns, 1994: 23; Thompson, 1996: 33–34; Heather, 1995 and 1996, chap. 4). Ammianus's words, however, have perhaps been made to sustain a greater interpretive weight than they can reasonably bear (Pohl, 1994: 75). Detailed studies of the actual modalities of the so-called barbarian incursions into the empire, beginning with Delbrück's revisionist analysis of the numbers involved, have shown that small-scale, recurrent local infiltrations of the frontier zone were the more usual threat to Roman frontiers. The revisionists assert that set battles were not typical of the multifarious confrontations between barbarian and Roman; rather, prevalent types of frontier violence were closer to petty raids and acts of brigandage, aimed at the immediate acquisition of booty (Whittaker, 1994: 152–191).

The Sassanid state, for which we know so much less, alas, was apparently no less prone to spates of civil or internal war, and for much the same causes as those that applied to the Roman empire. The king had preeminent significance as head of state, and because his position was sustained by being perceived as a successful war leader, failure to uphold this role was likely to provoke armed insurrections by pretenders (Whitby, 1994). When the strength of Bahram II was brought into question at the beginning of his reign by the successful attacks on Sassanid lands by the Roman emperor Carus (in 283), the response was an armed revolt of one of the eastern provinces, led by Bahram's brother Hormizd (Zonaras 12.30; Historia Augusta, *Carus,* 8). These internal wars were renewed in 293 with the death of Bahram II. His son ruled only a few months and was then overthrown by his uncle Narseh, who was then a general in Armenia. As in the Roman case, the prevailing tendency was for military commanders on the frontier to threaten a weakened center. The crises of the Sassanid state in the 5th century followed much the same pattern. Like Roman monarchs, Yazdgerd II (440–457), in his attempts to stabilize attacks on the northeastern frontier, was compelled to move both court and army to the periphery of empire. Alas, he met with no success, and his failure to control violence on the frontiers of the Sassanid empire only provoked the internal fragmentation of the state and civil war between his two sons, Hormizd and Peroz.

When Peroz became Shāhānshāh, however, he faced the same problems. His defeat by the Hephthalites in 482 produced internal dissension and armed rebellions by local men of power in the Sassanid empire, who appointed one of their own, Balāsh Valgāsh, as King of Kings. In a manner reminiscent of Aetius in the Roman west, Kavad, the son of Peroz, who had served time as a hostage among the Hephthalites, used his personal connections to mobilize the frontier peoples to assist him in the acquisition of central power. In 496, when Kavad was deposed in one of these internal wars, he managed to escape to the Hephthalites and engaged in large-scale recruiting of them to his army so he could restore himself to the throne. As in the Roman west, military dependency on the frontier peoples only served to increase the indebtedness of the state to them. These debts provoked Kavad to a series of aggressive moves against the Roman frontier on the northwest in 502–503 to extort from the Byzantine state the monies he needed to pay off the Hephthalites. Thus, the episodes of civil war within the Sassanid state produced much the same compulsion to recruit armed manpower from its northern periphery as did the internal conflicts of the Roman empire. The northern frontier was the important recruiting zone for the Sassanid state for the same reasons as Rome's own northern frontier was for the Roman empire: it harbored a large number of segmentary, dispersed, stateless societies whose main resource was their own population. The processes of war were comparable to those of the Roman state, but the precise conduct of it was different, since the populations of the Eurasian steppes were mainly pastoral nomads, with less dense populations dispersed over much larger geographic spaces, and the Sassanid state was more loosely structured than the Roman.

Although their imperial ideologies denied it, both the Roman empire and Sassanid Persia had internal frontiers which were potentially just as dangerous as many of their external ones. Indeed, all of the autonomous societies and polities located in the Mediterranean and the Near East were prone not only to external wars with foreign enemies, but also to warfare that involved internal components of the state or social order. The Roman empire offers the best evidence for this phenomenon and for understanding its significance, but this type of internal war was just as characteristic of the Sassanid state, and of the larger ethnic polities beyond the Rhine and Danube. Even within the outer frontiers of large states like Rome and Persia, however, there existed what might be called inner frontiers—large regions where the state's monopoly of violence was contested in a fashion comparable to that on the outer frontiers themselves. The existence of such inner frontiers has been doubted for the Sassanid state (Howard-Johnston, 1995: 184–185), but the paucity of evidence on the military history of the Sassanians makes one skeptical of the claim, especially since such recalcitrant inner frontiers are well documented for the Achaemenid period (Briant, 1976; 1982: 57–112). The most important reasons for the existence of the inner frontiers were ecological—a combination of climatic, topographic, demographic, and economic factors. And of the topographical factors, by far the most important were mountains. The highland zone of the Taurus mountain range called Isauria, located in the southeastern quadrant of Asia Minor, was a classic example of just such an autonomous land within the Roman empire (Shaw, 1990). All narrative accounts of war from late antiquity, including the representation of the province in the *Notitia dignitatum*, reveal not only the great difficulties that the Roman state had in controlling Isauria, but also its development as a kind of internal *limes* of the empire, marked by local effusions of state coinage typically associated with intrusive large-scale concentrations of the armed forces of the central state (Mitchell, 1989; 1995: 208–217).

Even modest mountain highlands seem to have presented the Roman state with considerable difficulties of armed control and political domination. The mountains of North Africa, especially the Qabiliyya (Kabyle) or "tribal lands" of the coastal ranges of Algeria, were a classic instance of the highland autonomy that presented the Roman state with constant problems of political integration. A late 4th century incident from North Africa reported in detail by Ammianus exemplifies the characteristic pattern: Since mountainous regions were known to be reservoirs of freedom, the local "big men" were constantly suspected of trying to enhance their own power at the expense of the central state. In the early 370s suspicions of rebellion and usurpation fell on one Firmus, son of Nubel (Kotula, 1970). "Flavius" Nubel was a paradigm of the frontier man who lived simultaneously in two worlds: he was at once an autonomous and powerful chieftain in his own community (*regulus per nationes Mauricas potentissimus*: Amm.Marc. 29.5.2) and a high-ranking officer *(comes)* in the late Roman army (*ILCV* 1822). Firmus, his son, became involved in a complicated set of machinations, mainly provoked by the problems plaguing a disintegrating central court (Matthews, 1976; 1989: 367–376). He tried to protest his loyalty to the central government, but to no avail. The incidents of guerrilla warfare and heavy policing that ensued were concentrated around Firmus's home terrain in the mountains of north central Algeria (Amm.Marc. 29.5). The general of the cavalry forces in Gaul, Theodosius, was dispatched to the area with a large expeditionary force that set sail from the port of Arelate. It is important to note that Theodosius's campaigns in North Africa stuck to the Roman roads that ran around the periphery of the mountains. He ultimately prevailed through constant patrolling of the lowlands immediately around the mountains and through imposing trade embargoes to convince Firmus's main followers that it was too costly to support him. In the end they abandoned him, and Firmus was compelled to commit suicide (Amm.Marc. 29.5.51–54).

Although large states like Rome and Persia could conduct their surrogate battles in a mountainous region like Armenia (or Lazica, Colchis, or Iberia), neither state ever managed finally to control the local dynasts, who were always able to retreat into ever more remote highland zones (Amm.Marc. 27.12, 368–70; Braund, 1994: 287–311). To the end of antiquity one encounters descriptions of zones of permanent insurgency in mountain highlands that were characterized, from the perspective of central states, by types of violence that they labeled "banditry" *(latrocinium, lēsteia)*. Such were the Tzanic people of Armenia, who could always be defeated by the Romans or the Persians in a set military confrontation, but who were never finally dominated as a people since they were always able to retreat into the mountain heights, only to return later to reassert their autonomy (*Wars* 1.15.21–15, 530). These internal highland frontiers were no less significant than the northern Rhine-Danube frontier had been in the 4th century, and played the same role as a provider of raw recruits for the Roman army. Indeed, the highland zones of Armenia, Isauria-Cilicia, and the mountains of the Lebanon and the Anti-Lebanon had been a regular source of manpower for imperial armies (Speidel, 1980, 1983; Kennedy, 1989; Mitchell, 1994). They became inland war zones of the empire, characterized by the same types of economic development as its outer frontiers (Mitchell, 1995: 212–214). The loss of the traditional Roman recruiting sources along the war frontier of the Rhine and Danube in the 5th century, however, only served to increase the importance of the eastern highlands in Isauria and Armenia for army recruiting, which brought them still more power as the eastern highlands became primary war zones. Isauria now provided the rising military men, like Longinus, Tarasikodissa, and Flavius Zenon, who became high-ranking military officers and even monarchs of the eastern empire in the third quarter of the 5th century (Shaw, 1990: 250–256).

The long-term history of warfare involving the large states that dominated Mesopotamia and the Iranian highlands—first the Parthians and then the Sassanians—is one of extraordinary stability. As long as Rome and Persia, the large states on either side, remained internally stable and were perceived to be strong militarily, then the relationships between the two, though based on a permanent armed confrontation, tended to be characterized by long periods of peace and stability. The fragmentation of the Roman state through a long spate of civil conflicts up to the middle of the 3rd century destabilized its extreme outer frontiers, both on the far east and the far west. Where the central state was not able to fulfill its critical war function of protection against invaders, local powerful figures arose to perform this task for their own regions. Thus on the western periphery the so-called local empire of the Gauls assumed this function for a long period (Drinkwater, 1987). The weakness and fragmentation of the Roman central state encouraged repeated Persian forays through the mid 3rd century, and with these the rise of a peripheral protector kingdom centered on Palmyra. The restabilization of the Roman state under Diocletian and Galerius at the end of the 3rd century, however, returned the eastern frontier to a long-term balance between the two empires. Despite the permanent marshaling of a large proportion of all the armed resources of either empire along their shared frontier, peace prevailed along the border between the two great states for over two centuries. The great peace was broken by occasional expeditionary forces and raids by either side, some of them of considerable scale (in 338–340, 358–360, and 363; and again in 421–422 and 441–442), but these sudden forays deep into each other's border zones are remarkable for their brevity and their infrequency. Every incident was rather quickly followed by a peace agreement.

War on this frontier also had an ethnic component, but the peoples who were open to recruitment by either side were locked in an interstitial zone—the large unsettled desert arch between the agricultural lands directly protected by Roman forces and the western limits of the settled areas of the Sassanid state. The interstitial desert zone was populated by ethnic groups first labeled Arabs, but later Saracens (Isaac, 1992: 235–236). Their leaders, recognized by the Roman or Persian states as rulers of their people, were granted the title of tribal chief or phylarch. Not wishing permanently to commit any sizable forces outside the zones of agricultural settlement, both the Roman and the Sassanid states forged links with the Arabic phylarchs as a means of patrolling the desert and harassing their opposites. Connections between pastoral nomadic groups and states in the region, which had a very long history, tended to be limited to the use of armed elements as surrogate policemen of the desert periphery. The long-term opposition of two great central states on either side of the Syrian desert, however, encouraged an increasing integration of warlike forces inside the desert zone itself (Isaac, 1992: 235–249). The formalization of these relationships seems to have reached a threshold of sorts in the aftermath of the long cycle of Roman civil wars that ended with Constantine. In the latter part of Constantine's reign one Imru' al-Qays, buried at Nemara in 328, was recognized as not just an isolated Arab tribal phylarch, but rather king of all the Arabs (Shahid, 1984b: 31–53; Isaac, 1992: 239–240). As Ammianus later remarked, before his time the previously disparate Arabic groups had come to unify in war and so were now seen as Saracens, a term which seems to be derived from a word that signified a larger conglomerate of ethnic groups (Bowersock, 1975, 1983: 138–

147; Graf and O'Connor, 1977; *contra:* Shahid, 1984a). By the 6th century, the heyday of these confederations, the two principal leaders—Arethas, whose Ghassanids were allied with the Romans; and al-Mundhir, whose Lakhmids cooperated with the Sassanians—assumed increasingly independent courses of action (Shahid, 1995: 209–235; 529–540). The fundamental difference between the armed ethnic servitors on this frontier and those on the northern frontiers of the Roman and Sassanid states, however, was that the former were firmly contained by the two major states in the region. The Arab allies of both states, even in the most ambitious moments of the larger war groups of the 6th century, remained contributors to the existing war system in the Near East.

Like the ethnic groups along the northern frontier, the Arab tribes were also segmentary lineage societies, and their power arrangements were structured accordingly. Only civil wars within one of the two larger states, or prolonged outbreaks of full-scale war between them, might have threatened the balance of the recruiting of the Arab tribes. Continuous wars between Rome and Persia, however, were not common until the 6th century, and even then the wars tended to be limited to the contact zone of Mesopotamia or to the Armenian highlands to the north. Neither the Sassanians nor the Romans had any serious possibility of recruiting each other's subject populations; by social and cultural disposition, the inhabitants of the settled areas on the borderlands of both empires were tied to the political structures and interests of their respective states. The crossover from one side to the other was truly minimal, and the desertion of a local big man, such as the Antoninus reported by Ammianus (18.5; 359), was usually balanced by the odd Persian nobleman who went in the opposite direction (*Wars* 8.26.13). Beyond these individual shifts, the dangers for the major states in the recruitment of Arabic ethnic groups were never that great. Because two states were competing for their resources, collaboration would tend to balance between the employers. Then again, the absolute population levels in the desert were low—certainly by comparison with those of the two large states. Even if most men of military age were co-opted (half by one side, half by the other), the immediate consequences for battlefield conditions between Rome and Persia were never great enough to change the basic nature of war on this frontier.

The northern contact zone between the lands north of the Rhine and Danube and north of the Black Sea, and the peripheries of the Roman and Sassanid states was different from the frontier between the two states. The European stretch of this long northern frontier can be divided into an eastern and a western zone incorporating the lands lying east and west of the Hungarian plain (Elton, 1996: 19–30). To the east of the European part of this northern frontier, and to the north of the Black and Caspian seas, were the great Eurasian steppelands. These different ecological zones tended to sustain different modes of war. Whereas the indigenous peoples in the western European zone conducted wars almost solely with infantry forces, in the eastern European zone, and further east to the Eurasian steppe, warfare was increasingly dominated by cavalry forces. Despite these distinctions in warfare, the societies that inhabited these zones shared some strong continuities. Ethnic groups were subdivided into small, sometimes very small, social groups. They had basic subsistence agro-pastoral economies, were illiterate, and had no complex state or bureaucratic structures through which they could marshal resources for war (Heather, 1994). Although descriptions of their social structures are few, biased, and difficult to interpret, it is reasonably certain that almost all of these societies functioned on the basis of segmentary lineage systems (Thompson, 1966; 1996: 36, 48–50, 64–66, 80). Their technologies of war were therefore exceedingly simple: "It is remarkable that despite fairly frequent contact with Roman frontier armies, and despite endemic intertribal disputes and private feuds, no great advances were made in arms and armor, with the exception of sword blades, during the centuries of the [Roman] empire" (Todd, 1972: 99-102; at 102; Raddatz, 1985). Warfare and low-level violence (feuding, raiding) seem to have been endemic to all of these societies, which had their own species of internal wars as well as larger-scale conflicts that involved the cumulated resources of their respective peoples (e.g., Orosius, *Adv.Pag.* 7.37.3 on wars involving the Huns, Alans, and Goths). Although a knowledge of these local indigenous wars is very important to a general understanding of war in late antiquity, the plain fact is that very little evidence about them has survived.

Usually, the wars waged by these northern peoples, even external ones, aimed at achieving a form of domination over other people that was analogous to the bonds of power within their own segmentary and illiterate societies: the production of a dependent following such as the "countless retinue" of the Gepid "king" Ardaric (Jordanes, *Getica,* 99). On the one hand, this politics depended on dramatic gestures and public assertion of personality (Pohl, 1994: 71). On the other hand, as Tacitus noted, the instruments of violence were of critical importance: "It is impossible to maintain a large following of warriors except by violence and war" (*Germ.* 14). Faith and trust—and one might add fear—held these men together. They tied Ardaric to the following of Attila and thereby reveal how the Huns could rapidly mushroom into a large ethnic war band. Successes in war encouraged larger numbers of adherents and solidified their loyalties. Failures, which were just as frequent, broke them. Thus warrior bands, such as that headed by Sarus the Goth at the beginning of the 5th century, could suddenly expand or diminish in size (Zosimus 6.2.4–5, 13.2, 36.2; Liebeschuetz, 1990: 38–39).

The dynamic composition of these ethnic war groupings made loyalty and motive critical to the attachment of component units to a single leader. One might think of the Gepids and their king Ardaric. In reality, his "Gepids" were a large conglomerate composed of Rugi, Heruls, Sarmatians, Suebi, Sciri, and others (Pohl, 1980: 260–261). The Longobard army that Alboin led into Italy in 568–69 was a composite band of Longobards, Saxons, Bulgars, Sarmatians, Pannonians, Suebi, Noricans, and others (*Hist.Lang.* 2.26; Christie, 1995: 64). Far from being the occasion of ethnogenesis or the forging of a specific and stable ethnic identity by means of violent confrontation with "others," war just as often impelled the creation of large polyethnic followings. Although their members might be called by a single name, like Gepid or Hun, in reality these groups were weak multiethnic conglomerates that constantly threatened to break down into their original ethnic and segmentary parts. No sooner did the Longobards conquer Italy than they redispersed and fragmented into the numerous segments *(Farae)* from which their society had been constituted (Christie, 1995: 65, 77–82).

The long-term benefits of the northern peoples' parasitic attachments to the Roman state were not inconsiderable. For their leaders, such links were probably necessary to maintain their position of superior power within their ethnic conglomerate. From the perspective of the Roman state, however, these frontier peoples posed a number of serious problems. The northern borderlands were inhabited by a great number of diverse ethnic groups, none of which were organized along state lines. Almost all of them were involved in intermittent warfare with each other, conflicts that occasionally threatened to spill over into the empire. Moreover, quite unlike the civil frontiers along the southern half of the empire, the northern frontiers had substantial population densities. The consistent Roman and Byzantine response to the serious threats posed in this war zone was the obvious one: to manipulate the local forces of violence, most often by using one ethnic group as a check on its neighbor. This response required constant readjustments, however, since the more the central state intervened with advice and exhortation, weaponry and material support, prestigious ranks and rewards, and large amounts of money and precious metals, the more violence increased. And the greater the intensity of the violence, the less predictable and controllable it became. The escalating rewards and the escalating violent behavior became part of frontier ethnic groups' learned behavior—and expectations. There was thus created along this frontier what might be aptly labeled a "parasitic economy," in which local chieftains and men of power came to depend on the acquisition of war rewards and prestige goods from their Roman employers as the critical economic means by which they sustained their own position with their followers (Pohl, 1980: 268; Todd, 1992: 86–87).

Compared to the eastern frontier, which was made unusually stable by the existence of bureaucracy, institutions, literacy, and the capability of setting fixed agreements that would hold for large geographical spaces and for long periods of time, the northern frontiers were continually threatened by war precisely because of their extreme instability. Any peace agreement on the Rhine or Danube was necessarily made with a finite ethnic group that covered only a relatively small geographic space and functioned wholly in an oral mode. The agreement had to be a spoken one between the Roman emperor and a specific ethnic head (the *rex, regulus, subregulus,* or *reiks*) who made spoken promises and swore oaths to keep his agreements (Amm.Marc. 17.1.13; 17.10.9; 30.6.2). The Roman state therefore had to deal with these peoples in the same oral mode in which they dealt with each other (Amm.Marc. 31.3.1: Huns and Alans, about 370). Alliances that were confirmed by what was said and heard by either side (Amm.Marc. 30.3.5, 374), however, were only as good as the individual chief who made them, and were based on the same networks of personal connections that constituted hierarchy in the local society—an order that constantly threatened to unravel with the provocation of some local feud or some other minor shift in local relationships that impaired the power of the individual who had made the promise to the Roman emperor. These attachments were also viewed on the ethnic side as highly personal. Gothic chieftains who made agreements with Constantine in the mid 330s passed these down to their descendants, who regarded themselves in a personal relationship with the familial descendants of that particular Roman and no other. Such a system of peace agreements was only as dependable as the oral and ritualistic personal links that sustained them from one generation to the next. The potential for misunderstanding was very great and sometimes involved the Roman emperor in grotesque scenes of farcical confusion as well as real danger, as when Constantius tried to stage a ritual ceremonial to confirm his relations with the Limigantes in 359, and almost lost his life in the ensuing wild melee (Amm.Marc. 19.11.10–13).

Warfare along the northern face of the empire, while it did involve both the congeries of ethnic groups and the massive resources of the Roman state, never produced a simple dichotomy of barbarians against Romans. The constant intrusion of the economic and political forces of the Roman state, and its exploitation of the frontier peoples for its own purposes, transformed the frontier between the two into an intensive war zone in which whole ethnic groups were repeatedly drawn into a vortex of violence. The powerful economic and social forces set in motion by these wars did on occasion contribute to the forging of new ethnic identities, in a process labeled ethnogenesis by modern-day historians—the Salian Franks being a striking example of a long-term identity defined in part by their military service for the Roman state (Anderson, 1995; see also Barlow, 1995). The identity of the whole generation of "Goths" that Alaric led across the northern war zone, from Illyricum into Italy, had been forged by the very processes of war and military service that made and unmade the circumstances of their daily lives (Liebeschuetz, 1990: 49–83). This was one of the creative faces of the northern war zone. But there was also a genocidal aspect to this frontier warfare—not, one must be careful to caution, in the sense of the physical extinction of all persons belonging to a given social group, but rather entailing the destruction of their social formations and identities. Ethnic groups were destroyed by the very forces of war that had initially helped to sustain them. As they were drawn into the vortex of violence that ground back and forth along the line of the middle Danube, Heruls, Huns, Rugi, Gepids, and others simply went out of existence as coherent and recognized peoples. It is difficult to describe this effect of war on cultural identity—the term ethnocide might be appropriate—but it was certainly no less pervasive than ethnogenesis.

The so-called Hun empire of Attila is one of the better attested cases of this general phenomenon. The factors that created an Attila were just stronger variants of those that had created Alaric half a century earlier on the same frontier. Various Hun groups had been drawn into warfare with other peoples along this northern periphery, including the Alans and the Tervingi; they began to coalesce into large coherent groups encouraged by Roman employment and by repeated invitations to intervene in civil wars within the Roman empire. The process accelerated the pyramiding of Hun clans and allied ethnic subgroups into a much larger collection of peoples under ever more powerful leaders in the period between Uldin (ca. 408–412) and Rua (420s), and culminated in the domination of Attila (ca. 435–450). Just as with the ethnic army commanded by Alaric in the late 390s and early 400s, however, even in the midst of their expansionist phase the Huns experienced several dramatic recessions of their power (Thompson, 1996: 33–35). Given the forces that made and unmade ethnic armies along this frontier, the acme of Hun power coincided with the large-scale employment of Huns by Aëtius in the court wars of the Roman state in the mid 420s to 440s (Heather, 1995: 17–19, 26–27; Thompson, 1996: 69–86). This Hun power and its social structure, however, were wholly parasitic. When the personal power relations and economic benefits of armed service that sustained it were removed, the whole edifice vanished more quickly than it had formed. In the decades after the collapse of the Hun domination, Rugi, Heruls, and others faced this same extinction of social identity in the violent gristmill of the Danubian war zone.

Contributing to the general matrix of violence in the north, war on this frontier was made more complex by internal wars, which were just as characteristic of the smaller ethnic groups as they were of the great empires. These local episodes of violence had serious implications whenever they became intermingled with the same processes within the Roman state. The expansion of any given ethnic group, such as that of the Longobards, generated internal pressures that encouraged the fission of the group's social structure and the outbreak of internecine conflicts over the appropriation of rewards and leadership—for example, in the Longobard case, in the war of Waccho against Tato and his son Hildechis fought around 510. Internal wars within the various ethnic congeries were characteristic of the system of personal power by which leaders of tribal cantons or segments built up their domination through the forcible incorporation of neighboring groups. They were also a natural result of the fission or fragmentation of an ethnic group into its smaller components.

These internal wars were just as important to the fate of any given ethnos as civil wars were to the larger states. A single case must suffice. The historian Socrates (*Hist.eccl.* 4.33) gives details of a civil war *(emphulios polemos)* between opposed segments of the "Goths" headed by Athanaric and Fritigern that broke out in the years before 370 (Lenski, 1995). The war was both cause and consequence of the fission of the Goths into two parts. When Athanaric appeared to be getting the upper hand in the war, Fritigern responded by trying to recruit Romans to assist him. In this case, Fritigern appealed for assistance from the Romans and Emperor Valens gave him the military aid that he needed. The civil war intertwined Roman and Gothic to the extent that when Fritigern and the large number of Goths attached to him won the war, they showed their gratitude to Valens by adopting his deity and his peculiar religious beliefs.

The great economic forces that flowed from the much more highly developed Mediterranean must also have contributed greatly to wars among the ethnic groups beyond the northern frontier. We cannot trace all the cause-and-effect relationships, but they included the routine redistribution of arms, luxury goods, and status symbols, and control of access to these (Todd, 1992: 86–103; Whittaker, 1994: 122–131). A particular sector of the northern frontier was rather special in this regard: the borderland zone across the lower Danube, extending northward and eastward into the present-day Ukraine. Both literary and archaeological evidence suggest that this was the premier "slaving frontier" of the Roman empire (Thompson, 1966: 38–39; Braund-Tsetskhladze, 1989). The deeply established business and power connections here went back through the period of the late Roman republic over a millennium or more, and involved all types of collusion, official and otherwise, on both sides of the frontier (Crawford, 1977). This trade (and the concurrent slaving operations of the Huns, Goths, and others) was likely to have had a considerable effect on the ethnic societies north of the Danube. It must have contributed substantially to the escalation of interethnic violence. Likewise, the sudden reduction of this enormously valuable trade in human commodities was bound to devastate the subsistence economies of the war zone that depended heavily for wealth and power on this monocrop economy (Amm.Marc. 27.5.7; 31.4.11; 31.5.1). Practically the only truly valuable "natural resource" this frontier had to offer the economy of the Roman state was its human population, whether for soldiers or for slaves (Todd, 1992: 19).

The northern frontiers of the Sassanid state were not greatly different in the typical results of interaction between the state and ethnic groups. The dimensions of the problem were different because the peoples in the Eurasian steppe, though just as segmented and as illiterate as their western counterparts, did not have as great a population density and faced more serious geographical barriers separating them from lands to the south—the great water barriers of the Black and Caspian seas, and the mountain ranges, above all the Caucasus. Yet the structure of the Sassanid state meant that responses would be modulated differently. Although so much less is known of the northern periphery of the Sassanid empire, it seems that it too was an important barbarian frontier, dominated by pastoral nomadic groups generally characterized as Hunnish, whose cultures were based on segmentary lineage structures (*Wars* 1.3.5–7). The comparable ecological and social forces meant that in the long run the warfare of the Persian state in the east tended to replicate that of Rome to the west. The hardening of the northern frontier by the building of large walls used to impede and to monitor the mobile pastoral populations, and the movement of the monarch and the royal court from Ctesiphon to the war zone itself, are but a few of the characteristic features that were duplicated by the Sassanids (Frye, 1983: 138–139; Howard-Johnston, 1995: 191–197).

There were two basic changes in the classic war system of late antiquity. The first centered on the war zone along the northern frontiers of the Roman empire and involved a complex and extended interplay of forces that were set in motion by the Augustan military restoration. Given the demographic resources and modes of social organization along this frontier, the massive militarization

of this periphery by the Roman state only contributed to its final destabilization. The prolonged internal or civil wars of the empire drew in one ethnic
group after another—a process which finally led to the disintegration of the
part of the Roman state that directly faced this frontier. The vortices of internal
conflict within the northern war zone, as well as their relationship to conflicts
within the central state, compelled the fragmentation of the basic operational
units of war into smaller regional units. The end of the process was marked by
the emergence of independent local warlords of the type perhaps best attested
for 5th and 6th century Gaul (Drinkwater, 1992; Liebeschuetz, 1993; Whittaker, 1993; 1994: 243–278). Viewed from the perspective of the system in
general, therefore, Piganiol's famous dictum (1972: 466) on the end of the
western empire—that "it was murdered" *(elle a été assassinée)*—could just as
usefully be rephrased as *elle s'est suicidée.*

Even as biological metaphors, however, the phrases are misleading representations of a process that involved not only both parties in the west, but other
parts of the organism in the east that survived rather well in consequence of the
demise of its "other half." For the other profound change transformed the
relationship between the two great states on the frontier between the Mediterranean and the Near East. The fundamental change was marked by the breakdown of the long stability between the Byzantine and Sassanid states, especially
in the first decades of the 7th century. The transformation of attitude was
reflected in an intensification of war aims, in which the leaders of each state
began to think more in terms of a "total war" aimed at the extermination of the
other (Isaac, 1992: 127; Howard-Johnston, 1995: 164). Neither state in its
much weakened state was prepared to meet the massive coalition of Arab forces
that came out of the Hijāz and struck at the southern faces of both states. There
is no evidence that they were even conscious of any special military threat
emanating from this direction. In their war preparations, which presumably
reflected their mental disposition, they continued to be obsessively concerned
with each other, and with the millennium-old frontier that converged on the
great fertile crescent that joined northern Syria and Mesopotamia.

The war system of the late antique Mediterranean and Near East was therefore determined by the resources of the large states. Rome, the power focused
on the Mediterranean, was counterpoised to Sassanid Persia, centered on the
great land masses of Mesopotamia and the Iranian highlands (Rubin, 1986b).
The geopolitical location of these states, and the manner in which they expanded militarily, caused them to leave open frontiers, mainly on their northern
flanks and along the narrow land frontier in Mesopotamia where they confronted each other. When the attacks of the Banu Quraysh erupted from the
Hijāz and the southern parts of the Syrian desert in 633–640—attacks that
were aimed no longer just at raiding and pillaging but at land conquest—the
basic shift in the direction and meaning of war was not expected by the major
contestants, who had hitherto defined the nature of war in the region. The
Arabs came out of a region that had never been considered a serious war frontier of the type shared by Rome and Persia during the preceding half millen-

nium. Whether centrally organized or not (Landau-Tasseron, 1995; *contra:* Donner, 1981; 1995), the Arab forces easily drove deep into the exposed civil undersides of both states and changed the war system of late antiquity forever. As with the successor states in the Roman west, this was another very successful case of violent parasitism. (See Heather, 1996, chaps. 7–10, for the parallel case of the Goths in the west.) But so little is known about how and why it happened that the conquest is as much a puzzle, and a surprise, to modern-day scholars as it was to the Byzantines and Sassanians when it happened. The same silence of the literary sources that bedevils our knowledge of war among the ethnic groups beyond the northern frontiers of the Roman empire also leaves us ignorant of the Arabs who achieved this great feat of violent appropriation.

For our mental image of war in late antiquity, we have therefore tended, almost by default, to adopt the classical interpretation so powerfully created by Edward Gibbon. It is a perspective that is Rome-centered, suffused with a vocabulary of decline, and marked by a dichotomy between the good internal forces of the state and the evil destructive forces of external enemies. It should perhaps be a matter of some concern that Gibbon himself, not long after the completion of his *Decline and Fall,* had serious misgivings about the division of war that he had offered his readers. He had already become convinced that problems of war internal both to Rome and Persia were as important as the classic battlefield clashes with external enemies (Bowersock, 1977). The whole problem of war, so critical to the making and the unmaking of the ancient world, must be viewed from a panoramic perspective that integrates the oecumenes of both the Mediterranean and the Near East, as well as the internal and external aspects of the social orders that were created and destroyed by violent force. Because of the peculiar interests of classical historiographies, ancient and modern, it is a subject on which considerable bodies of fact have been accumulated and analyzed. But the dominant paradigms of thinking have served to obscure a clearer view of the general dynamic of war itself. Despite the great assemblage of data for the Roman part of this story, one has the uneasy feeling that we are only beginning to understand the problematic nature of this "worst of all evils."

Works Cited

Anderson, T. A. 1995. "Roman Military Colonies in Gaul, Salian Ethnogenesis and the Forgotten Meaning of *Pactus Legis Salicae* 59.5," *Early Medieval Europe* 4: 129–144.

Austin, N. J. E. 1979. *Ammianus on Warfare: An Investigation into Ammianus' Military Knowledge.* Brussels.

Austin, N. J. E., and N. B. Rankov. 1995. *Exploratio: Military and Political Intelligence in the Roman World from the Second Punic War to the Battle of Adrianople.* New York.

Bachrach, B. S. 1993. "Logistics in Pre-Crusade Europe," chap. 4 in John A. Lynn, ed., *Feeding Mars: Logistics in Western Warfare from the Middle Ages to the Present,* 57–78. Boulder, Colo.

Barlow, J. 1995. "Kinship, Identity and Fourth-Century Franks," *Historia* 45: 223–239.

Barnes, T. D. 1979. "The Date of Vegetius," *Phoenix* 33: 254–257.

Bishop, M. C. 1985. "The Military *Fabrica* and the Production of Arms in the Early Principate," 1–42 in M. Bishop, ed., *Production and Distribution of Roman Military Equipment: 220–366*. Oxford.

Bivar, A. D. H. 1972. "Cavalry Equipment and Tactics on the Euphrates Frontier," *Dumbarton Oaks Papers* 26: 271–291.

Blockley, R. C. 1985. "Subsidies and Diplomacy: Rome and Persia in Late Antiquity," *Phoenix* 39: 62–74.

———— 1992. *East Roman Foreign Policy: Formation and Conduct from Diocletian to Anastasius*. Leeds.

Boak, A. E. R. 1955. *Manpower Shortage and the Fall of the Roman Empire*. London.

Bowersock, G. W. 1975. "The Greek-Nabataean Bilingual Inscription at Ruwwāfa, Saudi Arabia," 513–522 in *Le monde grec: Hommages à Claire Préaux*. Brussels. Repr. in Bowersock, *Studies on the Eastern Roman Empire*. Goldbach, 1994.

———— 1977. "Gibbon on Civil War and Rebellion in the Decline of the Roman Empire," *Daedalus* 105: 63–71. Repr. in G. W. Bowersock, J. Clive, and S. R. Graubard, eds., *Edward Gibbon and the Decline and Fall of the Roman Empire*. Cambridge, Mass., 1977.

———— 1983. *Roman Arabia*. Cambridge, Mass.

Braund, D. 1994. *Georgia in Antiquity: A History of Colchis and Transcaucasian Iberia, 500 BC–AD 562*. Oxford.

Braund, D., and G. R. Tsetskhladze. 1989. "The Export of Slaves from Colchis," *Classical Quarterly* 39: 114–125.

Briant, P. 1976. "'Brigandage', dissidence et conquête en Asie Achéménide et Hellénistique," *Dialogues d'Histoire Ancienne* 2: 163–258.

———— 1982. *État et pasteurs du Moyen-Orient ancien*. Cambridge, Eng.

Brunt, P. A. 1974. "Conscription and Volunteering in the Roman Imperial Army," *Scripta Classica Israelica* 1: 90–115. Repr. in Brunt, *Roman Imperial Themes*. Oxford, 1990.

Burns, T. S. 1994. *Barbarians within the Gates of Rome: A Study of Roman Military Policy and the Barbarians, ca. 375–425 A.D.* Bloomington-Indianapolis.

Bury, J. B. 1928. *The Invasion of Europe by the Barbarians*. London. Repr. New York, 1963.

Cameron, A. 1985. *Procopius and the Sixth Century*. Berkeley–Los Angeles.

————, ed. 1995. *The Byzantine and Early Islamic Near East, 3: States, Resources, and Armies*. Princeton.

Carrié, J.-M. 1986. "L'esercito, trasformazioni funzionali ed economie locali," chap. 12 in Andrea Giardina, ed., *Società romana e impero tardoantico*, vol. 1: *Istituzioni, ceti, economie*. Rome-Bari, 1986: 449–488; 760–771.

———— 1993. "Eserciti e strategie," 83–134 in A. Schiavone, ed., *Storia di Roma*, vol. 3: *L'Età tardoantica, 1: Crisi e trasformazioni*. Turin.

———— 1995. "L'état à la recherche de nouveaux modes de financement des armées (Rome et Byzance, IVe–VIIIe siècles," 27–60 in Cameron, 1995.

Christie, N. 1991. "Invasion or Invitation? The Longobard Occupation of Northern Italy, A.D. 568–569," *Romanobarbarica* 11: 79–108.

———— 1995. *The Lombards: The Ancient Longobards*. Oxford.

Christol, M. 1977. "Effort de guerre et ateliers monétaires de la périphérie au IIIe s. ap. J.-C.: L'atelier de Cologne sous Valérien et Gallien," 235–277 in Christol, *Armées et fiscalité dans le monde antique*. Paris.

Crawford, M. 1977. "Republican *Denarii* in Romania: The Suppression of Piracy and the Slave-Trade," *Journal of Roman Studies* 67: 117–124.

Crone, P. 1980. *Slaves on Horses: The Evolution of the Islamic Polity*. Cambridge.

Dagron, G. 1993. "Modèles de combattants et technologie militaire dans le *Stratègikon* de Maurice," 279–284 in F. Vallet and M. Kazanski, eds., *L'armée romaine et les Barbares du IIIe siècle au VIIe siècle*. Condé-sur-Noireau.

Delbrück, H. 1902/1921. *Geschichte der Kriegskunst im Rahmen der politischen Geschichte*, 2.1: *Die Germanen: Römer und Germanen*. Berlin: 1st ed., 1902; 2nd ed., 1909; 3rd ed., 1921. English ed.: *The Barbarian Invasions*, trans. W. J. Renfroe. Westport, Conn., 1980.

Demougeot, E. 1969–1979. *La formation de l'Europe et les invasions barbares*, 2 vols. Paris.

Dennis, G. T. 1985. *Three Byzantine Military Treatises*. Washington, D.C.

D'Huys, V. 1987. "How to Describe Violence in Historical Narrative," *Ancient Society* 18: 209–250.

Donner, F. M. 1981. *The Early Islamic Conquests*. Princeton, 1981.

—— 1995. "Centralized Authority and Military Autonomy in the Early Islamic Conquests," 337–360 in Cameron, 1995.

Drinkwater, J. F. 1987. *The Gallic Empire: Separatism and Continuity in the Northwestern Provinces of the Empire, AD 260–274* (Historia Einzelschriften 52). Wiesbaden.

—— 1992. "The Bagaudae of Fifth-Century Gaul," 208–217 in J. F. Drinkwater and H. Elton, eds., *Fifth-Century Gaul: A Crisis of Identity?* Cambridge, Eng.

Duncan-Jones, R. 1994. "The Imperial Budget," 33–46 in Duncan-Jones, *Money and Government in the Roman Empire*. Cambridge, Eng.

Eadie, J. W. 1967. "The Development of Roman Mailed Cavalry," *Journal of Roman Studies* 57: 165–169.

Elton, H. 1996. *Warfare in Roman Europe, 350–425*. Oxford.

Ferrill, A. 1986. *The Fall of the Roman Empire: The Military Explanation*. London. Repr. 1991.

—— 1991. *Roman Imperial Grand Strategy*. London-Lanham.

Flaig, E. 1992. *Den Kaiser herausfordern: Die Usurpationen im Römischen Reich*. Frankfurt–New York.

—— 1997. "Für eine Konzeptionalisierung der Usurpation im spätrömischen Reich," in F. Paschoud and J. Szidat, eds., *Usurpationen in der Spätantike*. Wiesbaden.

Frye, R. N. 1983. "The Political History of Iran under the Sasanians," 116–180 in E. Yarshater, ed., *The Cambridge History of Iran*, 3.1: *The Seleucid, Parthian and Sasanian Periods*. Cambridge, Eng.

Goffart, W. 1977. "The Date and Purpose of Vegetius' *De re militari*," *Traditio* 33: 65–100. Repr. in Goffart, *Rome's Fall and After*. London, 1989.

—— 1980. "The Barbarians in Late Antiquity," 3–39 in Goffart, *Barbarians and Romans*. Princeton.

—— 1989. "The Theme of 'The Barbarian Invasions' in Late Antique and Modern Historiography," 87–107 in Evangelos K. Chrysos and Andreas Schwarcz, eds., *Das Reich und die Barbaren*. Vienna-Cologne.

Goldsworthy, A. K. 1996. *The Roman Army at War, 100 BC–AD 200*. Oxford.

Goodburn, R., and P. Bartholomew, eds. 1976. *Aspects of the Notitia Dignitatum*. Oxford.

Gordon, C. D. 1949. "Subsidies in Roman Imperial Defence," *Phoenix* 3: 60–69.

Graf, D. F., and M. O'Connor. 1977. "The Origin of the Term Saracen and the Rawwāfa Inscription," *Byzantine Studies/Etudes Byzantines* 4: 52–66.

Haldon, J. F. 1979. *Recruitment and Conscription in the Byzantine Army, c. 550–950: A Study on the Origins of the Stratiotika Ktemata* (Österreichische Akademie der Wissenschaften, Philosophisch-historische Klasse: Sitzungsberichte, vol. 357). Vienna.

—— 1990. "The State and Its Apparatus: Military Administration," 208–253 in Haldon, *Byzantium in the Seventh Century: The Transformation of a Culture*. Cambridge.

—— 1993. "Administrative Continuities and Structural Transformations in East Roman Military Organisation, ca. 580–640," 45–53 in F. Vallet and M. Kazanski, eds., *L'armée romaine et les Barbares du IIIe siècle au VIIe siècle.* Condé-sur-Noireau.

Heather, P. J. 1991. *Goths and Romans, 332–489.* Oxford.

————— 1994. "Literacy and Power in the Migration Period," 177–197 in A. K. Bowman and G. Woolf, eds., *Literacy and Power in the Ancient World.* Cambridge, Eng.

————— 1995. "The Huns and the End of the Roman Empire in Western Europe," *English Historical Review* 110: 4–41.

————— 1996. *The Goths.* Oxford.

Hedeager, L. 1978. "A Quantitative Analysis of Roman Imports to Europe North of the Limes (0–400 AD) and the Question of Roman-Germanic Exchange," 191–216 in K. Kristiansen and C. Paludin-Muller, eds., *New Directions in Scandinavian History.* Copenhagen.

————— 1988. "The Evolution of Germanic Society, 1–400 A.D.," 129–143 in R. F. Jones et al., eds., *First Millennium Papers: Western Europe in the First Millennium AD.* Oxford.

————— 1992. *Iron-Age Societies: From Tribe to State in Northern Europe, 500 B.C. to A.D. 700.* Oxford.

Höckman, O. 1986. "Römische Schiffsverbände auf dem Ober- und Mittelrhein und die Verteidigung der Rheingrenze in der Spätantike," *Jahrbuch des Römisch-Germanischen Zentralmuseums* 33: 369–416.

Hoffmann, D. 1969–70. *Das spätrömische Bewegungsheer und die Notitia Dignitatum,* 2 vols. Düsseldorf.

Hollard, D. 1995. "La crise de la monnaie dans l'Empire romain au 3e siècle après J.C. Synthèse des recherches et résultats nouveaux," *Annales* 50: 1045–78.

Howard-Johnston, J. 1995. "The Two Great Powers in Late Antiquity: A Comparison," 157–226 in Cameron, 1995.

Iluk, J. 1985. "The Export of Gold from the Roman Empire to Barbarian Countries from the 4th to the 6th Centuries," *Münstersche Beiträge zur Antiken Handelsgeschichte* 4: 79–102.

Isaac, B. 1992. *The Limits of Empire: The Roman Army in the East,* rev. ed. Oxford.

James, S. 1988. "The *Fabricae*: State Arms Factories of the Later Roman Empire," 257–331 in J. C. Coulston, ed., *Military Equipment and the Identity of Roman Soldiers.* Oxford.

Jones, A. H. M. 1964. *The Later Roman Empire, 284–602: A Social, Economic, and Administrative Survey,* 3 vols. Oxford. Repr. in 2 vols., Baltimore, 1986.

Kaegi, W. E. 1992. *Byzantium and the Early Islamic Conquests.* Cambridge, Eng. Repr. 1995.

————— 1993. "Byzantine Logistics: Problems and Perspectives," 39–55 in John A. Lynn, ed., *Feeding Mars: Logistics in Western Warfare from the Middle Ages to the Present.* Boulder, Colo.

Kennedy, D. L. 1989. "The Military Contribution of Syria to the Roman Imperial Army," 235–246 in D. H. French and C. S. Lightfoot, eds., *The Eastern Frontier of the Roman Empire.* Oxford.

Kennedy, D. L., and H. I. MacAdam. 1985. "Latin Inscriptions from the Azraq Oasis, Jordan," *Zeitschrift für Papyrologie und Epigraphik* 60: 97–108.

Kolias, T. G. 1988. *Byzantinische Waffen: Ein Beitrag zur byzantinischen Waffenkunde von den Anfängen bis zur lateinischen Eroberung.* Vienna.

Kotula, T. 1970. "Firmus, fils de Nubel, était-il usurpateur ou roi des Maures?" *Acta Antiqua Academiae Scientiarum Hungaricae* 18: 137–146.

Kunow, J. 1986. "Bemerkungen zum Export römischer Waffen in das *Barbaricum*," *Limes: Studien zu den Militärgrenzen Roms,* 3, Stuttgart (1986): 740–746.

Landau-Tasseron, E. 1995. "Features of the Pre-Conquest Muslim Army in the Time of Muhammad," 299–336 in Cameron, 1995.

Lee, A. D. 1993. *Information and Frontiers: Roman Foreign Relations in Late Antiquity*. Cambridge, Eng.

Lenski, N. 1995. "The Date of the Gothic Civil War and the Date of the Gothic Conversion," *Greek, Roman, and Byzantine Studies* 36: 51–87.

Liebeschuetz, J. H. W. G. 1990. *Barbarians and Bishops: Army, Church and State in the Age of Arcadius and Chrysostom*. Oxford.

———— 1993. "The End of the Roman Army in the Western Empire," 265–276 in J. Rich and G. Shipley, eds., *War and Society in the Roman World*. London–New York.

———— 1994. "Realism and Fantasy: The Anonymous *De Rebus Bellicis* and Its Afterlife," 119–139 in E. Dabrowa, ed., *The Roman and Byzantine Army in the East*. Cracow.

Luttwak, E. 1976. *The Grand Strategy of the Roman Empire: From the First Century A.D. to the Third*. Baltimore.

MacAdam, H. I. 1989. "Epigraphy and the *Notitia Dignitatum*," 295–309 in D. H. French and C. S. Lightfoot, eds., *The Eastern Frontier of the Roman Empire*. Oxford.

MacMullen, R. 1980. "How Big Was the Roman Army?" *Klio* 62: 451–460.

———— 1984. "The Roman Emperor's Army Costs," *Latomus* 43: 571–580.

Matthews, J. 1976. "Mauretania in Ammianus and the *Notitia*," 157–186 in R. Goodburn and P. Bartholomew, eds., *Aspects of the Notitia Dignitatum*. Oxford. Repr. as chap. 11 in Matthews, *Political Life and Culture in Late Roman Society*, London, 1985.

———— 1989. *The Roman Empire of Ammianus*. London.

Millar, F. 1982. "Emperors, Frontiers and Foreign Relations, 31 B.C. to A.D. 378," *Britannia* 13: 1–23.

Milner, N. P. 1993. *Vegetius: Epitome of Military Science*. Liverpool.

Mitchell, S. 1989. "The Siege of Cremna, AD 278," 311–327 in D. H. French and C. S. Lightfoot, eds., *The Eastern Frontier of the Roman Empire*. Oxford.

———— 1994. "Notes on Military Recruitment from the Eastern Provinces," 141–148 in E. Dabrowa, ed., *The Roman and Byzantine Army in the East*. Cracow.

———— 1995. *Cremna in Pisidia: An Ancient City in Peace and in War*. London.

Musset, L. 1975. *The Germanic Invasions: The Making of Europe, A.D. 400–600*, transl. Edward and Columba James. London.

Patterson, W. F. 1966. "The Archers of Islam," *Journal of the Economic and Social History of the Orient* 9: 69–87.

Piganiol, A. 1972. *L'empire chrétien (325–395)*. Paris.

Pipes, D. 1981. *Slave Soldiers and Islam*. New Haven–London.

Pohl, W. 1980. "Die Gepiden und die *gentes* an der mittleren Donau nach der Zerfall des Attilareiches," 239–305 in H. Wolfram and F. Daim, eds., *Die Völker an der mittleren und unteren Donau im fünften und sechsten Jahrhundert*. Österreichische Akademie der Wissenschaften, Philosophish-Historische Klasse: Denkschriften, vol. 145. Vienna.

———— 1994. "La sfida Attilana: Dinamica di un potere barbaro," 69–89 in S. Blason Scarel, ed., *Attila: Flagellum Dei?* Rome.

Raddatz, K. 1985. "Die Bewaffnung der Germanen vom letzten Jahrhundert vor Chr. Geb. biz zur Völkerwanderungszeit," *ANRW* 2.12.3: 281–361.

Rubin, Z. 1986a. "Diplomacy and War in the Relations between Byzantium and the Sassanids in the Fifth Century A.D.," 677–695 in Philip Freeman and David Kennedy, eds., *The Defence of the Roman and Byzantine East*. Oxford.

———— 1986b. "The Mediterranean and the Dilemma of the Roman Empire in Late Antiquity," *Mediterranean Historical Review* 1: 13–62.

———— 1995. "The Reforms of Khusro Anushirwan," 227–297 in Cameron, 1995.

Schippmann, K. 1990. *Grundzüge der Geschichte des Sasanidischen Reiches*. Darmstadt.

Seeck, O., ed. 1876. *Notitia Dignitatum*. Berlin. Repr. Frankfurt, 1962.

Shahbazi, A. S. 1986. "Army (i) Pre-Islamic Iran," 489–499 in E. Yarshater, ed., *Encyclopedia Iranica* 2.5.

Shahid, I. 1984a. "The Term *Saraceni* and the Image of the Arabs," 123–141 in *Rome and the Arabs: A Prolegomenon to the Study of Byzantium and the Arabs*. Washington, D.C.

———— 1984b. *Byzantium and the Arabs in the Fourth Century*. Washington, D.C.

———— 1995. *Byzantium and the Arabs in the Sixth Century*, vol. 1. pt. 1: *Political and Military History*. Washington, D.C.

Shaw, B. D. 1990. "Bandit Highlands and Lowland Peace: The Mountains of Isauria-Cilicia: Parts I and II," *Journal of the Economic and Social History of the Orient* 33: 199–233; 237–270.

Speidel, M. 1980. "Legionaries from Asia Minor," *ANRW* 2.7.2: 730–746. Repr. in Speidel, 1992, vol. 1.

———— 1983. "The Roman Army in Asia Minor: Recent Epigraphical Discoveries and Researches," 7–34 in S. Mitchell, ed., *Armies and Frontiers in Roman and Byzantine Anatolia*. Oxford. Repr. in Speidel, 1992, 1:273–300.

———— 1984. "*Catafractarii Clibanarii* and the Rise of the Later Roman Mailed Cavalry: A Gravestone from Claudiopolis in Bithynia," *Epigraphica Anatolica* 4: 151–56. Repr. in Speidel, 1992, 2:406–11.

———— 1987. "The Roman Road to Dumata (Jawf in Saudi Arabia) and the Frontier Strategy of *Praetensione Colligare*," *Historia* 36: 213–221. Repr. in Speidel, 1992, 2:369–78.

———— 1992. *Roman Army Studies,* 2 vols. Stuttgart.

Stelten, L. F. 1990. *Flavius Vegetius Renatus: Epitoma Rei Militaris*. New York.

Thompson, E. A. 1952. *A Roman Reformer and Inventor, Being a New Text of the Treatise De Rebus Bellicis*. Oxford. Repr. New York, 1979.

———— 1966. *The Visigoths in the Time of Ulfila*. Oxford.

———— 1996. *The Huns*. Oxford.

Todd, M. 1972. *The Barbarians: Goths, Franks and Vandals*. London–New York.

———— 1992. *The Early Germans*. Oxford. Repr. 1995.

Traina, G. 1986–87. "Aspettando i barbari: Le origini tardoantiche della guerriglia di frontiera," *Romano-barbarica* 9: 247–280.

Treadgold, W. 1995. *Byzantium and Its Army, 284–1081*. Stanford, Cal.

Van Creveld, M. L. 1991. *Technology and War: From 2000 B.C. to the Present,* rev. ed. New York.

Waas, M. 1971. *Germanen im römischen Dienst*. Bonn.

Wheeler, E. L. 1993. "Methodological Limits and the Mirage of Roman Strategy, Part I and II," *The Journal of Military History* 57: 7–41, 215–240.

Whitby, M. 1994. "The Persian King at War," 227–263 in E. Dabrowa, ed., *The Roman and Byzantine Army in the East*. Cracow.

———— 1995. "Recruitment in Roman Armies from Justinian to Heraclius (ca. 565–615)," 61–124 in Cameron, 1995.

Whittaker, C. R. 1993. "Landlords and Warlords in the Later Roman Empire," 277–302 in J. Rich and G. Shipley, eds., *War and Society in the Roman World*. London–New York.

———— 1994. *Frontiers of the Roman Empire: A Social and Economic Study*. Baltimore–London.

Wickham, C. 1981. *Early Medieval Italy: Central Power and Local Society, 400–1000*. London.

Widengren, G. 1976. "Iran, der grosse Gegner Roms: Königsgewalt, Feodalismus, Militärwesen," *ANRW* 2.9.1: 219–306.

Empire Building

Christopher Kelly

On 11 May 330, Rome ceased to be the most important place in the Roman empire. Five hundred miles east of the Eternal City, on a site occupied by modern Istanbul, a new imperial capital was dedicated and (like Rome before it) named after its founder: Constantinople, the city of Emperor Constantine. The inauguration ceremonies were magnificent.[1] On the first of forty days of celebrations, parades, and largesse, the imperial court assembled at the foot of a tall porphyry column erected in the center of the city's new forum.[2] This column marked the place where six years earlier Constantine, in response to a vision from the Christian God, and with the advice of the Neoplatonic philosopher Sopater, had proclaimed the founding of the city and proceeded to mark out its territory.[3] The column also symbolized Constantine's claim that his new city's roots ran deep into the classical past. According to some, the column's seven smooth purple drums had come from Troy. Later Byzantine writers also claimed that the base of the column concealed the Palladium. This ancient Trojan statue of Pallas Athena, thought to ensure the safety of the city in which it was venerated, had been recovered from the Greeks and taken to Rome by Aeneas.[4] A thousand years later, Constantine—keen to secure a talisman which would protect his new capital and assert its antiquity—was believed to have had the Palladium secretly removed and brought to Constantinople.[5]

Constantine's column was also a Christian reliquary, whose sacred contents exotically multiplied with successive retellings of the city's foundation. In the column's base, along with the Palladium, was placed the stone Moses struck to provide water for the Israelites in the wilderness, the haft of the adze Noah used to build the ark, and the wicker panniers used by the disciples to distribute the loaves and fishes at the feeding of the five thousand.[6] The column itself was topped by a statue of Constantine in the likeness of Apollo. This golden image was raised on the day of Constantinople's inauguration, to the acclamation of the assembled crowd and the repeated chanting of the *Kyrie*.[7] The statue's head was crowned by a radiate diadem like the rising sun; each of its seven glittering rays contained a sliver from the nails used to crucify Christ.[8] Inside the statue, as a further guarantee of the city's security, was hidden a splinter from the True Cross.[9]

Following the dedication of the statue, the emperor and his entourage— senior officials, military commanders, and palace functionaries—processed in splendor to the imperial box in the Hippodrome to enjoy a day of chariot racing. Constantine himself was magnificently robed, standing out even amid such courtly brilliance. He wore, perhaps for the first time in his reign, a diadem encrusted with pearls and other jewels.[10] By all accounts, the high point of the day's events was the entry into the arena of a golden chariot bearing a gilded image of the emperor escorted by a crack company of the imperial guard in full ceremonial dress, all carrying long white tapers.[11] This stunning ritual was repeated each year on Constantine's orders to mark the anniversary of the city's dedication. For the next two hundred years, as the golden image rounded the turning-post of the Hippodrome and neared the imperial box, Roman emperors and their courtiers prostrated themselves before Constantinople's glittering founder.

The striking ceremonies and magnificent parades marking the inauguration of Constantine's new capital provide important insights into both the system of government and the political ideology of the later Roman empire. The empire's center was dominated by a godlike emperor, surrounded by high-ranking court officials, soldiers, and bureaucrats. The governance of empire largely depended on these groups. They channeled, mediated, and (on occasion) blatantly misdirected imperial power. Emperors moved to contain abuses as far as they were able. Against the ever present threat of courtiers' rival interests and inducements, they enforced, in both practical and symbolic terms, the dependence of all upon an imperial center. Loyalty was buttressed by the chance of reward; disloyalty threatened with horrific torture and public punishment.[12] In a delicate balancing of competing claims, emperors and their supporters continually emphasized, and in their ceremonies openly displayed, the advantages of upholding the prevailing regime. By and large, these tactics were effective. Later Roman emperors were remarkably successful in controlling both an elaborate court society and a sophisticated and highly complex bureaucracy. In the century after Constantine, that success permitted the central government to exercise a greater control over the human and economic resources of the Mediterranean world than at any time since the foundation of the Roman empire.[13]

But the effectiveness of later Roman government was only partially dependent on organizational rules which strengthened the position of emperors and helped to tip the balance of struggles in their favor. It was also underpinned by a political ideology which reinforced those rules. In electing to support Christianity in 312, Constantine adopted a religion whose monotheism presented a view of a heavenly kingdom ruled by one God. The theology of the incarnation of Christ offered a figure who blurred the distinctions between humanity and divinity and served in his inexpressible majesty as the sole mediator between this world and the next. Such images were not always easily accepted; but their attractiveness to a highly centralized, autocratic government is not surprising. Later Roman emperors sometimes represented themselves as Christlike, or offered subsidies and taxation immunity to the Christian church.[14] Of course, here as well, there were competing interests to be negotiated. The church, itself a highly complex organization vital to the dissemination of this new religion, could not be expected unquestioningly to be subordinate to secular authority. For many, too, deeply ingrained pre-Christian beliefs died hard. Part of Christianity's strength lay in its evident ability both to accommodate and to incorporate a wide variety of religious systems and ritual practices. That broad base of support made Christianity doubly effective: it helped promote a new system of rule without rejecting outright all that had gone before. It was crucially important to the success of Constantine's new religion as an effective political ideology that the transitions from Apollo to Christ to later Roman emperor not be too difficult.

The focus of the carefully choreographed ceremonies in Constantinople in May 330 was the emperor himself. According to the surviving, openly enthusiastic accounts, Constantine was the center of attention at the dedication of his statue in the city's principal forum, and he was loudly cheered as he processed to the Hippodrome where (before the races began) all eyes were turned toward him as he took his place amid the acclamations of the crowd. The exaltation of the emperor was the insistent theme of imperial ceremonial. The more loyal the crowd, the more worshipful the regime's historians, artists, and orators, the more magnificent the emperor. When, five years earlier, Constantine opened the Council of Nicaea (a conclave of bishops called to debate important doctrinal and credal matters), all present stood and in silence faced the entrance of the assembly chamber. The emperor—in the words of his Christian court-biographer, Eusebius of Caesarea—then appeared "like some heavenly messenger of God, clothed in a shining raiment, which flashed as if with glittering rays of light . . . and adorned with the lustrous brilliance of gold and precious stones."[15]

Court occasions demanded a similar splendor. Meetings of the *consistorium*, the most important imperial council of advisors, were conducted with all standing except the emperor.[16] Those formally introduced into the imperial presence were required, having prostrated themselves, to "adore the purple"—to kiss on bended knee the hem of the emperor's robe.[17] All approaches to the imperial person were hedged with similar protocols. A magnificent silver platter made to celebrate the tenth anniversary of the accession of Theodosius I in 388 shows the emperor enthroned between his junior colleagues Valentinian II and Arcadius. Behind stand the imperial bodyguard. In front, kneeling, a splendidly attired official receives in reverently veiled hands his letters of appointment. Beneath, a half-naked woman representing the fruitful earth reclines in a field of corn; around her playful *putti* romp joyously. The whole scene, skillfully constructed, displays to the viewer the prosperity and rewards of a world which revolves around the emperor as the personification of good order.[18]

To the regime's supporters, imperial ceremonies presented an ideal map of the political world. The emperor was at the center, and on that center the security, the position, and the magnificence of all depended. When, in 388, Theodosius I, victorious over the rebel general Magnus Maximus, entered the Slovenian town of Emona, he was greeted before the walls by its chief citizens and priests. In the version of the emperor's progress presented by the Gallic orator Pacatus before the court in Rome twelve months later, Theodosius was said to have passed through gates bedecked with garlands and, to the sound of choirs, paraded through streets hung with banners and lit with blazing torches.[19] In similar terms, the historian Ammianus Marcellinus described the entry of Constantius II to Rome thirty years before: the emperor, greeted by the senate and populace drawn up in strict order of precedence, proceeded through the city "in a golden chariot, shimmering in the glitter of various kinds of precious stones . . . on either side, there marched a double line of armed men, their shields and crests flashing with a dazzling light."[20] The appearance of an emperor imposed order on society. The status and importance of any individual or group could instantly be gauged by observing their distance from the imperial center. That subordinate position was acknowledged (most obviously) by those who participated in, or later favorably described, these ceremonies; but it was also affirmed by those who, dressed in their festival best, stood at the roadside shouting their approval or singing hymns as the emperor and the carefully graded ranks of his entourage passed by. For actors and onlookers alike, imperial ceremonies dramatically displayed the benefits and advantages of a particular system of rule. They represented perfect working models of centralized autocracy.[21]

Once seen, these magnificent events were never forgotten. Those who beheld Constantine in his golden raiment were said by Eusebius to be "stunned and amazed at the sight—like children who have seen a frightening apparition."[22] But away from court and capital, emperors rarely appeared in person. In the provinces, their presence was represented by statues and other images. Municipal squares were dominated by imperial statues; the portraits of emperors hung in official buildings, shops, theaters, and public porticoes.[23] The imperial likeness might also be used to decorate everyday items such as coins or medallions, or to add efficacy to rings or amulets.[24] An early 4th century silver ringstone shows the delicately carved profiles of Constantine and his mother Helena with the inscription FVRIVS VIVAS—"Long life to Furius!"[25] In the workplace, iron weights cast in the shape of imperial busts conveyed to the customer an impression of solidity, reliability, and accuracy.[26] Some imperial representations—like modern coronation plates, mugs, and dishtowels—were more garishly amusing. One of the most splendid pieces in the recently unearthed Hoxne treasure from Norfolk in eastern England is a silver pepper-pot, complete with its internal grinding mechanism, skillfully made to represent Helena, the mother of Constantine.[27]

In their range and variety, imperial images made emperors omnipresent. This presence was rendered all the more powerful by a continual confounding of the emperor's person and his image. That deliberate confusion was key to the ceremonies at the inauguration of Constantinople. In the forum, Constantine presided over the dedication of a statue of himself; in the Hippodrome, the crowd applauded not only the emperor but also his image as it was paraded before them, surrounded—like the emperor himself—by the imperial body-guard. Fifty years later, in an even more elaborate visual conceit, the base of an obelisk erected on the central spine of the Hippodrome facing the imperial box displayed an impressive bas-relief of Emperor Theodosius I and his court seated in the imperial box watching the chariot races in the Hippodrome.[28] These mirror images of majesty not only made permanent the transitory messages of imperial ceremonial, but were designed to blur the distinction between emperors and their representations. When Constantius's procession entered Rome in 357, the emperor (again in Ammianus Marcellinus's description) sat immobile in his golden chariot "as if his neck were firmly clamped, he kept his gaze fixed straight ahead . . . nor was he ever seen to spit, or wipe, or rub his face or nose, or to move his hands about." Onlookers saw not just an emperor, but an emperor who looked to them "as though he were a statue of a man."[29]

In the absence of a real emperor (and of such sophisticated metropolitan witticisms) a similar conflation of the emperor with his representations was achieved by a rigid insistence on the performance of the same rituals and ceremonies before imperial images as before the emperor himself. Those approaching an emperor's statue were required to prostrate themselves "not as though they were looking upon a picture, but upon the very face of the emperor."[30] A proper atmosphere of sanctity was to be maintained at all times. An imperial edict issued in 394 banned the posting of advertisements for plays or chariot racing "in public porticoes, or those places in towns where our images are accustomed to be dedicated."[31] These injunctions were not to be breached lightly. In 386, the citizens of Antioch in Syria rioted, pulling down the statues of Emperor Theodosius I, pelting them with filth, and dragging them through the streets of the city.[32] John Chrysostom, a future patriarch of Constantinople who was then a priest in the city, graphically described the fear of Antiochenes in the days which followed as they expected "the wrath of the emperor to come like fire from above." An ominous silence descended on the once busy public squares and porticoes as many fled to the desert: "For as a garden when the irrigation fails shows trees stripped of their foliage and bare of fruit, so now indeed is it with our city . . . she stands desolate, stripped of nearly all her inhabitants."[33]

The reverence accorded imperial images was in part the result of fear and coercion—as the so-called "Riot of the Statues" strikingly demonstrates. (The shattered visages of usurpers' images served as more permanent reminders of the consequences suffered by those who had unsuccessfully challenged the regime.)[34] But such deference also resulted from a keen awareness of the advantages which might accrue from supporting the prevailing system. In a beautifully illustrated calendar produced for a wealthy aristocrat in Rome, the magnificently bejeweled Constantius II is depicted seated in a rigid, statuesque pose. From his outstretched right hand cascades a ceaseless flow of gold coins.[35] The question which confronted many was how best to be placed to "dip into the stream" of imperial benefits.[36] Some thought it in their interests to advertise their loyalty publicly. In 425, following the elevation of Valentinian III to co-emperorship with Theodosius II, the town of Sitifis in Mauretania (modern Sétif in Algeria) erected a four-line metrical inscription which aimed to celebrate Valentinian's military prowess, to praise his mother Galla Placidia (the influential daughter of an emperor), and to compliment Theodosius's more bookish inclinations:

> Rising as the brightest star of this earthly realm,
> Valentinian, under the guardianship of the illustrious Placidia,
> Devoted to the clash of arms, preserved the empire:
> Theodosius, benefiting from the peace, pursued his learned studies.[37]

No doubt the townspeople in turning their popular image of these emperors into verse (although of no great pretension) hoped that they had got it right: in 425 Valentinian was, after all, only six years old. Regrettably, nothing is known of the reaction in Sitifis ten years later when Mauretania was sacked by the Vandals as they moved from Spain through North Africa.

All praise involves risk; public praise raised the stakes higher still. Well-judged support, if successful, might bring considerable benefits. The advantages of proximity to the emperor were well known. The rise of Valentinian I and Theodosius I to power in the late 4th century also saw the elevation of many of their provincial contacts to high-ranking military and administrative posts.[38] In similar fashion, Ausonius—a teacher of rhetoric from Bordeaux and tutor in the 360s to the future emperor Gratian—secured from his former pupil great offices for himself, his son, his son-in-law, and his octogenarian father.[39] More dramatically, the bureaucrat Flavius Eupraxius owed his rapid advance at court to his presence of mind at a ceremony in 367 where he was the first to cheer Valentinian's announcement of the elevation of Gratian to the rank of co-emperor.[40]

Lesser men could hope to emulate these tactics, if given the chance. In 340 an Egyptian soldier, Flavius Abinnaeus, petitioned Emperor Constantius II. The issue was a simple one: After thirty-three years' military service in Egypt, Abinnaeus had been selected to escort an embassy of Blemys (a Nubian tribe) to Constantinople. At court on at least one ceremonial occasion, kneeling in the imperial presence, he had "adored the purple." There followed promotion and a posting to the command of a cavalry detachment at Dionysias in the Fayum. But when, on his return to Alexandria three years later, Abinnaeus presented himself for service, he was told that there were other nominees for the same post, supported by Valacius, the commander of military forces in Egypt. Abinnaeus had only one claim for priority over these local rivals. He played it to the full. Petitioning the emperor, he explained the situation as he saw it: "But when your sacred letter was presented to Valacius, his office replied that other men had presented letters of promotion. Since it is clear they were advanced by influence, but I by your sacred decision . . . may your Clemency vouchsafe that I be appointed."[41] Abinnaeus was successful; by March 342 he was in place at Dionysias. His contact with the imperial court allowed him to cut through competing networks of influence and preference. It was a striking demonstration of the tangible benefits which might flow from a seemingly distant imperial center. Even so, it is unlikely that those who had been supported by Valacius and elbowed out of the queue for promotion were keen listeners to Abinnaeus's endless tales of the court and Constantinople.

It is worthwhile pausing for a moment to reflect on the delighted satisfaction of Flavius Abinnaeus in journeying to court, in securing his command, and in telling the story for years afterward; on the awestruck reaction of the crowds who chanced to see an emperor and his entourage; on the chill fear which ran through the people of Antioch as they contemplated the broken, mud-splattered statue of Theodosius; and on the reverence more usually shown toward imperial images. Such emotions—which must be taken seriously—strongly indicate an awareness of a powerful imperial center. No doubt many subjects of the empire were unable to name the current emperor, or to distinguish one emperor from another, or even to conceive of the magnificence of the court at Constantinople, but that does not mean that they were insensible to a model of society which placed at its apex the emperor and the *potestates excelsae* ("lofty powers") who surrounded him.[42] Success stories continually retold, like ceremonies repeatedly reenacted, helped both to construct and to reinforce a model of society dependent on an imperial center. The image of the emperor dominated the later Roman world as the statue of Constantine towered above his capital. In times of trouble a crowd might gather in an all-night vigil at the foot of the porphyry column to pray and sing hymns. The candle which each suppliant left burning at the column's base was, itself, a striking affirmation of imperial power, as well as a public declaration of the hope that such an affirmation might result in a glittering stream of imperial benefits as yet untold.[43]

There were (of course) severe limitations on the exercise of imperial power.[44] In an empire of sixty million people—stretching from Hadrian's Wall in the north to the river Euphrates in the east—in which, even at the best of times, it might take up to a month for an imperial edict issued in Constantinople to reach Antioch in Syria, emperors inevitably faced restrictions on their ability to rule.[45] Their difficulty was neatly summed up by Synesius, a late 4th century bishop of Ptolemais in Cyrene (modern Tulmaythah on the coast of Libya): "Now to seek to know each place, each man, and each dispute would require a very thorough survey, and not even Dionysius of Syracuse, who established his rule over a single island—and not even over the whole of that—would have been capable of performing this task."[46] Emperors were trapped. Faced with a Mediterranean-wide dominion, they had little option but to depend on secondhand advice or information; no choice but to rely on distant subordinates to carry out their commands. Delegation was an inescapable corollary of autocracy. To be sure, emperors ever since Augustus had relied on a staff of palace functionaries to collate incoming information, draft documents, and oversee the implementation of various imperial policies and projects.[47] But the continued growth of the state bureaucracy beginning with the reigns of Diocletian and Constantine significantly separated the nature of imperial rule in the early Roman empire from that of the later. The absolute number of bureaucrats was still tiny. The best estimates place the total of salaried officials in the whole of the later empire at somewhere around thirty-five thousand—roughly equivalent to the staff of the modern State Department in Washington.[48] But their impact should not be underestimated. Without a well-developed bureaucracy, imperial rule in the later Roman empire would have been considerably less pervasive, intrusive, and effective.

The formal structure of later Roman bureaucracy was concisely summarized in a document known as the *Notitia Dignitatum*. The *Notitia omnium dignitatum et administrationum tam civilium quam militarium* was, as its full title implies, a "list of all ranks and administrative positions both civil and military." The copy which survives provides a fairly comprehensive picture of the organization of imperial administration in the eastern half of the empire at the end of the 4th century.[49] The detail is complex, and—like most bureaucratic lists—the document does not make for interesting reading; but it does convey a strong impression of the meticulous classification of administrative tasks and the careful grading of imperial officials.[50] The basic unit of government throughout the empire remained the province: 114 are listed in the *Notitia,* each administered by a governor responsible for local judicial, financial, and administrative affairs.[51] The provinces were grouped into fourteen dioceses, each under the control of a *vicarius,* who had a general supervisory role and in some cases heard appeals from provincial courts. Dioceses, in turn, were grouped into four prefectures—Gaul (which included Britain and Spain), Italy (which included Africa), Illyricum, and the East—each in the charge of a praetorian prefect.

Praetorian prefects were the most powerful civil officials in later Roman government. They had overall responsibility for the administration of the empire, and in judicial matters, along with the emperor, were the final court of appeal. They also headed important financial departments, overseeing the levying of taxation to finance imperial public works, the administration, and the army (both wages and *matériel*), and to ensure the supply and transport of grain to the empire's capital cities.[52] Prefects, *vicarii,* and provincial governors each headed a permanent administrative department. The *officium* of the eastern praetorian prefect was divided into two branches: the administrative and judicial, and the financial. The former was headed by a *princeps officii* (with overall supervision of the branch's activities as well as of the department as a whole) and his deputy the *cornicularius;* beneath these officials, in descending order, were the *primiscrinius* or *adiutor* (responsible for the enforcement of judgments and court orders), the *commentarius* (mainly concerned with criminal trials), the *ab actis* (dealing with civil cases and judicial records), the *curae epistolarum* (in charge of the paperwork associated with official reports and of correspondence with *vicarii* and provincial governors), and the *regendarius* (responsible for issuing warrants for the use of the imperial postal system). Each of these officials—excepting the *princeps*—had three assistants *(adiutores)* who, in turn, were assisted by *chartularii*. These latter were drawn from the *excep-tores*, a *corps* of junior officials, divided into fifteen groups *(scholae)*, which formed the basic administrative staff of the prefecture. Below these were a set of subclerical grades—ushers, messengers, doorkeepers, and attendants—each, at least on paper, carefully organized with a similar precision and regimentation.[53]

Of course, late Roman officialdom, like any bureaucracy, was infinitely more subtle in its workings than any formal listing of administrative tasks and grades could reveal. One of the most important aspects of the system in operation was a continual tension between emperors and their officials. On the one hand, emperors were strong supporters of bureaucracy—the *Notitia Dignitatum* was, after all, drawn up by the *primicerius notariorum,* the head of the imperial secretariat (staffed by *notarii*) responsible directly to the emperor himself.[54] More broadly, imperial officials retained on retirement their high rank and status, had privileged access to the courts, and were granted taxation immunity for themselves and their families.[55] On the other hand, the increase in official-dom, with the inevitable growth of rules, regulations, and standard procedures, continually threatened to limit an emperor's right to intervene in any matter, at any time, for any reason, and without necessarily any justification. Imperial power depended in great part on an emperor's ability to reward or punish spectacularly and to do so on occasion without warning. Against the pressing strictures of administrative procedure, later Roman emperors felt an insistent need—as policy, desire, or whimsy took them—to assert their own authority, to break rules, or to subvert organizational hierarchies which on other occasions they might strongly uphold.[56]

This continual balancing of the institutional needs of autocracy and bureauc-racy can be seen in the selection, appointment, and promotion of imperial officials.[57] As in any administrative organization, seniority was a significant factor. In 331 Constantine affirmed this principle for the advancement of *excep-tores* in the eastern praetorian prefecture: "each shall succeed to a position according to his rank-order in the department and his merit, insofar as he would have deserved to obtain that position by length of service."[58] But on other occasions emperors issued laws upholding the right of retiring officials to appoint their sons to junior posts, or affirming that promotions were to be made on grounds of proficiency or competence.[59] These criteria were always difficult to define. Indeed, in a bureaucracy without entrance examinations or formal qualifications, assessment of a candidate's ability was unavoidably de-pendent on personal recommendation. *Suffragium*—the influence exercised by family or friends (and their well-placed connections)—was frequently key to ensuring a successful career. In the mid 4th century, Libanius, a famous teacher of rhetoric in Antioch who had an extensive network of contacts among high-ranking officials, frequently wrote recommendations on behalf of his pupils. In an elegantly phrased letter to Domitius Modestus, *comes orientis* (the title given to the senior *vicarius* in the eastern praetorian prefecture), Libanius was full of praise for the gracious support which some of his wealthier proteges had re-ceived, but also pointedly suggested that Modestus in his generosity might consider advancing others as well: "Of my young stock—led from the fields of the Muses—which I have given up to you, you see that there are those who have been favored by you, and those not as yet so favored. I am happy indeed for those who have received preferment at your hands, but I wish to bring the others to your notice . . . For you should turn your attention to all; to the wealthy so that they may gain honor, and to the poor, so that riches may come to them."[60]

Access to grand patrons and their connections, recommendations for office, and often even the position itself could sometimes also be secured through payment of money.[61] (Many wise aspirants no doubt relied on a judicious combination of all the tactics available to them.) In 362 Emperor Julian legislated to prevent litigation for the recovery of moneys paid out in exchange for recommendations by those who had benefited from such transactions.[62] In similar terms, in 394, Theodosius I affirmed that contracts to exchange gold, silver, movables, or urban or rural property in return for a recommendation were enforceable in the courts.[63] As these legal provisions indicate, such transactions might be concluded openly and officially sanctioned. That should come as no surprise. What mattered from an emperor's point of view was maintenance of a flexible system of criteria for promotion. A potentially threatening coalition of interests within the bureaucracy might be weakened by an emperor's insisting on promotion by seniority or merit, rather than by the recommendation of senior officers or other influential persons; candidates not part of existing networks might be brought into a department through the purchase of office. Conversely, a favored individual might be allowed to strengthen his position by recommending the appointment of friends, family, or associates. In such a system, emperors were able both to underline the degree to which a successful career depended upon imperial favor and, more significantly, to emphasize to all the importance of their own position at the center of government.

Yet inevitably not all matters were resolved to an emperor's best advantage. Some officials did not always enjoy—or could not always secure—imperial favor; some, understandably, attempted to reduce the risk of disfavor, while at the same time trying to protect their current position or advance their careers. When in the 340s Flavius Abinnaeus, back from Constantinople, presented his letters of appointment to the office of the military commander in Egypt, he was met with a cool response. Other, comparable documents had also been presented, documents obtained—as Abinnaeus claimed in his petition to the emperor—not as the result of imperial favor to one who had adored the purple, but *ex suffragio*, "as the result of influence."[64] Abinnaeus's success in using his courtly contacts to overcome his rivals must be seen in the light of others' expectations of promotion on the basis of documents issued (through connections or purchase) without imperial sanction and, in this case, against explicit imperial preference. For these officials, and those whom they helped, it was better for the emperor not to know what went on. After all, there was no particular reason to suppose that imperial intervention might result in the appointment of a better or more highly qualified candidate. For those at court, close to the center of government, "leakages" in imperial power could be even more deftly exploited. In 354, the decision to send to Antioch to recall Gallus

Caesar (Constantius II's heir apparent) and his subsequent execution in transit were rumored to be the result of a whispering campaign conducted by eunuchs in the royal household, who "while performing duties of an intimate nature" convinced Constantius that his son was plotting against him.[65] But such stories could also be turned. It was sometimes better too for emperors not to know. Constantius, subsequently accused of murder, forcibly retorted—with what truth it is impossible to say—that he had rescinded his order for Gallus's execution, but that regrettably his instructions had not been carried out.[66]

The continual see-sawing of advantage between emperors and the officials on whom they inescapably relied, and the tactics used by both sides to strengthen their positions, undoubtedly impaired the efficiency of later Roman bureaucracy. The resulting uncertainties and insecurities would not be considered good management practice in a modern organization. But they were the high cost emperors were prepared to pay to maintain a careful and delicately engineered balance between the establishment of a bureaucracy and the preservation of some measure of imperial autonomy. These "inefficiencies" did not necessarily render later Roman bureaucracy ineffective. Indeed, there is good evidence to suggest that officials were able to collect and present detailed information, to plan and execute complicated administrative tasks, and to record and monitor the results. On a grand scale, the *Notitia Dignitatum* provided a conspectus of the ranks and seniority of all senior officials in the empire. Likewise, the *Theodosian Code,* promulgated by Emperor Theodosius II in 438, was the first official consolidated collection of imperial edicts.[67]

Away from court, a telling picture of bureaucracy in action is provided by the instructions issued in advance of Emperor Diocletian's visit to Egypt in September 298. A papyrus roll, which preserves copies of some of the outgoing correspondence of the *strategos* of the Panopolite *nome* (the chief official in an administrative district roughly one hundred miles downstream from modern Luxor, near Sohag), contains a series of requisition orders issued to ensure that troops escorting the emperor were supplied with sufficient lentils, meat, chaff, bread, barley, wine, and vegetables.[68] A bakery, a smithy, and an armory were ordered to be made ready. Nile boats and their crews were to be kept on continual standby for the imperial post.[69] A similar, almost obsessive attention to detail marks the near contemporary work of Diocletian's land commissioners. In an edict promulgated in 297, the emperor sought to establish a single unit of assessment for all taxable land, based on its use and fertility. Officials were appointed to survey the empire accordingly and, as a necessary preliminary, to resolve ownership and boundary disputes. The evidence of their work in the form of a series of inscribed boundary stones, some in the most far-flung places, "shows that the demands and decisions of the state in this precise period penetrated into the most remote of country districts."[70] The state's new concern with the detailed assessment of tax liability was matched by an interest in accurate documentation and the surveillance of arrears. In July 372 Julius Eubulius Julianus, the governor of the Thebaid (the Egyptian province centered on modern Luxor), mounted an investigation, perhaps following the discovery of a shortfall in the province's revenue account. He sent a circular order to various cities instructing local magistrates that all officials in the villages who had been responsible for collecting taxes in the previous year, and in the three years prior to that, should be dispatched forthwith to the governor's headquarters for questioning.[71]

These are striking vignettes. The surviving documentation points toward a strong expectation on the part of central government that it would be able to exercise control both over its own personnel and over the resources of the Mediterranean world. It indicates too a significantly higher level of administrative activity than at any previous period under the empire. Of course, the overall impact of central government and its bureaucracy is difficult to gauge precisely; no doubt it varied markedly from time to time, and from place to place. Yet in broad terms it is worth bearing in mind that, in the 4th century, the Roman state raised enough revenue to enable it to pay for a professional standing army larger than that under the Principate, to fund a greatly increased bureaucracy, to support a new religion, to subsidize heavily barbarian tribes on its frontiers, and to found a second imperial capital at Constantinople. For a preindustrial empire, these achievements should not be underrated. Without some increase in the effectiveness of its officials, the later Roman government could not have operated in so many new areas or have hoped to pay for so many new obligations. Undeniably, the tense relationship between emperors and officialdom impaired administrative efficiency. Even so, from the reigns of Diocletian and Constantine, the growth in the number and responsibilities of imperial officials was an important element in the successful formation and financing of a highly centralized state. On balance, bureaucracy helped rather than hindered imperial rule. Despite its undoubted failings it was one of the most significant factors enabling later Roman emperors to establish a degree of control over empire not reached again in Europe until the 18th century absolutisms of France and Prussia.

In the late 4th century, the Christian mystic Dorotheus had a vision. He dreamed that he was transported to a heavenly palace. In the audience hall, guided by heaven's palace attendants, he saw God the Father and God the Son surrounded by their angelic courtiers. The archangel Gabriel stood next to a figure described by Dorotheus, in strict bureaucratic terminology, as "the Lord's *primicerius*"—head of the corps of secretaries *(notarii)* who staffed the imperial palace.[72] After a series of tests, Dorotheus found himself promoted through the ranks of God's palace guard and invested with a uniform familiar to anyone who had seen the troops flanking an emperor (or his image) on ceremonial occasions: "I did not have simple clothing . . . but I was wearing a cloak made for me from two different sorts of linen. I stood with a kerchief around my neck and around my legs I wore long breeches and a multicolored belt."[73]

Visions of the divine which commingled the outward and visible forms of sacred and secular power were not uncommon in the later Roman world. Atop its tall porphyry column in Constantinople, the shining golden statue with its radiate crown might be seen as Emperor Constantine, or Apollo, or Christ, or as some combination of all three. These carefully contrived confusions were deftly exploited by those keen to legitimate the position of the emperor as the undisputed center of a highly centralized state. In 336, in a speech celebrating the thirtieth anniversary of Constantine's accession, the emperor's biographer Eusebius of Caesarea described the emperor as "the friend of the all-ruling God; arrayed as he is in the image of the kingdom of heaven, he pilots affairs here below following with an upward gaze a course modeled on that ideal form."[74] Imperial ceremonies were given heavenly archetypes. Both emperors and divinities were cloaked in a distancing, awe-inspiring splendor. Eusebius congratulated his audience on appearing like a celestial court in its angelic array: "So let those who have entered within the sanctuary of this holy place—that innermost, most inaccessible of places—having barred the gate to profane hearing, narrate the sovereign's most secret mysteries to those alone who are initiated in these things."[75] For John Chrysostom, patriarch of Constantinople at the turn of the 4th century, the city of God was like an imperial palace adorned with innumerable courts and buildings: "Here angels stand not before a mortal king, but before him who is immortal, the king of kings and lord of lords."[76] Christ in the splendor of his second coming could be compared to an emperor surrounded by his retinue processing in full ceremonial panoply before an awestruck crowd: "the men in golden apparel, and the pairs of white mules caparisoned with gold, and the chariots inlaid with precious stones, and the snow-white cushions . . . But when we see the emperor we lose sight of these. For he alone draws our gaze: the purple robe, and the diadem, and the throne, and the clasp, and the shoes—all that brilliance of his appearance."[77] Colorful language was matched by magnificent art. From the mid 6th century, visitors to Ravenna in northern Italy could see in the church of S. Apollinare Nuovo a series of mosaics on gospel themes, each with Christ dressed in imperial purple.[78] In S. Vitale they saw images of Christ, Emperor Justinian, and his wife Theodora, all surrounded by similarly attired attendants, all staring with equal wide-eyed confidence past the viewer and into an eternity beyond.[79]

Images drawn from the new state religion helped sanctify a new system of rule. An empire is held together not only by military force and an efficient administration; it also requires an effective ideology to proclaim to all involved the rightness and legitimacy of its government. Christianity's monotheism and its vision of a hierarchical heaven ruled by an omnipotent divinity offered to the Roman state a means of comprehending and justifying an imperially dominated, centralized pattern of power. The ceremonial monarch, surrounded by the glitter of an immobile court, was presented as a potent icon of majesty whether in heaven or on earth. Whatever Constantine's personal motivations for conferring state patronage on Christianity, the theology and imagery of this new religion were undoubtedly useful for creating a political ideology which could complement changes in the nature, extent, and effectiveness of imperial government.[80] In addition, part of Christianity's success lay in its ability to accommodate itself to long-standing classical traditions. Arguably, one of the most significant factors in its growth throughout the 4th century was a recognition—in both liturgical practice and theology—of the value of pagan learning, philosophy, and ritual. This recognition was particularly attractive to members of the well-educated urban elite. The expensive classical education that marked their superior status was also an indispensable prerequisite for understanding and manipulating the highly rhetorical language of power which since Augustus had "provided a permanent background music to the consensus in favor of Roman rule skillfully fostered among the civic notables of the Greek world."[81] A Christianity in tune with classical culture provided an ideological framework which both shored up traditional urban hierarchies and gave the empire's municipal elite (on whose loyalty the stability of imperial rule ultimately depended) an appropriate language with which they could continue to exercise influence over central government and its representatives. In political and religious terms, the rise of Christianity in the later Roman world was dependent not only on its ability to attract adherents in the present, but also on its success in converting the empire's classical past.

But the advantages which this new religion offered the Roman state and its supporters did not go unchallenged. For the first three centuries after Christ, Christianity had survived as a close-knit sect firmly opposed to the religion and culture of the society which surrounded it. A classical education was regarded by many with suspicion. In a famous passage the 2nd century African writer Tertullian trenchantly asked: "What has Athens to do with Jerusalem? What has the Academy to do with the Church? . . . Away with all attempts to produce a Stoic, Platonic, and dialectic Christianity."[82] In the later empire, a dramatic rejection of the classical world and its learning—that "great dust cloud of considerations"[83]—remained important for those who sought holiness in the silence and solitude of the desert. Antony, one of the most famous of Egyptian monks, was said always to have worsted wily philosophers who sought to ridicule him for his professed illiteracy. Once a debate turned to a discussion of thought and writing. Antony asked which came first. The philosophers replied that, of course, thought was primary and through it writing and literature were generated. Antony pressed home the advantage: "Now you understand that in a person whose thought is pure there is no need for writing."[84] For those in the wilderness, that was a common theme. On turning forty, Arsenius, the highly educated son of a senatorial family and once tutor to the imperial princes Arcadius and Honorius in Constantinople, renounced the delights of high civilization for a monk's cell in the Egyptian desert. To those who would marvel at his rejection of such an influential position at court (perhaps thinking of the successes Ausonius enjoyed under his former pupil Gratian), Arsenius, pointing to his new teacher, would reply: "I once knew Greek and Latin learning; but with this peasant, I have not yet mastered my ABC."[85]

Aphorisms such as these were important in the presentation of a church militant, strongly resisting contamination in a world deeply wedded to its classical past. But against the rejection of classical learning advocated by holy men and monks must be set the conviction of those Christians who saw reverence for the classical past as a firm foundation for their own faith. For these deeply committed believers, Christ's teaching of his disciples could be envisioned as a philosopher's education of his pupils. In a beautiful early 5th century mosaic in the apse of S. Pudenziana in Rome, a seated Christ, holding a scroll in one hand, gestures didactically with the other; his disciples, decorously arranged in a semicircle on either side of their instructor, pay polite attention like well-bred students in some divine academy.[86]

The fusion of Christianity with classical learning illustrated by such images was perhaps best represented by the theological works of the Cappadocian Fathers. This group of highly educated bishops from Asia Minor drew freely on both classical literature and Neoplatonic concepts and vocabulary in their elucidation of Christian doctrinal problems. The justification for such an approach, they claimed, was firmly located in scripture. Writing in the late 390s, Gregory of Nyssa in his *Life of Moses* sought to demonstrate how the patriarch's great knowledge of "the wisdom of the Egyptians" had made him suitable to receive the divine law on Mount Sinai.[87] In the hands of the learned, argued Gregory, classical philosophy—"the wealth of Egypt"—might become "at certain times a comrade, a friend, and a lifetime companion for the higher way."[88] In that sense, Moses was a model for all educated men. Set afloat among the bulrushes in his papyrus coracle, he prefigured the true Christian, swaddled in classical learning, successfully navigating the hazards of "this stream of life."[89] The intellectual agility shown by the Cappadocian Fathers in sanctifying classical culture had a wide appeal, far beyond the abstruse subtleties of their weighty theological tracts. Once legitimated, a sophisticated synthesis of Christianity with traditional wisdom provided limitless opportunities for the display of knowledge and the erudite wittiness so prized by the *beau monde* of the Roman world. In the late 4th century, the well-educated elite of Kourion on entering the eastern portico of the house of Eustolius—no doubt to admire the splendid views along the Cypriot coast—might pause to admire an inscription neatly worked into the mosaic floor:

> This house in place of massy stones and solid iron,
> Burnished bronze and even adamant,
> Is now girt with the much hallowed signs of Christ.

The more learned would have been pleased to note that this forthright assertion of Christianity was couched in deliberately archaizing Greek. Perhaps too they paused to puzzle over some of the Homeric vocabulary, or to scan the elegant old-fashioned hexameter verses.[90]

The importance of this cultural fusion between paganism and Christianity was clearly evident in Constantine's carefully contrived ceremonies for the consecration of Constantinople in May 330. The emperor's statue (with its multiple possible meanings) looked out across a capital whose churches and cathedrals allowed it to lay claim to being a truly Christian city.[91] Yet the famous sculptures, bronzes, and monuments removed from towns and cult centers throughout the empire that crammed its public spaces must also have made it seem the ultimate classical city.⁹² The principal forum, itself dominated by the porphyry column taken from Troy, contained statues of Athena, Juno, the Judgment of Paris, Daniel in the lions' den, and the Good Shepherd.⁹³ Above all, the collection of relics believed to be hidden beneath the column's base—the Palladium taken from Rome, the holy nails, Noah's adze, Moses's stone, and the wicker panniers—symbolized the self-conscious incorporation of a classical and Hebrew past into a Christian present. This was a deliberate and elegantly constructed ambiguity, best epitomized in Constantine's own name for his imperial capital built on seven hills by the Bosphorus: "New Rome."⁹⁴

In one sense, the open display of Christianity in Constantinople was a striking indication of the effect of this new religion on the empire's government and its importance in the representation of imperial power. Equally, as the stress on "Roman" tradition indicated, the success of the Constantinian revolution depended on the continued loyalty and support of the empire's elites, understandably made nervous by an increasing concentration of authority in the hands of emperors and bureaucrats. The striking of a difficult balance between these two pressing concerns inevitably meant the survival of many traditional pagan institutions well into the new Christian empire: Constantine himself permitted the building of a temple to the imperial cult at Hispellum in Umbria; until well into the 5th century, emperors on their death were granted the title of *divus* ("deified"); the excited crowd which was said to have streamed out of Emona in 388 to greet the victorious Theodosius I included at its head municipal pagan priests *(flamines)* resplendent in their robes of office and distinctive tall conical hats.⁹⁵ But in the longer term, the assimilation of many traditional beliefs and practices hastened the acceptance of Christianity and the imperial regime which sponsored it.

Even in Rome itself—often seen as the last stronghold of a committed pagan aristocracy—by the mid 4th century there were clear signs of rapprochement. The Codex-Calendar of 354 produced for the wealthy Christian Valentinus included a meticulous record of pagan holidays and observances proper to the imperial cult.⁹⁶ The sarcophagus of Valentinus's contemporary, Junius Bassus, who died in office as urban prefect of Rome in 359, was decorated with scenes from the life of Christ juxtaposed with Bacchic cupids enjoying a plentiful grape harvest.⁹⁷ Like the ambiguities of Constantine's capital, this sophisticated melding of the old and the new had a strong political significance. An inscription on the upper edge of the sarcophagus clearly proclaimed Bassus's Christian belief and recorded his deathbed baptism.⁹⁸ It was complemented by flamboyant verses on the lid (neatly framed by representations of the sun and moon) which listed his offices and stressed his high social rank. As Bassus's cortege passed by, they proclaim,

> Even the roofs of Rome seemed to weep,
> And then the houses themselves along the way seemed to sigh.
> Grant him the highest honors of the living, grant these honors,
> Lofty is the height which death had assigned to him.⁹⁹

The public advertisement of Christian belief coupled with traditional iconography and the celebration of high office indicates that adherence to the new religion was compatible both with long-standing cultural expectations and with the maintenance of a superior social status. The success of Christianity among the empire's elite was linked closely with its ability to make sense of the present—in stark political as well as cultural terms—without rejecting the hard-won advantages of the past. Indeed, for confident Christian aristocrats like Junius Bassus, the surety of promotion under an emperor could be matched by an equally firm expectation of elevation to a lofty place in Christ's celestial hierarchy.

For members of the ruling elite throughout the empire the possibility that Christianity might help preserve their social and political clout (if only in this world) was unquestionably attractive. In the cities of the later Roman world, in growing numbers throughout the 4th century, the well-educated sons of the urban elite sought ordination and were in time raised to the episcopate.[100] As bishops, in time-honored upper-class fashion, they were in a position to support their family, to seek favors for their friends, and to secure preferment for their proteges. (In many of their concerns there is little to separate the letters of Basil of Caesarea from those of his pagan contemporary Libanius, the well-connected professor of rhetoric at Antioch.)[101] As bishops, these men continued also to fulfill the long-standing obligation of leading citizens to beautify their home towns. As their forebears had built splendid baths, temples, and porticoes, so their Christian descendants erected magnificent basilicas, churches, and hospices. An inscription set into the floor of the ambulatory in the early 5th century cathedral at Salona makes the point simply and clearly: "New things follow old; begun by Bishop Synferis, finished by his grandson Bishop Hesychius, with the help of the clergy and people, this gift of a church, O Christ, is freely given."[102] Finally, as bishops these municipal worthies remained well placed to cultivate a special relationship with the imperial government and its official representatives. Their advantageous position was publicly displayed in their rank, privileges, and immunities; in the grants of jurisdiction which allowed them to hear a range of civil and criminal matters; and in their role as spokesmen and advocates for the interests of their cities.[103] Imperial government continued to listen—as it had always done—to these civic grandees. It is no surprise to find that it was Basil, worried about the status and prosperity of Caesarea, who led a campaign against the division of the province of Cappadocia, or that, following the Riot of the Statues in Antioch, it was the intercession of the city's patriarch at court which secured the emperor's pardon.[104]

For the urban elite of the empire adherence to Christianity offered a way of confirming their traditional place at the head of municipal society; more widely, it gave them a recognizable place in the empire-wide hierarchy at whose distant apex stood both God and emperor. That security in both positions is reflected in a magnificent mosaic in the late 4th century cathedral at Aquileia in northern Italy. The central panels display portraits of the principal civic benefactors who had contributed to its construction. Their comfortable expressions—confident in the church as a guarantor of their identity and importance in local society—

are matched by the smug frankness of the inscriptions recording their generosity: "Januarius vowed this gift for God: 880 square feet of mosaic."[105] A similar certainty that the church could be invoked to uphold the existing social and moral order was neatly captured on a bronze tag from Rome once attached to the collar of a slave. Should the slave run away, the finder is asked to return the fugitive to his owner: "Seize me and return me to Maximianus the copyist in the Forum of Mars." For added efficacy (and Christian moral support) the inscription is neatly punctuated with the Chi-Rho monogram of Christ.[106]

The union of slavery and Christianity, churches decorated with portraits of wealthy benefactors, or the eclectic collection of relics under Constantine's porphyry column would have been unlikely to secure the approval of St. Antony or Arsenius. But away from the stark simplicities of the desert and its holy men who had turned their back on the cities of the Roman world, the accommodation between Christianity and the habits, customs, and social expectations of many in the empire was a vital factor in securing the widespread acceptance of the new imperial religion. On that acceptance the later Roman empire was substantially built. Christianity permitted the development of a sophisticated ideology of power; it was a key element in the establishment of a transcendent justification for the highly centralized rule imposed by the later Roman state. Earthly monarchy reflected heavenly archetypes: in churches, emperors appeared like Christ; in visions, angels appeared like bureaucrats; and in the expectations of many, the carefully graded hierarchies of this world prefigured the divinely ordained ranks of the next. Equally important, a Christianity which permitted the participation of leading members of the empire's elite (and, in many cases, helped secure their status within their own cities) provided both an ideological framework and an institutional structure for the exercise of influence on the actions of imperial government and its representatives. A shared language of power based on a coalition between Christianity and classical culture allowed emperors to emphasize their distant, godlike status while at the same time making possible the effective voicing of praise or disagreement by those whose cooperation and participation remained essential for the collection of taxes and the maintenance of good order in the provinces.

Despite the gloss of political and cultural unity which Christianity gave to the later empire, though, the shift toward a strong, centralized government should not be downplayed. One of the best indicators of that movement remains the expansion in the size and competence of the later Roman bureaucracy, particularly at the imperial court, and the change in the nature and scope of much of the surviving administrative paperwork. Of course, there were limits on both effectiveness and efficiency. Above all, emperors were wary of any restriction on their (sometimes capricious) freedom of action that might be imposed by a bureaucracy's inevitable reliance on rules, regulations, and standard procedures. While actively encouraging the growth of a more centralized system of rule, emperors insisted that the success and security of all was dependent on them alone. The importance of continued imperial favor was reflected in the vast ceremoniousness of later Roman government. Memorable rituals enacted before emperors or their images were designed to present an exemplary model of society which emphasized the dependence of all upon the imperial center and stressed the benefits which might flow from the recognition of an emperor's sovereignty. To be sure, ceremony had always played an important part in the representation of Roman imperial power, but in the later empire it acquired a heightened and more complex meaning.[107] Nowhere was this more clearly on show than in Constantine's new capital, a city consciously designed as a brilliant backdrop for the staged display of imperial power. Seven years after the city's inaugural celebration, another ceremony was played out before an awe-struck crowd in Constantinople. Under military escort, Constantine's body was carried through the grief-stricken city. Encircled by candles, the emperor lay in state in the main audience hall of the imperial palace, attended day and night by officials: "presenting a marvelous spectacle, and one such as no one under the sun had ever seen on this earth since the world began." Mourners were admitted in strict rank-order of precedence; the same court ceremony was observed before the dead emperor's golden coffin as before a living emperor's throne.[108] Constantius II, on his succession, commemorated his father's death by issuing a series of coins whose design explicitly drew on the classical imagery of Roman imperial apotheosis: Constantine was shown guiding a four-horse chariot across the sky as a veiled hand reached out to welcome him into heaven.[109] Yet the emperor was buried by his son in the Church of the Apostles, newly built on one of the most prominent hills in Constantinople: "this building he carried to a great height" and roofed with bronze, "and this too was splendidly and sumptuously adorned with gold, reflecting the sun's rays with a brilliance which dazzled the distant onlooker." At its center twelve splendid shrines "like sacred pillars" had been consecrated to Christ's apostles. In their midst, in a glittering catafalque, lay the magnificent sarcophagus of Constantine, the self-proclaimed thirteenth apostle of Christianity—a new official religion capable, when linked to proper reverence for the classical past, of both justifying and sanctifying a striking shift toward a more autocratic and highly centralized pattern of Roman rule.[110]

Notes

I should like to thank both Keith Hopkins and Richard Miles for their thoughtful, perceptive, and sympathetic comments on this essay.

1. There is no straightforward ancient account of these ceremonies: most versions were written later; many represent an almost baroque accretion of various stories; all contradict each other at some point. What follows draws substantially on the *Chronicon Paschale* (Easter Chronicle) for the years 328 and 330, and John Malalas 13.7–8; with the reconstruction of events by Gilbert Dagron, *Naissance d'une capitale: Constantinople et ses institutions de 330 à 451* (Paris, 1974), 32–47; Raymond Janin, *Constantinople Byzantine: Développement urbain et répertoire topographique* (Paris, 2nd ed., 1964), 18–19, 23–26; David Lathoud, "La consécration et de dédicace de Constantinople," *Échos d'Orient* 23 (1924): 289–314 and 24 (1925): 180–201; Richard Kraut-

heimer, *Three Christian Capitals: Topography and Politics* (Berkeley, 1983), chap. 2, esp. 55–56, 60–67, plates 51–53.

2. Cyril Mango, "Constantinopolitana," *Jahrbuch des Deutschen Archäologischen Instituts* 80 (1965): 305–336, at 306–313, repr. in Mango, *Studies on Constantinople* (London, 1993), chap. 2; id., "Constantine's Column," ibid., chap. 3; Janin, *Constantinople Byzantine*, 77–80. The column—known as the Çemberlitaş—or Colonne Brûlée— still stands; see Wolfgang Müller-Wiener, *Bildlexicon zur Topographie Istanbuls* (Tübingen, 1977), 255–257.

3. Sozomen, *Hist.eccl.* 2.3.3, ed. Joseph Bidez and Günther Hansen (Berlin: *GCS,* 1960); Nicephorus Callistus, *Ecclesiastical History* 7.48 (*PG* 145; 1324C); Philostorgius 2.9, ed. Joseph Bidez (Berlin, *GCS,* 3rd ed., 1981); John Lydus, *On Months* 4.2.

4. Procopius, *Gothic War* 1.15.9–14; Virgil, *Aeneid* 2.162–170.

5. Charles Diehl, "De quelques croyances byzantines sur la fin de Constantinople," *Byzantinische Zeitschrift* 30 (1929–30): 192–196, at 193–194; Andreas Alföldi, "On the Foundation of Constantinople: A Few Notes," *Journal of Roman Studies* 37 (1947): 10–16, at 11.

6. Nicephorus Callistus, *Ecclesiastical History* 7.49 (*PG* 145: 1325D); Hesychius 41 note, ed. Theodor Preger, *Scriptores originum Constantinopolitanarum,* 2 vols. (Leipzig, 1901–1907), 1: 17; A. Frolow, "La dédicace de Constantinople dans la tradition byzantine," *Revue de l'histoire des religions* 127 (1944): 61–127, at 76–78; Lathoud, *Echos d'Orient,* 23, 299–305.

7. *Breves Chronographicae* 56, ed. Preger, *Scriptores,* 1: 56–57; *Patria* 2.49, ed. Preger, *Scriptores,* 2: 177–178; Theodor Preger, "Konstantinos-Helios," *Hermes* 36 (1901): 457–469.

8. Zonaras 13.3.

9. Socrates, *Hist.eccl.* 1.17 (*PG* 67: 120B).

10. John Malalas 13.8; Richard Delbrueck, *Spätantike Kaiserporträts von Constantinus Magnus bis zum Ende des Westreichs* (Berlin, 1933), 59–61; Jules Maurice, *Numismatique Constantinienne,* 3 vols. (Paris, 1908–1912), 2: 486–487.

11. *Breves Chronographicae* 38, ed. Preger, *Scriptores,* 1: 42; *Patria* 2.42, ed. Preger, *Scriptores,* 2: 172–173.

12. Ramsey MacMullen, "Judicial Savagery in the Roman Empire," *Chiron* 16 (1986): 147–166, repr. in MacMullen, *Changes in the Roman Empire: Essays in the Ordinary* (Princeton, 1990), chap. 20.

13. A. H. M. Jones, *The Later Roman Empire 284–602: A Social, Economic, and Administrative Survey,* 3 vols. (Oxford, 1964; repr. in 2 vols, 1973), 1: 406–410; John Matthews, *The Roman Empire of Ammianus* (London, 1988), 253–262. For a contrasting view, see Ramsey MacMullen, *Corruption and the Decline of Rome* (New Haven, 1988), parts 3–4, esp. 167–170.

14. *C.Th.* 16.2.1–16; see Jean Gaudemet, *L'Eglise dans l'Empire romain (IVe–Ve siècles),* Histoire du droit et des institutions de l'église en occident, rev. ed. (Paris, 1989), 172–179, 240–245, 311–320; T. G. Elliott, "The Tax Exemptions Granted to Clerics by Constantine and Constantius II," *Phoenix* 32 (1978): 326–336.

15. Eusebius, *Life of Constantine* 3.10.3, ed. Friedhelm Winkelmann (Berlin: *GCS,* 1975).

16. Wolfgang Kunkel, "*Consilium, Consistorium,*" *Jahrbuch für Antike und Christentum,* 11/12 (1968/1969): 230–248, at 242–246; repr. in Kunkel, *Kleine Schriften: Zum römischen Strafverfahren und zur römischen Verfassungsgeschichte,* ed. Hubert Niederländer (Weimar, 1974), 405–440, at 428–437.

17. William Avery, "The *Adoratio Purpurae* and the Importance of the Imperial Purple in the Fourth Century of the Christian Era," *Memoirs of the American Academy in Rome* 17 (1940): 66–80.

18. Missorium of Theodosius I (now in the Real Academia de la Historia, Madrid): see Sabine MacCormack, *Art and Ceremony in Late Antiquity* (Berkeley, 1981), 214–

221; Richard Delbrueck, *Die Consulardiptychen und verwandte Denkmäler* (Berlin, 1929), 235–242.

19. *Latin Panegyrics* 11.37, ed. Édouard Galletier, 3 vols. (Paris, 1949–1955); for the background, see C. E. V. Nixon and Barbara Saylor Rodgers, *In Praise of Later Roman Emperors: The Panegyrici Latini, Introduction, Translation, and Historical Commentary* (Berkeley, 1994), esp. 441–447.

20. Amm.Marc. 16.10.4–10, with the useful remarks in MacCormack, *Art and Ceremony*, 39–45, and Matthews, *The Roman Empire of Ammianus*, 231–235.

21. MacCormack, *Art and Ceremony*, 1–14; Keith Hopkins, *Conquerors and Slaves* (Cambridge, Eng., 1978), 197–200; Michael McCormick, "Analyzing Imperial Ceremonies," *Jahrbuch der Österreichischen Byzantinistik* 35 (1985): 1–20.

22. Eusebius, *In Praise of Constantine* 5.6, ed. Ivar Heikel (Leipzig, 1902).

23. For a description of the Embolos, the principal commercial area of Ephesus in Asia Minor, see Clive Foss, *Ephesus after Antiquity: A Late Antique Byzantine and Turkish City* (Cambridge, Eng., 1979), 65–74; more generally on imperial statues, see Kenneth Setton, *Christian Attitude towards the Emperor in the Fourth Century Especially As Shown in Addresses to the Emperor* (New York, 1941; repr., New York, 1967), chap. 8; Helmut Kruse, *Studien zur offiziellen Geltung des Kaiserbildes im römischen Reiche* (Paderborn, 1934), chap. 2; Hopkins, *Conquerors and Slaves*, 221–231.

24. Coins: Delbrueck, *Spätantike Kaiserporträts*, 71–104; Medallions: Andreas Alföldi and Elizabeth Alföldi, *Die Kontorniat-Medaillons* (Berlin, 1976–1990), vol. 1, nos. 440–482, 148–156.

25. Gisela Richter, *Catalogue of Engraved Gems: Greek, Etruscan, and Roman, in the Metropolitan Museum of Art, New York* (Rome, 1956), no. 500, 109. The inscription is restored.

26. David Buckton, ed., *Byzantium: Treasures of Byzantine Art and Culture from British Collections* (London, 1994), nos. 31–32, 49; Kurt Weitzmann, ed., *Age of Spirituality: Late Antique and Early Christian Art, Third to Seventh Century* (New York, 1979), nos. 324–328, 343–345.

27. Roger Bland and Catherine Johns, *The Hoxne Treasure: An Illustrated Introduction* (London, 1993), 1, 25–26.

28. The Obelisk of Theodosius I: see Dagron, *Naissance d'une capitale*, 311–312, 323–324; Janin, *Constantinople Byzantine*, 189–191; the most comprehensive publication remains Gerda Bruns, *Der Obelisk und seine Basis auf dem Hippodrom zu Konstantinopel* (Istanbul, 1935), esp. 33–68. For the position of the imperial box, see Rodolphe Guilland, "Études sur l'Hippodrome de Byzance: Le palais du Kathisma," *Byzantinoslavica* 18 (1957): 39–76, repr. in Guilland, *Études de topographie de Constantinople byzantine*, 2 vols. (Berlin, 1969), 1: 462–498); Janin, *Constantinople Byzantine*, 188–189. The obelisk still stands on the site of the Hippodrome in Istanbul: see Müller-Wiener, *Bildlexicon*, 64–71.

29. Amm.Marc. 16.10.10.

30. Severianus of Gabala, *On the Holy Cross*, in John of Damascus, *On Images, Oration* 3.385 (*PG* 94: 1409A).

31. *C.Th.* 15.7.12 = *C.Just.* 11.41.4.

32. Glanville Downey, *A History of Antioch in Syria from Seleucus to the Arab Conquest* (Princeton, 1961), 426–433.

33. John Chrysostom, *Homilies on the Statues* 2.1 (*PG* 49.35); see Frans van de Paverd, *St. John Chrysostom, The Homilies on the Statues: An Introduction* (Rome, 1991), 15–159.

34. Gregory of Nazianzus, *Oration* 4.96 (*Sources chrétiennes* 309: 240).

35. Michele Renée Salzman, *On Roman Time: The Codex-Calendar of 354 and the Rhythms of Urban Life in Late Antiquity* (Berkeley, 1990), 34–35, fig. 13.

36. John Chrysostom, *On Vainglory* 4 (*Sources chrétiennes* 188: 78) with Peter

Brown, *Power and Persuasion in Late Antiquity: Towards a Christian Empire* (Madison, 1992), 83–84. The image was an old one; see Pliny the Younger, *Letters* 3.20.12.

37. *CIL* 8.8481 = *ILS* 802; on Sitifis, see Claude Lepelley, *Les cités de l'Afrique romaine au Bas-Empire*, 2 vols. (Paris, 1979–1981), 2: 497–503.

38. John Matthews, *The Roman Empire of Ammianus*, 271–274; id., "Gallic Supporters of Theodosius," *Latomus* 30 (1971): 1073–99, repr. in Matthews, *Political Life and Culture in Late Roman Society* (London, 1985), chap. 9.

39. Keith Hopkins, "Social Mobility in the Later Roman Empire: The Evidence of Ausonius," *Classical Quarterly*, n.s. 11 (1961): 239–249; Hagith Sivan, *Ausonius of Bordeaux: Genesis of a Gallic Aristocracy* (London, 1993), 131–141.

40. Amm.Marc. 27.6.14.

41. *P. Abinn.* 1.11–14. For Abinnaeus's career see E. G. Turner in H. I. Bell, V. Martin, E. G. Turner, and D. van Berchem, *The Abinnaeus Archive: Papers of a Roman Officer in the Reign of Constantius II* (Oxford, 1962), chap. 2; and the suggestions of Timothy Barnes, "The Career of Abinnaeus," *Phoenix* 39 (1985): 368–374, repr. in Barnes, *From Eusebius to Augustine: Selected Papers 1982–1993* (London, 1994).

42. Amm.Marc. 28.6.9.

43. Philostorgius 2.17; Theodoret 1.34.3, ed. Léon Parmentier and Felix Scheidweiler (Berlin, 1954).

44. Some of the arguments in the opening parts of this section are more fully worked out in Christopher Kelly, "Emperors, Government, and Bureaucracy," in Averil Cameron and Peter Garnsey, eds., *The Cambridge Ancient History, vol. 13: The Late Empire, A.D. 337–425* (Cambridge, Eng., 1998), chap. 5.

45. Richard Duncan-Jones, *Structure and Scale in the Roman Economy* (Cambridge, Eng., 1990), chap. 1.

46. Synesius of Cyrene, *On Kingship* 27, ed. Antonio Garzya (Turin, 1989).

47. For useful surveys, see P. R. C. Weaver, *Familia Caesaris: A Social Study of the Emperor's Freedmen and Slaves* (Cambridge, Eng., 1972), part 3; Nicholas Purcell, "The *Apparitores*: A Study in Social Mobility," *Papers of the British School at Rome* 51 (1983): 125–173, esp. 128–131.

48. Jones, *The Later Roman Empire*, vol. 3, n. 44, 341–342; Roger Bagnall, *Egypt in Late Antiquity* (Princeton, 1993), 66. See also MacMullen, *Corruption*, 144, roughly estimating a hundredfold increase in salaried officials from the early empire.

49. John Mann, "The *Notitia Dignitatum*—Dating and Survival," *Britannia* 22 (1991): 215–219; Werner Seibt, "Wurde die notitia dignitatum 408 von Stilicho in Auftrag gegeben?" *Mitteilungen des Instituts für Österreichische Geschichtsforschung* 90 (1982): 339–346. There are good introductions to the *Notitia* in Jones, *The Later Roman Empire*, 3: 347–380; Roger Goodburn and Philip Bartholomew, eds., *Aspects of the Notitia Dignitatum* (Oxford, 1976).

50. The most compact introduction to the formal structure of later Roman bureaucracy is Alexander Demandt, *Die Spätantike: Römische Geschichte von Diocletian bis Justinian, 284–565 n. Chr.* (Munich, 1989), 231–255; see also Jones, *The Later Roman Empire*, chaps. 11, 12, 16, 18. The functions of palatine departments—not described here—are well set out in Karl Noethlichs, "Hofbeamter," *Reallexikon für Antike und Christentum* 15 (1991): 1111–58.

51. *Not.Dig.(oc.)* i 57–128, *(or.)* i 50–121.

52. *Not.Dig.(oc.)* ii–iii, *(or.)* ii–iii; see Wilhelm Ensslin, "Praefectus praetorio," *Pauly-Wissowa: Realencyclopädie der classischen Altertumswissenschaft*, 22.2 (1954): 2391–2502, at cols. 2426–2478.

53. The details are disputed; see Ernst Stein, *Untersuchungen über das Officium der Prätorianerpräfektur seit Diokletian* (Vienna, 1922), esp. 31–77, repr. ed. Jean-Rémy Palanque (Amsterdam, 1962); Jones, *The Later Roman Empire*, 1: 586–590; Ensslin, *Pauly-Wissowa*, 22.2, cols. 2478–2495.

54. *Not.Dig.(oc.)* xviii 3–4, *(or.)* xvi 4–6; see Guido Clemente, *La "Notitia Dignitatum," Saggi di storia e letteratura* 4 *(Cagliari, 1968)*, 360–367; H. C. Teitler, *Notarii and Exceptores: An Inquiry into Role and Significance of Shorthand Writers in the Imperial and Ecclesiastical Bureaucracy of the Roman Empire* (Amsterdam, 1985), esp. chap. 6.

55. *C.Th.* 6.35.1 = *C.Just.* 12.28.1; *C.Th.* 8.4.1; Jones, *The Later Roman Empire*, 1: 525–530, 535–537, 543–545. The most useful survey of the evidence remains Emil Kuhn, *Die städtische und bürgerliche Verfassung des römischen Reichs bis auf die Zeiten Justinians*, 2 vols. (Leipzig, 1864–1865), 1: 149–226.

56. Christopher Kelly, "Later Roman Bureaucracy: Going through the Files," in Alan Bowman and Greg Woolf, eds., *Literacy and Power in the Ancient World* (Cambridge, 1994), chap. 11, at 166–168; Jones, *The Later Roman Empire*, vol. 1, 377. Karl Noethlichs, *Beamtentum und Dienstvergehen: Zur Staatsverwaltung in der Spätantike* (Wiesbaden, 1981), 3–18, 34–37, makes an instructive comparison between later Roman and modern western bureaucracies.

57. The evidence is discussed in Jones, *The Later Roman Empire*, 1: 383–396, 602–604; and in Fritz Pedersen, "On Professional Qualifications for Public Posts in Late Antiquity," *Classica et Mediaevalia* 31 (1970): 161–213, at 175–205, repr. as Pedersen, *Late Roman Public Professionalism* (Odense, 1976), at 23–46.

58. *C.Th.* 8.1.2.

59. *C.Th.* 6.27.8.2; 7.3.1.

60. Libanius, *Letters* 154; see Paul Petit, *Les étudiants de Libanius* (Paris, 1957), 158–166, 183–188; J. H. W. G. Liebeschuetz, *Antioch: City and Imperial Administration in the Later Roman Empire* (Oxford, 1972), 192–198. More generally, see Geoffrey de Ste. Croix, *"Suffragium*: From Vote to Patronage," *British Journal of Sociology* 5 (1954): 33–48.

61. For perceptive surveys of the evidence (and contrasting conclusions to those presented here) see Claude Collot, "La pratique et l'institution du *suffragium* au Bas-Empire," *Revue historique de droit français et étranger*, 4th ser., 43 (1965): 185–221, at 190–211; Detlef Liebs, "Ämterkauf und Ämterpatronage in der Spätantike: Propaganda und Sachzwang bei Julian dem Abtrünnigen," *Zeitschrift der Savigny-Stiftung für Rechtsgeschichte* 95 (1978): 158–186, at 170–183; Noethlichs, *Beamtentum und Dienstvergehen*, 69–72; MacMullen, *Corruption*, 150–151.

62. *C.Th.* 2.29.1, with Walter Goffart, "Did Julian Combat Venal *suffragium?* A Note on *C.Th.* 2.29.1," *Classical Philology* 65 (1970): 145–151; Timothy Barnes, "A Law of Julian," *Classical Philology* 69 (1974): 288–291.

63. *C.Th.* 2.29.2 = *C.Just.* 4.3.1.

64. *P. Abinn.* 1, line 12.

65. Amm.Marc. 14.11.3. Imperial eunuchs were frequently at the center of such stories; see, generally, Keith Hopkins, "Eunuchs in Politics in the Later Roman Empire," *Proceedings of the Cambridge Philological Society* 189 (1963): 62–80, repr. in Hopkins, *Conquerors and Slaves,* chap. 4; Peter Guyot, *Eunuchen als Sklaven und Freigelassene in der griechisch-römischen Antike* (Stuttgart, 1980), chap. 7.

66. Philostorgius 4.1.

67. See, generally, Tony Honoré, "The Making of the *Theodosian Code*," *Zeitschrift der Savigny-Stiftung für Rechtsgeschichte* 103 (1986): 133–222; Jill Harries and Ian Wood, eds., *The Theodosian Code: Studies in the Imperial Law of Late Antiquity* (London, 1993).

68. *P Panop. Beatty* 1, lines 241–248, 277–333; T. C. Skeat, *Papyri from Panopolis in the Chester Beatty Library, Dublin* (Dublin, 1964), xxii–xxiii.

69. *P Panop. Beatty* 1, lines 213–216, 252–255, 332–337, 342–346.

70. Fergus Millar, *The Roman Near East: 31 BC–AD 337* (Cambridge, Mass., 1993), 193–196 and appendix A, quoting 193.

71. *P Lips.* inv. no. 366; Bärbel Kramer, "Zwei Leipziger Papyri," *Archiv für Papyrusforschung* 32 (1986): 33–46, at 33–39.

72. *P Bodm.* 29, line 49. On this text see A. H. M. Kessels and P. W. van der Horst, "The Vision of Dorotheus (*P Bodm.* 29) edited with Introduction, Translation, and Notes," *Vigiliae Christianae,* 41 (1987): 313–359; Jan Bremmer, "An Imperial Palace Guard in Heaven: The Date of the Vision of Dorotheus," *Zeitschrift für Papyrologie und Epigraphik* 75 (1988): 82–88.

73. *P Bodm.* 29, lines 329–334. Generally on late antique uniforms see Ramsey MacMullen, "Some Pictures in Ammianus Marcellinus," *Art Bulletin* 46 (1964): 435–455, esp. 445–451, repr. in MacMullen, *Changes in the Roman Empire,* chap. 9, esp. 95–102.

74. Eusebius, *In Praise of Constantine* 5.4 and 3.5.

75. Ibid., *Prologue* 4. On Eusebius's political theology see Timothy Barnes, *Constantine and Eusebius* (Cambridge, Mass., 1981), esp. chap. 14; Raffaele Farina, *L'Impero e l'imperatore cristiano in Eusebio di Cesarea: La prima teologia politica del Cristianesimo* (Zurich, 1966), esp. 166–183, 195–203; Johannes Straub, *Vom Herrscherideal in der Spätantike* (Stuttgart, 1939; repr. 1964), 113–129; Setton, *Christian Attitude,* chap. 2.

76. John Chrysostom, *Homilies on the First Epistle to the Thessalonians* 6.4 (PG 62: 434).

77. Ibid. 14.10 (PG 60: 537); Setton, *Christian Attitude,* 187–195.

78. Friedrich Deichmann, *Frühchristliche Bauten und Mosaiken von Ravenna* (Wiesbaden, 1969), nos. 113 (Christ with Angels—with detail at 116–117), 156 (The Miracle of the Loaves and Fishes), 161 (Healing the Blind), 174 (Parable of the Sheep and Goats), 180 (The Last Supper), 184 (Gethsemane), 187 (Betrayal); for detailed description, see id., *Ravenna: Geschichte und Monumente* (Wiesbaden, 1969), 176–197.

79. Deichmann, *Frühchristliche Bauten und Mosaiken,* nos. 311, 351–353 (Christ), 358 (Theodora), 359 (Justinian); see also id., *Ravenna: Geschichte und Monumente,* 234–256; MacCormack, *Art and Ceremony,* 259–266; Marion Lawrence, "The Iconography of the Mosaics of San Vitale," *Atti del VI congresso internazionale di archeologia cristiana, Ravenna, 1962* (Vatican City, 1965), 123–140. Generally, on imperial imagery in Christian art, see Ernst Kitzinger, *Byzantine Art in the Making: Main Lines of Stylistic Development in Mediterranean Art, 3rd to 7th Century* (London and Cambridge, Mass., 1977), esp. chap. 2; André Grabar, *The Beginnings of Christian Art: 200–395,* trans. Stuart Gilbert and James Emmons (London, 1967), esp. chap. 1 and 193–207; and, challenging some of their approaches, Thomas Mathews, *The Clash of Gods: A Reinterpretation of Early Christian Art* (Princeton, 1993), esp. chap. 6; J. Elsner, *Art and the Roman Viewer: The Transformation of Art from the Pagan World to Christianity* (Cambridge, 1995), esp. 177–189.

80. There is a daunting literature on these themes. Recent discussions of some of their important aspects include Barnes, *Constantine and Eusebius,* part 3, reviewed by Averil Cameron, "Constantinus Christianus," *Journal of Roman Studies* 73 (1983): 184–190; G. W. Bowersock, "From Emperor to Bishop: The Self-Conscious Transformation of Political Power in the Fourth Century A.D.," *Classical Philology* 81 (1986): 298–307; Robin Lane Fox, *Pagans and Christians* (London, 1986), part 3; J. H. W. G. Liebeschuetz, *Continuity and Change in Roman Religion* (Oxford, 1979), 277–308; Garth Fowden, *Empire to Commonwealth: Consequences of Monotheism in Late Antiquity* (Princeton, 1993), chap. 4.

81. Brown, *Power and Persuasion,* 40, and chaps. 1–2.

82. Tertullian, *Prescription against Heresies* 7.9 and 11 (CCSL 1: 193).

83. *Life of Antony* 5 (PG 26.848A)

84. Ibid. 73 (PG 26.945A); see also 72 (PG 26.944B–C), 74–80 (PG 26.945B–956A).

85. *The Sayings of the Fathers: Arsenius* 6 (PG 65: 89A); on the holy effects of the Egyptian desert, see Peter Brown, "The Rise and Function of the Holy Man in Late Antiquity," *Journal of Roman Studies* 61 (1971): 80–101, at 82–84, repr. in Brown, *Society and the Holy in Late Antiquity* (London, 1982), 103–152, at 109–112.

86. Mathews, *The Clash of Gods,* 98–114, fig. 71. The best reproduction remains Joseph Wilpert, *Die römischen Mosaiken und Malereien der kirchlichen Bauten vom IV. bis XII. Jahrhundert,* 2nd ed., 3 vols. (Freiberg im Breisgau, 1917), 2: 1066–69, 3: plates 42–44.

87. *Acts* 7:22; Gregory of Nyssa, *Life of Moses* 1.18, ed. Jean Daniélou, 3rd ed. (Paris, 1968).

88. *Life of Moses* 2.112 and 37.

89. Ibid. 2.7–8. For Moses as a model of virtue to be emulated see 1.14–15 and 77; 2.48–50 and 319. For good introductions to the intellectual project of the Cappadocian Fathers, see Werner Jaeger, *Early Christianity and Greek Paideia* (Cambridge, Mass., 1962), esp. 68–102; Jean Daniélou, *Platonisme et théologie mystique: Essai sur la doctrine spirituelle de Saint Grégoire de Nysse* (Paris, 1944).

90. T. B. Mitford, *The Inscriptions of Kourion* (Philadelphia, 1971), 353–354 (with photograph); John Daniel, "Excavations at Kourion: The Palace," *University of Pennsylvania Museum Bulletin* 7:2 (1938): 4–10.

91. Eusebius, *Life of Constantine* 3.48.1; Dagron, *Naissance d'une capitale,* 388–401.

92. Jerome, *Chronicle* Olympiad 277, ed. John Fotheringham (Oxford, 1923); Eusebius, *Life of Constantine* 3.54.1–3.

93. *Life of Constantine* 3.49; Nicetas Chroniata, *On Statues* 3 (PG 139: 1044B); Janin, *Constantinople Byzantine,* 63; R. J. H. Jenkins, "The Bronze Athena at Byzantium," *Journal of Hellenic Studies* 57 (1947): 31–33.

94. Sozomen 7.9.2; Dagron, *Naissance d'une capitale,* 45–47; Janin, *Constantinople Byzantine,* 4–6, 22–23; Louis Bréhier, "Constantin et la fondation de Constantinople," *Revue historique* 119 (1915): 241–272, esp. 247–255; Lathoud, *Echos d'Orient,* 23, 296–297.

95. Hispellum: CIL 11.5265 = ILS 705 = ILCV 5; Mario de Dominicis, "Un intervento legislativo di Costantino in materia religiosa (Nota a C.I.L., XI, 5265)," *Revue internationale des droits de l'antiquité,* 3rd ser., 10 (1963): 199–211. Divus: *C.Just.* 5.17.9. Emona: *Latin Panegyrics* 11.37.4. Good discussions on the survival of the imperial cult into the later empire include Louis Bréhier and Pierre Batiffol, *Les survivances du culte impérial romain: A propos des rites shintoïstes* (Paris, 1920); G. W. Bowersock, "The Imperial Cult: Perceptions and Persistence," in Ben Meyer and E. P. Sanders, eds., *Jewish and Christian Self-Definition: vol. 3, Self-Definition in the Graeco-Roman World* (London, 1982), chap. 10, esp. 176–182; Lepelley, *Les cités de l'Afrique romaine,* 1: 362–369; Salzman, *On Roman Time,* 131–146.

96. Salzman, *On Roman Time,* 199–205 and chap. 4, esp. 118–131.

97. Elizabeth Struthers Malbon, *The Iconography of the Sarcophagus of Junius Bassus* (Princeton, 1990), gives a detailed description and analysis; diagram 1-1 on p. 6 presents, at one view, the complete iconographical scheme.

98. Ibid., 1.

99. Ibid., 114–115, quoting lines 7a–8b. For good discussions of the Christianization of the Roman aristocracy, see ibid., 136–153; Salzman, *On Roman Time,* chaps. 5–6; Peter Brown, "Aspects of the Christianisation of the Roman Aristocracy," *Journal of Roman Studies* 51 (1961): 1–11, repr. in Brown, *Religion and Society in the Age of St Augustine* (London, 1972), 161–182. A range of views is conveniently canvassed in Alan Cameron, "Forschungen zum Thema der 'heidnischen Reaktion' in der Literatur seit 1943," in Alföldi and Alföldi, *Die Kontorniat-Medaillons,* 2: 63–74.

100. Useful discussions include Werner Eck, "Die Episkopat im spätantiken Africa: Organisatorische Entwicklung, soziale Herkunft, und öffentliche Funktionen," *Historische Zeitschrift* 236 (1983), 265–295, esp. 284–293; Aline Rouselle, "Aspects sociaux du recrutement ecclésiastique au IVe siècle," *Mélanges d'archéologie et d'histoire de l'Ecole français de Rome* 89 (1977): 333–370, esp. 362–370; Frank Gilliard, "Senatorial Bishops in the Fourth Century," *Harvard Theological Review* 77 (1984): 153–175.

101. Barnim Treucker, "A Note on Basil's Letters of Recommendation," in Paul Fedwick, ed., *Basil of Caesarea: Christian, Humanist, Ascetic, A Sixteen-Hundredth Anniversary Symposium,* 2 vols. (Toronto, 1981), 1: 405–410.

102. *ILCV* no. 1843; Giuseppe Cuscito, "Vescovo e cattedrale nella documentazione epigrafica in Occidente: Italia e Dalmazia," *Actes du XIe Congrès international d'archéologie chrétienne,* 3 vols. (Rome, 1989), 1: 735–778, at 771–775, fig. 21.

103. Gaudemet, *L'Eglise dans l'Empire romain,* 230–240. Among recent discussions of the civic role of bishops, see Brown, *Power and Persuasion,* esp. chap. 3; Rita Lizzi, *Il potere episcopale nell'Oriente romano: Rappresentazione ideologica e realtà politica (IV–V sec. d.C.)* (Rome, 1987), chap. 3; Henry Chadwick, "The Role of the Christian Bishop in Ancient Society," in Edward Hobbs and Wilhelm Wuellner, eds., *Protocol of the Thirty-Fifth Colloquy (25 February 1979)* (Berkeley, 1979), 1–14, repr. in Chadwick, *Heresy and Orthodoxy in the Early Church* (London, 1991), chap. 3. There are also perceptive reflections on this wider context in some recent hagiographies: see Philip Rousseau, *Basil of Caesarea* (Berkeley, 1994), chap. 5, esp. 169–175; Neil McLynn, *Ambrose of Milan: Church and Court in a Christian Capital* (Berkeley, 1994), chap. 5; Timothy Barnes, *Athanasius and Constantius: Theology and Politics in the Constantinian Empire* (Cambridge, Mass., 1993), chap. 19.

104. Basil, *Letters* 74–77; Sozomen, *Hist.eccl.* 7.23.3–5; see also Thomas Kopecek, "The Cappadocian Fathers and Civic Patriotism," *Church History* 43 (1974): 293–303; Raymond Van Dam, "Emperor, Bishops, and Friends in Late Antique Cappadocia," *Journal of Theological Studies,* n.s. 37 (1986): 53–76.

105. Rita Lizzi, *Vescovi e strutture ecclesiastiche nella città tardoantica (L'"Italia Annonaria" nel IV–V secolo d.C.)* (Como, 1989), 139–145; Giovanni Brusin and Paolo Zovatto, *Monumenti Paleocristiani di Aquileia e di Grado* (Udine, 1957), 49–58, esp. fig. 21, and 79–89, esp. figs. 34–36; Heinz Kähler, *Die Stiftermosaiken in der konstantinischen Südkirche von Aquileia* (Cologne, 1962), esp. plates 1–14.

106. *CIL* 15.7190 = *ILS* 8730 = *ILCV* 712a; Giovanni Battista di Rossi, "Dei collari dei servi fuggitivi," *Bullettino di archeologia cristiana,* 2nd ser., 5 (1874): 41–67, 41, 51–55, 58–61. I thank Richard Duncan-Jones for his help in locating this reference.

107. MacCormack, *Art and Ceremony,* 116; see also Andreas Alföldi, "Die Ausgestaltung des monarchischen Zeremoniells am römischen Kaiserhofe," *Mitteilungen des Deutschen Archäologischen Instituts (Römische Abteilung)* 49 (1934): 3–118, at 3–6, repr. in MacCormack, *Die monarchische Repräsentation im römischen Kaiserreiche* (Darmstadt, 1970).

108. Eusebius, *Life of Constantine* 4.65–67, quoting 66.1; MacCormack, *Art and Ceremony,* 115–121.

109. Maurice, *Numismatique Constantinienne,* 2: 548, plate 16, no. 16; Leo Koep, "Die Konsekrationsmünzen Kaiser Konstantins und ihre religionspolitische Bedeutung," *Jahrbuch für Antike und Christentum* 1 (1958): 94–105, esp. 96–97, plate 6b; MacCormack, *Art and Ceremony,* 121–127; Bowersock, "The Imperial Cult," 178–179.

110. Eusebius, *Life of Constantine* 4.58–60, quoting 58 and 60.3; Sozomen 2.34.5–6; Socrates, *Hist.eccl.* 1.40 (*PG* 67: 180B). The details of Constantine's funeral are exhaustively discussed in Agathe Kaniuth, *Die Beisetzung Konstantins des Grossen: Untersuchungen zur religiösen Haltung des Kaisers* (Breslau, 1941, repr. Aalen, 1974); P. Franchi de' Cavalieri, "I funerali ed il sepolcro di Costantino Magno," *Mélanges d'archéologie et d'histoire de l'Ecole français de Rome,* 36 (1916–17): 205–261. For discussion of the Church of the Apostles, see Dagron, *Naissance d'une capitale,* 401–408; André Grabar, *Martyrium: Recherches sur le culte de reliques et l'art chrétien antique* (Paris, 1946), 1: 227–234; Suzanne Alexander, "Studies in Constantinian Church Architecture," *Rivista di archeologia cristiana* 47 (1971): 281–330, at 325–329, fig. 23; Müller-Wiener, *Bildlexicon,* 405–411.

CHRISTIAN TRIUMPH AND CONTROVERSY

Richard Lim

Under this sign conquer" *(en toutōi nikā)*—by this message, Emperor Constantine had understood the Christian God, his new patron, to be a bringer of victory in battles. Triumph in the context of traditional religions largely meant the military conquest of a people and therefore of its gods; polytheists rarely envisioned the victory of one set of beliefs over another. The rise of a universalistic monotheism altered this formula.[1] Persecuted Christians sometimes looked toward an eschatological settling of scores, while Lactantius's angry God struck down persecuting emperors. But Constantine's conversion in 312 lent impetus to more ambitious hopes than the mere redress of wrongs: Eusebius's ideal prince held out a thoroughgoing form of victory, for he was to promote the one faith throughout the empire and beyond. First promised by the house of Constantine and later realized by that of Theodosius I (379–395), the alliance of Christianity with the Roman state incorporated imperial victory ideology into ecclesiastical thinking and expectations. Following the end of the 4th century, Christ triumphant over death in resurrection scenes became a favorite iconographic subject.[2]

Yet even before Eusebius could fully articulate his theory of Constantinian triumph and proclaim the peace of the church, Christian communities had become polarized by proliferating disputes over discipline and belief. Conflicts between Donatists and Catholics in Roman North Africa nominally began in 311 over the status of *traditores*, priests who had surrendered sacred books during times of trouble. Around 319, Arius, presbyter of Alexandria, set into motion and defined the terms of an enduring theological dispute when he challenged his bishop's public doctrinal statements. These two developments, together with the Melitian schism in Egypt, posed a painful paradox: Why was it that the unlooked-for conversion of Constantine, a turn of events that portended such good, should coincide with the outburst of ever more fissiparous and inveterate controversies? And how could a church divided triumph in the world?

Rather than treat in detail and in historical order the ruptures that checked Christian triumphalism, I will paint in broad strokes certain aspects of Christian religious unity and diversity, techniques of controversy, and their consequences.[3] Theological disputes engendered fierce strife and bitter enmities, but more importantly, they sharpened doctrinal formulations—notions of orthodoxy and heresy—and eventually gave rise to stronger and more coherent religious communities. These conflicts also created a more elaborate set of rules for defining religious legitimacy. But creeds and anathemas, conciliar and episcopal authority, a bolstered ecclesiastical hierarchy, denunciation in heresiography and imperial edicts, together with outright religious coercion, finally served only to reinforce rather than reconcile divergent worldviews and group identities.

The religious landscape that emerged following the imperial imposition of orthodoxy under Theodosius I was neither tranquil nor monolithic, but oddly diverse and still pluralistic. Within a shrinking empire, establishment churches coexisted and competed with a variety of nonconforming communities. Sassanian Iran, with its resurgent militant Zoroastrianism, nevertheless tolerated autonomous Nestorian and Monophysite churches in its midst. The fragmentation of Rome's political universalism in the 5th century and the rise of successor Germanic kingdoms that retained Arian Christianity as an emblem of ethnic difference linked religious affiliation with regional or national identity.[4] Within these states, "dissident" groups continued to survive, aided not by openminded tolerance but by a religious taxonomy that marginalized minority communities, insulating them from each other. But even the reconquests and religious persecutions of Justinian failed to impose unity. Throughout a world on the brink of the Muslim conquest, many came to despair of complete victory or even of compromise; instead, Christians, although very much engaged in theological controversy, focused more on their own communities, tending to the business of survival.

Roman victory guaranteed cultural and religious pluralism in the Mediterranean world so long as the emperors chose to practice salutary neglect and shunned militant universalism. Polytheists' assimilative mythology, and their idiosyncratically diverse practices and multivalent religious claims, allowed them to coexist with even the oddest bedfellows so long as none challenged the *pax deorum* with provocative atheistic claims or sacrilegious acts.[5] Philosophers could likewise debate metaphysical issues or scorn traditional religion in the secluded privacy of the Academy and deliver diatribes against followers of other *haireseis* in the agora without fear of consequences.[6] Neither Graeco-Roman polytheism nor its philosophical tradition boasted the categories of orthodoxy and heresy in the later Christian sense—only differences, sometimes polemic, and always rivalry.[7]

Except in times of political insurrection, Romans freely allowed Jews, who flatly denied the gods' existence, to worship according to their ancestral custom.[8] Even though its adherents proselytized and attracted converts and sympathizers in places, Judaism was regarded by the Romans as a *Volksreligion* that had its own recognized hierarchy, distinctive laws, rituals, and institutions.[9] Thus for a nonconforming minority religion the secret to survival rested on being set apart and hedged by clear group boundaries. Whenever purveyors of religious ideas aggressively sought converts across established social and ethnic lines, their success met with stiffer opposition. Though universalistic in aspiration, the so-called mystery religions did not seek to monopolize religious devotion but offered added options under the rubric of polytheism. But the missionary efforts of Christians and later of Manichaeans, neither of whom could boast unambiguous ethnic identities, posed a more threatening challenge to the existing order; their brand of transgressive proselytism alarmed local opponents and caused them to be intermittently persecuted by the state.

Imbued with an imperative to prevail over others by spreading the gospel, early Christians had deliberately and repeatedly engaged in controversy. First they had to differentiate themselves from the matrix of Graeco-Roman Judaism and to claim the legitimacy and heritage of *verus Israel*.[10] Conflicts between Christians and Jews often assumed the form of competing exegesis of biblical prophecies because both sides readily accepted the authority of the Hebrew Bible.[11] Such contests, ranging from face-to-face verbal jousts to literary skirmishes, provided the *mise en scène* for Tertullian's *Adversus Judaeos* and Justin Martyr's *Dialogue with Trypho,* gentle precursors to a long-lived war of pamphlets and innuendo that soon turned ugly.[12] This *Adversus Judaeos* literature, compiled by Christians from a growing collection of arguments and *catenae,* chains of biblical proof-texts, supported their claims to scriptural prophecies and to the social respectability that Romans begrudgingly granted Judaism, a *religio licita*.[13]

Christians sought to subordinate Jews, but they had to win over pagans. Since Christianity moved, within the Roman empire at least, within predominantly gentile circles, Jewish-Christian controversy ultimately aimed not to convert Jews, whose "hard-heartedness" had been accepted by the gospel writers and allowed for in Christian soteriology, but to impress polytheists, especially those who harbored sympathies for Judaism.[14] Unable to engage in formal controversy because they lacked a shared biblical culture, Christians and pagans competed with each other over claims to power. The mystery religions attracted adherents by *son et lumière*—through processions, ceremonies, and aretalogies. According to Ramsay MacMullen, "signs, marvels and miracles" were the primary vehicle for converting pagans.[15] Easily graspable signs of power, divine miracles demonstrated the Christian God's superiority to a plethora of pagan deities. In the *Acts of Peter,* Peter confronts Simon Magus before a pagan audience by working a miracle that wins the people's acclamation: "There is but one God, the God of Peter!"[16] In a more true-to-life scenario in the Pseudo-Clementine literature, Peter debates Simon Magus but fails to win decisively; likewise, Barnabas, who only tells stories of miracles and does not perform them, receives a mixed reception from his audience. In literary accounts, public miracles ensured instant triumphs, but such narrated victories leave a loose thread: How might Christians show that their god was the one and only true deity when such a cognitive claim could not be proved by power alone? Surely, the *kerygma* still had to be based on the *logos* and the persuasion of words.

Public preaching and set disputations appear in the early literature as favored missionary tactics, whereas it was mostly in smaller and humbler settings and through tightly knit networks of households that Christians disseminated their beliefs and persuaded others.[17] Thus Celsus accused Christians of being able to impress only women, children, and old men, individuals who according to contemporary elite opinion were ill equipped to judge.[18] At times, Christian reliance on miracles and paradoxes turned the contest for converts into an intellectual debate over rational demonstration.[19] Some Christians sought to answer pagan critiques by condemning the irrationality of ancient myths and cultic observance, using chiefly "off-the-rack" philosophical *topoi*; the multivalence of set arguments, textually transmitted, remained a persistent feature of ancient religious controversy. Christian apologists made ample use of the contrast between their own alleged universalism and *homonoia*, and the manifest lack of unity among pagan philosophers, who contradicted and refuted each other: since the truth is one, the consensus of Christians proves beyond doubt that they alone possess it.[20] Confident of their triumph over the entire polytheist tradition, some Christians even asked whether the whole purpose of the *pax romana* was not to prepare for Christ's coming.[21]

Late antique Christians looking back from a vantage point after the late 4th century might see their victory over polytheism as ideologically clear-cut and unproblematic. Events such as the violent destruction of the Serapeum in 391 merely confirmed Christ's triumph over the powers of the lower world. Likewise, they thought that Jews, with their laws superseded by a new dispensation and their fortunes in steady decline since the Temple was destroyed, would ultimately be converted when Christ returned.[22] But these same Christians could find no such comforting assurance when examining their own history, marked by factionalism and divisions. Indeed, later explanations for why Eusebian hopes of Christian triumph soon turned to ashes point to the success of the devil's ruse of sowing seeds of internal discord, a last-ditch attempt to delay Christianity's final victory.[23] What determined Christian unity and disunity, and how did Christian communities resolve disputes before and after the reign of Constantine?

Frequently sectarian in a sociological sense, early Christian communities endured institutional fragmentation, schisms, and mutual accusations of heresy. Recurring admonitions to beware of "false teachers" and their *heterodidaskalia* in early Christian texts bespeak a dynamic climate of claims and counterclaims. In this environment, the church universal and apostolic succession were ideals favored and promoted by certain Christians in their struggle for advantage or survival. Recent scholarship, following the influential work of Walter Bauer on orthodoxy and heresy, shuns the anachronistic and partisan bias that the wholesale acceptance of these ideals necessitates, and accepts instead a plurality of Christianities and the conclusion that those later deemed heretical often once represented a local "catholic" majority.[24]

Clustered in isolated small groups, sometimes in semi-autonomous house-churches, early urban Christians easily accommodated a variety of different beliefs and practices. Gnostic Christians questioned the authority of ecclesiastical hierarchy and apostolic tradition, preferring a living wisdom rooted in revealed scriptures, and for this reason did not concern themselves much with the integrity of the *ekklēsia* as a social body.[25] While Ignatius of Antioch had theorized on the monarchical episcopacy, and Cyprian of Carthage, another champion of episcopal authority, had rejected the notion of the plurality of churches on the basis of a strictly defined *disciplina,* only a few pre-Constantinian bishops were able to impose conformity.[26] Instead, emerging factionalism in a Christian community normally required careful treatment by a combination of moral persuasion and authority. A regional synod might be convened so that those in disagreement could discuss their differences in the open.[27] Origen of Alexandria (ca. 185–254) employed his charisma and exegetical acumen to help reconcile various divided Christian communities after he debated and refuted a number of other Christians without shaming them.[28] Dionysius (bishop 247–ca. 264), his pupil, traveled from Alexandria to confront a millenarian movement in the Fayum that justified itself by a literal interpretation of the Apocalypse of John.[29] He finally succeeded in persuading his interlocutors to accept his views because he spent three trust-building days arguing with them: his reminiscences of the event dwell on the deference and eagerness for truth that both sides displayed.[30]

Dionysius's employment of patience and mutual deference was rarely repeated by his successors, who more and more relied on the direct exercise of authority. At the same time, the willingness of church members to defer to authority diminished as the right and ability to expound on scriptures ceased to be a monopoly exercised by a privileged few; rather, the commitment to a *via universalis*—in Momigliano's words, "the Christian abolition of the internal frontiers between the learned and the vulgar"—made virtually every Christian a potential exegete and theologian.[31] The early Arian controversy began when the presbyter Arius (ca. 250–336) dared to challenge the ecclesiastical authority of his bishop because he thought the latter had incorrectly explained Christian doctrine.[32] Perhaps all would have been well if only Arius had deferred to Alexander of Alexandria (313–328) instead of publicizing and popularizing their disagreements; indeed, later traditions would blame this rift on Arius's prideful ambition, even—anachronistically—on his dialectical cunning.

The Christian *oikoumenē* adopted by Constantine thus contained a church monolithic and universal in name only. Diversity had been a fact of life for Christians, partly resulting from their widespread diffusion and the lack of central organization. Even within each city, the indeterminacy of Christian authority, distributed among charismatic ascetics and confessors, scriptures, synods and communal consensus, and holders of ecclesiastical offices, gave ample room for differences to arise while also making them difficult to resolve. The success of local attempts to settle intra-Christian disputes depended on the initiatives and strengths of particular individuals and communities.

Constantine, to whom Christian divisions appeared bewildering and unnecessary, repeatedly urged the parties to reasonable compromise, especially during the first few years of the Donatist and early Arian controversies.[33] Drawing on their own experience with provincial synods, *koina* and *concilia,* emperors chose to invest the collective decisions of assemblies of bishops, which were already becoming important in the 3rd century, with imperial dignity.[34] Constantine's personal presence and his exhortations to *homonoia* at Nicaea in 325 prevailed upon most disputants to sign on to a compromise solution. By promoting the products of the conciliar process as reflecting a *consensus omnium gentium,* and by exiling opponents who refused to sign on, Constantine and his successors mistakenly believed they could forestall future ruptures.

Yet the emperor's selective patronage did strengthen episcopal authority, counterbalancing the centrifugal forces exerted by charismatic ascetics and confessors and the aristocratic patronage of household communities. Adapting the imperial tradition of relying on the leading men of local cities to rule, emperors dealt primarily with bishops as ranking heads of a hierarchy and as Christian spokesmen.[35] The emperors' support and their expectation that such men, now in principle given judicial authority over internal Christian disputes, would keep their own houses in order caused local bishops to aspire to more effective control over their communities.[36]

While many modern studies have been concerned with the theoretical underpinnings of imperial religious interventions, the notion of Caesaropapism, and the constitutional relationship between church and state, recent works examine the practical aspects of imperial religious policies and the precise historical interactions between emperors and bishops.[37] Thanks to the efforts of T. D. Barnes and others, understanding of imperial involvement in Christian controversy has gained greater definition.[38] The imperial presence after Constantine altered the course and aims of Christian religious controversies. Formerly, disputants who lacked formal powers of coercion and thus also the prospect of outright triumph had two main options: to follow the pattern of traditional dispute settlement in which persuasion, compromise, and consensus building represented a normative ideal, or to boycott and rhetorically condemn their opponents. Now protagonists on either side could hope for an enforceable decision in their favor when they appealed to the emperor's arbitration. Such dreams of victory too frequently chased away the willingness to compromise.

Beyond perpetuating Christian controversies, imperial patronage actually inflamed them by giving protagonists more booty to fight over. Grants of liturgical exemptions and endowed basilicas to qualified priests turned the possession of the *nomen christianum* from a badge of belonging for any who dared claim it to a title even more worth having. Disputed successions to the episcopacy were a common cause of violence and disorder, as rival parties sought to install their candidates. On occasion a number of communities within the same city would lay claim to the same real estate. A Christian quarrel over the own-ership of a church was first heard by Aurelian (270–275), a pagan. Christian disputes turned into competitions over concrete possessions and imperial recog-nition during the 4th century as control over large urban churches became a coveted prize that could not be shared, as Ambrose of Milan's involvement in the basilica conflict of 386 shows.[39]

But by this I do not mean to suggest that theological controversies were only about politics, wealth, and vested interests, or that the disputed ideas served merely as excuses for Christians to engage along established lines of civic fac-tional rivalry. Edward Gibbon had early on credited Christianity with making "the abstruse questions of metaphysical science" that elite philosophers once meditated in quiet leisure a preoccupation of the masses: "These speculations, instead of being treated as the amusement of a vacant hour, became the most serious business of the present, and the most useful preparation for the future, life. A theology which it was incumbent to believe, which it was impious to doubt, and which it might be dangerous, and even fatal, to mistake, became the familiar topic of private meditation and popular discourse. The cold indiffer-ence of philosophy was inflamed by the fervent spirit of devotion."[40] In its crudest and most reductive form, an approach to these disputes through the history of ideas might see them as struggles between monotheism and dualism, rationalism and mysticism, Platonism and Aristotelianism, or Greek philoso-phy and Christian *paideia*.[41] But, as Gibbon knew equally well, not every theological controversy was a clash of rarefied ideas. Even though Christian controversies were not uncommonly fed by the tensions between divergent strands of the classical tradition and the need to reconcile scriptural expres-sions, which often undergirded communal beliefs and practice, with Greek philosophical precepts, the motivations of the individuals involved were rarely pure and never simple. Positions on such issues were seldom taken in the abstract, particularly by those who played a public role.[42] The individual pref-erences of the protagonists tended to reflect specific concerns; the need to argue against immediate rivals frequently determined the manner in which individual Christians eclectically appropriated past traditions.

Even so, the theoretical element of Christian controversies remains crucial and should not be brushed aside as mere window dressing for age-old rivalries. At a minimum, the importance of biblical warrants to Christian actions al-lowed individuals and groups who disagreed for any number of reasons to conduct their mutual contest by means of a scriptural debate.[43] Scriptures could serve established authority or challenge it, justify a social movement or delegit-imize it. Many Christians in practice insisted on applying rules of faith or creeds to circumscribe the scope of exegesis; biblical interpretation unrooted in tradi-tion might easily give impetus to radical changes.

A particular kind of argument based on scriptures became a source of wide-spread disorder for Christians. Aristotelian dialectic emerged as an important element in the later Arian controversies of the late 4th century and remained prevalent until much later, as Christians who engaged in Trinitarian and Chris-tological controversies needed to find a precise logic for defining the relationship among nouns, adjectives, and predicates.[44] The doctrinal controversies surrounding the figures of Aetius the Syrian (ca. 313–370) and Eunomius of Cappadocia (ca. 335–394), variously called Neo-Arians or Anomoeans today, encapsulate the competitive environment that the unregulated social use of dialectic might entail.[45] Aetius had learned to pose philosophical and theological *aporiai* publicly in the form of syllogisms, and made available his method through his *Syntagmation*, a collection of alternating questions and answers that enabled readers to reproduce or adapt deductive syllogisms that were irrefutable in controversy.[46] His disciple and associate Eunomius so developed and propagated the use of dialectic and syllogisms that he gained from adversaries the label of *technologos*, in grudging recognition of his turning theological discourse into a precise yet popular *technē*.[47] The agonistic flavor of dialectic and the necessity of syllogistic reasoning, together with the logical principle of the excluded middle, allowed the identification of winners and losers in arguments; but by rendering outright victory possible they also decreased the likelihood of patient compromise.[48]

Exacting dialectical questions stripped Christian leaders of the security of their office and social standing. The anxious requests for help from Amphilochius of Iconium (ca. 340–395) to Basil of Caesarea, and Gregory of Nyssa's famous observation regarding the widespread culture of questioning in late 4th century Constantinople, are but two examples of the challenges this verbal culture presented.[49] Called to account by those of lower or no rank who no longer deferred to authority, elites found themselves susceptible to challenge from those who claimed *isēgoria* based on a competitive form of knowledge; moreover, the solidarity of the communities they led was disrupted as individuals bandied urgent and challenging questions at each other, undermining accepted certainties, established friendships, and loyalties.[50] For a brief moment, it was feared that even Theodosius might be swayed by the arguments of Eunomius if Empress Flacilla were to succeed in securing an audience for him.[51]

A number of ad hoc textual weapons were sent into the fray, often for defense. Ready-made responses or retorts, often in the form of catechetical or question-and-answer dialogues, were provided to arm common as well as elite Christians against anticipated questions;[52] creeds were also sometimes put to use in this context to quell further discussion.[53] Later, Anastasius of Sinai (d. ca. 700) combined text and icon in his *Hodēgos*, a multimedia prophylactery designed to put a stop to provocative Monophysite questions.[54] In short, no effort was spared to prevent Christians from engaging in frank and unmediated exchanges over particular theological issues. A growing selection of theological writings, ranging from catechetical pamphlets such as Theodoret of Cyrrhus's *Eranistes* to more ponderous system-building treatises, provided individuals with ready-made arguments against challenges from familiar quarters. The authority of this literature delineated and patrolled the boundaries of theological communities; it also helped harness dialectic to the task of defending a group's position against outside attacks.

The ideological strategies for managing conflict in such situations were fundamental to the development of the later orthodox identity and culture. Such

tactics included appeals to the authority of simple but steadfastly faithful ascetics, who abhorred sophistry and dialectical disputation; reliance on the traditional authority of patristic consensus expressed in *florilegia* and in councils;
and the elaboration of a mystical theology—all of them a part of the ideological
fence, erected to contain freewheeling theological debates, that finally helped
solidify Christian communities formed around set theological ideas.

Sometimes treated as marginal to theological controversy, the phenomenon
of asceticism first entered the fray as certain Christians began to validate their
own claims by invoking the charisma and *virtutes* of ascetics, who were represented as paragons of orthodoxy; rival groups, who portrayed them as itiner-
ants and Manichaeans, regarded them as purveyors of dangerous teachings.
The positive emphasis on the *habitus* of these ascetics served as a counterpoint
to the ad hominem ethical invective against adversaries castigated as sophistic
dialecticians, whose allegedly dissolute way of life only confirmed their scant
regard for truth.[55] Christians who asserted that simple and God-loving ascetics
professed the same true faith which they also embraced thus exploited the
cultural capital of ascetics in "antiheretical" polemics.[56] A story connected with
the Council of Nicaea has an unlearned confessor put an end to ongoing dialectical disputations by challenging those present to confess together to a short
and simple creed.[57]

In this story, the bishops at Nicaea found themselves in such disarray that
they had to be rescued from their war of words by a charismatic confessor.[58] But
the ability of individuals to challenge authority with dialectical questions at
councils would be checked by patristic consensus as the authority of *florilegia
patrum* came to be more widely accepted. These collections of sayings from
eminent "Fathers of the church" were often used with *catenae* of proof-texts
culled to establish particular interpretations of scriptures; together they became a fixture of conciliar proceedings, whereby a particular *florilegium* would
be affirmed by the acclamations of attending bishops.[59] This combination of
diachronic and synchronic consensus circumscribed the ability of individuals,
even trained dialecticians, to pose fresh questions and arguments in council.
When those engaged in controversy expected their own arguments to be measured against authoritative precedents, they would be less likely to argue dialec-
tically from first principles or from a few scriptural premises. By thus removing
theological formulations from close questioning and constant reexamination,
a precious element of stability could be introduced into these controversies—
even as protagonists soon learned to compile their own partisan *florilegia* and
catenae. Now transposed to the level of written authorities, Christian disputes
became less sharply agonistic: victory would go to those who championed
views that accorded with established consensus, allowing for the operation of
analogical reasoning.

As growing weight was placed on the examination of written evidence in
conciliar proceedings, similar to senatorial and legal methods, the principle of
agreement with established norms became a criterion for judging orthodoxy.
Later traditions would represent the scriptures enshrined as the ultimate
authority at the Council of Constantinople in 381. Theodosius I, who allegedly

asked for written statements of faith from disputing Christian groups so that he could render judgment based on them, decided after prayer to accept only those that agreed with the Nicene creed.[60] At the Council of Ephesus in 431, Nestorius received the collective anathemas of the assembled bishops after his views were found by Cyril's partisans to conform not to the Nicene creed but rather to the condemned views of Paul of Samosata, who had been branded a heretic at the Council of Antioch in 268.[61]

Authoritative creeds were both a tool and a product of controversy. What later came to be known as the Nicene creed had been subsequently modified or even set aside in numerous councils until it was reestablished by imperial fiat as the canon of orthodoxy at Constantinople 381.[62] As the language of theological controversy became ever more complex and convoluted, short credal statements could rarely serve, on their own and without specifically attached interpretations, as an adequate guarantee of orthodoxy.[63] But a creed whose language was extremely precise would also likely be exposed to criticism, leading to an unending cycle of controversy.

Concerned that every championed idea provoked a response, particularly if the precise terms used lent themselves to dialectical and syllogistic reasoning, some Christians turned to a strategy of mystification. The Cappadocians, in their argument against Eunomius, had insisted that human language and thought were inadequate for grasping the divine essence.[64] John Chrysostom (ca. 347–407) and Gregory of Nazianzus (329–389), who as priest and bishop came into intimate contact with the culture of dialectical questioning, opposed what they termed *polupragmosunē*, meddlesome curiosity, with a robust assertion of divine mystery that put the knowledge of God's attributes beyond the reach of ordinary believers.[65] Their homilies on the incomprehensibility of the divine essence, occasioned by immediate controversies, later developed into the mystical theology of Pseudo-Dionysius the Areopagite (ca. 500), according to whom the hierarchical chain of beings could know God only anagogically and in part through intermediary signs. That this view came to the fore when Aristotelian dialectic was being employed by both sides during the ongoing Monophysite controversy may not be sheer coincidence.[66]

Borrowing ideas from a venerable philosophical tradition of apophaticism, the Christian *via negativa,* instead of being seen as a form of irrationalism that blocked advances in theology and science, may be considered the price that a society had to pay for greater social harmony. By asserting that unaided human reason could not grasp the divine essence, mystics established the need for Christians to adhere steadfastly to creeds and to participate in liturgical prayer and worship. Such strategies enhanced rather than undercut Christian solidarity. Competitive forms of knowledge such as Aristotelian dialectic were subordinated to an apophatic, mystical *theōria* that stressed the importance of a hierarchical status quo and the mediation of priests in the spiritual anagogy.[67] Christian communities, thus rallied around local priests and bishops, became more unified bodies with distinct group identities and boundaries. Competition and conflict between Christians did not cease; but they increasingly took place at the edges of communities: as the battle-lines were drawn, contests tended to take place between rival congregations rather than within groups. In fact, with the heightened sense of belligerence that controversy bred, differences between encapsulated communities tended to become even more intractable.

H. I. Marrou speaks of the 4th century as "a century of strong personalities, men of steel who knew how to withstand the powerful forces of the day and oppose violence with the firmness of their faith."[68] This statement betrays a prevalent bias of patristic scholarship. To examine religious controversies as a historical phenomenon, it is not enough to focus just on select patristic figures, or even on the more colorful "heresiarchs." The nature of Christian leadership must be placed under careful scrutiny. Beginning with the 4th century, bishops increasingly hailed from the upper strata of society, entering ecclesiastical office with firmer notions about the exercise of power. As part of a macrosocial elite, these bishops knew that they had to seek allies abroad and build on their own power bases at home to secure their own future in an uncertain, fractious world.

Somewhat sweepingly, W. H. C. Frend has portrayed the religious controversies of the 4th century as sustained by bishops, while those of the 5th were pursued by the populace as a whole.[69] Though the importance of individual Christian leaders and later ecclesiastical parties (frequently connected with the imperial court) in religious disputes in the 4th century has been overstated, it did pale in significance in the course of the 5th century as popular participation expanded, a result of deliberate efforts by the leaders to widen the controversies. The process had in fact already begun in the 4th century, if not even earlier: Arius was said to have popularized his views through metrical songs contained in his *Thalia,* while Athanasius of Alexandria, a consummate political fighter and an ideologue equally capable of mobilizing a community, appealed with simple words to monks in the Egyptian desert.[70] More concrete involvements of communal organizations in religious rivalry included popular acclamations and the singing of antiphonal songs during processions through cities such as Antioch and Milan.[71] Chanting provocative words served as a clarifying ritual that rallied the catholic congregations, giving them a visible and solid identity and openly challenging Arian Christians. As Christian leaders embroiled in controversy sought to increase their bases of support by securing regional constituencies, bishops of Alexandria such as Cyril and his successor Dioscoros (bishop 444–454) mobilized the desert monks outside the city, whose biblical fundamentalism and unquestioning adherence to the Nicene creed made them stalwart allies against Nestorius once the latter's views had been recast by the Alexandrians in simple terms and encapsulated in slogans.[72] Without taking into account how leaders shaped the controversies as well as both the intended and unintended consequences of popularization, historians will continue to pose moot questions such as whether the majority of Christians understood the intellectual issues in dispute.[73] As certain leaders deployed demagogic rhetoric and tailor-made appeals to create or galvanize communities, it is impossible to examine doctrinal disputes as having a single underlying cause. These leaders' actions have greatly vexed the longstanding scholarly discussion concerning whether the Christian heresies were also national or regional movements.[74]

The consequences were reaped in the 5th century, when monastic participation and activism in controversy became much more noticeable: monks accused their own bishops of heresy and even violently disrupted the Council of Ephesus in 431.[75] Monks did not always have a predetermined inclination to particular theological views (many in Syria were Chalcedonian while those in Egypt were mostly Monophysite), yet their tendency to starkly dualistic worldviews added uncertainty and volatility to already difficult situations. The involvement of unlettered monks, who attacked heretics as they would a polluted pagan temple—with hatred and determination—exacerbated intra-Christian contests by giving protagonists without imperial support the option of prevailing through physical violence. A patriarch of Alexandria might even turn to the strong right arms of the 500 *parabalani* (hospital attendants) under his charge to impose his will.[76] The Christians' incitement of popular violence against each other soon made imperial repression of disputes more palatable, which in turn led to further resistance. Emperors might prevail upon individuals and crush ecclesiastical parties by cajoling, threatening, or exiling leaders, but a *dēmos* or *populus* in arms was a tougher nut to crack.[77] The operation of imperial pressure and consensual politics behind closed doors became well-nigh impossible.

But the inability of conciliar proceedings to resolve disputes and prevent further controversies cannot be blamed entirely on those who disrupted the proceedings of particular councils. The councils' transformation from occasions for consensual compromise and moral exhortation into a forum for the exercise of authority weakened their ability to settle differences. Because many councils were openly partisan, interested groups that failed to prevail at them quickly sought to undercut their authority. The lack of a disinterested and neutral broker was another problem: as emperors became more embroiled in religious controversies, rival parties turned the imperial court into an arena for ecclesiastical political maneuvers, through persuasion or even bribery.[78] But although protagonists in controversy increasingly learned to play the game and gained sophistication in shaping such proceedings, select councils were still regarded by later Christians as inspired. Those who opposed their decisions, as Arius and Nestorius were said to have done, came to be called *theomachoi,* those who resisted God, in the later orthodox tradition. Councils such as Nicaea and Constantinople became sanctified icons for most Christians, while Monophysites anathematized Chalcedon.[79] As Cyril's victory at that council was won by questionable means, its decisions served only to entrench divisions among Christians and eventually split the empire. In vain, emperors tried to close the book after such a general council. Marcian (450–457) forbade future discussion of the subject three years after Chalcedon to protect its decisions.[80] Zeno (474–491) issued his *Henoticon* in 482 containing the twelve anathemas of Cyril of Alexandria, the creeds of Nicaea and Constantinople, and a ban on further debate. Two subsequent imperial attempts at compromise, including Heraclius's *Ecthesis* in 638 and Constans II's *Typus* in 647/48, came too late because the rival communities had by then become far too well established and entrenched in their differences. Instead a separate and increasingly important discourse of Christian consensus grew up in the form of hagiography, especially of the *saloi,* "fools for the sake of Christ": the holy men of the late empire embodied a positive, broad-based religiosity that overrode the effects of theological controversy on many Christian communities.[81]

While Christians had long entertained a notion of orthodoxy, the state's support gave it definition and weight. How was one to identify orthodox Christians, who alone could claim considerable privileges and imperial gifts? For a half-century after Nicaea, a fixed and precise definition of orthodoxy did not yet obtain, as emperors and bishops continued to revisit the decisions of 325, but closure began to be achieved under the reign of Theodosius I: orthodox Christians held communion with named bishops; they adhered to specific short creeds; and they accepted the conclusions of designated councils.[82]

Theodosius I tried and failed to create a thoroughly Christian society.[83] He prohibited polytheists' sacrifices, both private and public, and demanded the closing of temples.[84] Groups that had existed at the margins of catholic communities, such as the Manichaeans and those who had sympathies with the theological views and methods associated with the Anomoeans Aetius and Eunomius, were pushed out and doors shut behind them.[85] The emperor's sanction of the use of physical force to address religious nonconformity enshrined a practice that had been selectively applied by Constantine, Constantius, and Valens. Now entitled to apply coercion against rivals, some Christian bishops such as Augustine quickly rationalized its use.[86] Pagans and their temples were the most immediate target, but the momentum of growing zeal caused Donatist Christians, who had earlier been treated as schismatics, to be indiscriminately lumped with heretics.[87] Deprived of churches, their priests exiled and suffering other indignities, nonconforming Christians nevertheless found ways to survive. As polytheists had once learned, religious persecution rarely succeeded in extirpating its target; instead, well-organized dissident groups merely hardened under pressure, as they developed their own internal hierarchies, textual authorities, communal rituals, and group memory.

Imperial edicts against named heresies, which relied on the religious taxonomy and labels generated by disputing Christians, turned mud-slinging among them into a far more consequential enterprise.[88] Heresiologues such as Epiphanius of Salamis (ca. 315–403), Filaster of Brescia (d. ca. 397), and Augustine drew on earlier precedents to present a taxonomy of Judeo-Christian sects that splintered from the one original truth by coupling descriptions of sectarian fragmentation with explanations of each group's peculiar beliefs and customs.[89] By naming sects after supposed eponymous founders or by caricaturing an aspect of their beliefs, these compendia of religious ethnography reflect a clear bias toward orthodox views; any sect that bore a particularistic name could not be catholic or true. But ultimately they generate a cognitive map that contains carefully delineated spaces even for dissenting "heretics."

Demonizing opponents appealed to "God-bearing" desert monks accustomed to contending with the devil in the wilderness, yet it also appeared in cities, where a different set of conditions encouraged the stigmatization of rivals. Urban Christianity, with its plurality of study groups and networks of patronage and friendship, furnished fertile ground for peripheral diversity in domestic spaces even as centers were being formed by bishops around basilica churches.[90] As bishops encouraged the homogenization of Christian beliefs and practices through preaching *ex cathedra,* direct supervision over liturgical life, and administration of communion, their practical hold over the large urban community long remained incomplete. The unsupervised networks of people and information that continued to exist became the targets of polemic: slanders against Manichaeans, for instance, focused on their performance of unspeakable crimes in closeted spaces, just as libelous claims against Christians at an earlier period had done. By mobilizing public opinion, by allowing rumors to spread and pamphlets that cast aspersions on the private activities of such marginal groups to circulate, those in authority hoped to undercut their legitimacy and appeal, and perhaps even to force them to justify themselves in a public forum that Christian bishops could control.[91] The tactic that Augustine used against the Manichaeans while he was bishop of Hippo combined the pressure of rumors, the threat of coercion, an imposing episcopal presence, and the use of stenography to record the victorious proceedings for later use and for posterity; the shift in the locale of the disputations from public baths to the bishop's palace is equally suggestive of the constriction of civic dialogue.[92]

The heresiological discourse increasingly cast the orthodox community as a body that was assailed by the disease of heresy, for which it prescribed dismemberment—shunning and excommunication—to protect the whole when the infected part was thought beyond cure. Once the social lines between the orthodox community and named heresies had been drawn, intra-Christian controversy continued between rival communities. Creeds, anathemas, and abjuration formulas, common weapons in the arsenal of war, implied above all inclusion and exclusion from social bodies.

Yet symbolic forms could enable sanctioned and outlawed groups to co-exist ideologically, particularly if the leaders of nonconforming groups, even polytheists, belonged to the social elites and accepted their own subordinate status.[93] Such a *modus vivendi* with local Arians was important to Roman emperors before the reign of Justinian because, with Arian Germanic peoples ruling over large catholic populations of *Romani* in the west and as *foederati* at home, persecutions against Arians on imperial soil might occasion reprisals against one's own people, as indeed happened in Vandal Africa. Justinian's reconquest had reclaimed Italy and North Africa for the *imperium,* making possible the assertion of Roman political and religious universalism.[94] After the Burgundians and the Suebi converted to catholic Christianity, the Visigoths, who under Euric (466–484) had persecuted Catholics, turned to orthodoxy. Reccared convened a council at Toledo in 589 to mark the change, at which the king and his nobles swore to uphold the creeds established at Nicaea, Constantinople, and Chalcedon, burned Arian books, and anathematized Arian beliefs. By establishing Chalcedonian Christianity as its *Reichskirche,* Visigothic Spain aimed to become a fully Christian society, a rival to Byzantium.[95] The time for pluralism was past: efforts were made to forcibly convert Jews within the kingdom to Christianity.[96]

But even with these changes, and with the widespread forced conversion of pagans under Justinian, the Christian *oikoumenē* did not suddenly become unified in one confession. As religion and society became harder to separate, religious controversies and endemic civic and intercity rivalry also tended to come together. The dispersal of religious authority into often rival centers further perpetuated and accentuated theological differences among the Christian population.[97] The growing confidence expressed by bishops of metropolitan sees such as Alexandria, Antioch, Constantinople, Jerusalem, and Rome added fuel to the flames of controversy. Rome intervened more actively and was repeatedly appealed to by eastern prelates about to lose an ongoing struggle at home. While often seen as naives by modern scholars, Roman bishops such as Leo asserted their own voices in the definition of orthodox doctrine, sometimes derailing imperial efforts to achieve compromise and unity. Heraclius (610–641), anxious to rally Monophysite communities in the face of the Persian threat, promoted his *Ecthesis* as a compromise document.[98] It was immediately derided in Monophysite Egypt and rejected the following year in Rome at a synod convened by Pope Martin (649–655), attended by a large number of eastern bishops who approved instead a mainly Greek *florilegium* compiled by Maximus the Confessor (ca. 580–662).[99] This assertion of Roman primacy was premature, as Martin was soon exiled from the city by imperial order.

The theological controversies that continued from the 5th century onward tended to have heavier regional accents. But as long as marginal groups retained hopes of being one day accepted by the emperor, they continued to remain loyal to the empire. After Nestorian Christians were deprived of the Christian name in 435, they began to move eastward and eventually crossed into the Persian empire in 457, from which they were to expand into Central Asia and China.[100] Monophysites became alienated from the Chalcedonians championed by Constantinople after numerous attempts at reconciliation failed; but only more determined persecutions under Justinian caused them to create their own churches. When pressured further, these dissident communities retreated into the remoter regions of the empire and even into Persian territory with their own full-fledged ecclesiastical hierarchy, organized monasteries, and schools.[101]

Originally, categories of heresy and orthodoxy operated differently in the Sassanian empire than in the Christianized Roman empire. Zoroastrians prized orthopraxy above all and condemned as heretics only those who refused to acknowledge Ahura Mazda with appropriate rites. While the magi, whose worship at the fire temples safeguarded the prosperity of the state, remained alert to challenges from others—especially Manichaeans—the *zindīq*s, kings of kings from Yazdegird (399–420) onward, normally acknowledged the Christians' right to exist, supporting their synods and confirming the bishop of Seleucia-Ctesiphon as their *katholikos* and spokesman.[102] The later success of Nestorians in converting Iranians away from Zoroastrianism and their ill-advised destruction of fire temples provoked repressive measures. Periodically persecuted, Nestorian and Monophysite communities, as sizable subject minorities like the established Jewish population in Mesopotamia, nonetheless found in the Sassanians reasonably tolerant masters, even while the Chalcedonians were singled out for intense persecution as imperial allies in conquered Byzantine lands.

It is salutary to remind ourselves that religious controversies of the sort described here were not unique to Christians in the Mediterranean world.[103] A religion of the book, Islam accepted Jews and Christians as subject peoples but insisted on the conversion of pagans; for this reason the polytheists of Harran famously attempted, ultimately without success, to pass themselves off as Sabians.[104] Membership in the 'umma, the Islamic community, could be gained by anyone who professed the belief that God was one and that Muhammad was his last and most eminent prophet; in practice, it was largely limited to Arabs in the first century or so after the hijra. The Umayyad caliphs, who combined religious and political authority, had no reason to desire mass conversion because it could result in a loss of revenue; taxes raised from the conquered population served as the financial basis of the state. While Muslim heresiographers, perhaps following Christian predecessors, noted in retrospect the continuous fragmentation of the true faith, no reliable source portrays an Umayyad caliph as having sought to impose religious uniformity. Beliefs regarding doctrine remained open to question, though there were already hints that the scriptural authority of the Qur'ān was becoming a source of contention.[105] Interestingly, the intellectual roots of important sectarian political movements that the state attempted to suppress were downplayed: the Azāriqa (a splinter group of the Khārijites) and Shī'i Muslims were viewed by what became the Sunnī majority community as schismatics and religious extremists respectively, not heretics.[106] Bid'a, arbitrary theological innovation, was frowned upon rather than condemned. Persecution against zindīqs, such as the Manichaeans, intensified under al-Mahdī (775–785) and came closest to the categorical rejection of heretics in contemporary Byzantium; but this exception rather proves the rule.[107]

The loose association between the Umayyad caliphate and Muslim theologians safeguarded the freedom of doctrinal discussions. The Abbasids, particularly during the reign of al-Ma'mūn (813–833), the first caliph also to claim the imamate, began to form a tighter bond between the state and an established religion.[108] Al-Ma'mūn's adviser was a chief advocate for Mu'tazilism and through him an alliance was forged between the caliphate and those individuals who championed the view that the Qur'ān was created rather than coeternal with God, who alone was transcendent. Sometimes characterized as rationalists, Mu'tazilites believed that God, and hence correct belief about him, could be discovered by applying reason to the exegesis of Qur'ānic revelation. The caliph, using inquisitorial procedures, sought to compel the major religious scholars in Baghdad and elsewhere to accept this doctrine and transformed the matter into a litmus test for political loyalty as well as religious orthodoxy. The resulting controversy spread far beyond the intellectual circles of theologians as communities coalesced in support of or in opposition to the imposed dogma. Such a precedent soon resulted in a backlash beginning in 848, as a succeeding caliph, al-Mutawakkil (847–861), the Islamic Theodosius, gave the Muʿtazilites a taste of their own medicine; his zeal went beyond this controversy to the persecution of Jews and Christians, who had previously been left alone if they would pay a poll tax. This setback encouraged the Muʿtazilites to settle into more coherent schools based in Basra and Baghdad, which in the 10th century developed their own distinctive traditions; they also found safe havens in rival centers on the Iranian plateau where local rulers lent them support. The history of Muʿtazilism shares the same ingredients with the earlier history of Christian religious triumph, controversy, and survival: state formation, revealed scriptures, Greek philosophical rationalism, regional diversities, and an initial dichotomy between theologians and ordinary believers that was later overcome through popularization.

Notes

My warmest thanks go to Peter Brown, Keith Lewinstein, and Jennifer M. Miller for their generous help in the preparation of this essay.

1. On the connection between monotheism and intolerance, see E. Peterson, *Der Monotheismus als politisches Problem: Ein Beitrag zur Geschichte der politischen Theologie im Imperium Romanum* (Leipzig, 1935); A. Momigliano, "The Disadvantages of Monotheism for a Universal State," in id., *On Pagans, Jews, and Christians* (Middletown, Conn., 1987), 142–158; and G. Fowden, *Empire to Commonwealth: Consequences of Monotheism in Late Antiquity* (Princeton, 1993).

2. A. Grabar, *Christian Iconography: A Study of Its Origins* (Princeton, 1968), 123–127; on Roman triumphalist ideology, see M. McCormick, *Eternal Victory: Triumphal Rulership in Late Antiquity, Byzantium and the Early Medieval West* (Cambridge, Eng., and Paris, 1986), esp. 100–111.

3. For general accounts, see S. L. Greenslade, *Schism in the Early Church* (London, 1953); id., "Heresy and Schism in the Later Roman Empire," in D. Baker, ed., *Schism, Heresy and Religious Protest* (Cambridge, Eng., 1972), 1–20; and J. Meyendorff, *Imperial Unity and Christian Divisions: The Church from 450–680 A.D.* (Crestwood, N.Y., 1989). J. Stevenson, *Creeds, Councils and Controversies: Documents Illustrative of the History of the Church to AD 337* (2nd ed., London, 1987), provides a selection of pertinent texts in translation,

4. M. Meslin, "Nationalisme, état et religions à la fin du IVe siècle," *Archives de sociologie des religions* 18 (1964), 3–20, and *Les ariens dans l'occident, 335–430* (Paris, 1967).

5. A. Momigliano, "La libertà di parola nel mondo antico," *Rivista storica italiana* 4:83 (1971): 499–524; and P. Garnsey, "Religious Toleration in Classical Antiquity," in W. J. Shiels, ed., *Persecution and Toleration* (Oxford, 1984), 1–27.

6. See J. Hahn, *Der Philosoph und die Gesellschaft: Selbstverständnis, öffentliches Auftreten und populäre Erwartungen in der hohen Kaiserzeit* (Stuttgart, 1989); on philosophical polemics, see G. E. L. Owen, "Philosophical Invective," *Oxford Studies in Ancient Philosophy* 1 (1983), 1–25; on philosophical sectarianism and schools, see J. P.

Lynch, *Aristotle's School: A Study of a Greek Educational Institution* (Berkeley, 1972); and D. Runia, "Philosophical Heresiography: Evidence in Two Ephesian Inscriptions," *Zeitschrift für Papyrologie und Epigraphik* 72 (1988), 241–243.

7. See M. Simon, "From Greek *hairesis* to Christian Heresy," in W. R. Schodel and R. L. Wilkens, eds., *Early Christian Literature and the Classical Intellectual Tradition in honorem Robert M. Grant* (Paris, 1979), 101–116. On the management of conflict in Late Platonist circles, see Richard Lim, *Public Disputation, Power, and Social Order in Late Antiquity* (Berkeley, 1995), 31–69.

8. See J. G. Gager, *The Origins of Anti-Semitism: Attitudes towards Judaism in Pagan and Christian Antiquity* (Oxford, 1985), 39–66; and A. M. Rabello, "The Legal Condition of the Jews in the Roman Empire," in H. Temporini and W. Haase, eds., *ANRW* II.19.662–762; for the later period, see the fine overview in N. de Lange, "Jews and Christians in the Byzantine Empire: Problems and Prospects," in D. Wood, ed., *Christianity and Judaism* (Oxford, 1992), 15–32.

9. For diaspora Judaism, see P. R. Trebilco, *Jewish Communities in Asia Minor* (Cambridge, Eng., 1991); for Palestinian Judaism, see M. Avi-Yonah, *The Jews under Roman and Byzantine Rule: A Political History of Palestine from the Bar Kokhba War to the Arab Conquest* (New York, 1984). On conversion to Judaism, see M. Goodman, "Proselytizing in Rabbinic Judaism," *Journal of Jewish Studies* 40 (1989): 175–185; on god-fearers, see J. Reynolds and R. Tannenbaum, *Jews and God-Fearers at Aphrodisias: Greek Inscriptions with Commentary* (Cambridge, Eng., 1987).

10. See M. Simon, *Verus Israel: Etude sur les relations entre chrétiens et juifs dans l'empire romain (135–425)*, rev. ed. (Paris, 1964). M. S. Taylor, in *Anti-Judaism and Early Christian Identity: A Critique of the Scholarly Consensus* (Leiden, 1995), now argues that there was no actual direct competition between Jews and Christians in the first two centuries and that Christian anti-Judaism was wholly an ideological construct.

11. See O. Skarsaune, *The Proof from Prophecy: A Study of Justin Martyr's Proof-Text Tradition* (Leiden, 1987).

12. W. Bousset, *Jüdisch-christlicher Schulbetrieb in Alexandria und Rom* (Göttingen, 1915); on Jewish-Christian dialogues, see M. Hoffmann, *Der Dialog bei den christlichen Schriftstellern der ersten vier Jahrhunderte* (Tübingen and Leipzig, 1966); and B. R. Voss, *Der Dialog in der frühchristlichen Literatur* (Munich, 1970).

13. A. L. Williams, *Adversus Judaeos: A Bird's Eye View of Christian Apologetic until the Renaissance* (Cambridge, Eng., 1955); and H. Schreckenberg, *Die christlichen Adversus Judaeos Texte und ihr literarisches und historisches Umfeld (1.–11. Jahrhunderte)*, 2nd ed. (Frankfurt am Main, 1990).

14. H. Remus, "Justin Martyr's Argument with Judaism," in S. G. Wilson, ed., *Anti-Judaism in Early Christianity II: Separation and Polemic* (Waterloo, Ont., 1986).

15. R. MacMullen, *Christianizing the Roman Empire (A.D. 100–400)* (New Haven, 1984), 25.

16. *Acta Petri* 8.26. See J. Colin, *Les villes libres de l'orient gréco-romain et l'envoi au supplice par acclamations populaires* (Brussels, 1965), 109–152.

17. R. MacMullen, "Two Types of Conversion to Early Christianity," *Vigiliae Christianae* 37 (1983): 174–192.

18. Origen, *Contra Celsum* 2.55.

19. See, e.g., R. Walzer, *Galen on Jews and Christians* (London, 1949), 15–16; and S. Benko, "Pagan Criticism of Christianity during the First Two Centuries," *ANRW* II.23.2.1055–1118. On Christian paradoxical discourse, see Averil Cameron, *Christianity and the Rhetoric of Empire: The Development of Christian Discourse* (Berkeley, 1991).

20. K. Oehler, "Der Consensus Omnium als Kriterium der Wahrheit in der antike Philosophie und der Patristik: Eine Studie zur Geschichte des Begriffs der allgemeinen Meinung," *Antike und Abendland* 10 (1961): 103–130. The pagan Celsus used this argument against Christians: Origen, *Contra Celsum* 3.11–12.

21. See Eusebius, *Praeparatio evangelica* (compiled ca. 318).

22. Eusebius, *Hist.eccl.* 2.26, 3.5–6.

23. Evagrius Scholasticus, *Hist.eccl.* 1.1; Nicetas, *Encomium of Gregory of Nazianzus* 16.

24. W. Bauer, *Orthodoxy and Heresy in Earliest Christianity,* trans. R. A. Kraft and G. Krodel (Philadelphia, 1971).

25. G. Levesque, "Consonance chrétienne et dissonance gnostique dans Irénée 'Adversus haereses' IV, 18, 4 à 19,3," *Studia Patristica* 16 (Berlin, 1985): 193–196.

26. Ignatius, *Ep. ad Eph.* 3–5 and Cyprian, *Ep. 66; De ecclesiae catholicae unitate* 3–24.

27. C. J. Hefele, *Histoires des conciles* (Paris, 1907–1908), vols. 1–2. For the ideology of early councils, see H. J. Sieben, *Die Konzilsidee der Alten Kirche* (Paderborn, 1979), 384–447; and C. Vogel, "Primalialité et synodalité dans l'église locale durant la periode anténicéenne," in M. Simon, ed., *Aspects de l'orthodoxie: Structure et spiritualité* (Paris, 1982), 53–66.

28. Eusebius, *Hist.eccl.* 6.18 and 6.33; Origen, *Dialogue with Heraclides,* J. Scherer, ed., *Entretien d'Origène avec Héraclide,* Sources Chrétiennes 67 (Paris, 1960). See Lim, *Public Disputation,* 16–20, and "Religious Disputation and Social Disorder in Late Antiquity," *Historia* 44 (1995): 204–231, at 209–210.

29. Eusebius, *Hist.eccl.* 7.24. See Lim, *Public Disputation,* 20–22, and "Religious Disputation," 211–215.

30. R. MacMullen, "Personal Power in the Roman Empire," *American Journal of Philology* 107 (1986): 513–524. See also E. P. Thompson, "Patrician and Plebeian Society," *Journal of Social History* 7 (1974): 382–405, and *Customs in Common* (London, 1991); and J. G. A. Pocock, "The Classical Theory of Deference," *American Historical Review* 81 (1976): 516–523.

31. A. Momigliano, "Popular Religious Beliefs and the Later Roman Historians," in G. J. Cuming and D. Baker, eds., *Popular Belief and Practice* (Cambridge, Eng., 1972), 1–18, at 17.

32. Arius has recently been rehabilitated by scholars as a rigorous ascetic with deep theological convictions. On Arius and early Arianism, see R. C. Gregg and D. E. Groh, *Early Arianism: A View of Salvation* (Philadelphia and London, 1981); R. Williams, "The Logic of Arianism," *Journal of Theological Studies* n.s. 34 (1983): 56–81, and *Arius: Heresy and Tradition* (London, 1987); R. C. Hanson, *The Search for the Christian Doctrine of God: The Arian Controversy 318–381* (Edinburgh, 1988). For later developments, see essays in M. R. Barnes and D. H. Williams, eds., *Arianism after Arius: Essays on the Development of the Fourth Century Trinitarian Conflicts* (Edinburgh, 1993).

33. Lim, "Religious Disputation," 217–219.

34. F. Millar, *The Emperor in the Roman World (31 B.C.–A.D. 337)* (London, 1977), 385–394.

35. P. R. L. Brown, *Power and Persuasion in Late Antiquity: Towards a Christian Empire* (Madison, Wis., 1992), 3–34.

36. H. von Campenhausen, *Ecclesiastical Office and Spiritual Power in the Church in the First Three Centuries* (Stanford, 1969; orig. German ed. Tübingen, 1953); E. W. Kemp, "Bishops and Presbyters at Alexandria," *Journal of Ecclesiastical History* 3 (1952): 125–142; H. Chadwick, "The Role of the Christian Bishop in Ancient Society," in *Protocol of the 35th Colloquy,* Center for Hermeneutical Studies (Berkeley, 1980) = *Heresy and Orthodoxy in the Early Church* (London, 1991), III; G. W. Bowersock, "From Emperor to Bishop: The Self-Conscious Transformation of Political Power in the Fourth Century, A.D.," *Classical Philology* 81 (1986): 298–307; R. Lizzi, *Il potere episcopale nell'oriente romano* (Rome, 1987); and Brown, *Power and Persuasion,* 71–117.

37. E.g., E. Schwartz, *Kaiser Constantin und die christliche Kirche,* 2nd ed. (Leipzig, 1936); F. Dvornik, "Emperors, Popes and General Councils," *Dumbarton Oaks Papers* 6 (1951): 1–27; C. Pietri, "La politique de Constance II: Un premier 'césaropapisme' ou l'*imitatio Constantini?*" *L'église et l'empire au IVe siècle,* Entretiens sur l'antiquité classique 34 (Vandoeuvres, 1989), 113–172; and G. Dagron, *Empereur et prêtre: Étude sur le 'césaropapisme' byzantin* (Paris, 1996), esp. 141–168.

38. T. D. Barnes, *Constantine and Eusebius* (Cambridge, Mass., 1981), and *Athanasius and Constantius: Theology and Politics in the Constantinian Empire* (Cambridge, Mass., 1993).

39. See A. Lenox-Conyngham, "Juristic and Religious Aspects of the Basilica Conflict of A.D. 386," *Studia Patristica* 18 (Kalamazoo, Mich., 1985), I, 55–58; D. H. Williams, "Ambrose, Emperors and Homoians in Milan: The First Conflict over a Basilica," in Barnes and Williams, *Arianism after Arius,* 127–146; and N. McLynn, *Ambrose of Milan: Church and Court in a Christian Capital* (Berkeley, 1994), 187–196.

40. E. Gibbon, *Decline and Fall of the Roman Empire* (New York, 1932) 1:682.

41. See, e.g., A. Meredith, "Orthodoxy, Heresy and Philosophy in the Latter Half of the Fourth Century," *Heythrop Journal* 16 (1975): 5–21; essays in G. Vesey, ed., *The Philosophy in Christianity* (Cambridge, Eng., 1989); and the fine survey in C. Stead, *Philosophy in Christian Antiquity* (Cambridge, Eng., 1994).

42. In Basil's *Hexaemeron* and Augustine's *De Genesi contra Manichaeos.* See Lim, "The Politics of Interpretation in Basil of Caesarea's *Hexaemeron,*" *Vigiliae Christianae* 44 (1990): 351–370. Arian Christians, sternly opposed by Basil and Augustine (both of whom had once rejected allegory), also opposed allegories in favor of literal readings that legitimated their subordination of the Son to the Father (their attachment to literalism was such that they even accused their Nicene opponents of introducing nonscriptural terms such as *ousia* and *hypostasis*). See T. E. Pollard, "The Exegesis of Scripture and the Arian Controversy," *The Bulletin of the John Rylands Library* 41 (1989): 289–291.

43. A. H. Armstrong, "Pagan and Christian Traditionalism in the First Three Centuries, A.D.," *Studia Patristica* 15 (Berlin, 1957), 414–431.

44. J. de Ghellinck, "Quelques appréciations de la dialectique d'Aristote durant les conflits trinitaires du IVe siècle," *Revue d'Histoire Ecclesiastique* 26 (1930): 5–42; on scriptural traditionalism, see A. H. Armstrong, "Pagan and Christian Traditionalism in the First Three Centuries, A.D.," *Studia Patristica* 15 (Berlin, 1957), 414–431.

45. See R. P. C. Hanson, *The Search for the Christian Doctrine of God: The Arian Controversy 318–381* (Edinburgh, 1988), 594–636; Lim, *Public Disputation,* 109–148.

46. See L. R. Wickham, "The *Syntagmation* of Aetius the Anomean," *Journal of Theological Studies* n.s. 19 (1968): 532–569.

47. M. Wiles, "Eunomius: Hair-Splitting Dialectician or Defender of the Accessibility of Salvation?" in R. Williams, ed., *The Making of Orthodoxy: Essays in Honour of Henry Chadwick* (Cambridge, Eng., 1989), 157–172.

48. See Lim, "Religious Disputation," 204–231, esp. 222–228.

49. Basil of Caesarea, *Ep.* 234–235; and Gregory of Nyssa, *De deitate filii et spiritus sancti* (PG 46.557).

50. E.g., Gregory of Nazianzus, *Or.* 27.2.

51. Sozomen, *Hist.eccl.* 4.18.

52. On this issue, see Averil Cameron, "Texts as Weapons: Polemic in the Byzantine Dark Ages," in A. Bowman and G. Woolf, eds., *Literacy and Power in the Ancient World* (Cambridge, Eng., 1994), 198–215; and Lim, *Public Disputation,* 165–166. See also J. A. Munitz, "Catechetical Teaching-Aids in Byzantium," in J. Chrysostomides, ed., *Kathegetria: Essays Presented to Joan Hussey on Her 80th Birthday* (Camberley, 1988), 78ff.

53. Gregory of Nazianzus, *Or.* 29.21.

54. A. D. Kartsonis, *Anastasis: The Making of an Icon* (Princeton, 1986), 40–67.

55. R. P. Vaggione, "Of Monks and Lounge Lizards: 'Arians', Polemics, and Asceticism in the Roman East," in Barnes and Williams, *Arianism after Arius,* 181–214; and Lim, *Public Disputation,* 144–149, 182–216.

56. See *Vita Danielis* 90.

57. See E. Jugie, "La dispute des philosophes païens avec les pères de Nicée," *Échos d'Orient* 24 (1925): 403–410; and Lim, *Public Disputation,* 182–216.

58. Skill in debate was not a monopoly of Arians; see *Altercatio Heracliani,* in C. P. Caspari, ed., *Kirchhistorische anecdota nebst neuen Ausgaben patristischer und kirchlichmittelalterlicher Schriften* (Christiania, 1883), 1:133–147.

59. M. Richard, "Notes sur les florilèges dogmatiques du Ve et du VIe siècle," in *Actes du VIe Congrès Internationale d'Études Byzantines* (Brussels, 1950), 1:307–318.

60. See J. Taylor, "The First Council of Constantinople (381)," *Prudentia* 13 (1981): 47–54, 91–97.

61. *Acta Oecumenicorum Conciliorum* I.1.1, 18 (Schwartz, ed., 101).

62. See A. de Halleux, "La réception du symbole oecuménique, de Nicée à Chalcédoine," *Ephemerides Theologicae Lovanienses* 61 (1985): 5–47.

63. On increasingly exact definitions of orthodoxy, see *C.Th.* 16.5.14 (388) on the targeting of Nicene Apollinarians who opposed Cappadocian Christology.

64. Gregory of Nyssa, *Contra Eunomium* 1.683 (Jaeger, ed., 1:222).

65. See Lim, *Public Disputation,* 149–181.

66. Corpus of Pseudo-Dionysius: *PG* 3, 119–1064; see also R. Roques, *L'univers dionysien: Structure hiérarchique du monde selon le pseudo-Denys* (Paris, 1954).

67. Lim, *Public Disputation,* 175–177.

68. H.-I. Marrou and J. Daniélou, *The Christian Century I: The First Six Hundred Years,* trans. V. Cronin (London, 1964), 234.

69. W. H. C. Frend, *The Rise of the Monophysite Movement: Chapters in the History of the Church in the Fifth and Sixth Centuries* (Cambridge, Eng., 1972), 141: "The Chalcedonian crisis was not only a crisis of the intellectuals. It was a crisis involving the totality of Christians in the eastern Mediterranean. This marks it off from the Arian controversy a century before for the latter was primarily a crisis of bishops. Throughout the Monophysite dispute, the key role was always to belong to the monks." Frend's characterization of the elite nature of the Arian controversy is now increasingly under challenge.

70. W. H. C. Frend, "Athanasius as an Egyptian Christian Leader in the Fourth Century," *New College Bulletin* 8 (1974): 30–27; reprinted in Frend, *Religion Popular and Unpopular in the Early Christian Centuries* (London, 1976).

71. Socrates, *Hist.eccl.* 6.8.

72. Frend, *Rise of the Monophysite Movement,* 137.

73. H. J. Carpenter, "Popular Christianity and the Theologians in the Early Centuries," *Journal of Theological Studies* n.s. 14 (1963): 294–310.

74. E. L. Woodward, *Christianity and Nationalism in the Later Roman Empire* (London, 1916); W. H. C. Frend, *The Donatist Church* (Oxford, 1952); J. P. Brisson, *Autonomisme et christianisme dans l'Afrique romaine* (Paris, 1958); A. H. M. Jones, "Were the Ancient Heresies National or Social Movements in Disguise?" *Journal of Theological Studies* n.s. 10 (1959): 280–295; W. H. C. Frend, "Heresy and Schism as Social and National Movements," in D. Baker, ed., *Schism, Heresy and Religious Protest* (Cambridge, Eng., 1972), 37–56. See survey of these approaches by R. A. Markus, "Christianity and Dissent in Roman North Africa: Changing Perspectives in Recent Work," in Baker, ed., *Schism, Heresy and Religious Protest,* 21–36.

75. S. H. Bacht, "Die Rolle des orientalischen Mönchtums in den Kirchenpolitischen Auseinandersetzungen um Chalkedon (432–519)," in A. Grillmeier and H. Bacht, eds., *Das Konzil von Chalkedon* (Würzburg, 1953), 2:193–314. On the effects of having

monks living near cities, see G. Dagron, "Les moines et la ville: Le monachisme urbain à Constantinople," *Travaux et Mémoires* 4 (1970): 229–276.

76. *C.Th.* 16.2.42–43.

77. T. Gregory, *Vox Populi: Popular Opinion and Violence in the Religious Controversies of the Fifth Century* (Columbus, Oh., 1979); R. MacMullen, "The Historical Role of the Masses in Late Antiquity," in MacMullen, *Changes in the Roman Empire: Essays in the Ordinary* (Princeton, 1990), 25–76, 384–393; and N. McLynn, "Christian Controversy and Violence in the Fourth Century," *Kodai* 3 (Tokyo, 1992), 15–44.

78. P. Batiffol, "Les présents de saint Cyrille à la cour de Constantinople," in *Etudes de liturgue et d'archéologie chrétienne* (Paris, 1919), 159–173; and Brown, *Power and Persuasion*, 15–17.

79. On the Monophysite rejection of Chalcedon, see Michael the Syrian, *Chron.* 9.26. On the liturgical celebration of select councils, see S. Salaville, "La fête du concile de Nicée et les fêtes de conciles dans le rite byzantin," *Echos d'Orient* 24 (1925): 445–470, and "La fête du concile de Chalcédoine dans le rite byzantin," in Grillmeier and Bacht, *Das Konzil von Chalkedon*, 2:677–695.

80. *C.Just.* 1.1.4 (Krueger, ed., *Corpus Iuris Civilis*, II, 6).

81. See, e.g., V. Déroche, *Études sur Léontios de Néapolis* (Uppsala, 1995), 270–296; see also 226–269 on the miracle as a consensual symbol of holiness.

82. *C.Th.* 16.1.2 (= *Cunctos populos*, 380); 16.1.3 (= *Episcopis tradi*, 381).

83. N. Q. King, *The Emperor Theodosius and the Establishment of Christianity* (London, 1961); T. D. Barnes, "Religion and Society in the Age of Theodosius," in H. A. Meynell, ed., *Grace, Politics and Desire: Essays on Augustine* (Calgary, 1990), 157–160.

84. *C.Th.* 16.10.11–12 (391–392). G. Fowden, "Bishops and Temples in the Eastern Roman Empire, A.D. 320–425," *Journal of Theological Studies* n.s. 29 (1978): 62–69.

85. Lim, *Public Disputation*, 103–108.

86. Brown, "St Augustine's Attitude to Religious Coercion," *Journal of Roman Studies* 65 (1964): 107–116; J. Vanderspoel, "The Background to Augustine's Denial of Religious Plurality," in Meynell, *Grace, Politics and Desire,* 179–193. On pagan reactions, see F. Paschoud, "L'intolérance chrétienne vue et jugée par les païens," *Cristianesimo nella storia* 11 (1990): 545–577.

87. Brown, "Religious Coercion in the Later Roman Empire: The Case of North Africa," *History* 48 (1963): 283–305; and B. Shaw, "African Christianity: Disputes, Definitions and 'Donatists,'" in M. R. Greenshields and T. A. Robinson, eds., *Orthodoxy and Heresy in Religious Movements: Discipline and Dissent* (Lewinston, Queenston, Lampeter, 1992), 5–34. See Augustine's new sermons, in F. Dolbeau, "Nouveaux sermons de S. Augustin sur la conversion des païens et des Donatistes," *Revue des études Augustiniennes* 37 (1991): 37–78 and *Recherches Augustiniennes* 26 (1992): 69–141.

88. On moral categorization, see L. Jayussi, *Categorization and the Moral Order* (Boston and London, 1984).

89. A. Le Boulluec, *La notion d'hérésie dans la littérature grecque (IIe–IIIe siècles* (Paris, 1985); and R. Lyman, "A Topography of Heresy: Mapping the Rhetorical Creation of Arianism," in Barnes and Williams, *Arianism after Arius,* 45–62.

90. Peter Brown, "The Patrons of Pelagius: The Roman Aristocracy between East and West," *Journal of Theological Studies* n.s. 21 (1970): 56–72; E. Clark, *The Origenist Controversy: The Cultural Construction of an Early Christian Debate* (Princeton, 1992); H. O. Maier, "Private Space as the Social Context of Arianism in Ambrose's Milan," *Journal of Theological Studies* n.s. 45 (1994): 72–93, and "The Topography of Heresy and Dissent in Late Fourth-Century Rome," *Historia* 44 (1995): 232–249.

91. Mark the Deacon, *Life of Porphyry of Gaza,* 85–91, in H. Grégoire and M.-A. Kugener, *Marc le diacre: Vie de Porphyre évêque de Gaza* (Paris, 1930), 66–71; and Augustine, *Contra Felicem* (in CSEL 25).

92. Lim, *Public Disputation*, 93–102.

93. Brown, *Authority and the Sacred: Aspects of the Christianization of the Roman World* (Cambridge, Eng., 1995), 29–54.

94. See Cyril of Scythopolis, *Vita Sabae* 72 on the religious aspects of the reconquest.

95. J. Herrin, *The Formation of Christendom* (Princeton, 1987; rev. ed., 1989), 228–229.

96. Isidore of Seville, *Historia de regibus Gothorum, Vandalorum et Suevorum* 52–53 (on the Council of Toledo), 60 (on the conversion of Jews).

97. See Herrin, *Formation of Christendom,* 90–127, 250–290.

98. See Meyendorff, *Imperial Unity,* 336–380.

99. *Acta Oecumenicorum Conciliorum* II.1 (= R. Riedinger, ed., *Concilium Lateranense a. 649 celebratum,* Berlin and New York, 1974), 2–29 (the proceedings according to the *primus secretarius*), 425–436 (the *florilegium* = *Codex Vaticanus Graecus* 1455, fol. 165r–176r).

100. *C.Th.* 16.5.66 (435).

101. On the school of Nisibis, see J.-B. Chabot, "L'école de Nisibus, son histoire, ses statuts," *Journal Asiatique* 9 (1896): 43–93; A. Vööbus, *Statutes of the School of Nisibis* (Stockholm, 1961/62), and *History of the School of Nisibis,* CSCO 266 (Louvain, 1965).

102. On Christian synods in Persia, see J.-B. Chabot, ed., *Synodicon orientale ou recueil de synodes nestoriens* (Paris, 1902).

103. Fundamental studies include J. Wellhausen, *Die religiös-politischen Oppositionsparteien im alten Islam* (Berlin, 1901); T. Nagel, "Das Problem der Orthodoxie im frühen Islam," *Studien zum Minderheitenproblem im Islam* (Bonn, 1973), 1:7–44; M. Cook, *Early Muslim Dogma* (Cambridge, Eng., 1981); and J. van Ess, *Theologie und Gesellschaft im 2. und 3. Jahrhundert Hidschra: Eine Geschichte des religiösen Denkens im frühen Islam* (Berlin, 1991–1992), vols. 1–2. W. M. Watt, *The Formative Period of Islamic Thought* (Edinburgh, 1973), provides an accessible introduction to the subject.

104. See M. Tardieu, "Sābiens coraniques et 'Sābiens' de Harrān," *Journal Asiatique* 274 (1986): 1–44.

105. W. Madelung, "The Origins of the Controversy concerning the Creation of the Koran," in J. M. Barral, ed., *Orientalia Hispanica sive Studia F.M. Pareja octogenario dicata* (Leiden, 1974), 1:504–525 = *Religious Schools and Sects in Medieval Islam* (London, 1985), V.

106. K. Lewinstein, "The Azâriqa in Islamic Heresiography," *Bulletin of the School of Oriental and African Studies* 44 (1991): 251–268.

107. See G. Vajda, "Les *zindiqs* en pays d'Islam au début de la période abbaside," *Rivista degli studi orientali* 17 (1937–38): 173–229; Van Ess, *Theologie und Gesellschaft,* 1:136–137, 416–458, 2:4–41; and S. Shaked, *Dualism in Transformation: Varieties of Religions in Sasanian Iran* (London, 1994), 58–59: Manichaeans were called *zindīqs (zanadaqa)* because of their "twisted" exegesis of the Avesta *(Zand).*

108. Madelung, "Imāmism and Muʿtazilite Theology," in T. Fahd, ed., *Le Shīʿism imāmite* (Paris, 1979), 13–29 = *Religious Schools,* VII.

Islam

Hugh Kennedy

Of all the dividing lines set up between academic disciplines in the western intellectual tradition, the frontier between classical and Islamic studies has proved among the most durable and impenetrable. Great monuments of scholarship like A. H. M. Jones's *Later Roman Empire* and the *New Cambridge Ancient History* take it as axiomatic that the coming of Islam in the early 7th century marked a change so complete that there was no advantage in pursuing the topics that had been discussed into the new era. To a certain extent this is simply a result of linguistic difficulties—the coming of a new language of high culture and historiography (Arabic) meant that the source material was simply incomprehensible—but it is also cultural in a broader sense: whereas late antiquity can be seen as part of the broader history of western civilization, the history of the Islamic world cannot. Yet reflection will soon suggest that the changes cannot have been so sudden and dramatic, especially at the level of the structures of everyday life, and that the Islamic was as much, and as little, a continuation of late antiquity as was western Christendom.

It would be easy to see late antiquity as a unit in the history of the Near East and to see broad continuities from the 4th century to the beginning of the 7th century. The development of a Greek-Christian high government and culture would support this. Yet more than three centuries elapsed between the adoption of Christianity as the official religion and the coming of Islam, and in this period the structures of everyday life continued to evolve and develop. Insofar as the Muslims were the heirs of late antiquity, they inherited the world of Heraclius, not of Constantine; the cities and villages they came to rule were those of the early 7th, not the 4th century; and comparisons which look back from the formation of the early Islamic world to a homogenous late antiquity can be either unhelpful or actually misleading.

To examine these issues, I have chosen to concentrate on greater Syria, the lands the Arabs call Bilad al-Sham—that is to say, the lands of the eastern

Mediterranean from Antioch in the north to Gaza in the south and their hinter-
lands. There are good reasons for choosing this area. The literary and archaeological evidence allows us to form a fuller impression of what the end of
antiquity and the coming of Islam entailed than in any other area of the empire
and this wealth of evidence provides a much more nuanced picture than we can
find in Egypt or North Africa.[1] The changes which took place in this area
between the 6th and the 8th centuries affected all aspects of society. In this essay I will discuss ethnic change, political and administrative change, religious
change, and change in the patterns of settlement and the built environment.

The Muslim conquest of the Near Eastern lands of the Byzantine empire was
neither particularly violent nor particularly destructive. That does not mean, of
course, that there was not bloodshed and disruption: the Byzantine armies were
defeated, cities like Damascus and Caesarea were taken by siege and storm,
refugees were driven from their homes, and some clerics were forced to flee to
Constantinople or even Rome. However, compared with later invasions, like
those of the Crusaders or the Mongols, or even of the Persian invasions which
immediately preceded the coming of Islam, neither the literary sources (such as
they are) nor the archaeological records show evidence of extensive destruction.
The Muslims came not as a *Volkswanderung*, nor as tribes migrating with their
families and their beasts, but rather as organized armies with commanders and
strategic objectives. The Muslim conquest was a stage in the long-term penetration of Arabic-speaking peoples into the Near East which seems to have begun
in about 200 c.e. and continued to the 10th and 11th centuries. Certainly the
Muslim conquest, bringing as it did a new religion and a new language of high
culture, marks an important stage in this process—but a stage nonetheless.

The early Islamic state in Syria may have been the heir of late antiquity but it
also inherited from the *jāhilīya*, the world of pre-Islamic tribal Arabia with its
cult of poetry and warrior heroes and fierce loyalty to tribe and kin. This
heritage was temporarily eclipsed by the coming of Islam, which rejected its
values, but was rediscovered and to an extent reinvented in the first century
after the Prophet's death. In the 8th century the collection of poems and stories
relating to the *ayyam*, the "days" or battles of the pre-Islamic tribes, were studied with almost as much love and veneration as the traditions of the Prophet
himself, and the world of the pagan Arabian nomad became as integral to the
history of Islam as the works of classical pagan authors did to the Christian
intellectual tradition.

Many of the early Muslim conquerors of the Near East were not nomads at
all but came from the settled fertile areas of highland Yemen, from a world of
stone-built towns and carefully terraced mountainsides. The Muslims who first
settled in Egypt and Spain largely came from tribes like the Khawlan, Madhhij,
Ma'afir, and Hadramawt, long settled in south Arabia. The people of this area
were used to irrigation culture and had produced, in the Marib dam, one of the
most impressive hydraulic works of the ancient world. They also had a political
tradition of powerful monarchy, and memories of the lords of Himyar and Dhu
Raydan who had ruled as kings when the ancestors of the Umayyad caliphs
were no more than shepherds and peddlers.

Closer to Syria itself had been the pre-Islamic kings on the desert margin of the crescent: the Lakhmids of Hira in southern Iraq, who had guarded the lands of the Sassanian kings, and the Ghassanids, who had performed the same service for the Byzantines. Around both these courts, a Christian Arabic culture had developed, a world of palaces, hunting, and poetry. Though the political independence of both groups had ended in the late 6th century, the memory of their rule and their style persisted in literature and tales and was probably a potent source of inspiration for Umayyad court life.

It was the monarchy of Sassanian Persia, however, which provided the most pervasive of the legacies to the Islamic world.[2] Here again there was an ancient cultural tradition, a memory of kings like Khosro and heroes like Rustam whose more or less mythical stories were to provide material for poets and painters for centuries. There was also a more practical legacy of political and administrative structures and theories of statecraft from the well-remembered Sassanian monarchy of the 6th and early 7th centuries, not to speak of the presence of administrators who had actually worked for the old kings. These competing influences diluted the culture of late antiquity, but it still remained important, especially in Syria and Egypt, which had been so thoroughly Hellenized.

Although the Muslim conquests swept away the superstructure of Byzantine power, the emperor and the governors he had appointed, the early Muslims took on much of the lower-level Byzantine administrative practice. The provincial boundaries of the Byzantine empire largely disappeared, to be replaced by a system of *jund*s (military provinces) based on the need to supply troops. Attempts to discover the origins of these *jund*s in the nascent *theme* system of the Byzantine empire have not met with favor but the logic behind the new Muslim divisions remains obscure.[3] Each of the new divisions stretched from the seacoast on the west to the desert in the east, and the Arab population had different tribal and regional origins. From the beginning, the Muslims recognized two major administrative areas, Syria (al-Sham) and Palestine (Falastin), which were in turn subdivided. Instead of two Syria provinces based on Antioch and Apamea, two Phoenicias based on Tyre and Damascus, three Palestines based on Caesarea, Scythopolis and Petra, and the Provincia Arabia with its metropolis at Bostra there were now *jund*s of Palestine, Jordan (Urdunn), Damascus, Homs (Emesa), and Qinnasrin (Chalcis). While the *jund* of Qinnasrin covered some of the same territory as Syria I and Homs the same as Syria II, the frontiers were significantly different. Farther south, Damascus, Tiberias, and from the early 8th century Ramla were the new provincial capitals.[4] Most of this area had been conquered by the Persians in the first decade of the 7th century and restored to Byzantine rule only in 628, less than ten years before the Muslim conquest. It is likely that the old Byzantine administrative divisions had not been fully reestablished and that the Muslims were working with a *tabula rasa* when it came to local boundaries.

If the boundaries had been eroded or had disappeared, there were still people who had operated the late antique administrative systems who were in a position to help the newly arrived Muslim rulers make the best use of the resources of their new-won lands. Until the reign of 'Abd al-Malik (685–705) Greek remained the language of administration. We know this not just from references in the Arabic chronicles but also from the evidence of papyri from Egypt and Nessana in the Negev, where we can see this early Islamic, Greek-using administration in action.[5] It seems as if even the *diwan,* which recorded the names of the Muslim soldiers and their entitlement to stipends, was sometimes compiled in Greek.[6]

The use of Greek in the administration meant that knowledge of the language continued to be a valuable skill; throughout the 7th century and into the 8th a Greek culture continued to thrive in Palestine and Syria, perhaps more vigorously than in Constantinople itself. The most important figure in this culture was of course St. John of Damascus (d. ca. 754), who came from an Arab family with a tradition of working in the Byzantine administration and whose name before he entered the church was Mansur. He had worked for the Byzantine administration before taking service with the Umayyads. Despite working for a Muslim court he retained the faith of his ancestors and his defense of the use of icons in Christian worship was perhaps the most important contribution to Greek theology in the 7th and 8th centuries. When Greek ceased to be an official language, Greek education withered, as it was no longer a qualification for a lucrative career, and became confined to a few monasteries. By the 9th century, Christian intellectuals like Theodore Abu Qurra (ca. 740–ca. 820) and the historian Agapius of Manbij (d. ca. 950) were writing in Arabic even when discussing questions of theology and Christian doctrine.[7]

Early Islamic administration may have inherited the language and some of the forms of late antique government but it put them to rather different use. The Muslims came with their own ideas about administration and taxation and they felt no need to look to late Roman models. These ideas were certainly only half-formed in the early days, but it must not be forgotten that the Prophet was the ruler of a small state as well as the Messenger of Allah and that even this small state had developed a rudimentary fiscal structure. The Muslims may have not had a fully worked-out taxation system but they did have an ideology of taxation; reference to late antique practice carried no weight to devotees of the new religion.

In reality, the Muslims probably borrowed more from late antiquity in this area than they normally admitted. The fiscal system developed in Medina in the time of the Prophet was based on booty from war, the taxes paid by the protected non-Muslims *(dhimmī)* and the tithe *('ushr)* that richer Muslims were enjoined to pay for the support of widows, orphans, and Muslims in need. In both the Byzantine and Sassanian empires, the main source of revenue was the land-tax paid on all cultivated property. At first the Muslims took this over for their own purposes and obliged non-Muslims to pay it to them. As the pace of conversion increased, however, an ever higher proportion of the population claimed immunity. By the end of the 8th century Muslim rulers demanded the land-tax, now generally known as the *kharaj,* of almost all landowners, very much as it had been in the great empires of antiquity.[8]

In most preindustrial states, the proceeds of taxation were largely used to support the ruler and the military and elite elements who sustained his power. The Byzantine empire in late antiquity and the early caliphate both shared this common characteristic, but there were significant differences. In late antiquity, Syria was a provincial area, a rich and culturally significant area certainly, but it did not support an independent court and bureaucracy. Although we have no figures, it must be assumed that a considerable proportion of the taxes raised in Syria were exported to Constantinople. While emperors and the imperial government could and did spend money on ecclesiastical and military buildings in the province, we would probably be correct to assume that Syria was a net exporter of wealth.

In the earliest phases of Islamic rule Syria remained a province of a larger empire, but in the chaotic conditions of the years immediately after the conquests it is unlikely that much revenue was exported from Syria to the Muslim government in Medina. After the Umayyad Mu'āwiyya ibn Abi-Sufyān became governor in 639 it is probable that the revenues of Syria were spent in the province itself. The seizure of the caliphate by Mu'āwiyya in 661 changed the province's position yet again and Syria now become the capital of an empire which stretched from the Atlantic to Central Asia and the Indus valley. In its early phases, the administration of this empire was very decentralized and most of the revenue raised in the various provinces was distributed to the Muslim conquerors and their descendants in the province without ever having been sent to the capital.

Successive Umayyad caliphs attempted to break down this fiscal autonomy and secure at least a proportion of the tax revenues for the caliph. The leading figures in this policy of centralization were 'Abd al-Malik and Hishām (721–743). They encountered stiff and sometimes violent opposition, but the evidence suggests that they did secure a share of the revenues of the rest of the caliphate. For the first and only time in its millennial history, Syria became the center of a widespread empire; the wealth which flowed into the country is reflected in great prestige building projects like the Umayyad mosque in Damascus and the development of the Dome of the Rock and the Aqsa mosque in Jerusalem. Nothing on this scale was ever attempted in the later Islamic history of Syria, and it is striking testimony to the importance of its imperial role that the two major Muslim monuments of Syria and Palestine were built within twenty years at the end of the 7th century and the beginning of the 8th.

The Muslim conquerors brought with them the outlines of a new system of rewards for the military which owed nothing to Byzantine models. The Byzantine army had been paid out of tax revenue by the imperial treasury. Until the middle of the 6th century, the frontiers had been defended by *limitanei,* who were assigned lands in exchange of their military services. This system seems to have been abolished, or simply fallen into disuse under Justinian (527–561). Maintaining the security of the desert frontier was now the responsibility of the

Ghassanid phylarchs, Arab leaders who acted as intermediaries between the Bedouin tribes and the Byzantine authorities. The Persian and Muslim invasions marked the end of the late antique military system in the Byzantine empire as well as in the Muslim world. It is true that the Byzantines did still have paid soldiers based in Constantinople, but the reduced resources of the battered empire could no longer sustain a regular salaried army in the provinces. Instead the land was divided into *themes* and peasant soldiers were enrolled to defend their native soil against outside attack. In many rural areas, the slide to a nonmonetary economy meant that there was no longer any paid army in the area.

The Muslim military finance system owed nothing to late antique models and was a direct product of the settlement which followed the initial Muslim conquests.[9] The early stages of this development are difficult to recreate but its beneficiaries ascribed it to the decisions of the caliph 'Umar ibn al-Khattāb (634–644), thus elevating it above criticism and change. According to this traditional story, 'Umar had decreed that the victorious Muslims should not disperse through the conquered lands, settling as proprietors or farmers, but should establish Muslim cities known as *amṣār* (singular *miṣr*). The revenues from the subject people would be collected and distributed to the Muslims as *ata'* (salaries) and *rizq* (supplies). In this way the Muslims would remain a small elite "tax-eating" caste and so retain their religion and culture.

In Iraq, Kufa and Basra became the main centers of Muslim habitation; in Egypt it was Fustat or Old Cairo; and in Ifriqiya (Tunisia), Qayrawan was founded as the local *miṣr*. In Syria too a *miṣr* was founded at Jabiya in the Golan Heights, but the Muslim conquerors never settled in it in large numbers and were instead dispersed through the ancient cities, notably Damascus, Homs, and Qinnasrin. Why this should have happened in Syria is not clear but it may have been a result of the Arabization of the population before the coming of Islam. Many of the Muslim conquerors came, in fact, from tribes already resident in Syria or its frontier districts, like the Kalb of the Palmyrena or the Lakhm and Judham of southern Palestine. It was inconceivable that they should reside as outsiders, isolated from the local population of which they were in a sense part and with which they had well-established links.

Nonetheless in Syria, as elsewhere in the Muslim world, the pattern of a caste of conquerors paid from local revenues was the ideal if not the practice. Soon, however, this system came under increasing strain and pressure, even in those areas where it was well established. The problems stemmed ultimately from the fact that membership of the *diwan*, the register of the names of the tax-eaters, was hereditary. Furthermore, salaries varied greatly according to the *sabiqa* or precedence in Islam of the family concerned; early converts and their descendants were highly paid whereas late arrivals to the Muslim fold were at the bottom of the scale. This may have been acceptable in the first generation when men were rewarded for their own faith and commitment, but as the conquerors died off and their privileges were inherited by their sons and grandsons, it caused increasing resentment.

The system could function only as long as the Muslims were a small minority and there was no provision for new, post-conquest converts to enter the *diwan*. As conversion gathered pace, the pressure from those outside the system increased until it became irresistible. At the same time, the hereditary militia whose names did appear on the *diwan* became increasingly militarily ineffective. Like 18th century janissaries in the Ottoman empire, they rarely took up arms except in defense of their own privileges and even then they were not especially successful. As a military force for policing and defending the empire, they were virtually useless.

Unable to rely on this cumbersome and inflexible system, the Umayyad and early Abbasid rulers tried to step outside it. The later Umayyads recruited troops from the Bedouin tribes of the Syria desert, whether or not their ancestors had fought in the original conquests, and set about finding resources to pay them. The Abbasids, unable to draw on the Syrian tribes who had supported their rivals, looked outside the Muslim world entirely and began to employ Turkish mercenaries and slaves, recruited in Central Asia.

By the reign of the caliph al-Mu'tasim (833–842), the old *diwan* system had broken down almost entirely. The hereditary Muslim militia had been replaced by a professional army paid from the land-tax *kharaj* imposed on Muslim and non-Muslim alike (though, of course, non-Muslims were still obliged to pay the *jizya* or poll tax). In a curious way the raising of taxes and armies had come full circle; the Muslim rulers of the 9th century operated a system broadly similar to that of their Byzantine and Sassanian predecessors in late antiquity.

Nor was this similarity entirely unconscious. Muslim rulers and, even more, their bureaucrats knew that they were following pre-Islamic models of statecraft and they became proud of it. However, the legacy they looked to was not Byzantine but Sassanian.[10] This was partly because many of the bureaucrats were themselves of Persian origin, although in Umayyad and even in Abbasid times considerable numbers of Syrians were still employed in the bureaucracy. The Byzantine empire still existed, of course, and it was perhaps controversial for any Muslim ruler to admit that he was following the practices of the ancient enemy. The Sassanians, however, posed no such threat and their memories could be called on to sanction present practice. "Anushirvan the Just" (largely based on Khosro I Anushirvan, 531–579) was the figure to whom Muslim rulers felt able to appeal to legitimize their practice. Indeed it would be possible to argue that Khosro I and Muhammad shared the honor of being the two great begetters of Muslim statecraft. But we may perhaps see, lurking in the shadows, the image of the Roman empire of late antiquity from which, it can be suggested, Khosro himself received his political education.

The end of late antiquity meant the coming of a new religion of government and power. The Byzantine empire was fiercely Christian, so loyalty to religion could have consolidated resistance to the invaders even if ties of blood and language drew many Syrians to the new Muslim arrivals. In the event things were not as simple as this: the Christians were not as homogenous nor the new religion as clear-cut and aggressive as might have been imagined. By the end of antiquity, it is likely that the vast majority of the population of Syria were either Christians or Jews. Paganism had continued to flourish well into the 5th century and classical mythology was familiar to the designers of mosaic floors even in quite remote rural areas like the Hawran; a few pockets, notably the Sabaeans of Harran (Carrhae), maintained their ancient beliefs into the Islamic period.[11] The triumph of Christianity did not, however, mean that religious conflict had disappeared.

Relations between Jewish communities and the Byzantine authorities were marked by periods of persecution by the government and unrest among the Jews. In 556 an uprising of Jews and Samaritans resulted in the death of the governor of Caesarea, but the accusations that the Jews supported the Persian attack on Jerusalem in 614 probably owe more to the imagination of later Christian apologists, seeking to explain away the successes of Persian and Muslim conquerors, than to contemporary historical fact. There were also violent Samaritan revolts in 484 and in 529, when Scythopolis, the capital of Palestine II, was sacked. There is no doubt that Jews and Samaritans were second-class citizens in late antiquity and that, from time to time, decrees were issued that they should be converted to Christianity. Archaeological evidence, however, suggests that the fearsome legislation was not enforced with any vigor and that many Jewish populations, especially in Galilee, shared in the general prosperity of late antiquity.[12]

The Jews remained second-class citizens after the Muslim conquest, being classed as *dhimmīs* or protected people.[13] The great difference, however, was that they were no longer alone: the Christians too were now *dhimmīs*; indeed, *dhimmīs* formed the overwhelming mass of the population. The Muslim conquest certainly did not bring the two communities together in adversity, and Christian-Jewish controversy and polemic continued to be as shrill as ever, but the Jews were no longer the targets of legislation directed solely at them. We cannot be certain whether the poll tax demanded by the Muslims was more or less than the taxes required by the Byzantines, but we do not hear of large-scale Jewish unrest. In some ways the situation of the Jews did improve: though Tiberias still remained the most important Jewish city, Jews were allowed once more to settle in Jerusalem itself, though the bulk of the population of the Holy City remained Christian.

The Christian church was far from united in late antiquity. Syria was the scene of a fierce and prolonged struggle between the Monophysites and the Dyophysites.[14] The dispute centered on the nature of the incarnation, the Dyophysites maintaining that Christ had two distinct and complete natures, one human and one divine. The Monophysites regarded this as blasphemy and claimed that Christ had a single, divine nature and only took on the appearance of humanity. This apparently technical dispute went to the heart of Christian belief and aroused violent passions, each sect regarding its opponents as the vilest of heretics. These theological differences were compounded by cultural conflicts. Though there were important exceptions, the Dyophysites were mostly to be found among the Greek-speaking inhabitants of the towns and coastal areas, the Monophysites among the Syriac-speaking populations of the inland rural areas: the Monophysites were strongest in the north of Syria, while Palestine was almost entirely Dyophysite.

The broad outlines of the dispute had developed during and after the church council at Chalcedon in 541, which had adopted a Dyophysite position (hence the Dyophysites were often known as Chalcedonians), but the dispute did not become a real schism until the 6th century. Emperor Justinian tried to enforce Chalcedonian uniformity and this led militant Monophysites like Jacob Bar ʿAdai (Baradaeus) to break away and after 536 to set up an alternative church with a parallel hierarchy. This church is often referred to as Jacobite. Despite attempts to reach a compromise in the second half of the 6th and early 7th centuries, the church in Syria was painfully divided and many Syrian Christians were alienated from the official church. There is no evidence that the Monophysites were disloyal to the empire in the face of Persian and Muslim attacks. They wanted an empire which was Christian and, as they saw it, orthodox, but their disaffection with the empire may account for the lack of popular resistance to the Muslim conquest in many areas.

The coming of Islam radically affected the status of the Christian churches.[15] The Chalcedonian church, from being the religion of the elite, became simply another sect among several and the links with the emperor, which had ensured its success in earlier days, now became an embarrassment rather than a help.[16] The conquests shattered the hierarchy; we do not even know if the patriarchates at Antioch and Jerusalem were filled during the later part of the 7th century. However, as long as Greek remained the language of administration, the Chalcedonian church still had wealthy patrons; there is archaeological evidence that new churches continued to be built in the Umayyad period. From the mid 8th century, the Christians' position became more precarious and the general insecurity and impoverishment of Syria from 750 onward caused increasing problems.

In these circumstances, the Chalcedonian church reinvented itself. Whether intentionally or not, it was cut off from Constantinople and the Greek heritage. The liturgical language changed to Syriac and then to Arabic, which also became the language of Christian religious writing and polemic. Priests and bishops were recruited from the members of the local churches. This church, commonly referred to as the Melkite or Royal church (in memory of its ancient links with the Byzantine emperors), has survived to the present day, and, despite the constant attrition of converts to Islam, remains the most numerous of the Christian denominations of Syria.

The Muslim conquests significantly improved the status of the Jacobite church in the short term. For the first time in a century, the Jacobite patriarch of Antioch was able to reside in the city from which he took his title, and the Muslim authorities granted the Jacobites the same status as the Melkites, with the added advantage that their church was not tainted by association with the Byzantine enemy. The Jacobites were now free to preach and make converts, which had been forbidden under Byzantine rule. However, Syriac was never a language of government and the Jacobites seem to have been slower to adopt Arabic than their Melkite rivals. The church remained firmly entrenched in the villages of northern Syria and the areas of the Byzantine frontier but failed to achieve any ascendancy over its hated competitors.[17]

The most obvious feature of the Muslim conquest was that it brought a new elite religion; yet despite the military ascendancy of the Muslims the spread of the new religion was slower and more hesitant than might be imagined. Not only were many of the bureaucrats Christian but so were some of the Syrian Bedouin, like the leaders of the Kalb, who supported the Umayyads against their Muslim rivals. It is very difficult to assess the progress of conversion. Bulliet's model, which is based on statistics from Iranian biographical dictionaries of Muslim scholars, suggests that conversion in the first century and a half of Islam was very slow, and that it was not until the 10th century that the Muslim element in the population began to increase rapidly.[18] There is little if any evidence of forced conversion except among the Christian Bedouin, though churches and monasteries certainly did suffer in periods of general lawlessness, like the disorders and rebellions which followed the death of the caliph Hārūn al-Rashīd in 809.

The new religion needed high-status architecture to assert its identity against the surviving monumental architecture of Christianity. Almost miraculously, the two most important of these buildings have survived, with some alterations, down to the present day: the Dome of the Rock in Jerusalem and the Umayyad Mosque in Damascus.[19] The Dome of the Rock, constructed during the reign of the caliph 'Abd al-Malik (685–705), is a centrally planned, domed structure; it stands over the rock that projects in the middle of the great paved terrace which had once supported Herod's Temple and which the Muslims know as the Haram al-Sharif. The purpose of the building remains a subject of controversy. It was probably both a pilgrimage center and a conspicuous rival to the Christian Church of the Holy Sepulcher, whose dome could easily be seen across the narrow streets of the city. In both construction and decoration, it owed much to the late antique building traditions of Syria. The overall design has a number of precursors in the centrally planned churches of Christian architecture. The construction, with its thin walls, classical columns, and wooden roofing and dome, derives directly from the ecclesiastical architecture of the 5th and 6th centuries. The decoration, too, is heavily Byzantine in style, as is shown by the veined and patterned marble panels which decorate the lower parts of the walls and the glass mosaics on the drum of the dome. Only the absence of representations of the human figure and the Arabic dedicatory inscription reveal this building as a mosque.

The Umayyad mosque in Damascus, built by the caliph al-Walīd (705–715), stands on the site of the cathedral of St. John, which in turn stood within the *temenos* of the ancient temple of Haddad/Jupiter, whose origins go back to remotest antiquity. It is striking evidence of the continuity of cult centers that the Muslims decided to take over this ancient holy place. Unlike the Dome of the Rock, this is a congregational mosque, where the Muslims could gather in large numbers to worship together on Fridays. As well as being a religious center, it had a political function, for it was here that caliphs and governors could address the Muslims, and it soon acquired judicial functions, as the setting for the court of the Muslim judge *(qāḍī)* and as a center of Muslim education. In one direction, the design of the mosque looked back to the origins of Islam, for the first such mosque and community center had been the house of the Prophet himself in Medina, built, as it was, around a large courtyard where the Muslims could gather. Yet the mosque, with its open court and three-aisled prayer hall, also derived from the forum and the basilica of antiquity. Nowhere is this clearer than in Damascus, where the great rectangular court of the mosque still constitutes the only formal open space with the old city walls and whose architecture, despite the vicissitudes it has suffered, still reflects its origins in the antique townscape.

Mosques were of course built in most towns, but the great structures of the Dome of the Rock and the Umayyad mosque in Damascus give a somewhat misleading impression of the relative importance of these structures. The mosque at Jerash (Gerasa), a town of some prosperity in the Muslim Umayyad period, was little more than a large room with a *miḥrāb* in the shadow of the giant remains of antiquity and large numbers of Christian churches. In Subeita in the Negev, the mosque was a very modest hall fitted into a corner of the narthex of the splendid south church, more tentative than triumphant. In other cities, like Hims, the Muslims continued to share the main church with the Christians, as indeed they had done at Damascus until the time of al-Walīd.

Muslim government arrived in Syria with dramatic suddenness in the decade after 632, but the new religion was much slower to establish itself among the people. The decline of Christianity can be attributed to many causes. Among these were certainly the grinding burden of the poll tax, the fierce rivalries between Christian sects, often eager to appeal to the Muslim authorities for support against their hated opponents, and the tendency of ambitious figures in the Christian community to convert for career reasons. The Christian populations, being largely unarmed and unmilitarized, also suffered disproportionately from the impoverishment and Bedouinization of the country in the 9th and 10th centuries. Despite these problems, there were still important Christian populations, especially in northern Syria, at the coming of the crusaders in 1099, and the Christian society of late antiquity only gradually gave way to the Muslim society of the later Middle Ages.

The Islamic city conjures up visions of winding, narrow streets; crowded, bustling *sūq*s; calm and spacious mosques; and secluded houses, presenting only blank walls to the outside world but enclosing private courtyards where domesticity and even luxury flourish, unseen by the outside world.[20] How different such a city appears from the monumental city of antiquity. There we find broad, straight, colonnaded streets; open fora; magnificent temples, theaters, and baths; and, in general, an atmosphere of spacious, ordered elegance. Of course this is a simplistic view but it has achieved a certain scholarly respectability, and the Islamic city has been the object of considerable academic discussion. As in so many investigations into late antiquity and Islam, the true picture is much more complex and the differences much less clear-cut.[21] The Muslims did not inherit the classical city. No new theater had been constructed in Syria for four hundred years before the Muslims invaded, and the temples had been closed three centuries before al-Walīd ibn ʿAbd al-Malik began the construction of the Umayyad mosque in Damascus. Instead the Muslims inherited the cities of late antiquity, which had evolved significantly.

Two factors lay behind this evolution. The first was the prolonged period of civil war and disturbance in the mid 3rd century. This had brought to an end the great building boom of the 1st and 2nd centuries. When the emperors recovered their authority under Aurelian, Diocletian, and Constantine, the civic autonomy which had characterized and made possible the construction of the classical city had largely disappeared: city treasuries were confiscated, and the cities of Syria no longer minted the bronze coins which had advertised their individuality and status. The second major change was the coming of Christianity, which became the official religion in 313 with the Edict of Milan: by the end of the 4th century most of the temples in the cities had been closed. The main buildings in many cities thus had become derelict, and the courts which surrounded them and the ceremonial ways which led up to them were now redundant. In Gerasa, for example, the ceremonial way which led from the river up to the temple of Artemis was blocked off, and part of what had been a colonnaded street was roofed over and converted into a church.

Other public buildings in the city were allowed to decay. It is difficult to tell from the archaeological evidence when the great baths of antiquity or the aqueducts and nymphaea which supplied running water to the city fell into disuse. The construction of new, much smaller baths in Gerasa in the mid 5th century suggests that the two huge ancient structures in the city were no longer in use. Theaters survived rather longer, as the setting for the performances the early Christians so strongly condemned but also as a site of political occasions, where a governor could hear the acclamations (and complaints) of the people. But even so, it is likely that most theaters were in an advanced state of decay before the coming of the Muslims.

The loss of civic self-government and the end of paganism changed not just the physical structures of the city but the ideological environment which supported it. The classical city was dependent on the generosity of its citizens, who demonstrated their status by paying for and maintaining public buildings and were, in return, commemorated by inscriptions and statues. The cult of the city was the essential underpinning of this beautiful but fragile urban environment.

The Christians of late antiquity had other priorities.[22] The building of churches was the most obvious, and cities of any size were endowed with a fair number of them. In Gerasa for example some fifteen have been discovered, and there were no doubt others now lost, varying in size from the great city center churches of the cathedral and St. Theodore to much smaller structures which may have been little more than local chapels. It is arguable that Christianity put more emphasis on the family and hence on the family house. It almost seems that the people of late antiquity turned their backs on the public open spaces which their ancestors had seen as the setting for their lives and retreated inside, locking the doors and windows on the street scene.

The character of the streets themselves began to change. The wide straight streets with colonnaded sides and covered pavements were gradually encroached on as shops and houses invaded the previously public open spaces. The streets narrowed as pack animals came to replace wheeled vehicles as the main means of transporting goods. There were attempts to turn the clock back: when Justinian built his great Nea Church in Jerusalem, he extended the ancient colonnaded *cardo* to the south and constructed a broad straight city street which any Hellenistic builder would have been proud of. But without the intervention of a revivalist emperor, such projects were doomed; commercial pressures and social indifference gradually eroded the fabric of Hippodamian (rectilinear) planning.

The Muslim conquerors inherited this late antique city, with its narrow streets and blank-walled houses, a city whose only public buildings were the churches. The first century of Muslim rule saw the continuation and completion of many of the developments of the previous three centuries. The Muslims kept up the ancient tradition of bathing, but the Muslim *hammam* looked much more like the Byzantine bath of the mid 5th century than the great structures of antiquity. Hypocausts were still used and the procession of rooms from cold to hot was maintained but the palaestra and social areas were gone and the scale was more intimate, the business more commercial: baths became a source of revenue for mosques and other religious endowments (*awqāf*, singular *waqf*) rather than a subsidized relaxation for the citizens.

The theater was now entirely useless. The public life of early Muslim cities contained no dramatic performances of any sort. The political function of the theater was transferred to the mosque; it was there that the governor would lead the people (at least the political classes, that is, the Muslims) in prayer and address them from the pulpit. If theaters were still used at all, it was as the setting for pottery kilns.

The most noticeable changes occurred in the street pattern. The houses and shops continued to intrude on the pavement as the streets became narrow, winding, and in some cases blocked entirely. But there was nothing specifically Islamic about these changes; they were the continuation of trends which had begun in late antiquity. Clear evidence of the process has emerged in a number of recent excavations: at Jerash, where extensive and well-built Umayyad houses have been discovered that spill out from the hillside onto the sidewalk and use the pillars of the colonnade as the cornerstones of the front wall. This privatization of previously public spaces can be seen again at Beisan/Scythopolis, where the Umayyad buildings occupy the sidewalk and parts of the main carriageway.

Market areas underwent the same sort of transformation. In 1934 Sauvaget published a famous model, demonstrating how the broad, colonnaded street of antiquity slowly evolved into the narrow, crowded *sūqs* of the premodern Near Eastern city.[23] It was a classic piece of theoretical archaeology but until recently there was no site where the crucial stages of this transformation could be directly observed. Excavations at Palmyra have, in a sense, provided the missing link.[24] Palmyra boasted one of the grandest of all classical street layouts.

The vast porticoed way which forms the spine of the plan was unsurpassed in its scale and the richness of its decoration. In the Umayyad period a *sūq* was built on the paving of the main street, consisting of narrow but substantially built stone booths which used the pillars of the classical design to frame their entrances. The main surface of the street was now completely blocked and passage was allowed only on the old sidewalk or along a narrow alley behind the shops.

More than thirty years after his death, Sauvaget's theory was triumphantly vindicated, except in its chronology. He argued that the "degradation" (as the value-laden language of the day put it) of the classical street had taken place in the Fatimid period in the 10th century, when, he argued, civic government disappeared, allowing traders to usurp the public spaces. Archaeological evidence has since proved beyond all reasonable doubt that this process began in late antiquity and gathered pace in the first Islamic century. But the legacy of antiquity was not entirely obliterated: in the three greatest cities of Syria—Jerusalem, Damascus, and Aleppo—the Roman street plan underlay and determined the street plan, not just in early Muslim times, but right down to the present day.

The Muslims did not simply occupy and develop ancient cities; they founded new ones as well. The most important of these were the major *amṣār* at Kufa and Basra in Iraq, Fustat in Egypt, and Qayrawān in North Africa, as well as the failed *miṣr* at Jabiya in Syria. The archaeological record for these *amṣār* is not very helpful. Fustat has produced a good deal of evidence, mostly from later periods but, as in the Iraqi examples, the early phases of urban development can be discerned only in very general outline from the written sources. Qayrawān is a stone-built town whose origins go back to the first century of Islam, but the urban history and topography of the site have not been investigated in depth.

The Islamic new towns in Syria are on a much smaller scale.[25] Two sites can be singled out for discussion: Anjar, near Baalbek in the Biqaa Valley; and Ayla (Aqaba), on the gulf of that name in the Red Sea. Both sites are comparatively small and very obviously planned, more or less square in shape and surrounded by walls with round interval towers and four gates, one in the center of each side. The plan within the walls at Anjar is well preserved, showing straight streets crossing in the center in a very classical manner. Another example of such planning is the small madina at Qaṣr al-Hayr al-Sharqi: again the city is surrounded by walls with towers.[26] Inside there is a regular pattern of dwellings and a mosque. At the center there is a large, square courtyard which originally had an arcade around it. The striking feature of all these foundations is the concern with formal urban planning.

How far such planning was a reflection of antique practice is doubtful: settlements of comparable size in late antiquity—Umm al-Jimal in the Hawran, or Subeita in the Negev, for example—show no such concern for order. As we have seen, the formal regularities of the classical city may not have been very apparent to the incoming Muslims. The distinction is probably not between late antique order and Muslim chaos but between planned and informal, organic growth in both cultures. The square enclosures with their regularly spaced towers are certainly reminiscent of Roman structures like the legionary fortresses of Lajjun, but before we assume that this form was entirely derived from ancient practice we should consider the evidence from Arabia.

At a site known today as Qaryat Faw, on the road from Najd and Yamama to Yemen, excavations have uncovered a *sūq* probably dating from the 3rd to the 5th century.[27] It consists of a square, walled enclosure about 30 × 25 m, with small square towers at the corners and on the middle of each side. There is one entrance. In the interior, shops, which in their present form postdate the enclosure wall, are arranged around a sub-rectangular court which contains a deep cistern. Outside the enclosure a secondary market has been found, less strongly defended but still within a rectangular wall. Qaryat Faw demonstrates that planned fortified settlements could be found in Arabia well before the coming of Islam or the Muslim conquests. Like the architecture of early mosques, the development of these fortified settlements seems to represent a fusion, or at least an interaction, of Arabian and antique forms.

One of the features which makes the archaeology of late antique Syria so interesting and important is the wealth of rural settlement. Remains of numerous villages have survived in areas such as the limestone massif of northern Syria and the Hawran. As far as we can tell from dated structures, most of these villages were constructed approximately between 350 and 550. These villages seem to reflect a thriving rural economy; much of the domestic architecture seems to demonstrate considerable affluence, with simple and massive but curiously elegant houses being found in large numbers, even in the most out-of-the-way communities. Most of the surviving examples of these villages are found in marginal areas, where there was little or no settlement in antiquity and none since the 8th or 9th centuries. The best known and most fully researched of these areas of rural settlement are to be found in the rolling limestone hills of northern Syria, between Antioch and Aleppo.[28] This distribution may be due to accidents of survival; settlements in more obviously inviting areas, like the plains around Tripoli or the vale of Jezreel, have been overbuilt. However, it is clear that late antiquity was an era of expanding settlement and it seems likely that the Syrian countryside was more densely populated in the 5th and early 6th century than at any period before the present century.

The importance of villages in this pattern of rural settlement should be noted. There are many affluent-looking houses in villages like Serjilla or Refada, but little evidence of large estates or latifundia. It is possible that estates and villages were owned by the numerous monasteries in the area. The only aristocratic rural residence which can be clearly identified is the mid 6th century complex of palace and church at Qaṣr Ibn Wardan, on the edge of the desert northeast of Hama. This was obviously the residence of a large landowner or military commander but, unfortunately, we have absolutely no indication who the builder might have been. The thriving village economy may have faltered in the late 6th century. These is very little evidence for the construction of new houses after this date (possibly simply reflecting that people no longer inscribed dates on their dwellings), and the series of plagues which ravaged the area from 540 onward must have taken their toll. Archaeological evidence from Dehes in northern Syria, the only site which has been subjected to systematic excavation, suggests that the houses continued in use during the first two centuries of Muslim rule, even if new houses were not being built.[29]

The early Islamic period also saw an expansion of rural settlement in marginal areas, but one very different in character. Whereas the settlements of late antiquity were largely villages inhabited by free peasants—a social structure reflected in the high quality of individual houses combined with a lack of overall planning—the settlements of the Umayyad period took the form of large estates with high-status buildings. These developments were undertaken and financed in the early 8th century by important members of the Umayyad family.

There were good fiscal reasons why they should do this. Because the early Islamic fiscal system assigned revenues from conquered lands to those people whose names were entered in the *diwan* for the area, there was a strong feeling—vigorously, sometimes violently defended—that money raised in a given province should be disbursed among the Muslims of that province. This feeling made it difficult for the Umayyad caliphs in Damascus to tap into provincial resources, and though they did secure a share of the revenues, it was never as much as they hoped for or needed. Even in Syria itself, much of the revenue was already hypothecated in this way and the opportunities for expanding the caliphs' resource bases were very limited. It was a principle of both Roman and Islamic law that "dead lands" which were brought into cultivation belonged to the cultivator. For the Umayyad ruling elite, bringing new land on the desert margins into cultivation was the most effective, sometimes the only, way of providing much-needed resources. Hence the need for large-scale agricultural development projects.

Such activities gave rise to what can fairly be described as the cult of the gentleman farmer in Umayyad times. The anecdotes which reflect this are mostly centered on the caliph Hishām, a figure renowned for his shrewdness in administrative and financial matters. He is often portrayed as a farmer or gardener, inspecting crops himself and giving instructions to his subordinates about the harvesting and marketing of produce. The literary evidence for the expansion of agriculture is fullest from Iraq, where we have descriptions of the building of new canals and the irrigation of large, previously uncultivated areas. As often, however, the best archaeological evidence comes from Syria. Two sites illustrate this phenomenon, Qaṣr al-Hayr West and Qaṣr al-Hayr East.

Qaṣr al-Hayr West lies on the course of the old highway between Damascus and Palmyra, in an area where dry farming on a large scale is impossible.[30] The Romans had built a dam at Habarqa in the nearby mountains to retain water for the use of troops in frontier garrisons but this fell into disuse in late antiquity. In Byzantine times a monastery was founded in the plains by the road where the later palace was to be. In the 720s the area was extensively developed. The reservoir behind the dam, which had become silted up, was brought back into use and a canal dug to bring water to the plains, where it was distributed to gardens, a watermill, a khan, a bathhouse, and a luxuriously decorated palace.

Qaṣr al-Hayr East lies deep in the Syrian desert, halfway between Palmyra and the Euphrates in an almost completely arid landscape. The site consists of two square buildings, both surrounded by walls with interval towers and a central courtyard. There is also a freestanding bathhouse. The larger complex was described in a (now lost) inscription as a madina or city and consists of a series of dwellings, a mosque, and an olive press, arranged in strict symmetry around a central court. The smaller enclosure has a series of chambers arranged around a court and has been interpreted as a khan or possibly as a palace. As with Qaṣr al-Hayr West, the water-harvesting arrangements are impressive. In this case rainwater was gathered in the shallow wadis around the site and canalized into a walled enclosure. The olive press and the possibility that the site was called Zaytuna, or olive grove, point to an agricultural function.

In both these estates, we can see the careful management of water allowing agriculture in areas which were not cultivated either before or since. The village civilization of late antiquity was replaced by a demesne farming regime in the early Islamic period but agricultural development continued. It was not until after the fall of the Umayyads and the creation of a centralized, land-tax-based government by the Abbasids in the 9th century that investment in these large-scale projects became unprofitable and was abandoned.

The transition from the world of late antiquity to that of early Islam was gradual and multifaceted. Society and culture in the area changed slowly but markedly between the 4th century coming of Christianity and the fall of the Umayyads in 747–750. Despite the change in official language and elite religion, early Islamic society built on and developed the late antique legacy. In many ways the great earthquake of 747 and the coming of the Abbasids in 750 mark a bigger break than the coming of Islam; they spelled the real end of late antiquity and with it the end of the prosperity of Syria's golden age. Perhaps the archaeological record shows it most clearly: between the death of Hārūn al-Rashīd in 809 and the coming of the Fatimids in 969 there is not a single extant dated monument in the entire area of greater Syria. The contrast with the vast building activity of late antiquity and the Umayyad period could not be more striking.

Notes

1. There is a large and growing literature on Syria in late antiquity. For a helpful introduction, see Clive Foss, "The Near Eastern Countryside in Late Antiquity: A Review Article" in J. Humphrey, ed., *The Roman and Byzantine Near East* (Journal of Roman Archaeology, Supplementary Series 14, 1995), 213–234. See also the three volumes of *The Byzantine and Early Islamic Near East*, ed. A. Cameron, L. Conrad, and

G. R. D. King (Princeton, 1992, 1994, 1995). For the Islamic conquest of Syria, see Fred Donner, *The Early Islamic Conquests* (Princeton, 1981), 91–155, and Walter Kaegi, *Byzantium and the Early Islamic Conquests* (Cambridge, Eng., 1992).

2. The Sassanian legacy to the early Islamic state is fully discussed in Michael Morony, *Iraq after the Muslim Conquest* (Princeton, 1984).

3. Irfan Shahid, "Heraclius and the Theme System: New Light from the Arabic," *Byzantion* 57 (1987): 391–403, and "Heraclius and the Theme System: Further Observations," *Byzantion* 59 (1989): 208–243.

4. The best English-language guide to the geography of Muslim Syria is still Guy Le Strange, *Palestine under the Moslems* (Cambridge, Eng., 1890).

5. C. J. Kraemer, ed., *Excavations at Nessana*, vol. 3: *Non-Literary Papyri* (Princeton, 1958).

6. For this suggestion see H. Kennedy, "The Financing of the Military in the Early Islamic State" in Cameron, *Byzantine and Early Islamic Near East III* (Princeton, 1995), 361–378.

7. On this Christian Arab tradition see Sidney H. Griffith, *Arabic Christianity in the Monasteries of 9th-Century Palestine* (Aldershot, 1992).

8. On taxation in early Islam, see D. C. Dennett, *Conversion and Poll-Tax in Early Islam* (Cambridge, Mass., 1950).

9. On this system see H. Kennedy, "The Financing of the Military in the Early Islamic State," in Cameron, *Byzantine and Early Islamic Near East*, 361–378.

10. See H. Kennedy, "The Barmakid Revolution in Early Islamic Government," in *Pembroke Papers*, ed. C. Melville (Cambridge, Eng., 1990), 89–98.

11. For a good recent discussion, see G. W. Bowersock, *Hellenism in Late Antiquity* (Cambridge, Eng., 1990).

12. There is a considerable literature on the Jews in late antique Palestine: see M. Avi-Yonah, *The Jews of Palestine: A Political History from the Bar Kokhba War to the Arab Conquest* (Oxford, 1976); G. Alon, *The Jews in Their Land in the Talmudic Age (70–640 C.E.)*, 2 vols. (Jerusalem, 1980; repr. Cambridge, Mass., 1988); and Averil Cameron, "The Jews in Seventh Century Palestine," *Scripta Classica Israelica* 13 (1994): 75–93.

13. For the Jews in early Islamic Palestine, see Moshe Gil, *A History of Palestine, 634–1099* (Cambridge, Eng., 1992), 490–776.

14. See William H. C. Frend, *The Rise of the Monophysite Movement* (Cambridge, Eng., 1972) and J. Meyendorff, *Imperial Unity and Christian Divisions* (New York, 1989).

15. For a general survey, see Gil, *History of Palestine*, 430–489.

16. For the Chalcedonian (Melkite) church in this period, see H. Kennedy, "The Melkite Church from the Islamic Conquest to the Crusades," in *17th International Byzantine Congress: The Major Papers* (New Rochelle, N.Y., 1986), 325–343.

17. There is no good survey of the Jacobite church in Syria in the early Islamic period, but see Morony, *Iraq after the Muslim Conquest*, 372–380, and the discussion of the Tur Abdin area (southern Turkey) in Andrew Palmer, *Monk and Mason on the Tigris Frontier* (Cambridge, Eng., 1990), 149–181.

18. Richard Bulliet, *Conversion to Islam in the Medieval Period* (Cambridge, Mass., 1979), 104–113.

19. The literature on these two buildings is vast. For a concise discussion of the early development of the mosque, see Robert Hillenbrand, *Islamic Architecture* (Edinburgh, 1994), 31–74. See also Oleg Grabar, *The Formation of Islamic Art* (New Haven, 1973).

20. For an overview of this subject, see H. Kennedy, "From Polis to Madina: Urban Change in Late Antique and Early Islamic Syria," *Past and Present* (1985): 3–27.

21. The fullest archaeological survey of an indivdual city in this period remains C. H. Kraeling, ed., *Gerasa: City of the Decapolis* (New Haven, 1938). For other important urban sites see Y. Tsafrir, "Beisan/Scythopolis" in King and Cameron, *Byzantine and*

Early Islamic Near East II (Princeton, 1994); Maurice Sartre, *Bostra: Des origines à l'Islam* (Paris, 1985); G. Downey, *Antioch in Syria* (Princeton, 1961). For the smaller towns of the Negev, see J. Shereshevski, *Byzantine Urban Settlements in the Negev Desert* (Jerusalem, 1991).

22. See the recent discussion of changing values in the late antique city in Annabel Wharton, *Refiguring the Post Classical City* (Cambridge, Eng., 1995).

23. Jean Sauvaget, "Le plan de Laodicée-sur-Mer," *Bulletin d'études orientales* 4 (1934): 81–116.

24. K. al-As'ad and F. M. Stepniowski, "The Umayyad Suq in Palmyra," *Damaszener Mitteilungen* 4 (1989): 205–223.

25. For these smaller towns, see A. Northedge, "Archaeology and New Urban Settlement in Early Islamic Syria and Iraq," in King and Cameron, *Byzantium and Early Islam,* II.

26. See the classic account: Oleg Grabar, *City in the Desert,* 2 vols. (Cambridge, Mass., 1978).

27. Described in A. R. Al-Ansary, *Qaryat al-Fau: A Portrait of Pre-Islamic Civilisation in Saudi Arabia* (London, 1981).

28. See the classic account: G. Tchalenko, *Villages Antiques de la Syrie du Nord,* 3 vols. (Paris, 1953–1958), and the more recent discussion in G. Tate, *Les campagnes de la Syrie du Nord du IIe au VIIe siècle* (Paris, 1992).

29. See J.-P. Sodini et al., "Dehes (Syrie du Nord) Campagnes I–III (1976–78): Recherches sur l'habitat rural," *Syria* 57 (1980): 1–304.

30. For this site, see D. Schlumberger, *Qasr El-Heir El Gharbi* (Paris, 1986).

The Good Life

Henry Maguire

In his tenth homily on Paul's Epistle to the Philippians, John Chrysostom, at that time patriarch of Constantinople, gave a vivid description of the good life as it was flaunted by the wealthy and powerful of his day. The preacher criticized the extravagance of the rich man's house, with its display of porticoes, columns, and precious marbles, its gilded ceilings, and its pagan statues. He spoke of the elaborate confections served in the dining room, made to satisfy the pleasure and vanity of the host. He complained of the clothes of the well-to-do, costing a hundred pieces of gold and worn in many layers, so that the wealthy appeared sweating beneath their finery. Finally, he ridiculed the rich men's wives, weighed down with jewelry and decked out like their mules and horses with gold.[1] This characterization of the prosperous lifestyle during late antiquity was not mere rhetorical exaggeration, for archaeology has shown that the picture painted by John Chrysostom was true. This essay reviews a selection from the abundant material evidence of domestic prosperity in late antiquity, including the interior furnishings of houses, the silver vessels used for eating, drinking, and bathing, silk clothing, and jewelry. I also look at imitations of these objects made in cheaper materials, through which the less fortunate emulated the success of the rich. The second part of the essay turns from the objects themselves to the images used to decorate them, which evoked the idea of prosperity in various ways, primarily through personifications, motifs drawn from nature, and mythology. Finally, I consider the attitudes toward those images that were adopted by Christianity, Judaism, and Islam, and the degree to which each religion opposed, assimilated, or rejected the visual expressions of domestic prosperity in late antiquity.

In the Roman and Byzantine worlds, marble was always an important emblem of wealth and consumption. The effect of this material upon the clientele of the wealthy aristocrats of Rome was described in scathing terms by the 4th century historian Ammianus Marcellinus: "Idle gossips frequent their houses, people who applaud with various flattering fictions every word uttered by those whose fortune is greater than their own . . . In the same way they admire the setting of columns in a high facade and the walls brilliant with carefully selected colors of marble, and extol their noble owners as more than mortal" (Amm.Marc. 23.4.12). Such late antique houses, featuring arcades with marble columns and walls expensively clad with marble revetments, have survived in nearby Ostia; a well-preserved example is the House of Cupid and Psyche, which featured a marble-lined dining room and a columnar arcade, as well as statuary of the type criticized by John Chrysostom, including the group of Cupid and Psyche that gave the house its modern name (fig. 1).[2] Many wealthy homes had floors covered with colorful tessellated mosaics. Among the best preserved are the 6th century pavements discovered in the Villa of the Falconer at Argos in Greece, which had a dining room looking out onto a courtyard that was surrounded on two sides by columnar porticoes. The floor of the *triclinium* (dining room) was decorated with a mosaic of Dionysus with satyrs and maenads, which was placed so that it could be admired by diners reclining on the couch set at the back of the room (fig. 2). The position of the semicircular couch is marked on the mosaic floor, together with that of the sigma-shaped table in front of it. Even the meal of two fish on a platter was indicated in the center of the table. The porticoes of the courtyard also were paved with mosaics. In front of the dining room were scenes of hunting with dogs and falcons, activities which provided food (ducks and hares) for the table (fig. 3). The other portico was decorated with personifications of the months holding their seasonal attributes (figs. 4 and 5).[3]

Textiles were very important in the decoration of late antique houses, although their effect is more difficult to visualize today than that of the splendid mosaic floors that have survived in their original locations. A luxurious copy of the poems of Virgil, possibly produced in Ravenna during the 6th century, contains a painting of Dido entertaining Aeneas in her palace which gives some idea of the contribution made by textiles to the late antique dining room: blue, green, and red hangings and swags cover the walls, white and purple cloths decorate the couch (fig. 6).[4] A number of domestic wall-hangings executed in tapestry weave, some of considerable size, have been excavated from graves in Egypt, where they had been used to wrap corpses for burial when they were no longer needed in the house. The rich imagery of these tapestries includes beneficent personifications (fig. 7); bearers of gifts (fig. 8); servants (fig. 9); trees, fruits, and flowers (fig. 10); animals and hunting scenes; and figures from mythology. Houses were also decorated with curtains, which were hung in doorways and between the columns of arcades. As may be seen from the example illustrated in figure 11, curtains were made of a lighter weight material than the wall-hangings, being typically woven of linen with intermittent repeat patterns executed with dyed woolen threads.[5] Such a curtain, decorated with a repeating pattern of flowers on a neutral ground, may be seen hung across a doorway in the 6th century mosaic of Empress Theodora and her retinue from the church of S. Vitale in Ravenna.[6]

Diners in late antiquity well appreciated the aura of luxury that finely woven textiles brought to a dining room. In one of his poems, the 5th century Gallic aristocrat Sidonius Apollinaris wrote how his experience of a feast was enriched by the red- and purple-dyed cloths of wool and linen that adorned the couch. He describes a textile woven with hunting scenes, showing hills and "beasts rushing over the roomy cloth, their rage whetted by a wound well counterfeited in scarlet," so that "at the seeming thrust of a javelin, blood that is no blood issues." On the same textile he admired the motif of the Parthian shot, in which "the Parthian, wild eyed and cunningly leaning over with face turned backwards, makes his horse go [forward] and his arrow return, flying from or putting to flight the pictured beasts" (*Epistulae* 9.13.5; trans. W. B. Anderson). Such couch-covers, woven with scenes of horseback riders hunting in landscapes, are depicted on the lids of some 3rd century Attic sarcophagi.[7] As for the Parthian shot, it is depicted in surviving textiles, such as a fragment of draw-loom silk now preserved in the treasury of St. Servatius at Maastricht, which dates to the 8th century (fig. 12).[8] Besides hunting scenes, textiles used to cover household furnishings were woven with many other figural subjects, as may be seen in the fragment of wool and linen tapestry weave in figure 13, which may have come from the border of a couch cover showing a series of beneficent personifications.[9] The rich 4th century silk shown in figure 14, depicting the Nile in his chariot accompanied by *putti*, aquatic creatures, and waterfowl, could also have been part of a spread or a cover, although its original function is uncertain.[10]

One further element of the furnishing of the late antique houses should be mentioned here, even if it is preserved only in the imagery of poets and weavers: in the aristocratic dining room a profusion of greenery and flowers provided color and fragrance, as is described in the poem by Sidonius: "Let the round table show linen fairer than snow, and be covered with laurel and ivy and vine-shoots, fresh and verdant. Let cytisus, crocus, starwort, cassia, privet, and marigolds be brought in ample baskets and color the sideboard and couches with fragrant garlands" (*Epistulae* 9.13.5).

Another feature of entertaining in late antiquity was the display and employment of a large variety of silver vessels for serving drink and food. The discovery of several hordes of late antique silver has shown the astonishing richness and variety of this ware; the 4th century treasure discovered at Kaiseraugst, on the river Rhine in Switzerland, for example, included a big rectangular salver, large circular and polygonal platters (fig. 15), dishes specially shaped for serving fish, bowls of various sizes, long- and short-handled spoons, wine strainers, beakers, an elaborate candlestick, a handbasin, and even toiletry implements such as toothpicks and ear cleaners.[11] Other treasures have contained silver jugs of various shapes and sizes, as well as sauce bowls equipped with lids and handles. The painting of Queen Dido's banquet in figure 6 shows some of this ware in use. The servant on the left offers a silver beaker of wine to the guests, which he has filled from the silver jug in his right hand (the artist has indicated the purple liquid at its brim). The servant on the right, who holds another silver jug and a long-handled silver bowl, is probably preparing to pour water over the hands of the guests to clean them. A good host was expected to keep his silver well polished, as we learn again from Sidonius Apollinaris, in a letter praising the Gothic king Theoderic II: "When one joins him at dinner . . . there is no unpolished conglomeration of discolored old silver set by panting attendants on sagging tables . . . The viands attract by their skillful cookery, not by their costliness, the platters by their brightness, not by their weight" (*Epistulae* 1.2.6). Much of this silver tableware was decorated, either with chasing or with motifs executed in relief; often the designs were enriched with niello or gilding. Fine examples of such pieces are the great platters from the Kaiseraugst and the Mildenhall treasures, which portray, respectively, scenes from the early life of Achilles (fig. 15) and a Bacchic revel surrounding a central mask of Ocean (fig. 16).[12] This kind of decoration, also, was described by Sidonius: "Let the attendants bend their heads under the metal carved in low relief, let them bring in lordly dishes on their laden shoulders" (*Epistulae* 9.13.5). Nor should one forget the repeated pleasures of the food that was served with such splendor: "I have overextended myself by eating everything," wrote the poet and bon vivant Venantius Fortunatus in the 6th century, "and my belly is swollen with various delicacies: milk, vegetables, eggs, butter. Now I am given dishes arranged with new feasts, and the mixture of foods pleases me more sweetly than before" (*Carmina* 11.22).

Silver vessels also played a prominent role in bathing, another luxury enjoyed in the houses of the rich. Late antique villas were frequently equipped with their own private bathhouses, some of which contained floor mosaics illustrating the rituals of cleanliness and beautification. One such mosaic has been preserved in the baths of a large villa discovered at Sidi Ghrib, in Tunisia (fig. 17). The mosaic, which dates to the late 4th or early 5th century, shows the lady of the house at her toilette. On the left, a maid proffers jewelry in a silver tray, while her mistress tries on an earring. Another maid holds up a mirror, so that the resulting effect can be admired. On either side of the mosaic appears the silver that has been used in bathing: to the left is a scalloped washbasin, similar to one that survives in the Kaiseraugst treasure, and a silver-gilt chest containing a towel or a garment.[13] A similarly shaped gilded chest was preserved in the mid 4th century treasure found on a slope of the Esquiline hill in Rome (fig. 18).[14] Such silver vessels, made expressly for bathing, were described about one hundred and fifty years earlier by the early Christian writer Clement of Alexandria, who wrote scornfully that women went to the public baths with "a great paraphernalia of vessels made of gold or silver, some for drinking the health of others, some for eating, and some for the bath itself . . . Parading with this silverware, they make a vulgar display of it in the baths" (*Paedagogus* 3.31).

Another way of publicly displaying one's wealth was through clothing, and especially through the wearing of patterned silks. Both pagan and Christian writers criticized the extravagance of such garments. Ammianus Marcellinus described the extreme fineness of the mantles worn by the Roman senators, which "were figured with the shapes of many different animals" and which shone when their wearers moved (14.6.9). A contemporary of Ammianus, Asterius, bishop of Amaseia, condemned the luxury of silks and the vanity of those who wore garments decorated with "lions and leopards, bears, bulls and dogs, forests and rocks, hunters and [in short] the whole repertory of painting that imitates nature." He also castigated those who wore garments decorated with scenes from the gospels. Such people, he declared, "devise for themselves, their wives and children gay-colored dresses decorated with thousands of figures . . . When they come out in public dressed in this fashion, they appear like painted walls to those they meet."[15]

The fashions evoked by these texts are borne out by images and by survivals of the textiles themselves. The mosaic of Theodora with her retinue in S. Vitale shows the ladies of her court wearing draw-loom silks with repeating patterns, including flowers and ducks. The empress herself has a gospel scene, the Adoration of the Magi, embroidered into the hem of her cloak. As for the male garments, a late 4th century silk tunic has been preserved in relatively good condition in the church of S. Ambrogio in Milan (fig. 19). Even if it may not have been the garment of the saint himself, as tradition would have it, the textile is almost certainly of his date. The tunic had a linen lining, over which was an outer layer of white silk damask woven all over with repeating designs of lions being hunted by men and dogs in a landscape evoked by trees and bushes.[16] Less expensive tunics had applied bands and roundels of silk rather than a continuous surface of the costly material, but the effect of these garments could still be rich (figs. 20 and 21).

As in the villa at Sidi Ghrib, late antique floor mosaics demonstrate the importance of jewelry in the self-image of the rich (fig. 17). A similar scene appears in the famous late 4th century mosaic of Dominus Iulius, which was found in a house at Carthage. Here scenes of the life of an estate revolve around the main house, depicted with its columned porticoes and its domed baths (fig. 22). At the lower left appears the mistress of the domain, leaning on a column and gazing at herself in a mirror, while she stretches out her hand languidly to receive a necklace proffered by a maid who holds the box containing her jewelry.[17] Magnificent examples of jewelry from late antiquity still survive. Two necklaces from the 7th century are illustrated in figures 23 and 24, one composed of eleven openwork plaques of gold set and hung with pearls and precious stones, and another adorned with a pendant portraying a golden Aphrodite in a lapis lazuli shell.[18]

The accouterments of the good life—the marbles, the silver, the silks, the gold, and the gems—were well enough appreciated to inspire imitation in cheaper materials. In North Africa, for example, panels of floor mosaic frequently imitated the veining of marble, which was a more expensive material; figure 25 illustrates a mosaic of the second half of the 4th century found at Thuburbo Majus which reproduces green "cipollino," a marble imported from Greece.[19] Such false marble panels were frequently installed at important places in the floor, such as at thresholds. On occasion, mosaic itself might be imitated in the medium of fresco. This occurred in the early Islamic period at the Umayyad palace of Qaṣr al-Hayr West, where there are floors paved with frescoes whose designs, characterized by hard-edged contrasts of color, imitate the effect of tessellated pavements (fig. 26).[20] Even the great tapestry wall-hangings, luxurious in themselves, imitated the greater luxury of spacious marble arcades and porticoes. This emulation explains the popularity of textile compositions that framed their subjects beneath arches or between columns, as seen in figures 8–10.

The imitation of silverware in ceramic is a phenomenon well attested for many periods and cultures, but it was especially pronounced in North Africa during late antiquity. Here potters decorated their earthenware vessels with raised motifs in imitation of the repoussé decoration of silver, and even went so far as to reproduce the shapes of rectangular silver vessels in clay, a form that could not be manufactured on the potter's wheel. They also copied the iconography associated with silverware, as can be seen in figure 27, which reconstructs part of a rectangular earthenware tray decorated in relief with scenes from the life of Achilles, similar to those appearing on the 4th century polygonal dish from Kaiseraugst (fig. 15). Even though these pottery dishes were cheaper imitations of more precious models in silver, they were prized by the poorer folk who owned them; in several cases there is evidence that the ceramics were repaired in antiquity.[21]

Silk-weaving was often imitated in less precious materials, as is shown by a medallion of the 7th century showing two mounted lion hunters which originally adorned a domestic textile such as a tunic (fig. 28). This piece, a tapestry weave of dyed woolen threads on linen, carefully reproduces the bilateral symmetry characteristic of silks produced on the draw loom.[22] The red ground and the border containing floral motifs are also copied from silks; compare the fragmentary silk medallion at Maastricht (fig. 12). The manufacturers of tapestry weaves even went so far as to imitate gold and jewelry in their humble materials. A particularly striking example is a fragment of a tunic woven in linen and wool with gold threads (fig. 29). This garment was decorated with two imitation necklaces at the neckline, one of which has pendants like the real piece of jewelry in figure 23.[23]

The houses and objects possessed by the rich and the would-be rich were adorned with images that expressed the prosperity projected and desired by their owners. It would be inaccurate to call these motifs decoration, which implies they had no function other than to provide visual delight to the beholder. Often these designs were invested with a stronger significance, which approached a numinous power; that is, the images were both an expression and an assurance of abundance.

In many cases the prosperity of the late antique house was illustrated literally, in compositions such as the Dominus Iulius mosaic from Carthage (fig. 22). In this mosaic the activities of the estate are focused on the ease and comfort of the owners, in a cyclical composition that evokes the gifts of the seasons. Immediately above the representation of the villa sits the lady, fanning herself as she receives offerings from her servants: ducks and a basket of olives on the left, and a lamb on the right. At the lower left she is presented with jewelry, as we have seen, and also with a fish and a basket full of roses, while on the right sits the master of the estate, who receives birds, a basket of grapes, and a hare. Similar imagery of servants or personifications bringing gifts can be found on tapestry hangings. In one example we find two attendants under jeweled arches, one carrying a fish and three pomegranates, and the other holding a bowl and a small elongated flask of a kind that could have contained scent for sprinkling over the hands of guests (fig. 8). (This recalls the line "iuvat ire per corollas / alabastra ventilantes" ["It is pleasant to pass through garlands while swinging perfume boxes"] in Sidonius's description of a feast, *Epistulae* 9.13.5.) A fragment of another hanging shows a servant pulling back a curtain hanging between two columns (fig. 9); it evokes a privileged setting, where, at the appointed time, curtains are drawn aside by the hands of half-hidden minions.[24]

Beneficent female personifications were a popular presence in the household. While many of these personifications alluded to moral qualities, and may have had Christian overtones, they also evoked material wealth, prosperity, and security. They include Ktisis (Foundation or Creation), Kosmēsis (Ordering or Adornment), Ananeōsis (Renewal), and Sotēria (Security or Salvation). To these may be added personifications more directly associated with physical prosperity, such as Tychē Kalē (Good Fortune), Apolausis (Enjoyment), and Hestia Polyolbos (the Blessed Hearth). The last-named is depicted in a splendid 6th century wool tapestry that was woven to be fitted into an arched niche (fig. 7). As often with these personifications, Hestia Polyolbos is richly dressed. She wears a heavy jeweled necklace and pendant earrings, and is enthroned like the mistress of an estate flanked by her attendants. The six boys who approach her on either side hold disks inscribed with her blessings, namely "wealth," "joy," "praise," "abundance," "virtue," and "progress."[25] Hestia Polyolbos is clearly identified by an inscription above her head, but frequently the richly attired female personifications were left unnamed, as unspecific beneficent presences. Such a figure, wearing a pearl headband, a pearl necklace, and pearl pendants on her earrings, can be seen in the fragment of tapestry band illustrated in figure 13.

Another group of propitious personifications evoked nature and its cycles: the earth, the ocean, the seasons, and the months. The seasons and months were often depicted in floor mosaics, as in the 6th century villa at Argos, where each of the personified months holds the attributes appropriate to it (fig. 4). Since many of these attributes are in the form of seasonal produce enjoyed by the owner of the villa—such as ducks from February, a lamb from April, a basket of flowers from May, and grain from June—the months in effect take the place of the servants who catered to the owners' pleasure on the Dominus Iulius mosaic from Carthage (fig. 22). A similar promise was embodied in the personifications of the earth and the ocean, which occurred not only in floor mosaics but also on a smaller scale in textiles worn as clothing. The fragment of silk illustrated in figure 20 originally formed half of one of the two sleeve bands of a tunic. The complete band depicted the earth surrounded by the ocean;

Earth was personified by four repeated busts of a crowned woman wearing a heavily jeweled collar and holding up a fruit-laden cloth in front of her chest, and the ocean was signified by means of fishes and water plants in the border. A similar personification of Earth was portrayed elsewhere on the garment, in medallions at the ends of the four bands that descended from the shoulders, and in four small circles that were affixed to the lower part of the tunic at the level of the knees.[26] These motifs, which miniaturized the abundance of the whole earth into a small charm repeated sixteen times on the same garment, illustrate the magical potential of these personifications of the power of nature. The silk tunic band in figure 21 shows at the bottom a similar female personification, wearing a crown and a jeweled collar; here she accompanies birds, plants, and hunting scenes, which signify the terrestrial domain.[27] Ocean, also, appeared on household objects, such as the magnificent platter from the 4th century Mildenhall treasure, where he appears as a mask with dolphins leaping from his hair and beard at the center of a marine *thiasos* of nereids riding upon sea beasts (fig. 16). Like the personification of Earth, Ocean had both a metaphorical and a magical value. According to John Chrysostom, in 4th century Antioch a public benefactor could be compared by grateful citizens to the ocean on account of his generosity: "he in his lavish gifts is what the Ocean is among waters."[28] But it was also possible for the personification to have protective value, as is demonstrated by a mosaic discovered at Ain-Témouchent, near Sétif, in Algeria. Here a head of Ocean with enlarged eyes is accompanied by an inscription invoking the gaze of the mask as protection from the misfortunes caused by envy (fig. 30).[29]

Another subject that conveyed good fortune was the river Nile with its flora and fauna, for the flooding of the Nile was seen as emblematic of prosperity not only in Egypt itself but in much of the Mediterranean world. The imagery of Nilotic abundance was evoked in a pagan hymn, written around the year 300:

> Fishes and not oxen dwell in the plain,
> for the Nile inundated the land formerly accessible by foot . . .
> Dark earth, you flourish in your water which produces corn.
> Be gracious king of the rivers, Nile nourisher of children . . .
> You are present bringing to mortals full baskets.[30]

The motifs of this hymn—the fishes, the children, the baskets, the abundance of produce—were reproduced on textiles, on tableware, and on floors. In the 4th century silk illustrated in figure 14, the personified river is accompanied by *putti* holding wreaths and garlands and by a variety of aquatic creatures. Sometimes the Nilotic subject matter is accompanied by an inscription specifying its propitious value. This can be seen in the case of a large 5th or 6th century mosaic, recently excavated in a secular building at Sepphoris, in Galilee. It displays a variety of conventional motifs, including the personified Nile accompanied by the usual aquatic plants and birds; a personification of Egypt reclining on a basket full of fruit and holding a cornucopia; and boys engaged in engraving the high-water mark on a nilometer. All of this is accompanied by an inscription in the border enjoining the viewer to "Have good fortune."[31]

The wealth of earth and sea was invoked not only by personifications, but also by the numerous portrayals of animals and plants throughout the home. The rich acanthus borders of the floor mosaics in the Villa of the Falconer at Argos are inhabited by a variety of creatures, including birds such as ducks and waders, reptiles such as snakes and lizards, and mammals such as rabbits and deer, together with fruits and vegetables (fig. 5). While these motifs undoubtedly provided visual pleasure to the beholder, they also gave an assurance of continuing life and prosperity. Birds were especially favored as a decoration on textiles, whether curtains (fig. 11) or the silks worn by the ladies at court. Plants and their products appeared in numerous guises. Large tapestry hangings portrayed lines of trees (fig. 10)—in one case at least eight in a row.[32] The significance of such representations is indicated by a fragment of a curtain which depicts a tree in full leaf with the invocation *Euphori* ("Flourish!") written upon its trunk (fig. 31).[33] Sometimes the imagery of plants was enhanced by the richness of gems, as can be seen in the case of the 6th or 7th century tunic band in figure 21, where the central motif, a stylized plant crowned by a pomegranate, rises from a jeweled vase.

In this evocation of plenty and abundance through images drawn from nature, there was a supporting role for the old pagan deities, even if the patrons were Christian. The domestication of pagan gods in Christian households can be seen both in art and in literature. The epithalamia of Dioscorus of Aphrodito, a 6th century Egyptian lawyer whose father had founded a monastery, strikingly combine references to Zeus, Ares, Apollo, Heracles, Dionysus, Ariadne, Demeter, and other deities with invocations to the Christian God. In the poem for the wedding of Count Callinicus and Theophile, for example, which he wrote sometime before 570, he declared: "You [the bridegroom] raise up the honey-sweet grape-cluster, in its bloom of youth; Dionysos attends the summer of your wedding, bearing wine, love's adornment, with plenty for all, and blond Demeter brings the flower of the field . . . They have woven holy wreaths round your rose-filled bedroom." In another epithalamium, for the wedding of Isakios, Dioscorus invokes "garlanded Dionysos" and "the Nile with his many children," before exclaiming "Go away, evil eye; this marriage is graced by God."[34] This easy combination of nature imagery with the evocation of pagan deities in the context of a Christian wedding finds a parallel two centuries earlier in the reliefs on the casket of Projecta, where the toilette of the bride is mirrored by a marine Venus portrayed on the lid (fig. 18). Here, in spite of the explicit evocation of the pagan goddess, the Christian orientation of bride and groom is not in doubt, for on the rim of the casket's lid appears the inscription *Secunde et Projecta vivatis in Chri[sto]* ("Secundus and Projecta, may you live in Christ").

The appearance of pagan deities on domestic furnishings from late antiquity should not, therefore, necessarily be taken as evidence of outright paganism on the part of their owners; rather, the pagan motifs should be read as embodying ideas of plenty and good fortune. The 4th century treasure from Mildenhall in

Suffolk contained both spoons engraved with the Christian Chi-Rho monogram and dishes decorated with figures from pagan mythology. The latter included the great platter with its central mask of Ocean surrounded by a Bacchic
revel portraying the drinking contest of Dionysus and Hercules in the company
of dancing satyrs and maenads (fig. 16). These subjects, in the eyes of many
Christians as well as pagans, evidently signified the respective gifts of the waters
and the earth, the seafood and the wine that should accompany a feast.[35]
Likewise, the woman of the 7th century who wore the gold and lapis lazuli
pendant portraying Aphrodite was probably a Christian (fig. 24); but she may,
nevertheless, have hoped that her charm might bring her some good things.
Such a wish is expressed by a 5th century mosaic discovered in a bath building
at Alassa on the island of Cyprus, which depicts the goddess beautifying herself
under the inscription EP AGATHOIS ("for a good cause").[36]

The late antique repertoire of images drawn from nature was not confined to
the homes of pagans and Christians; some of it survived into the decoration of
early Islamic palaces. It formed a common cultural frame of reference, evocative of well-being and prosperity, which was not the exclusive preserve of one
faith. For example, the offering of the products of the land, a theme depicted in
floor mosaics and textiles (see figs. 4, 8, and 22), also appears in the 8th century
stucco reliefs set into the courtyard facades of Qaṣr al-Hayr West, where there
are attendants holding, among other things, pomegranates, birds, lambs, and
vases filled with flowers.[37] One of the frescoed floors in the palace at Qaṣr
al-Hayr West even portrays a personification of the Earth (fig. 26). As in the silk
tunic ornaments discussed above (fig. 20), she is portrayed in a medallion as a
bust-length figure holding a scarf in front of her, while the surrounding ocean is
evoked by aquatic creatures, in this case marine centaurs. The fresco is bor-
dered by vine scrolls containing bunches of grapes, a motif also frequently
encountered in pre-Islamic art (compare the borders of the casket of Projecta,
shown in fig. 18). Although it would certainly be possible to read into this
fresco a political meaning of conquest and hegemony, given its presence in a
palace of the Umayyad rulers, its motifs also belonged to a common vocabulary
of abundance inherited from late antiquity.[38]

Even though the evidence of material culture demonstrates that many Christians were perfectly happy to accept pagan imagery into their houses, there was
also an undercurrent of opposition and unease. Sidonius Apollinaris, in a description of a villa at Avitacum, praised its bath building because its walls were
unadorned concrete: "Here no disgraceful tale is exposed by the nude beauty of
painted figures, for though such a tale may be a glory to art it dishonors the
artist . . . there will not be found traced on those spaces anything which it
would be more proper not to look at; only a few lines of verse will cause the
new-comer to stop and read" (*Epistulae* 2.2.5–7). This somewhat puritanical
viewpoint, with its disapproval of nudity and pagan myth, finds some confirmation in the archaeological record, for there are a few instances in which figural
images were removed from the floor mosaics of houses. A case in point is the

so-called House of the Sea Goddess at Seleucia, near Antioch. In one of the rooms of this villa, the late 5th or early 6th century floor mosaic exhibited the heads of four female personifications set in medallions, which were excised at a later period and replaced with slabs of marble.³⁹ A similar intervention occurred in a pavement of the baths of a Roman house at El Haouria, in Tunisia, where there was a frontal mask of Ocean accompanied by an apotropaic inscription against envy, similar to the mosaic of the same subject at Ain-Témouchent (fig. 30). Some time after the setting of the mosaic at El Haouria, the face of the mask was carefully picked out, leaving behind only Ocean's curved beard and the claws that had projected from his hair. The images that had framed the mask in the four corners of the composition, *erotes* and hippocamps, were allowed to remain, presumably because they were deemed to be more innocuous.⁴⁰

Such archaeologically attested instances of the destruction of mosaics with pagan connotations in private houses give credence to certain stories in the saints' lives that might otherwise be dismissed as pure fantasy. One is found in the biography of St. Eutychius, a 6th century patriarch of Constantinople, which was written by his pupil Eustratius. It relates the story of a young artist residing at Amaseia in the Pontos, who was made to remove an old mosaic representing the story of Aphrodite from the walls of a private house. The mosaic was inhabited by a demon, who got his revenge upon the young man by causing his hand to become so severely infected that it had to be amputated. Eventually, the hand was restored through the agency of St. Eutychius, after which the grateful artist set up the saint's image in the house, in the place of the pagan goddess.⁴¹ The story demonstrates that some Christians of the 6th century opposed and feared the pagan imagery that was still current in domestic contexts, even while other Christians were prepared to accept it.

In addition to these instances of domestic iconoclasm, there are other cases in which it may be possible to speak of private patrons manipulating traditional iconographic schemes so as to avoid the representation of pagan deities. For example, a curious mosaic survives on the floor of one of the three apses of a luxurious dining room attached to a large house north of the Antonine baths in Carthage (fig. 33). According to the latest investigations, the mosaic probably dates to some time after the beginning of the 5th century. The central subject of the floor was an open domed *tholos,* beneath which four boys danced with a garland held in their outspread hands against a background scattered with flowers. On either side of the *tholos* were projecting wings, above which grew fruiting vines.⁴² This scene, which appears to make the domed building the central focus of the design, has no direct parallels in North African art. It is, however, reminiscent of later mosaics from Christian Monophysite and Islamic contexts, which eschewed portrayals of sacred figures in favor of buildings and plants (see fig. 42).⁴³ The mosaic at Carthage can be related to a composition that was relatively frequent in North African mosaics of the 4th century, namely a central shrine containing the image of a pagan deity, flanked by motifs such as creatures, plants, and dancers that were suggestive of abundance. Such a mosaic was excavated in another house at Carthage (fig. 33). Dating to the first half of the 4th century, it shows Venus sitting on an island beneath an open domed structure supported on columns, with flowers and garlands spread at her feet, and with a chorus of dwarfs and musicians dancing in boats on either side.[44] We know that pagan art was an especially sensitive subject in Carthage at the turn of the 4th and the 5th centuries; archaeology shows that at this time it was even necessary for some householders to hide their pagan statuary in the basement.[45] It is possible, therefore, that the mosaic of the *tholos* represents one patron's solution to the problem. He has preserved the ebullient motifs of the frame—the elaborate domed building, the flowers, and the dancers—but the offending deity has been removed.

If Christians were occasionally unsure about the suitability of personifications and pagan deities as decoration for their houses, it might be assumed that they would be even more reluctant to admit such images to their places of worship. However, after a brief phase at the end of the 4th century during which aniconic floors were in favor, the repertoire of images from nature that had expressed domestic well-being began to make itself increasingly at home in churches.[46] By the 6th century, in spite of earlier condemnations of domestic luxury, ecclesiastical buildings were displaying much of the visual splendor that was characteristic of a magnate's villa or palace.[47] They avoided explicit portrayals of pagan myths, but minor pagan deities such as Pan might occasionally slip into the decoration of church pavements.[48] The naves and aisles of church buildings, which Christian cosmographic interpretations identified with the earth, exhibited nature personifications as well as a rich repertoire of creatures and plants, motifs that could be subject to Christian allegorization on the part of the patron or the viewer.[49] A good example of such decor is provided by the newly excavated church at Petra, in Jordan. Here the nave, the sanctuary, and the central apse were covered with an expensive *opus sectile* pavement of purple sandstone and imported marble, but the two side aisles were carpeted in the 6th century with the cheaper medium of tessellated mosaic. The mosaic in the north aisle displayed a vine scroll filled with a rich assortment of motifs evocative of the earth and its produce, including birds and beasts of various kinds, trees, baskets and fruits, and vases, goblets, and bowls. The south aisle portrayed more creatures of land, air, and sea, together with personifications of the earth, the ocean, the four seasons, and wisdom. The season of summer appeared as a bare-breasted woman wearing earrings and brandishing a sickle (fig. 34), while Ocean was portrayed as a half-nude man distinguished, as in the domestic mosaics, by claws growing from his hair.[50] These bold personifications have parallels in other 6th century churches, for example in the nave mosaic of the East Church at Qaṣr-el-Lebia in Libya, dated to 539–540, where the four rivers of Paradise (Gihon, Pishon, Tigris, and Euphrates) are portrayed as reclining nude figures, in the same manner as pagan river gods; they are joined in this composition by the pagan oracular spring Castalia, now converted by the power of Christ (fig. 35).[51] Several churches preserve Nilotic scenes, among the finest examples being the 5th century floor mosaics in the transepts of the

Church of the Multiplication of the Loaves and the Fishes at Tabgha in Galilee,[52] and the carvings on the westernmost of the wooden beams over the nave
of the church at Mount Sinai, which date from between 548 and 565 (fig. 36).[53]

Such evocations of the powers of nature in the context of Christian churches
became possible because of a new way of thinking which saw them as subjects,
rather than as rivals, of Christ. In one of his epithalamia, the 6th century poet
Dioscorus of Aphrodito bound the power of the Nile to Christ in order to
convey a blessing on the bride and groom: "Easily protecting . . . the Nile with
his many children, may God grant a superlative marriage free from the accursed
envy of others."[54] A 6th century papyrus from Antinoe in Egypt contains a
hymn addressed to the Nile which begins in a manner reminiscent of pagan
invocations, but closes with an appeal to the Christian deity:

> O most fortunate Nile, smilingly have you watered the land;
> rightly do we present to you a hymn . . .
> you are full of wonders in all Egypt, a remedy for men and for beasts;
> [you have brought] the awaited season . . .
> the fruit of your virtue is very great . . .
> you have displayed to us a strange miracle;
> you have brought the benefits of the heavens . . .
> True illumination, Christ, benefactor, [save] the souls of men, now and
>   [forever].[55]

There is nothing explicitly Christian about most of this poem. Only at its end is
there a prayer to Christ, the true source of the river's power. It is as if the
supplicant is appealing to the river as Christ's agent, almost in the same way
one might appeal to a saint.

By the 5th century a nave pavement decorated with creatures and plants was
considered to be a typical part of a church, as is demonstrated by a tomb
mosaic from a church at Tabarka, in Tunisia (fig. 37). The mosaic depicts a
basilica labeled Ecclesia Mater, symbolizing the reception of the deceased into
the eternal repose of the church. In an "exploded" view, we are shown the apse,
the altar, the interior colonnades, the clerestory windows, and the tiles of the
roof. Only the further line of columns, on the south side of the building, is
depicted at full height, from the bases to the capitals. The nearer line of columns, on the north side of the church, is cut off at half height, so as not to
obscure the south side of the church from the spectator's view. Between the
truncated columns appear glimpses of the floor mosaic, which is composed of
different types of birds and plants.[56] While one might assume that the creator of
this panel, being himself a mosaicist, would have a particular interest in floors,
it is striking that the pavement, with its motifs drawn from nature, is the only
part of the building's decoration to have been shown. But such motifs, as we
have seen, were not confined to floors. They flourished also on the fittings of the
church, whether they were carved in wood, such as doors and ceiling beams
(fig. 36), or in stone, such as chancel screens, pulpits, and capitals. Walls and

vaults also received decoration evoking the profusion of terrestrial creation, as is shown by the mid 6th century mosaic that arches over the chancel of S. Vitale in Ravenna (fig. 38).[57] This composition in green and gold, with its scrolling plant rinceaux bearing fruit and flowers and framing several species of beasts, birds, and reptiles, is a richer version of the borders of the mosaics in the provincial villa at Argos (fig. 5).

A similar imagery of abundance was incorporated into the decoration of Jewish synagogues during the late antique period, although with a somewhat more restricted repertoire than in Christian churches. A popular composition for the floors of synagogues, which has been found at several locations, is represented by a 4th century pavement discovered at Hammath Tiberias. Here the widest of the four aisles of the hall, leading to the raised alcove that contained the Torah chest, displays a handsome mosaic divided into three sections (fig. 39). The southern section, closest to the Torah niche, contains signs of the Jewish faith, such as the Ark of the Law, menorahs, and other ritual objects. The northern section contains inscriptions naming founders or donors, flanked and watched over by two lions which also serve as guardians of the entrance. The largest of the sections represents at its center Helios, shown as a young man with a halo, riding in his chariot within a circular frame containing the signs of the zodiac. The circular border is itself framed by a square, in the four corners of which appear personifications of the seasons holding their attributes.[58] Thus the biggest section of the floor evokes the cycle of the year and the good things brought by the seasons. Even though it is set beside a panel containing cultic images and another invoking blessings upon members of the congregation, it has few specifically Jewish elements; most of its subjects can be found depicted in the houses of the pagans.[59] A similar composition—Helios surrounded by the signs of the zodiac and the four seasons, the Ark of the Law, and the menorahs—is found in the 6th century floor mosaic of a synagogue at Na'aran, but here with the addition of a geometric carpet of octagons and circles filled with fruits, baskets, and creatures of earth, sea, and air. In addition, this pavement contains a biblical subject: the Prophet Daniel is depicted standing in prayer in front of the Ark, flanked by two large lions.[60]

Another composition that is found on several synagogue floors is the inhabited vine scroll, which occurs at Gaza, Ma'on, and Beth Shean. The medallions framed by these vines contain a wide variety of creatures, both the more common species such as snakes and hares, and relatively exotic ones such as zebra and giraffe. In addition, the vines at Ma'on and Beth Shean contain specifically Jewish symbols, such as the menorah. Other motifs displayed on these floors include bowls, vases, baskets, and fruit. Inscriptions set into the medallions of the mosaics or adjacent to them commemorate the donors of the pavements and, at Beth Shean, the artist ("Remembered be for good the artisan who made this work").[61] These floors, which all date to the 6th century, closely resemble depictions of inhabited vines appearing in Christian churches, such as the basilica discovered at Shellal, which is dated by an inscription to the year 561–62.[62]

Such figured floors were not confined to synagogues in Palestine. A pavement presenting a large repertoire of creatures was found in a synagogue at Hamman Lif (Naro), eleven miles from Tunis (fig. 40). Here the main hall was carpeted with mosaics depicting, among other motifs, fishes hooked on lines; ducks, quails, and peacocks; a lion, a hare, and a bull; as well as palm trees and baskets of fruit and possibly bread. All of these images surrounded the inscription of the donor, Juliana, which stated that she had at her own expense provided the mosaic for her salvation.[63]

As in the case of the Christian churches, these motifs from nature were capable of specific symbolic interpretation on the part of the faithful. Lions, for example, could represent Judah, or, as at Na'aran, they could refer to the salvation of Daniel. The continuing underlying message, however, was always of well-being and prosperity. And among the Jews, as among the Christians, there was a current of opposition to these motifs. In a recently discovered synagogue at Sepphoris there is a pavement depicting the chariot of the sun surrounded, as at Hammath Tiberias, by the signs of the zodiac and the seasons. In this case, however, the chariot is not driven by the personified Helios, but instead carries the sun itself, represented by a circle surrounded by rays.[64] It may be surmised that those who commissioned the mosaic were uncomfortable with the portrayal of the sun as a human figure. In this case an image redolent of paganism was avoided at the initial creation of the mosaic, but there were also several cases of floors whose images were removed after they had been laid, as can be seen in the mosaics at Na'aran, where not only the human figures but even the beasts and the birds were carefully picked out of their frames. The date at which these interventions took place has not yet been determined, but since the iconoclasts were often at pains to preserve the Hebrew letters, it seems to have been the Jews themselves who undertook the destruction.[65]

Islamic attitudes to figural representations excluded much of the late antique imagery of abundance from their religious architecture, where the portrayal of living creatures was scrupulously avoided. This absence of figural motifs left only plants and vegetation to evoke the fecundity of organic nature within the confines of cult buildings. Such a decoration may be seen in the late 7th century wall mosaics of the Dome of the Rock in Jerusalem, where plant forms of various kinds spring from jeweled vases and cornucopias (fig. 41).[66] In their design, some of these plants and gems recall the ornaments of tunics, such as the one illustrated in figure 21. The most extensive employment of plant forms in the decoration of an early Islamic religious building is to be found in the courtyard mosaics of the Great Mosque at Damascus, which date to the early 8th century (fig. 42). These mosaics, which present lines of trees, some with fruit and some without, interspersed with buildings, are devoid of any portrayal of living creatures, but show a striking variety of arboreal species.[67] Their overall effect recalls not only the earlier floor mosaics of villas set in bucolic surroundings (fig. 22), but also the tapestry hangings, displaying different varieties of trees together with architectural features such as columns, that were displayed on the walls of wealthy houses (fig. 10).[68] Whatever the symbolic meanings that could be projected upon the Jerusalem and Damascus mosaics by Muslim viewers, their ancestry lay in the imagery of well-being that had characterized the domestic environment of late antiquity.

At Damascus portrayals of living creatures were avoided, but in mosques there were also instances in which figural elements were deliberately destroyed. This happened at the Great Mosque of Kairouan, constructed in the 9th century, which contained sculptures appropriated from earlier Byzantine buildings, most of which must have been churches.[69] Many of the reused Byzantine capitals were of the two-zone type with projecting animal protomes at the corners. The Islamic builders of the mosque carefully cut off the features of the birds and beasts of the protomes, ingeniously converting them into nonfigural elements of the capital, such as volutes (fig. 43). The other decorative elements of the capital, however, such as leaves and cornucopia filled with fruits, they allowed to remain; in some cases the wings of the birds were recut and redrilled to become leaves. As in the mosaics of the Great Mosque of Damascus, some elements of the late antique imagery were preserved—the foliage and the horns of plenty— while the objectionable figural motifs were excised.

The material trappings of the good life in late antiquity, especially as it was enjoyed in the domestic sphere, displayed a rich imagery of personifications and motifs drawn from nature that evoked prosperity in the homes of the well-to-do. This imagery was a common frame of reference for pagans, Christians, Jews, and Muslims alike, but it was not completely neutral; it was sufficiently powerful to provoke opposition, demonstrated both by texts and by iconoclastic interventions in the monuments themselves. Nevertheless, many of the motifs that expressed abundance and well-being were eventually incorporated into the decoration of cult buildings after the removal of elements that were deemed unacceptable—such as the major pagan deities in the case of the Christians, or living creatures in the case of the Muslims. The Christians went the furthest in introducing the imagery of abundance into their places of worship; their permissiveness in this respect may even have contributed, by way of reaction, to the later adoption of stricter stances on the part of Jews and Muslims.[70] Borrowing much of the iconography of secular abundance and pleasure, the Christian authorities converted the good life dominated by the late Roman aristocrats into a good life that was controlled by the church. Thus, while the deities changed, the rich frames within which they had been presented survived.

Even among the Christians, however, there was an undercurrent of unease at this assimilation, and in the end the frames themselves came under increasing suspicion. The iconoclastic controversy of the 8th and 9th centuries, although primarily concerned with sacred portraiture, sensitized Christians anew to the issue of the suitability of motifs drawn from nature as a decoration for churches. John of Damascus wrote in the 8th century: "Is it not far more worthy to adorn all the walls of the Lord's house with the forms and images of saints rather than with beasts and trees?"[71] A famous passage in the iconodule Life of St. Stephen the Younger accuses the iconoclast Emperor Constantine V of scraping the pictures of Christ's miracles off the walls of the church at the Blachernae, and replacing them with mosaics representing "trees and all kinds of birds and beasts, and certain swirls of ivy leaves [enclosing] cranes, crows, and peacocks," thus turning the building into a "store-house of fruit and an aviary."[72] After iconoclasm, there was little place in medieval Byzantine churches for elaborate tessellated floors with animals and personifications from nature; these motifs were, in many churches, replaced by aniconic compositions in intarsia, which did not compete with the sacred company depicted upon the walls.[73] Hereafter, the good life was to be lived with the saints, not with the wealth imaged by the material world.[74]

Notes

I thank Stephen Zwirn for his critical reading of this essay.

1. *PG* 62.259–264.
2. G. Becatti, "Case Ostiensi del Tardo Impero," *Bollettino d'Arte* 33 (1948): 105–107.
3. Gunilla Åkerström-Hougen, *The Calendar and Hunting Mosaics of the Villa of the Falconer in Argos* (Stockholm, 1974).
4. Vatican Library, ms. lat. 3867, fol. 100v. Facsimile and commentary: Carlo Bertelli et al., *Vergilius Romanus, Codex Vaticanus Latinus 3867*, 3 vols. (Zurich, 1985–1986).
5. Eunice Dauterman Maguire et al., *Art and Holy Powers in the Early Christian House* (Urbana, 1989), 48.
6. Friedrich Wilhelm Deichmann, *Ravenna: Hauptstadt des spätantiken Abendlandes*, vol. II, 2, *Kommentar* (Wiesbaden, 1976), 180–187.
7. Friedrich Matz, *Die dionysischen Sarkophage* (Berlin, 1968), vol. 1, nos. 11–11A, pls. 18, 22.
8. Annemarie Stauffer, *Die mittelalterlichen Textilien von St. Servatius in Maastricht* (Riggisberg, 1991), 102–103.
9. Maguire, *Art and Holy Powers*, 51.
10. Mechthild Flury-Lemberg, *Textile Conservation* (Bern, 1988), 412–420.
11. Herbert A. Cahn and Annemarie Kaufmann-Heinimann, *Der spätrömische Silberschatz von Kaiseraugst* (Derendingen, 1984).
12. Ibid., 1: 225–315; K. S. Painter, *The Mildenhall Treasure* (London, 1977), 26.
13. Abdelmagid Ennabli, "Les thermes du thiase marin de Sidi Ghrib," *Monuments et Mémoires*, Fondation Eugène Piot, 68 (1986): 42–44.
14. Kathleen J. Shelton, *The Esquiline Treasure* (London, 1981), 72–75.
15. *Homilia I; PG* 40.165–168; trans. Cyril Mango, *The Art of the Byzantine Empire, 312–1453* (Englewood Cliffs, N.J., 1972), 50–51.
16. Alberto de Capitani d'Arzago, *Antichi tessuti della Basilica Ambrosiana* (Milan, 1941), 15–67; Hero Granger Taylor, "The Two Dalmatics of St. Ambrose?" *Bulletin de Liaison du CIETA* 57/8 (1983): 127–173.
17. Wulf Raeck, "Publica non despiciens," *Mitteilungen des Deutschen Archäologischen Instituts, Römische Abteilung*, 94 (1987): 295–308.
18. Kurt Weitzmann, *Age of Spirituality* (New York, 1979), 310, 313–314.

19. Margaret A. Alexander et al., *Corpus des Mosaiques de Tunisie*, vol. 2.4, *Thub-urbo Majus* (Tunis, 1994), 100.

20. Richard Ettinghausen, *Arab Painting* (Geneva, 1962), 33–35.

21. J. W. Salomonson, "Late Roman Earthenware," *Oudheidkundige Mededelingen* 43 (1962): 56, 74–81, 89.

22. W. Fritz Volbach, *Il tessuto nell'arte antica* (Milan, 1966), 74–76.

23. Jutta-Annette Bruhn, *Coins and Costume in Late Antiquity* (Washington, D.C., 1993), 33–34.

24. Larry Salmon, "An Eastern Mediterranean Puzzle," *Boston Museum of Fine Arts Bulletin* 67 (1969): 136–150.

25. Paul Friedländer, *Documents of Dying Paganism* (Berkeley, 1945), 1–26.

26. Margaret T. J. Rowe, "Group of Bands Adorning a Tunic: Dossier," *Bulletin de Liaison du CIETA* 17 (1963): 9–13.

27. Annemarie Stauffer et al., Textiles of Late Antiquity (New York, 1996), 45, no. 24.

28. *De inani gloria*, 4; cited by Peter Brown, *Power and Persuasion in Late Antiquity* (Madison, 1992), 83.

29. Katherine M. D. Dunbabin, *The Mosaics of Roman North Africa* (Oxford, 1978), 151–152.

30. Raffaella Cribiore, "A Hymn to the Nile," *Zeitschrift für Papyrologie und Epigraphik* 106 (1995): 97–106; translation on 100.

31. Ehud Netzer and Zeev Weiss, *Zippori* (Jerusalem, 1994), 46–51.

32. On this class of tapestries, see Annemarie Stauffer, *Textiles d'Egypte de la collection Bouvier* (Fribourg, 1991), 35–53.

33. Henry Maguire, "Garments Pleasing to God: The Significance of Domestic Textile Designs in the Early Byzantine Period," *Dumbarton Oaks Papers* 44 (1990): 217.

34. Leslie S. B. MacCoull, *Dioscorus of Aphrodito: His Work and His World* (Berkeley, 1988), 88–89, 111–112; translations by MacCoull.

35. Lambert Schneider, *Die Domäne als Weltbild: Wirkungsstrukturen der spätantiken Bildersprache* (Wiesbaden, 1983), 150.

36. D. Michaelides, *Cypriot Mosaics*, 2nd ed. (Nicosia, 1992), 93, no. 51.

37. Daniel Schlumberger, "Les fouilles de Qasr el-Heir el-Gharbi (1936–1938)," *Syria* 20 (1939): 330, fig. 25, pl. 47.3.

38. Ettinghausen, *Arab Painting*, 36.

39. The personifications, whose inscriptions survived, were Ktisis, Ananeōsis, Euandria, and Dynamis; Doro Levi, *Antioch Mosaic Pavements* (Princeton, 1947), 349–350, pl. 132.

40. Louis Poinssot, "Mosaïques d'El-Haouria," *Revue Africaine* 76 (1935): 183–206.

41. *Vita S. Eutychii*, 53; PG 86.2333–36.

42. Dunbabin, *Mosaics of North Africa*, 142–144; Margaret A. Alexander, Aïcha Ben Abed, and Guy P. R. Metraux, "Corpus of the Mosaics of Tunisia, Carthage Project, 1992–1994," *Dumbarton Oaks Papers* 50 (1996).

43. On aniconic mosaics of the early 6th century preserved in a Monophysite church, see Ernest J. W. Hawkins and Marlia C. Mundell, "The Mosaics of the Monastery of Mar Samuel, Mar Simeon, and Mar Gabriel near Kartmin," *Dumbarton Oaks Papers* 27 (1973): 279–296.

44. From the Maison d'Ariane; Dunbabin, *Mosaics of North Africa*, 156.

45. Katherine M. D. Dunbabin, "A Mosaic Workshop in Carthage around A.D. 400," in John Griffiths Pedley, ed., *New Light on Ancient Carthage* (Ann Arbor, 1980), 77–78; Henry Maguire, "Christians, Pagans, and the Representation of Nature," *Riggisberger Berichte* 1 (1993): 151–152.

46. Maguire, "Christians, Pagans," 132–136.

47. See André Grabar, "Recherches sur les sources juives de l'art paléochrétien, II: Les mosaïques de pavement," *Cahiers archéologiques* 12 (1962): 115–152, esp. 132–134.

48. Elisabeth Alföldi Rosenbaum and John Ward-Perkins, *Justinianic Mosaic Pavements in Cyrenaican Churches* (Rome, 1980), 41–42, pl. 11.3.

49. Henry Maguire, *Earth and Ocean: The Terrestrial World in Early Byzantine Art* (University Park, Pa., 1987); Marek-Titien Olszewski, "L'image et sa fonction dans la mosaïque byzantine des premières basiliques en Orient: L'iconographie chrétienne expliquée par Cyrille de Jérusalem (314–387)," *Cahiers archéologiques* 43 (1995): 9–34.

50. Zbigniew T. Fiema, Robert Schick, and Khairieh 'Amr, "The Petra Church Project: Interim Report, 1992–94," in J. H. Humphrey, ed., *The Roman and Byzantine Near East: Some Recent Archaeological Research* (Ann Arbor, 1995), 294–295.

51. Maguire, *Earth and Ocean*, 45–51.

52. Alfons M. Schneider, *The Church of the Multiplying of the Loaves and Fishes* (London, 1937), 58–63, figs. 2–17.

53. Maguire, *Earth and Ocean*, 29, figs. 32–33.

54. MacCoull, *Dioscorus of Aphrodito*, 111–112.

55. M. Manfredi, "Inno cristiano al Nilo," in P. J. Parsons and J. R. Rea, eds., *Papyri Greek and Egyptian Edited by Various Hands in Honour of Eric Gardner Turner* (London, 1981), 56.

56. Noël Duval, "La représentation du palais d'après le Psautier d'Utrecht," *Cahiers archéologiques* 15 (1965): 244–247.

57. Deichmann, *Ravenna*, vol. II, 2, *Kommentar,* 177–178.

58. Moshe Dothan, *Hammath Tiberias* (Jerusalem, 1983), 33–60.

59. See, for example, a floor from the Maison de Silène at El Djem depicting busts of the sun and the moon accompanied by the four seasons (Dunbabin, *Mosaics of North Africa,* 160, pl. 159), and another from the *oikos* of a villa at Bir-Chana showing the planetary deities surrounded by the signs of the zodiac (ibid., 161, pl. 162).

60. Michael Avi-Yonah, "Na'aran," in Ephraim Stern, ed., *The New Encyclopedia of Archaeological Excavations in the Holy Land* (Jerusalem, 1993), 3: 1075–1076.

61. A. Ovadiah, "The Synagogue at Gaza," in Lee I. Levine, ed., *Ancient Synagogues Revealed* (Jerusalem, 1981), 129–132; Dan Barag, "Ma'on," in *The New Encyclopedia of Archaeological Excavations in the Holy Land,* 3: 944–946; D. Bahat, "A Synagogue at Beth-Shean," *Ancient Synagogues Revealed,* 82–85.

62. A. D. Trendall, *The Shellal Mosaic* (Canberra, 1957).

63. Jean-Pierre Darmon, "Les mosaïques de la synagogue de Hammam Lif," in Roger Ling, ed., *Fifth International Colloquium on Ancient Mosaics* (Ann Arbor, 1996), 7–29.

64. Netzer and Weiss, *Zippori,* 56–58.

65. Avi-Yonah, "Na'aran," 1076.

66. K. A. C. Creswell, *Early Muslim Architecture* (Oxford, 1969), vol. I, 1, 213–322, pls. 7–37; Oleg Grabar, *The Formation of Islamic Art* (New Haven, 1987), 55–62.

67. Creswell, *Early Muslim Achitecture,* vol. I, 1, 323–372, pls. 50–58; Grabar, *Formation of Islamic Art,* 88–89; Gisela Hellenkemper Salies, "Die Mosaiken der Grossen Moschee von Damaskus," *Corsi di cultura sull'arte ravennate e bizantina* 35 (1988): 295–313.

68. Tadeusz Sarnowski, *Les représentations de villas sur les mosaïques africaines tardives* (Wroclaw, 1978); Stauffer, *Textiles d'Egypte,* 45–46.

69. K. A. C. Creswell, *Early Muslim Architecture* (Oxford, 1940), 2: 220.

70. See Ernst Kitzinger, "The Cult of Images in the Age before Iconoclasm," *Dumbarton Oaks Papers* 8 (1954): 130, n. 204; Grabar, *Formation of Islamic Art,* esp. 94.

71. *De imaginibus oratio I, PG* 94.1252.

72. *Vita S. Stephani iunioris, PG* 100.1120; trans. Mango, *Art of the Byzantine Empire,* 152–153.

73. On the archaeological evidence for the destruction of such motifs in the pavements of churches in Jordan, which seems to have occurred not earlier than the 8th century, see Michele Piccirillo, *The Mosaics of Jordan* (Amman, 1993), 41–42, and

Michele Piccirillo and Eugenio Alliata, *Umm al-Rasas Mayfa'ah,* vol. 1, *Gli scavi del complesso di Santo Stefano* (Jerusalem, 1994), 121–164. See also Urs Peschlow, "Zum byzantinischen opus sectile-Boden," in R. M. Boehmer and H. Hauptmann, eds., *Beiträge zur Altertumskunde Kleinasiens: Festschrift für Kurt Bittel* (Mainz, 1983), 435–447, pls. 89–93.

74. See Peter Brown, *The Rise of Western Christendom* (Oxford, 1996), esp. 250–253.

1 Ostia, House of Cupid and Psyche
(photo: Henry Maguire)

2 Floor mosaic from the dining room
of the Villa of the Falconer, Argos
Museum (from G. Åkerström-
Hougen, *The Calendar and
Hunting Mosaics of the Villa
of the Falconer in Argos*
[Stockholm, 1974])

3 Hunting with falcons, detail of a floor mosaic from the Villa of the Falconer (Åkerström-Hougen, *Calendar and Hunting Mosaics*)

4 May (holding a basket of flowers) and June (holding a sheaf of grain), detail of a floor mosaic from the Villa of the Falconer (Åkerström-Hougen, *Calendar and Hunting Mosaics*)

5 Acanthus border, detail of a floor mosaic of the months from the Villa of the Falconer, Argos Museum (photo: Henry Maguire)

6 Dido's feast (Biblioteca Apostolica Vaticana, MS. lat. 3867, fol. 100v., Roman Virgil)

7 Hestia Polyolbos, tapestry weave hanging (Dumbarton Oaks, Washington, D.C.)

8 Bearers of gifts, fragment of a tapestry weave hanging (Dumbarton Oaks, Washington, D.C.)

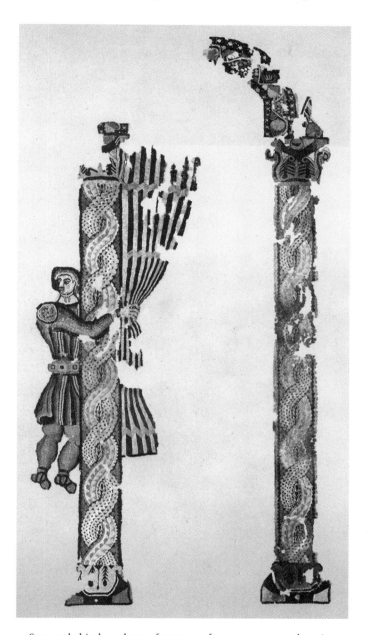

9 Servant behind a column, fragment of a tapestry weave hanging
(Museum of Fine Arts, Boston)

10 Fruiting trees,
fragment of a
tapestry weave
hanging (State
Hermitage Museum,
St. Petersburg)

11 Curtain fragment (Walter Massey Collection, Royal Ontario Museum, Toronto)

12 Rider making the "Parthian" shot, fragment of a silk roundel (Treasury of St. Servatius, Maastricht)

13 Female personification, fragment of tapestry weave (University of Toronto Malcove Collection)

14 Nilotic themes, silk fragment (Abegg-Stiftung, Riggisberg)

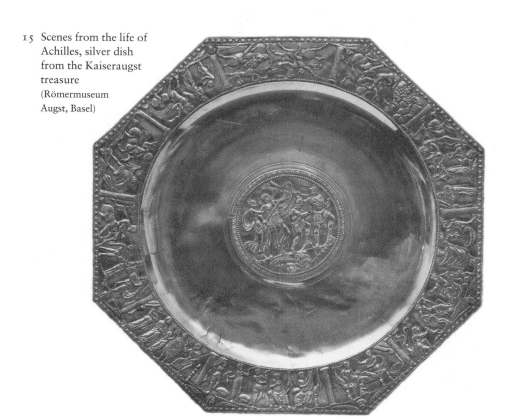

15 Scenes from the life of Achilles, silver dish from the Kaiseraugst treasure (Römermuseum Augst, Basel)

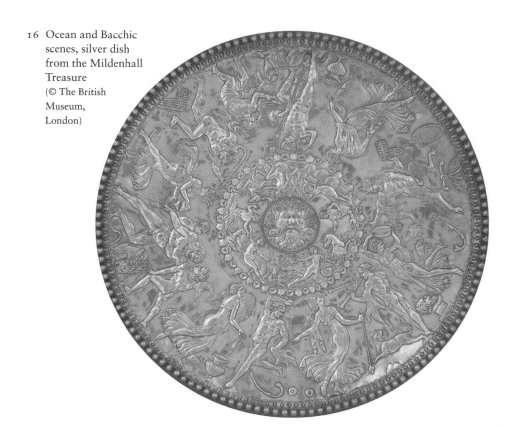

16 Ocean and Bacchic scenes, silver dish from the Mildenhall Treasure (© The British Museum, London)

17 The lady's toilette, floor mosaic (from Abdelmagid Ennabli, "Les thermes du thiase marin de Sidi Ghrib," *Monuments et Mémoires* 68 [1986], pl. 14)

18 "Projecta Casket," silver casket from the Esquiline treasure (© The British Museum, London)

19 Lion hunt, detail of silk tunic (from Alberto de
Capitani d'Arzago, *Antichi Tessuti della Basilica
Ambrosiana* [Milan, 1941], fig. 20)

20 Personifications of Earth, surrounded by the ocean, fragment
of silk sleeve band (Yale University Art Gallery, New Haven)

21 Lion hunters, plants,
and personification, silk
band (Metropolitan Museum
of Art, New York)

22 Estate of Dominus Iulius, floor mosaic from Carthage (Bardo Museum, Tunis)

23 Gold necklace with gems and pearls (Staatliche Museen, Berlin)

24 Shell-shaped pendant with
    Aphrodite, necklace
    (Dumbarton Oaks,
    Washington, D.C.)

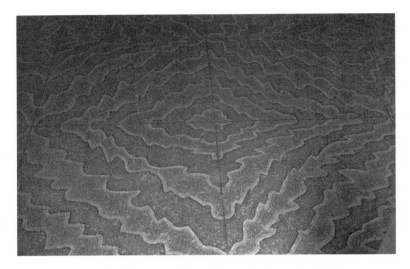

25 Imitation marble, floor mosaic from Thuburbo Majus (Bardo Museum, Tunis)

26 Personification of Earth, floor fresco, Qaṣr al-Hayr West (© 1962 and 1977 by Editions d'Art, Albert Skira SA, Geneva)

27 Scenes from the
life of Achilles,
reconstruction of
North African
pottery *lanx*
(National
Museum of
Antiquities,
Leiden)

28 Lion hunters, tapestry
woven medallion
(Cooper-Hewitt
National Design
Museum/Art Resource,
New York)

29 Imitation necklaces, neckline
of a tunic (Museum of Fine Arts, Boston)

30 Mask of Ocean, floor mosaic from Ain-Témouchent (photo: Katherine Dunbabin)

31 Flourishing tree, curtain
fragment (Museum of Fine
Arts, Boston)

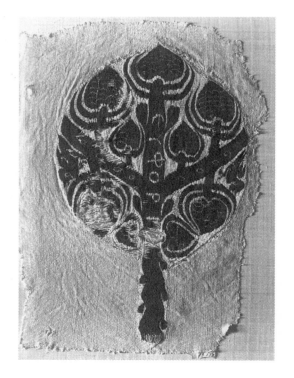

32 *Tholos* with dancers, floor mosaic, house north of the
Antonine baths, Carthage

33 Venus and dancers, mosaic from the Maison d'Ariane in Carthage (Bardo Museum, Tunis; photo: Margaret Alexander)

34 Summer, detail of floor mosaic in the south aisle, church east of the Temple of the Winged Lions, Petra (photo: Henry Maguire)

35 Detail of floor mosaic in the
nave, East Church, Qaṣr el-Lebia
(from Elisabeth Alföldi- Rosenbaum,
*Justinianic Mosaic Pavements in
Cyrenaican Churches* [Rome, 1980])

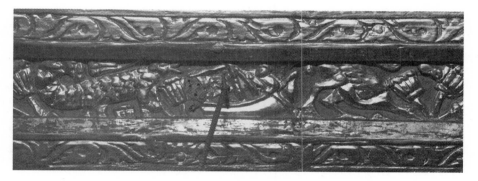

36 Nilotic motifs (crocodile, boat, and ostrich), detail of carved ceiling beam over the nave,
St. Catherine, Mount Sinai (Michigan-Princeton-Alexandria Expedition to Mount Sinai)

37 View of a church with its floor mosaic, tomb mosaic from Tabarka (Bardo Museum, Tunis)

38 Mosaics in the vault over the chancel, S. Vitale, Ravenna (Hirmer Fotoarchiv, Munich)

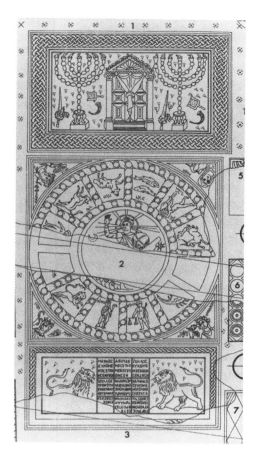

39 Floor mosaic in principal aisle,
synagogue, Hammath Tiberias
(from Moshe Dotha, *Hammath
Tiberias* [Jerusalem, 1983])

40 Floor mosaic in main hall,
synagogue, Hamman Lif (Naro)
(from Erwin Goodenough, *Jewish
Symbols in the Greco-Roman
Period,* © 1988 by Princeton
University Press)

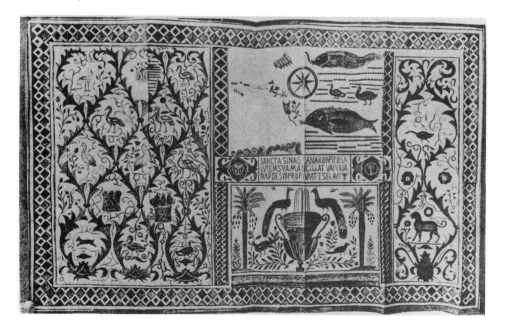

41 Plant and jewels, wall mosaic in the drum, Dome of the Rock,
  Jerusalem (photo: B. Brenk)

42 Trees and buildings, wall mosaic in the western portico, Great Mosque, Damascus (photo: B. Brenk)

43 Bird converted into leaves and volutes, reused Byzantine capital, Great Mosque, Kairouan (photo: Henry Maguire)

Habitat

Yizhar Hirschfeld

The dwellings of the inhabitants of the empire in late antiquity express various and at times contradictory trends. During this time the gap between the aristocratic class and the simple folk widened. Yet there was also a significant increase in the economic power of the middle class, which comprised landowning free farmers as well as city dwellers dealing in small industry, commerce, and services. The high point of private construction came in the 4th century, which saw the building of magnificent urban complexes and of fortified villas in rural areas. The prevailing economic prosperity also found expression in the houses of simpler people. The decline that followed was not uniform: in the west, prosperity ended in the 5th century, in contrast to the east, where it continued until the mid 8th century.

The Roman villa of late antiquity, both urban *(villa urbana)* and rural *(villa rustica)*, underwent a renaissance. The end of the 3rd century and beginning of the 4th witnessed a dynamic process of consolidating properties into private hands. This process, which was initiated in part by the emperors, created an affluent social stratum across the empire. The wealth of the elite found expression in the villas they built—which functioned not only as dwellings, but also as centers of social and economic activity. The existence of substantial villas, both in the city and village, attest to a high standard of living. Their regular plan and high-quality construction (including architectural decoration) reflect the economic resources of members of the middle class. Many of the houses of this period contained facilities for the processing of agricultural produce; this private enterprise also helped raise the standard of living.

The abundance that earlier, in the Roman period, was at the disposal of the few became widespread among the residents of settled lands and also extended to outlying areas. Farmhouses of varying sizes have been discovered in regions that were previously sparsely settled or not settled at all. These well-constructed buildings often served as the production centers of local landowners. In the east the construction of farmhouses in peripheral areas continued into the 8th century. There the economic prosperity of this period influenced the nomadic desert population to make the transition to seminomadic or permanent settlements.

On the outskirts of settled areas we also find the dwellings of monastic communities—an innovation on the landscape of late antiquity. The communal monasteries *(coenobia)* were for the most part very similar to the villa rustica, but they always preserved their special function as institutions of prayer as well as hospitality. The monasteries of the recluses *(lavrae)* and individual monks' places of seclusion, or hermitages, were unlike any secular buildings. The use of the natural landscape—cliffs, caves, and rock shelters—as dwellings emphasized the importance of monks as spiritual patrons. These people, many of whom gained admiration as holy men, were immeasurably more accessible than the landowning patrons living in the city, who offered financial sponsorship. The contrast between these two forms of patronage is among the signs of late antiquity.

Our information about dwellings and domestic life in late antiquity comes from an array of sources. Hagiographic literature contains various references to houses, primarily in the rural settlements, as well as detailed descriptions of monastic dwellings transmitted to us in the written lives of the saints. Other literary works from the 4th and 5th centuries, such as the descriptions of banquets in the writings of Ausonius or Paulinus of Nola, inform us of daily life in the villa. Relevant information regarding private building is occasionally found in imperial laws as well. For example, in the writings of Julianus of Ascalon, a 6th century architect who composed a book about the laws of construction, we learn about the urban bylaws regulating the height of construction, distances between houses, the location of windows, and so on.

Rabbinic literature is a rich historical source for the lifestyle of dwellings in the east. The corpora of halakha (Jewish law), such as the Mishnah, Tosefta, and Talmuds, and of midrash written by the Jewish religious leadership in Palestine and Babylonia, reflect daily life in the Roman-Byzantine period. In them we find references to almost every aspect of existence, including the most intimate ones concerning the home. Although this literature was written in the cities of Palestine, such as Sepphoris, Tiberias, and Caesarea, it expresses the way of life of the Jewish population as a whole, the majority of whom lived in rural areas.

In addition to literary sources, a trove of information about rural life in Egypt can be derived from papyrological evidence. These documents usually deal with landed property and estates; the descriptions of houses are incidental. This valuable material is found in the papyri of Oxyrhynchus, the capital of the desert located about 180 km south of Cairo. Detailed references to estates—dwellings and landed property—are found in the papyri of Petra in Jordan from the 6th century and in the papyri of Nessana in the Negev, which date a bit later (6th and 7th centuries). These documents complement what we know from the papyri discovered in Nahal Hever in the Judaean desert, which date to the 2nd century C.E. These papyri inform us of various details about the dwellings of the inhabitants of the desert oases around the Dead Sea, such as Ein Gedi and Zoar.

Epigraphical evidence is particularly important because it includes dedicatory inscriptions that provide names of homeowners and construction terms. So, for example, we learn about the various elements of the house, such as the *triclinium* (dining hall), *stablon* (stable), or *aulē* (courtyard), from inscriptions found on the walls or ceilings of houses.

The archaeological evidence of dwellings from late antiquity is very rich. Although the study of archaeological sites in the west is quite developed and has a relatively long tradition, it naturally has focused on villas and manor houses, the better preserved remains of the period; details of the homes of simple farmers in the west, which were often constructed of brick, are not so readily studied. In contrast, remains of all types of dwellings in the east have been preserved, both in cities and rural regions, since their construction was largely of stone. Moreover, in the peripheral areas of the east, human activity after antiquity waned; therefore many of the dwellings from the Roman-Byzantine period were left in the relatively good state of their last occupation. In the desert areas of North Africa and the Negev, for instance, many houses were preserved intact to a height of over one story, while Hauran houses from the Roman-Byzantine period were inhabited by the local population until recently. Archaeological finds enable us to trace the dynamics of expansion and renovation, as well as those of reduction, abandonment, and destruction.

Another important source of information is the depiction of houses and manors in mosaics of the 5th century, primarily from North Africa. In the urban villas of North Africa's upper classes, very precise, almost photographic depictions of their rural manors have been found. These mosaics, and mosaics from sites throughout the empire, also contain scenes of banquets and social events that were held in halls intended for these purposes *(convivia)*. These scenes appear alongside the images from Greek mythology favored by upper classes in the 3rd–4th centuries.

The wealth accrued by the urban aristocracy supported the building of dwelling complexes of outstanding splendor and size. Much simpler dwellings, and occasionally even houses bearing a rural character, stood side-by-side with these urban complexes.

Remains of houses of the well-to-do have been found throughout the empire, in both the east and west. These houses were usually located in the center of the city, following the local Roman tradition, or on the city's periphery, where there was ample building space. Although the houses of the urban aristocracy varied in their layout and details, they all had some combination of two elements: an apsidal reception hall *(oikos)*, and a central courtyard surrounded by columns (peristyle). The peristyle courtyard was the heart of the house. The entrance hall leads from the street to the courtyard, from which one gains access to the reception hall and dining rooms (triclinia), where the homeowners received their guests. This is a departure from the design of the Pompeiian house of the Roman period, in which the peristyle courtyard was situated at the back. In the center of the courtyard, or in one of its corners, a fountain or pond containing exotic fish was almost a standard fixture. In the west, the peristyle courtyard disappears in the 5th and 6th centuries, but in the east we know of examples of houses with peristyle courtyards that were in use until the 8th century, such as those at Pella and Gerasa, cities of the Decapolis in Jordan.

The reception hall and dining hall opened directly onto the courtyard (through one wide entry or three narrower ones), so guests could enjoy the air and light as well as the pond or fountains in the courtyard. Opposite the entrance facing the courtyard, on the other side of the hall, there was almost always an apse or an arrangement of three apses (in this case, the hall is termed *triconchos*). The apse occasionally framed the official seat of the homeowner. It was in the reception hall that the homeowner would receive his guests. Since according to the system of patronage that characterized late antiquity many people were dependent upon a wealthy person's sponsorship, the reception hall served in the daytime as a place to receive people seeking help. The ceilings in such rooms were often supported in the center by two rows of columns; inscriptions found on mosaics called these halls *basilica*.

Next to the reception hall was the triclinium, where business or social dinners were held. It also served as the place of reception in houses that lacked a separate oikos. The social function of rooms of this type was depicted in the magnificent mosaic floors decorating them. These floors were characteristically divided into four colored panels arranged in a T shape: three panels forming a horizontal row with a fourth, larger panel perpendicular to them. The diners would sit around the mosaic panels and look out at the view through the courtyard entrance.

The banquets held in these rooms are depicted on many mosaic floors. In the triclinium of the Orpheus House—a large dwelling recently discovered in Sepphoris in the Lower Galilee—a festive banquet is depicted. The central panel depicts four members of the dining party sitting on a semicircular sofa *(stibadium)*, of the type that was fashionable in the 5th–6th centuries. This semicircular sofa surrounds a three-legged dining table, next to which stands a three-legged urn *(milliarium)* for heating wine. The triclinium in which this mosaic is found is a large hall measuring 6 × 8 m. The house is named after the figure of Orpheus appearing in the center of the mosaic.

Another element often found in the villa urbana is the private bathhouse, sometimes added on to an existing structure. At Ostia, large houses with halls heated by a hypocaust were found, as were private bathhouses with toilets. It appears that aristocratic homeowners saw a need to separate themselves from the masses that frequented the public bathhouses. Such private bathhouses were also found in the large manors in the rural areas.

The rooms of the villa urbana were arranged in various configurations, although the villas of the west continued to uphold the strict Roman tradition of symmetry. The homeowner's living quarters were usually on the ground floor, while the second floor held the rooms of servants and others in the homeowner's employ, and those considered part of the household's *familia*. The villa also accommodated its owners' commercial occupations: the facade of the villa urbana often contained shops that sold agricultural produce from the rural manors of the homeowners, who were also large landowners. Some of these shops were rented to the highest bidder. Often at the entrance to the house there was a stone-paved courtyard for the loading and unloading of merchandise. Sometimes a room for a guard who watched those entering and leaving the premises was positioned next to the entrance.

Houses of the urban aristocracy have been found at a large number of sites. Near the Athenian agora, spacious houses of the well-to-do from the 4th–5th centuries have been uncovered. These houses range between 1000 and 1300 sq m (unlike houses in Roman Athens, whose area is 350–420 sq m). Magnificent villas have been uncovered at Antioch and its nearby port of Seleucia. The focus of these houses was their triclinia, which were decorated with colored mosaics. It appears that the importance of the triclinium was expressed by its size; whereas the average width of the 2nd century triclinium was 4–5 m, in the 5th century it was 7–8 m. Other impressive houses of the urban aristocracy were discovered at Sepphoris in the Galilee (Dionysius House) and at Nea Paphos in Cyprus, among other places.

The most beautiful examples of the houses of the wealthy come from the cities of Africa Proconsularis. The villas of the local aristocracy, who had accrued much wealth, were exceptionally large and magnificent. Their triclinia usually contained three or more apses; in the Bacchus House in Djemila we find a triclinium with seven apses. This complex, which stretches over an area of 7000 sq m, is one of the largest dwellings found in North Africa. Another complex is the 4th century House of the Hunt uncovered at Bulla Regia. The area of this complex is 2800 sq m and includes a front courtyard for carriages at the entrance to the house and a peristyle courtyard in its center. Signs of renovations and additions are evident in these houses.

From the late 2nd century until the end of the 4th, various cities in the west saw the building of villas with peristyle courtyards. An impressive aristocratic house from the 4th century was uncovered near the Cologne cathedral. In its center was a huge courtyard with a fountain lying on the same axis as the triclinium, which was adorned with scenes from the life of Dionysius. At the front of the house were a large portico and a row of shops. Aristocratic houses from the 4th century have been found in other cities as well, such as Bordeaux, Ravenna, Ostia, and Rome. Late Roman Ostia, the port town of Rome, marks a breaking away from the Roman *insula* (apartment block) and a preference for the *domus* (freestanding house). When the city's decline beginning in the 2nd century caused the prices of rented apartments in the insulae to plummet, these buildings were abandoned and destroyed. In contrast, this period witnessed a flourishing of the peristyle dwelling, the domus. This house is characterized by marble floors, gardens, and fountains in a peristyle courtyard, as well as a frequently used warm-air heating system beneath the floors. One such domus is the House of Cupid and Psyche, built around 300. A magnificent garden with a nymphaeum and a privy occupied one-third of the ground floor. The rear of the garden opened onto a large hall paved with floors worked in beautiful colored marble *(opus sectile)*, next to which were three bedrooms. In the course of the 5th and 6th centuries these houses were abandoned, some converted into monasteries.

Near the urban peristyle aristocratic houses were various types of simpler dwellings. A densely built residential quarter from the 6th century has been uncovered in Jerusalem, south of the Temple Mount. In this quarter, twenty-two houses were found built one next to the other. Most of them were two stories high; the rooms on the ground floor were used for storage and services, while those on the upper floor served as living quarters. Bordering these were single-story houses with one or two rooms, and bordering them, agricultural tracts that were worked by their owners. Another example of an urban dwelling with a rural character was found at Pella in Jordan. In the eastern quarter of the city, archaeologists uncovered a house that was built in the 4th century and destroyed in the great earthquake of 749. The rooms on the ground floor of this two-story house served as stables and storerooms. The remains of a horse, two cows, and a goat were found beneath the rubble of the earthquake.

The central courtyard was a prominent feature in the dwellings of late antiquity. The extended family, which was the primary social unit in this period, lived in apartment buildings arranged around a common courtyard. An apartment building typical of the 7th–8th centuries has been discovered at Gerasa. In the front of the building, which faced the *decumanus,* were three shops and an entranceway leading into an irregularly shaped inner courtyard. Around it, five or six separate dwelling units were built for members of one family. Each unit had two rooms: a front room for daily living and a back room for sleeping. The area of the complex was about 600 sq m.

Workplace elements were found in many urban houses. A good example of this are the houses from the 4th–7th centuries uncovered in Alexandria. The houses' facades were integrated with shops that served simultaneously as workshops *(ergasteria),* equipped with kilns, dye vats, a glass factory, and so on. Various workshop facilities were found inside the houses as well, which required the homeowners to enlarge their dwelling complexes. The expansion at times came at the expense of the street area; this process marked the appearance of the Oriental *sūq* (bazaar) in the cities of the east as early as the 6th century. Dwellings with shops and workshops are known from the 7th–8th centuries (Umayyad period) at Apollonia on the coast of Palestine, north of Tel Aviv.

In many cities, especially in the east, monasteries had become a new type of dwelling. These were communal institutions (coenobia), complexes containing enclosed inner courtyards and surrounded by a wall, housing for the most part modestly sized monastic communities. An example is the 6th century Monastery of the Lady Mary discovered in Beth Shean/Scythopolis, which was named after one of the donors mentioned in the mosaic floor. It was situated not in the city's center, but rather next to the northern wall. The plan of the monastery is reminiscent of the aristocratic houses of the period: a central courtyard (though not peristyle) and a church paralleling the apsidal reception hall (oikos) of the secular villa. The remaining rooms of the monastery—the monks' cells, dining room, and kitchen—are arranged around the courtyard. As in the villas, here too the floor is composed of colored mosaic depicting animals and agricultural scenes. These subjects were close to the hearts of the monks, many of whom worked in agriculture (producing wine and oil) while living in the monastery.

Thousands of sites with manor houses and farmhouses have been found throughout rural areas of the empire, both in the east and west. In the east some of these survived after the urban centers had waned. For example, farmhouses in the Negev continued to be used in the 8th and 9th centuries, although the main settlements of Avdat, Nessana, and Shivta ceased to exist at some point in the 7th century. A similar phenomenon occurred in the west. At the end of the 4th century and during the 5th, some cities lost their function as commercial centers, and the economic center of gravity shifted to the rural areas. The simple dwelling that characterized the rural areas of the west in late antiquity continued to be used in the early Middle Ages as well. This "aisled house" contains a main hall divided by two rows of wooden posts into a central nave flanked by two side aisles. The internal division of these spaces depended upon the needs of the residents of the house.

The countryside of late antiquity was characterized by large rural manors which usually served as the hub of vast estates. We know of examples of urban villas that were built according to Roman tradition—on beautiful landscapes, on the coast (in North Africa), or along large rivers (in Germany and Belgium)—but they are in the minority. The dominant type of manor house in late antiquity was the fortified villa which, influenced by military architecture, continues the eastern Hellenistic tradition of fortified courtyard houses, equipped with up to four towers. The tower, rising to a height of three or four stories, was a status symbol; it was also functional, as it enabled the homeowner or estate manager *(villicus)* to oversee and supervise the manor.

The large rural manor houses are familiar to us first and foremost from depictions on mosaics from North Africa. These mosaic floors, dating to the 4th and 5th centuries, were usually found in the dining rooms of large aristocratic urban houses such as the ones in Carthage, Cherchel, Tabarka, and elsewhere. The wealth of these homeowners was derived from their rural manors, which were clearly a source of pride. We can imagine these aristocrats dining with their guests and, during the banquet, proudly pointing to the depictions of their manors in the mosaic. The manor houses are depicted standing in an open landscape surrounded by orchards and fields. Occasionally, as in the famous mosaic of Dominus Iulius in Carthage, the lord of the manor and his wife are depicted. The manor building in this mosaic is typical: a fortified structure with two towers. The arched entrance gate leads into the central courtyard, where the reception hall and adjacent private bathhouse are depicted. The reception hall was used by the lord of the manor for receiving his guests and subjects, as was the custom in the city. The bathhouse is depicted as a structure with domes venting smoke from the heating system.

The typical villa rustica, which had three components, is depicted in detail in

a 4th–5th century mosaic discovered at Tabarka. The mosaic adorned a trifoli-
ate triclinium, so that each of the room's three apses depicted one part of the
villa. The central apse shows the main structure, the *pars urbana,* where the
owner lived when he was in residence. This was an enclosed structure with a
main gate leading into an inner courtyard. One can see the domes of the
bathhouse inside the courtyard, and opposite them the two-story residential
wing with its portico and two towers. The side apses depict portions of the *pars
rustica,* that is, the parts of the manor that served as living quarters for the
workers and animals and for food storage and the processing of agricultural
produce; the right-hand apse pictures the main structure, with a horse tethered
to it; the left-hand apse, a simple farmhouse with storerooms, animal pens, and
barns.

The manor house symbolized the wealth of the homeowner. In the Dominus
Iulius mosaic, the lord of the manor is seen on the left coming to visit his manor
and, on the right, leaving for a hunt—a popular occupation of the elite. Above
and beneath the manor house are detailed depictions of agricultural activity
according to the seasons of the year. The entire image illustrates the patronage system, as the lord and his wife receive presents from the tenant farmers
(coloni) who live on the manor. The coloni dwellings were much more modest,
as attested by the mosaic floor at Oudna, which depicts a tent that apparently
served as their seasonal home. Next to the tent a shepherd stands at the entrance to a simple farmhouse.

The villas in the mosaics from North Africa are the fortified villas that were
widespread from the 4th century on. They are characterized by high walls on
the ground floor, windows and porticoes on the upper floors, and towers in the
corners. The fortified villa of late antiquity may be viewed as the prototype of
the medieval château.

Archaeological finds confirm the mosaic depictions of villas. At Nador, which
lies in the rural area of Mauretania, stood a large (2000 sq m) 4th century
complex surrounded by walls. The front wall, facing north, boasted an arched
gate with round towers in each corner, similar to the facades of fortified farms
depicted in mosaics. Inside the complex is a large courtyard surrounded by
various installations associated with the processing of agricultural produce:
wine presses, olive presses, and storerooms for food. The residential section of
the farm (pars urbana) occupies less than one third of the structure's area,
indicating that the lord of the manor was an absentee owner, an urban dweller
who was away from the manor most of the year. Fortified farms like the one at
Nador became an integral part of the rural landscape of North Africa. In
various inscriptions, such a farm was called *turis* or *centenarium,* terms borrowed from the realm of military architecture. It was apparently designed to
defend its inhabitants and property from invasions by barbarians or local theft.

The remains of dozens of much simpler farmhouses have been found next to
the fortified farms. In an archaeological survey conducted in Tunisia, 67 farmhouses were discovered within an area of 47 sq km, which is 0.7 sq km per
structure. These farmhouses were built and used from the 2nd to 7th centuries.
The preferred structure was long and narrow, with the length varying according

to the number of rooms (usually 1 or 2); in contrast, the house's width was more or less fixed at 3.5–4 m, according to the length of the wooden beams that were available to the builders. The entrance facade to the houses generally face east or south, to ensure maximal exposure to sunlight and minimal penetration of cold winds in the winter. Next to the house there was always a large courtyard with various agricultural installations. One surprising find in this Tunisian survey was the discovery of 15 to 20 rural bathhouses, most of which were built in the 4th–5th centuries. This phenomenon is a clear sign of Roman urban cultural influence on the rural populations.

A unique type of tower-like farmhouse was developed in the semiarid peripheral areas of the empire. Dozens of structures of this type were discovered in the semidesert strip of Libya, about 200 km south of the coastline. These dwellings, called *gusr* in Arabic, were built in the 3rd and 4th centuries by local landowners. They are fortified tower-like structures rising to a height of two to three stories and ranging in area between 70 and 240 sq m. In their center is a compact courtyard surrounded by rooms. The quality of the construction and the stone ornamentation attest to the employment of professional builders. Next to the main tower-like structure are the remains of courtyards, annexes, agricultural installations, and terraces. The gusr were thus dwelling complexes for the extended family, numbering up to fifty people. Dedicatory inscriptions found above the entrance lintels to the gusr mention the centenarium, originally a military term, but in this context referring to a fortified dwelling place for landowners. The Negev of southern Palestine was also dotted with similar dwellings.

Various versions of fortified villas have been discovered throughout the empire. At Ramat Hanadiv, northeast of Caesarea in Palestine, a fortified villa built sometime between the 5th and 7th centuries has been discovered. This complex, measuring 520 sq m, was built around a central courtyard flanked by wings on three sides: two two-story wings and one single-story wing. The rooms on the ground floor were used for various functions, including food storage and sleeping quarters for animals, while the rooms on the upper floor were living quarters. This layout characterizes private rural construction. A fortified farm similar to the one at Ramat Hanadiv was discovered at Monte Birro in southern Italy; it also dates from the 5th and 6th centuries.

The manor houses of the west prospered in the 4th century. A 2nd century villa in Chedworth, England, for instance, added a portico, triclinium, and two private bathhouses in the 4th century. Another example is the villa rustica excavated at Gadebridge Park in England. This house was also initially built in the 2nd century, but its principal period of construction was in the 4th. The main structure consisted of a number of rooms joined by a portico in the front. Like the farmhouses of North Africa, it was flanked by two towers. The notable additions of a private bathhouse and large swimming pool were among the house's 4th century modifications, attesting to the high standard of living enjoyed by the villa's residents.

The Gadebridge house is a typical example of the corridor villa that characterized the northwestern provinces of the empire (Britain, Germany, and Bel-

gium). In Gaul (southern France) and Spain, villa design was influenced by the
Mediterranean concept of the central courtyard. The enormous villa excavated
in Lalonquette, France, has at its center a wide peristyle courtyard, surrounded
by living quarters, halls, and other amenities.

The most impressive manors perhaps in the entire empire have been found in
Sicily; famous among them is Piazza Armerina, a striking complex covering an
area of over 5000 sq m. This manor house, which belonged to a wealthy landowner, was built in the early 4th century in central Sicily. The house displays the
repertoire of components characteristic of the villa urbana, such as an enormous peristyle courtyard, apsidal reception halls, and magnificent triclinia. The
entire complex is covered with a colored mosaic floor containing depictions of
daily life inside and outside the manor.

The intricate layout of the Piazza Armerina complex and the exceptional
opulence of its mosaics have led to various theories regarding its owners.
Among other suggestions, it has been proposed that this site was the palatial
dwelling of the emperors of the west in the early 4th century, although not a
single piece of evidence has been found to justify this claim. Parallels from other
sites in Sicily support the more reasonable assumption that the owner of the
Piazza Armerina complex was a local wealthy senatorial nobleman.

For an example of imperial dwellings in late antiquity we can look at Diocletian's palace in Split. This huge complex (160×200 m), erected around the
year 300 on the Adriatic coast, is surrounded by a wall with four corner towers.
The interior is distinguished by its symmetrical division into intersecting streets
around large courtyards. Adjoining the courtyards were the dwelling quarters
of the emperor's coterie and personal military guards, as well as large reception
halls and the emperor's residential wing overlooking the sea. This wing contained a private bathhouse. The construction of the palace was influenced by
the military architecture of the era, but it also continued the eastern Hellenistic
tradition of building fortified palaces with four corner towers—*tetrapyrgia*, as
they are called in the sources.

Both Piazza Armerina in Sicily and the palace in Split were surrounded by the
hundreds of modestly built farmhouses that typically stood nearby to magnificent complexes. Thus in the countryside one would find settlements containing: (1) The *small farm*, a simple rectangular structure containing 7–15 rooms,
without amenities, 300–400 sq m in area, the dwelling of a small farmer or
tenant; (2) the *medium farm*, 500–2500 sq m, including a courtyard house or a
house with a double hall and 20–50 rooms (and often a separate wing with a
bathhouse), the property of landowners of medium estates; (3) the *large farm*,
extending over an area of over 2500 sq m, an enormous complex containing
dozens of built structures surrounding two or three courtyards. The opulence of
these structures is evident in the mosaic floors, decorative fountains, and other
installations. The owners of these palatial centers lived in the city.

In a study conducted of about two hundred sites of this type, it became clear
that most of the complexes were built in the 2nd century, underwent a period of
decline in the 3rd, and prospered again in the 4th. In the early 5th century, the
scope of the settlements began to contract, and toward the end of that century

most of the sites were abandoned. It therefore appears that there was a high rate of settlement in the 3rd and 4th centuries, mostly an increase in the number of medium farms. There are no signs of the creation of huge estates, *latifundia,* at the expense of the small farmers; indeed, the number of large manors diminished in relative terms. There was also a decrease in the number of small farms, in contrast to the rise in the number of medium farms belonging to independent landowning farmers. This pattern is repeated in all the provinces of the west (England, France, and Spain) and also characterizes rural settlement in the northern provinces of the Danube region (Moesia, Pannonia, Noricum, and Dalmatia).

This phenomenon also characterized the provinces of the east (Syria, Jordan, Palestine); the prosperity of the 4th, 5th, and 6th centuries found expression in the construction of well-built and adorned dwellings, similar to the medium farm in the west. This construction attests to an increase in the broad class of independent farmers who had established themselves financially. However, unlike in the west, where settlement was primarily in the farm setting, the dominant settlement in the east was (and still is) the village.

The rural dwellings of the east suggest a homogeneous rural society without distinctive class differences. The houses are built one next to the other, without preconceived plan. The difference in the sizes of the houses expresses the difference in the farmers' economic standing. The large dwellings of more prosperous families are usually located in the center of the village next to the house of prayer (synagogue or church). At Chorazin, north of the Sea of Galilee, five or six large courtyard houses (900 sq m each) were discovered next to the synagogue. These houses contained many rooms, as well as storerooms and stables. Simpler rural houses, with an adjacent courtyard, were found next to them. Another example is the village of Behyo in northern Syria, which blossomed in the 5th–6th centuries. In this period, spacious courtyard houses, with portico facades facing the courtyards, were built in the center of the village. These houses were the dwellings of wealthy landowners, while the simple rural houses were occupied by the rest of the farmers, who worked as tenants or hired day-laborers.

The modest rural house was a square or rectangular structure facing a courtyard. The 4th–5th century house excavated at Horvat Shema' in the Upper Galilee is composed of two rooms built one on top of the other; the room on the ground floor (2.3 × 3.6 m, or 8.3 sq m) served as a storeroom and workshop, while the room above it functioned as a dwelling. A stone staircase outside the house connected the two rooms. The main activity of the house's inhabitants took place in the courtyard: a raised surface in the corner of the courtyard served as a place for sitting, working, and sleeping; the center of the courtyard contained a cistern. Rabbinic sources inform us that most domestic activities, such as cooking and laundry, were performed in the courtyard, which also housed farm animals.

The dominant trend in the design of rural houses in late antiquity was the transition toward a more closed plan, an inclination toward separating parts of the house by function, and the establishment of the family living unit around a courtyard. Thus we witness development of large courtyard houses that served as dwellings for extended families. A good example of this are the dwellings preserved at Umm el-Jimāl, which in the 6th century numbered 128 complexes built to a height of two or three floors. Each house had a clear separation between the ground floor, which was reserved for work and agricultural purposes, and the floors above it, which served as living quarters. The large rooms of the ground floor were roofed with a single arch and used as a silo and animal pens or stable. Five to ten stone troughs attest to the presence of animals. In the corner of the room there was often a toilet. It is possible that these stables also accommodated the hired day-laborers. A typical example is house no. 119, a relatively modest complex measuring 40 × 40 m built around a large central courtyard. There are seven rooms on the ground floor, including a large stable (7 × 8 m) containing troughs for horses and cows. The complex was built in the 4th century and remained in use until its destruction in the great earthquake in the mid 8th century.

A rise in the rural standard of living is evident from the interior plan of the house. The functional separation between different parts of the house, usually achieved by building a second story, characterizes private construction in the east after the Hellenistic period. The ground floor, opening onto the courtyard, was used as a service area and for storing food and stabling animals, while the floor above it served as living quarters. The rooms on this floor were well illuminated, open to the landscape, allowing cool breezes to stream through them. The area of the second story was often smaller than that of the ground floor. In this case, the rest of the roof may have been used as a veranda for sitting or as an area for drying food (for example, raisins and figs). The two floors were connected by an exterior stone, or sometimes wooden, staircase. A characteristic feature of the two-story houses is the portico—a row or two of columns standing parallel to each other at the front of the house. The columns supported the veranda that gave access to the rooms on the upper floor of the house. The shaded area created beneath this porch gave shelter to the workers on the ground floor.

Another separation instituted in rural private construction was the partition between the sleeping quarters and the dining area (triclinium). The larger triclinia were gracefully built spaces that usually had a separate entrance. A rural dwelling discovered at Horvat Susiya in southern Judaea, built in the 6th century and used continuously until the 8th century, is a single-story house with a regular plan (160 sq m). The front of the house facing the courtyard had two entrances: a northern one leading into three residential rooms and a southern one leading into a spacious room that served as a dining room. In the rear of the house, two shops were built facing the street. We may therefore conclude that the homeowners dealt not only in agriculture, but also in commerce. The incorporation of shops into dwellings was a widespread phenomenon in the villages. In Shivta in the Negev, a courtyard house adjoining three shops facing the street was discovered. Two of them were connected by entrances into the house, while the third shop was isolated and possibly intended for rental.

The rural dwellings of northern Syria exhibit the prosperity of the 4th, 5th, and 6th centuries. These were stone houses with simple plans, but well built and decorated with great opulence. Most of the houses are rectangular two-story buildings with two or three rooms on each floor. Galleries as well as cellars and olive presses were constructed in many houses. No triclinia were found, not even in the large houses. The high point of private construction in Syria was in the 5th century, although these structures remained in use until the 8th century. The architectural uniformity of these houses expresses a homogeneous society with limited class distinctions.

A similar situation characterizes private building in the large settlements of the Negev—Shivta, Nessana, and Rehovot. These are large, densely built villages without preconceived plan. The superior construction exploited the local limestone. The dominant type of structure is a spacious courtyard house, ranging in area between 200 and 400 sq m. The courtyard of each house had a cistern. The living quarters surrounding the courtyard included one larger room that served as a dining room. The larger houses had towers similar to those of the rural manor houses. Division of the villagers by family is reflected in the Nessana papyri, which deal almost entirely with familial property of modestly sized tracts of land.

The rural settlement of the Negev in the 4th through 7th centuries is characterized, among other things, by a wide distribution of hamlets, or clusters of modest farmhouses. These are small settlements of five to ten dwelling units at an average distance of 20–25 m. The houses are simple rectangular structures consisting of two or three rooms facing a courtyard. Occasionally, another wing was built perpendicular to the existing structure. Hundreds of structures of this type that have been surveyed in the Negev and elsewhere in the east attest to the safe conditions prevailing in the remote peripheral areas of the empire. These conditions apparently did not change after the Muslim conquest, since these hamlets and farmhouses continued to exist until the end of the Umayyad period.

In addition to the villages, hamlets, and farmhouses in the peripheral areas, a new settlement phenomenon involved the desert nomads. During the 6th, 7th, and 8th centuries, nomads working in agriculture established seasonal settlements. The dwellings characterizing these settlements are round stone huts with a diameter of 4–8 m. The walls were built to a height of 1.5–2 m without bonding materials. The huts were roofed with foliage. The inhabitants of these huts worked in agriculture in the winter and spring months, while in the summer and fall they herded their flocks. The Negev surveys have yielded hundreds of sites of this type, occasionally including 20–30 dwelling units. Next to some of them were open mosques that are considered among the earliest in Islam. The nomadic settlements continued until the 9th century and then ceased completely.

Another new settlement phenomenon characterizing the rural areas in late antiquity is the various monasteries and hermitages. Among monasteries we can distinguish two types: the communal monastery (coenobium) and the monastery of recluses (lavra). The coenobium, built in an open rural area, is in many respects reminiscent of the fortified villa. It was surrounded by a wall with one or two entrances leading into a large inner courtyard. Around the courtyard were living quarters, as well as a dining room, kitchen, and church hall. The construction was often two stories high, in the plan characterizing the large farms.

A marvelous example of a coenobium may be found at the Martyrius monastery in the Judaean Desert, 5 km east of Jerusalem. It was erected at the end of the 5th century and assumed its final form in the 6th. Like the fortified villas of North Africa, it is a large complex surrounded by a wall. An entrance gate leads into a large courtyard occupying about 40 percent of the monastery's area. A large church was built east of the courtyard, and a large dining hall (refectory) at the north. The monks' dwellings were located in various rooms on the building's upper floor, above the service quarters (including stables) on the ground floor. A private bathhouse was found at the west side of the courtyard (according to monastic regulations, only sickly monks or monastic leaders were allowed to use the bathhouses). Well-tended vegetable gardens and orchards adorned the interior and exterior of the monastery; from afar it would have appeared like one of the fortified villas depicted in the mosaics of North Africa.

The lavra, in contrast, is reminiscent of a desert hamlet. It consisted of a cluster of cells surrounding communal structures, including a small church and a storehouse for food and supplies. The monks' cells, small structures with one or two rooms, were separated from one another. Often next to the cells were garden plots worked by the monks. The distance between the cells was about 30–35 m and a path (Greek: *lavra*) connected the cells with the church and the communal structures. The lavra could have looked like an idyllic, well-cared-for village with fruit and vegetable gardens.

In addition to the lavrae, monastic places of seclusion can be found in the remote desert areas, or between cliffs or in caves or rock shelters in the hills. An example is the secluded site of Sousakim (el-Quseir) in the Judaean Desert, where the holy man Cyriac lived; it consisted of a cave and a fenced garden plot with a cistern in front of it. At a later stage, a dwelling cell with a prayer niche was built for the holy man. Such a dwelling was part of its natural surroundings and open to visitors. Here Cyriac received his many admirers among the monks and the local rural population. The phenomenon of patronage, which became institutionalized in this period, took on a completely new dimension. Unlike the urban patron, who was difficult to approach, and to whom entrance was blocked by officers and bodyguards, the holy man in his remote dwelling place was easily and immediately accessible. Here his admirers could receive spiritual healing as well as relief from pain. The monastic simplicity of early Christianity was a new phenomenon in late antiquity.

The dwellings throughout the Roman empire reflect several of the main characteristics of late antiquity. The economic prosperity that followed the resolution of the 3rd century crisis affected the quality of housing construction in all social strata and in all forms of settlement. From the 4th century onward, existing dwellings were expanded and renovated, while new houses were built at sites hitherto unsettled. Although this prosperity in the western empire lasted only until the 5th century, in the east it continued until the end of the Umayyad period in the 8th century.

The discovery of dwellings in remote, previously unsettled areas—where we find the diverse dwellings of farmers, nomads, and monks—is an impressive aspect of private building in this period. This development expresses a shift of the cultural center of gravity from the city to the rural areas. In this respect, the dwellings of late antiquity express the character of the period as moving from the classical world into the culture of the early Middle Ages.

Bibliography

Barker, G., J. Lloyd, and J. Reynolds, eds. *Cyrenaica in Antiquity* (Oxford, 1985).

Dietz, S., L. L. Sebai, and H. Ben Hassen, eds. *Africa Proconsularis: Regional Studies in the Segermes Valley of Northern Tunisia* (Copenhagen, 1995).

Dunbabin, K. M. D. "Triclinium and Stibadium," in W. J. Slater, ed., *Dining in a Classical Context* (Ann Arbor, 1991), 121-148.

Ellis, S. P. "The End of the Roman House," *American Journal of Archaeology* 92 (1988): 565-576.

Frantz, A. "The Athenian Agora," in *Late Antiquity A.D. 267-700* (Princeton, 1988), 30-45.

Hirschfeld, Y. "Farms and Villages in Byzantine Palestine," *Dumbarton Oaks Papers* 51 (1997): 33-72.

——— *The Palestinian Dwelling in the Roman-Byzantine Period* (Jerusalem, 1995).

Lefort, J. "Rural Economy and Social Relations in the Countryside," *Dumbarton Oaks Papers* 47 (1993): 101-113.

Lewit, T. *Agricultural Production in the Roman Economy A.D. 200-400* (Oxford, 1991).

Mattingly, D. *Tripolitania* (London, 1995).

Nowicka, M. *Les maisons à Tour dans le monde grec* (Wroclaw, 1975).

Possiter, J. "Convivium and Villa in Late Antiquity," in W. J. Slater, ed., *Dining in a Classical Context* (Ann Arbor, 1991), 199-214.

Sodini, J.-P. "Habitat de l'antiquité tardive," *Topoi* 5 (1995): 151-218; 7 (1997): 435-577.

Stillwell, R. "Houses of Antioch," *Dumbarton Oaks Papers* 15 (1961): 47-57.

Tate, G. *Les campagnes de la Syrie du nord du IIe au VIIe siècle*, I (Paris, 1992).

Thébert, Y. "Private Life and Domestic Architecture in Roman Africa," in P. Veyne, ed., *A History of Private Life*, I: *From Pagan Rome to Byzantium* (Cambridge, Mass., 1987), 313-409.

Tsefrir, Y. *Eretz Israel from the Destruction of the Second Temple to the Muslim Conquest*, II: *Archaeology and Art* (Jerusalem, 1984), 133-142, 301-316. In Hebrew.

Villeneuve, F. "L'économie rurale et la vie des campagnes dans le Hauran antique (Ier siècle av. J.-C.–VIIe siècle ap. J.-C.): Une approche," in J.-M. Dentzer, ed., *Hauran I: Recherches archéologiques sur la Syrie du sud à l'époque hellénistique et romaine* (Paris, 1985), 63-136.

ABBREVIATIONS

Adv.Haer.	Irenaeus, *Adversus Haereses*	*Against Heresies*
AE	*Année épigraphique*	
Aed.	Procopius, *De aedificiis*	*On Buildings*
Aen.	Virgil, *Aeneis*	*Aeneid*
Amm.Marc.	Ammianus Marcellinus, *Res Gestae*	*History*
ANRW	*Aufstieg und Niedergang der römischen Welt*	*Rise and Fall of the Roman World*
Anth.Pal.	*Anthologia Palatina*	*Palatine Anthology*
Apoph.patr.	*Apophthegmata patrum*	*Sayings of the Desert Fathers*
Bell.Goth.	Claudian, *De bello gothico*; Procopius, *Wars,* Books 5–7: *De bello gothico*	*On the Gothic War*
Bell.Iug.	Sallust, *Bellum Iugurthinum*	*The Jugurthine War*
Bell.Pers.	Procopius, *Wars,* Books 1–2: *De bello persico*	*On the Persian War*
Bell.Van.	Procopius, *Wars,* Books 3–4: *De bello vandalico*	*On the Vandal War*
Bibl.	Photius, *Bibliotheca*	*Library*
C.Cels.	Origen, *Contra Celsum*	*Against Celsus*
C.Just.	*Codex Justinianeus*	*Justinianic Code*
C.Th.	*Codex Theodosianus*	*Theodosian Code*
Carm.	*Carmen; Carmina*	*Poem; Poems*
Carm.min.	Claudian, *Carmina minora*	*Minor Poems*
CCSL	*Corpus Christianorum, Series Latina*	*Corpus of Christian Writers, Latin Series*
CH	*Corpus Hermeticum*	*Corpus of Hermetic Writings*
Chron.	*Chronicon*	*Chronicle*
CIG	*Corpus Inscriptionum Graecarum*	*Corpus of Greek Inscriptions*
CIL	*Corpus Inscriptionum Latinarum*	*Corpus of Latin Inscriptions*
Clem.	Seneca, *De clementia*	*On Clemency*
CSEL	*Corpus Scriptorum Ecclesiasticorum Latinorum*	*Corpus of Latin Ecclesiastical Writers*
De abstin.	Porphyry, *De abstinentia*	*On Abstinence*
De civ.Dei	Augustine, *De civitate Dei*	*City of God*
De fac.	Plutarch, *De facie in orbe lunae*	*On the Face in the Lunar Orb*
De mort.pers.	Lactantius, *De mortibus persecutorum*	*On the Deaths of the Persecutors*
De vir.ill.	Jerome, *De viris illustribus*	*Lives of Illustrious Men*
Dem.evang.	Eusebius, *Demonstratio Evangelica*	*Proof of the Gospel*
Enarr. in Ps.	Augustine, *Enarrationes in Psalmos*	*Commentaries on the Psalms*
Ep.	*Epistula*	*Epistle*
Ep. ad Eph.	Ignatius, *Epistula ad Ephesios*	*Letter to the Ephesians*
Etym.	Isidore of Seville, *Etymologiarum libri*	*Etymologies*
GCS	*Die griechischen christlichen Schriftsteller*	*The Greek Christian Writers*
Gen. c. Manich.	Augustine, *De Genesi contra Manichaeos*	*On Genesis against the Manichaeans*

Germ.	Tacitus, *Germania*	*Germania*
Gramm.Lat.	*Grammatici Latini*	*Latin Grammarians*
HGM	*Historici Graeci Minores*	*Minor Greek Historians*
Hist.	Gregory of Tours, *Historia Francorum*	*History of the Franks*
Hist.Ar.	Athanasius, *Historia Arianorum*	*History of the Arians*
Hist.eccl.	*Historia ecclesiastica*	*Ecclesiastical History*
Hist.Lang.	Paulus Diaconus, *Historia Langobardorum*	*History of the Longobards*
Hist.Laus.	Palladius, *Historia Lausiaca*	*Lausiac History*
Hom.	*Homilia*	*Homily*
IG	*Inscriptiones Graecae*	*Greek Inscriptions*
IGUR	*Inscriptiones Graecae Urbis Romae*	*Greek Inscriptions of the City of Rome*
ILCV	*Inscriptiones Latinae Christianae Veteres*	*Ancient Christian Latin Inscriptions*
ILS	*Inscriptiones Latinae Selectae*	*Selected Latin Inscriptions*
In Ruf.	Claudian, *In Rufinum*	*Against Rufinus*
In Tim.	Proclus, *In Timaeum*	*On the Timaeus*
Inst.	*Institutiones*	*Institutes*
Itin.Anton.	*Itinerarium Antoninianum*	*Antonine Itinerary*
Ling.	Varro, *De lingua latina*	*On the Latin Language*
Mag.	John Lydus, *De magistratibus*	*On Magistracies*
Mens.	John Lydus, *De mensibus*	*On the Months*
Met.	Ovid, *Metamorphoses*	
MGH	*Monumenta Germaniae Historica*	
Myst.	Iamblichus, *Abammonis responsio* = *De mysteriis*	*On the Mysteries*
Nat.Hist.	Pliny, *Naturalis Historia*	*Natural History*
Not.Dig. (oc.) (or.)	*Notitia Dignitatum*	*List of Offices* (West) (East)
Nov.	*Novella*	*Novel*
Orat.	*Oratio*	*Oration*
P	Papyrus	
P Oxy.	*Oxyrhynchus Papyri*	
Paed.	Clement of Alexandria, *Paedagogus*	*The Schoolmaster*
Pan.Lat.	*XII Panegyrici Latini*	*Twelve Latin Panegyrics*
Peri strat.	*Peri strategias*	*On Strategy*
PG	*Patrologia Graeca*	*Writings of the Greek Fathers*
PGM	*Papyri Graecae Magicae*	*Greek Magical Papyri*
Phil.	Cicero, *Orationes philippicae*	*Philippics*
PL	*Patrologia Latina*	*Writings of the Latin Fathers*
PLRE	*Prosopography of the Later Roman Empire*	
PO	*Patrologia Orientalis*	*Writings of the Eastern Fathers*
Praep.evang.	Eusebius, *Praeparatio evangelica*	*Preparation for the Gospel*
Prin.	Origen, *De principiis*	*On First Principles*
Quaest.conv.	Plutarch, *Quaestiones conviviales*	*Table Talk*
RE	*Paulys Realenzyklopädie der classischen Altertumswissenschaft*	Pauly-Wissowa, *Encyclopedia of Classical Antiquity*
Rep.	Cicero, *De re publica*	*Republic*
RLM	*Rhetores Latini Minores*	*Minor Latin Rhetoricians*
Sat.	Macrobius, *Saturnalia*	*Saturnalia*
SEG	*Supplementum epigraphicum graecum*	
Serm.	*Sermo*	*Sermon*
SH	Procopius, *Anecdota*	*Secret History*

SHA	*Historia Augusta*	*Augustan History*
Strom.	Clement of Alexandria, *Stromateis*	*Miscellanies*
Tact.	Arrian, *Tactica*	*Tactics*
Theol.Platon.	Proclus, *Theologia platonica*	*Platonic Theology*
Trin.	Augustine, *De Trinitate*	*On the Trinity*
Tusc.	Cicero, *Disputationes tusculanae*	*Tusculan Disputations*
VA	Philostratus, *Vita Apollonii*	*Life of Apollonius of Tyana*
Vera Relig.	Augustine, *De vera religione*	*On True Religion*
Verr.	Cicero, *Orationes in Verrem*	*Verrines*
Vit.Ant.	Athanasius, *Vita Antonii*	*Life of Antony*
Vit.Const.	Eusebius, *Vita Constantini*	*Life of Constantine*
VS	Eunapius, *Vitae philosophorum et sophistarum*	*Lives of the Philosophers and Sophists*

CONTRIBUTORS

G. W. Bowersock, School of Historical Studies, Institute for Advanced Study, Princeton

Peter Brown, Department of History, Princeton University

Averil Cameron, Keble College, University of Oxford

Béatrice Caseau, Collège de France, CNRS, and Université de Paris IV–Sorbonne

Henry Chadwick, Christ Church, University of Oxford

Garth Fowden, National Hellenic Research Foundation, Research Centre for Greek and Roman Antiquity, Athens

Patrick J. Geary, Director, Medieval Institute, University of Notre Dame

Oleg Grabar, School of Historical Studies, Institute for Advanced Study, Princeton

Yizhar Hirschfeld, Institute of Archaeology, Hebrew University of Jerusalem

Christopher Kelly, Corpus Christi College, Cambridge University

Hugh Kennedy, Department of Mediaeval History, University of St. Andrews

Richard Lim, Department of History, Smith College

Henry Maguire, School of Art and Design, University of Illinois at Urbana-Champaign

Brent D. Shaw, Department of Classical Studies, University of Pennsylvania

INDEX